U0035665

The Collected Works of Margaret C. Fung, Ph.D.

Showwe Information Corporation

Taipei, Taiwan, ROC

TO

My Dear Family

John

Helen, Kang-chien

Freda, Felicia, Frank, Peter

Nicholas, Matthew

Preface

At the time of my stepping into seventy years' existence in the world, I tried to organize my files collected during my teaching/library administration profession and civil services work to be sent to the National Archives of the Republic of China for safekeeping as historical records. I found that many of my writings and speeches published previously in conference proceedings, journals, newsletters, etc. have not been included in the other four publications: *Library and Information* (published by Feng Cheng Publishing Company in 1979), *On Library and Information Science* (published by Taiwan Student Book Company in 1982), *A Primer of Library Automation* (published by Library Association of China in 1987 and 1991) and *Reflection of Civil Service System and Library/Information Science* (published by Taiwan Student Book Company in 1996).

These writings covering a wide range of subjects – information policy, library history, Sino-American librarianship, library/information status of the Republic of China, library automation, library/information science education, etc. – might be dated, but they are descriptions and facts to be possibly used as historical records. Some of my viewpoints and comments might be useful to researchers when they pursue further studies on the subjects discussed. It is indeed a true record of my efforts contributed to the arena of library/information science and to the promotion of global international understanding. Some corrections have been made on the texts to ensure accuracy. Parts of the contents are redundant because they were written for different occasions with added information or from different perspectives. All Chinese papers or books referred in the Notes/Bibliography are first stated in Wade-Giles romanization followed by Chinese characters and English translation (in brackets) for easy identification.

I wish to thank the following people and institutions for the permission to reprint these papers: the Editorial Committee of the *Journal of Library and Information Science*; Ms. Stacy F. Salling, Journals Rights

& Permissions/Circulation Manager, University of Texas Press; Library Association of China; Dr. John V. Richardson Jr., Professor of Information Studies, University of California, Los Angeles and Dr. Jinnie Y. Davis, Library Consultant and Librarian Emeritus, North Carolina State University; Dr. Ching-chih Chen, MicroUse Information; Mr. Richard B. Hill, Executive Director, American Society for Information Science and Technology; the National Library of Korea; Dr. Hwa-Nien Yu, editor of 1990 *Chinese American Academic and Professional Convention Proceedings*, and National Central Library.

I would like to express my heartfelt thanks to: the Dean of the Graduate Institute of Library & Information Science, National Taiwan Normal University, Dr. Mei-mei Wu for her most valuable suggestions, planning and encouragement; to Ms. Ophelia Chun-yin Liu, Chief Librarian, Institute of Chinese Literature and Philosophy, Academia Sinica, for her invaluable assistance in transliteration of titles, indexing and double checking the citations; to the Division Heads of the National Taiwan Normal University Library, Ms. Shih-chao Lin, Ms. Hsiu-ching Chang, Ms. Hai-yen Chang and Ms. Mei-lan Kuo for their tireless efforts in proof reading; to Mr. Tate Fu, Chief Editor and Ms. Ares Chang of Showwe Information Corporation for the efficiency in publishing this book. I also like to express my appreciation to Miss Shu-hua Wu, Miss Lucy Y. T. Chang, and Miss Hua-yu Hsu for their multi-faceted assistance.

Last but not least, I am immensely grateful to Dr. David Kaser for his invaluable guidance and advice given me in preparation of this work and in all of my endeavors for the past three decades.

Contents

Part III Databases Information Systems/Services

Part IV Miscellaneous

Part I

INFORMATION POLICY
LIBRARY HISTORY

1

National Information Policy - Some Basic Considerations

ABSTRACT

Recognizing the value of information as an asset to national development, this paper attempts to identify the need of a coordinated national information policy, identify an appropriate definition among many connotations, and explore related issues in a broad sense with succinct descriptions of American, Australian, British, Indian, and Western European countries' viewpoints and their pertinent endeavors.

Attention is directed to some of the basic considerations involved in developing such a policy, especially those relevant to the formulation of national information policy in the Republic of China.

Analysis of the ROC information-related efforts and brief recommendations are presented with discussions on some of the basic considerations such as centralized leadership, hierarchical upgrading of responsible sub-units, participation of public and private sectors, issues of standardization, and comprehensive, continuous, and coordinated efforts.

INTRODUCTION

While the world has already stepped into the "Post-Industrial Society," the society is built upon a sophisticated, information-based and capital-intensive production system;[1] people gradually come to appreciate that information is viewed both as power and wealth.[2]

Similar to that of the American society as depicted by Peter Drucker, the world has changed rapidly from an economy of pure goods to a knowledge economy;[3] we thus have entered a so-called information age in which information is a chief ingredient of knowledge.

The advent of computer and communication technology has certainly prompted human beings entering into this revolutionary age of information. This was evidenced by the fact that over 60% of the United States work force is involved in information-related jobs and there has been a worldwide increase of information workers from 10 to 60 million during the last decade.[4] Continuous increase of information, speedy innovation of information technology, and overall dependence upon information have enhanced the need for many national leaders to react to the needs generated by these dynamic phenomena.

Information, being instrumental to productivity, to modernization of society, and to the well-being of any individual or group, serves as the foundation for national development and policy making.[5] "A country's creativity, visions, and insights, are fueled by the analysis of information and data."[6] UNESCO has long stressed that information is now considered as a vital resource for national development.[7]

Treating information as a nation's vital resource, constant creation, collection, processing, dissemination, transferring, availability, access, analysis, and utilization of information are indispensable for efforts in national development. Cognizance of the value of information is especially true in countries which are confronted with both internal and international crises.

As identified by Victor Rosenberg, most nations assume that information activities are essential or at least significantly contribute to their economic growth.[8] The importance of information has gained worldwide recognition; it is certainly the case in the Republic of China.

THE NEED FOR A NATIONAL INFORMATION POLICY

While the value of information is ascertained so affirmatively, the most effective collection, processing, dissemination, transferring, availability, access, analysis, and utilization of information depend greatly upon a workable, long-range, multi-faceted national information policy. "Throughout the world policymakers are establishing national policies to promote their information industries and to protect against potential negative effects on the information age."[9] "Information is at the very heart of public policy," stated by Hubert H. Humphrey, illustrates the prominent position of information policy in the United States.[10] Universally, attention given to national information policy is indeed on the upswing. All these concerns indicate that only with a well thought out and coordinated national information policy, can a nation really be benefited from information.

CONNOTATIONS AND DEFINITION

The term "information policy" has many connotations depending upon different viewpoints and various interpretations. "To some, it is that body of statutes and regulations that governs the telecommunications industry. To others, it is concerned with the issues of privacy and freedom of information. To still others, it is those laws and policies affecting libraries and government printing and publication."[11]

As identified by the National Commission on Libraries and Information Science (U.S.A.), information policy should be a policy which governs the way information affecting our society.[12]

It deals with various components of information which are interrelated and interdependent.

ISSUES AND BASIC CONSIDERATIONS

The interrelationships and interdependences of the various components of information, which can be seen in communication, technology, economics, privacy of information, and among information management, information networks and information/library science, are indeed key issues confronting us. A sound, comprehensive, and coordinated national information policy, therefore, should be determined with a broad concept and should deal with every facet of information: creation, collection, organization, supplies, processing, dissemination, transfer, and usage. In effectively and successfully formulating a national information policy, centralized high-level leadership, hierarchical upgrading of responsible sub-units, participation of public and private sectors, issues of standards, and comprehensive, continuous, and coordinated efforts are the basic considerations.

SOME NATIONAL INFORMATION POLICY ENDEAVORS

Numerous examples of attempts have been made on the formulation of national policies throughout the world. Some of them aim at the overall national information policy as a whole; some of them address national library/information services in particular. As illustrations of the diversity of the types of national information policy, a few such endeavors are described as follows:

A decade ago in the United States, the Domestic Council Committee on the Right of Privacy was commissioned by the U.S. President in 1976, to review and to define the information policy issues which confront federal policymakers, and to ascertain the status of information policy studies then going forward within a number of agencies in the Executive Branch. That was the first serious U.S. attempt to assemble the salient issues with a comprehensive discussion on related issues. This charge resulted in a report- -*National Information Policy* which emphasized the following needs:[13]

1. To examine communications regulatory practices,
2. To review copyright law,
3. To clarify the role of public and private sectors in developing computerized databases and,
4. To establish standards for the interchange of computer information issues pertaining to national information policy.

Among many of the endeavors, two American legislative propositions, which address many of the information issues, deserve our attention: 1) H. R. 744 Information Science and Technology Act proposed by Representative George E. Brown, Jr., features the establishment of an Institute for Information Policy and Research to study information science and technology and 2) S786, Information Age Commission Act calls for the creation of an Information Age Commission to handle related research on the topic.[14]

In Australia, the Australian Advisory Council on Bibliographic Services (AACOBS) has been the moving force in its initiation of a national library/information policy in cooperation with the National Library. Borchardt indicated that national information policy will have to be considered by a statutory authority charged with the execution of a national information policy.[15] This group emphasized the establishment of norms and standards, the economics of automation, and the measurement of user satisfaction.

In Western Europe, "in none of the Member States does there seem to be a single coherent 'horizontal' information policy."[16] C. Jansen van Rosendaal, Director, Commission of the European Communities, indicated that the lack of a general policy framework, both at the national and community levels, is considered by many as a real constraint to the favorable development of the information market. He advocated that "...... new rules of the game have to be formulated!"[17]

L. J. Anthony traced the history of information policy in the United Kingdom back to its genesis in 1963.[18] In spite of several changes of responsibilities and organizations, the Fourth Report from the Education, Science and Arts Committee, Session 1979-80, made a good move. It recommended:[19]

1) As soon as possible the Government should appoint a Minister of Cabinet rank to take responsibility for information policy and should provide him with the necessary staff ......2) The Government should set up, as a matter of urgency, a Standing Commission representative of the wide range of interests ...... 3) Examine on a continuing basis the problems of developing a national information network to formulate national requirements, to relate them to international developments, to investigate possible solutions, and to make proposals for their implementation by appropriate bodies.

In India, Nagpur University organized an All-India Seminar on National Policy on Library and Information Science in September of 1983, with sessions to discuss the following topics: 1) Need for a national policy and areas to be covered; 2) Levels or training and agencies that should handle it; 3) Bibliographic organization and control in library/information science; and, 4) Policy for research and training in LIS monitoring, evaluation and standardization. It concluded by recommending a national policy for library and information services.[20]

The above are some of the important endeavors in the last decade. All of them do indicate a need for coordinated efforts and an authorized body to handle such a high level venture. Well summarized by Michel J. Menou, most policy papers...... tend to proceed from various specialized points of view rather than from a comprehensive and integrated "informationalization" strategy.[21] This, together with the common lack of appropriate coordination mechanisms among the many interested government and private organizations which all countries have inherited from the industrial society, might account for their frequent lack of effectiveness.[22]

INFORMATION-RELATED EFFORTS IN THE ROC

The public and private sectors of the Republic of China have paid considerable attention to information-related activities/ programs. It is most commendable that the efforts in the Republic of China are well under way. The following are some of the highlights of these accomplishments:

1. Under the direction of Drs. K. T. Li and H. T. Chou, Ministers Without-Portfolio in the Executive Yuan, the Information Development and Promotion Task Force has been established with five decentralized working groups: a) Integrated Planning (Research, Development and Evaluation Commission), b) Information Industry (Ministry of Economic Affairs), c) Personnel Training and Recruitment (Ministry of Education), d) Networking Technology (Ministry of Communications) and, e) Evaluation (Auditing Department).[23] Among many of its innovative and policy-making endeavors, the most popular program initiated by the Task Force is its annual Information Week/Month, and its annual information technology exhibition which does accomplish many missions. A social consciousness of information and public education/orientation of information industry/technology/science are definitely the applauding results of such a nationwide endeavor.
2. Under the auspices of the Research, Development and Evaluation Commission of the Executive Yuan, six national management information systems created to provide management information to various levels by different organizations consist of: a) General Administration Information System, b) Economical Information System, c) Scientific and Technological Information System, d) National Defense and Security Information System, e) Communication Information System, f) National Status or

Facts Information Systems.[24]

3. Under the planning of the Council for Cultural Affairs, Executive Yuan, library/information systems have been developed jointly with the Library Automation Planning Committee (LAPC), which is organized by the National Central Library in cooperation with the Library Association of China.[25] Library laws, legal supports, community cultural centers, local library information services and policies have been the concerns of the Council for Cultural Affairs; automated library services and their related standards are the chief concerns of the LAPC.

OBSERVATIONS AND RECOMMENDATIONS

It is most encouraging to note that these three major information-related endeavors, in one way or another, are the responsibilities assumed by the Executive Yuan, which is the highest executive branch of the government in the Republic of China. Each of them has achieved considerable success. However, more coordination among them should be encouraged. Such diversity of efforts does indicate growing attention and developing interest; it also reveals policy fragmentation. More effective handling and retrieval of information resulted from compatibility of computerized information systems, clear identification of public and private participation in information activities, various pertinent but non-redundant standards, and encouraged coordination of efforts within the information environments are of great concern.

While the Scientific and Technological Information System has the blessings of the Research, Development and Evaluation Commission of the Executive Yuan, at least two separate systems stand out by themselves, having nothing to do with the national library information system. Between these two systems, compatibility is needed.[26]

While libraries do constitute an important component of the

entire national information network, national information policy should also concern itself with various issues confronting library/ information entities.

The National Central Library has an outstanding proposal developed by Director C. K. Wang for national library/information services.[27] These proposals pertaining to library policies and development need to be considered by the overall national information policy. The national library should be authorized to coordinate and supervise library services at all levels, and the national library, to be elevated to a higher administrative echelon, should be a unit contributing to the process of national information policy making.

We are very much encouraged by the initiatives that the Research, Development and Evaluation Commission of the Executive Yuan has already taken. It has quickly recognized the importance of legal issues confronting information, and has recently completed research on the topic.[28] This study certainly has provided some background information helpful to move the Republic of China closer to the task of formulating a national information policy.

Because of the uniqueness of each nation, policies should be formulated based on its individuality. However, to adapt a sound idea is to be encouraged; paraphrasing some of the recommendations made by the Domestic Council Committee on the Right of Privacy a decade ago seems to be worthy of our consideration:

1. Identifying the development of a coordinated national information policy as a national goal,
2. Refocusing and expanding the current responsibilities of the Task Force of the Executive Yuan by formally charging it to coordinate and consolidate functions of several existing entities and to upgrade the hierarchy of certain responsible entities. This Task Force should be inter-agency in nature, and consist of high-level agency representatives,
3. Creating an advisory committee to assist the Task Force in performance of its duties. This committee must consist of

representatives from the private sectors, local governments, and academic and professional disciplines concerned with information policy issues.

CONCLUSION

A sound, well-rounded, and far-sighted national information policy can only be developed if a top-level executive body is organized, or is given the authority to either coordinate or to consolidate all efforts involved, on a centralized, high-level, and continuing basis.

Only through such efforts, can a rational framework for a national information policy be accurately articulated and coordinately formulated. National library and information service policy can then be logically and effectively derived from the framework of this overall national information policy aiming at handling assorted issues of information communication, information technology, information economics, information privacy, laws pertinent to information related activities, information management, information networks, information/library services and information education. With the ROC's firm commitments to the information environments, the fruits of a true national information policy are indeed forthcoming.

NOTES

1. Daniel Bell, *The Coming of Post-Industrial Society* (New York: Basic Books, 1976), 49-119.
2. Tefko Saracevic, "Tzu Hsun Shih Tai Chung Te T'u Shu Kuan Chiao Yu 資訊時代中的圖書館教育 [Library Education in the Information Age]," trans. Mei-hua Yang 楊美華 譯, *T'u Shu Kuan Hsueh Yu Tzu Hsun K'o Hsueh 圖書館學與資訊科學 [Journal of Library & Information Science]* 8, no. 2 (October 1982): 221-228; Margary J. McCauley, "Information Policy and the National Audiovisual Center," *Government Publications Review* 8A (1981): 215; R. ElHadidy and E. E. Horne, *The Infrastructure of an Information Society* (North-Holland: Elsevier Science Publishers BV, 1985), 83.
3. Peter Drucker, *The Age of Discontinuity* (New York: Harper and Row, 1969), 263.
4. G. Feketekuty; J. D. Aronson, "Meeting the Challenges of the world Information Economy," in *The World Economy* 7, no.1 (March 1984): 63-86.
5. Margaret C. Fung, "Planning Resources of National Information System-Some Issues and Considerations," in *The Infrastructure of an Information Society*, by R. ElHadidy and E. E. Horne (North-Holland: Elsevier Science Publishers BV, 1984), 83.
6. M. J. McCauley, "Information Policy and the National Audiovisual Center," *Government Publications Review* 8A (1981): 215-220.
7. UNESCO. "International Governmental Conference on Scientific and Technical Information for Development," in *UNISIST II. Final Report* (Paris: UNESCO, 1979), Recommendation no.1, pp.17-19; Recommendation no.2, pp.19-20; Recommendation no.3, pp.20-23.
8. Victor Rosenberg, "National Information Policies," in *Annual Review of Information Science and Technology* XVII (White Plains, N.Y.: Knowledge Industry Publication, 1982), 16.
9. Jane Bortnick, "National and International Information Policy," *Journal of the American Society for Information Science* 36, no. 3 (May 1985): 164-168.
10. Robert Lee Chartrand, "National Information Policy," *Bulletin of the American Society for Information Science* 12, no. 5 (June/July 1986): 10.
11. Marilyn Killebrew Gell, "Washington Update: Information and Public Policy," *Library Journal* (July 1981): 1357.
12. Domestic Council Committee on the Right of Privacy, ed., *National Information Policy: Report to the President of the United States* (Washington,

D.C.: National Commission on Libraries and Information Science, 1976).

13. Ibid.
14. Robert Lee Chartrand, "National Information Policy," *Bulletin of the American Society for Information Science* 12, no. 5 (June/July 1986): 10.
15. D. H. Borchardt, "Australian Information Policy," *Australian Academic and Research Libraries* 11 (March 1980): 226-40.
16. C. Jansen Van Rosendaal, "European Information Policy Situation," *ASLIB Proceedings* 36, no. 1 (January 1984): 15-23.
17. Ibid.
18. L. J. Anthony, "A National Information Policy for the United Kingdom," *ASLIB Proceedings* 35, no. 3 (March 1981): 73.
19. Ibid.
20. H. R. Chopra, "National Policy on Library and Information Science Education: All-India Seminar," *Herald Library Science* 24 (January-April 1985): 70-4.
21. Michel J. Menou, "An Overview of Social Measures of Information," *Journal of the American Society for Information Science* 36, no. 3 (1985): 169-177.
22. Ibid.
23. Tzu Hsun Kung Yeh Ts'e Chin Hui Pien 資訊工業策進會 編 [Institute for the Information Industry, ed.], *Chung Hua Min Kuo Ch'i Shih I Nien Tzu Hsun Kung Yeh Nien Chien 1982 中華民國七十一年資訊工業年鑑 [Information Industry Yearbook of the Republic of China, 1982]* (Taipei: Institute for the Information Industry, 1982), 4-5.
24. Yung Wei 魏鏞, *Fa Chan Tzu Hsun T'i Hsi, Ch'iang Hua Chueh Ts'e Kung Neng: Wo Kuo Hsing Cheng Tzu Hsun T'i Hsi Chih Chien Li Yu Chan Wang 發展資訊體系，強化決策功能：我國行政資訊體系之建立與發展* (Taipei: Research, Development and Evaluation Commission, Executive Yuan, n.d.): 14-15.
25. Chinese MARC Working Group, Library Automation Planning Committee, ed., "Chinese MARC Format and Bibliographic Database," in *Symposium on Computer Processing of Chinese Library Materials and Computer-Assisted Chinese Language Instruction at ASIS-82: Proceedings*, Columbus, Ohio, 19 October 1982. (Taipei: ASIS Taipei Chapter, 1982), 5-1-27.
26. T. S. Fang, "The Establishment and Use of Information System on Science and Technology in ROC," in *Symposium on Computer Processing of Chinese Library Materials and Computer-Assisted Chinese Language*

Instruction at ASIS-82: Proceedings, Columbus, Ohio, 19 October 1982. (Taipei: ASIS Taipei Chapter, 1982), 10-1-3; W. J. Wu et al., "Agri-Thesaurus: A Chinese Thesaurus for the Agricultural Science and Technology Information Management System," in *Symposium on Computer Processing of Chinese Library Materials and Computer-Assisted Chinese Language Instruction at ASIS-82: Proceedings*, Columbus, Ohio, 19 October 1982. (Taipei: ASIS Taipei Chapter, 1982), 6-1-6.

27. Hsing Cheng Yuan Yen Chiu Fa Chan K'ao He Wei Yuan Hui Pien 行政院研究發展考核委員會 編 [Research, Development and Evaluation Commission, Executive Yuan, ed.], "Wo Kuo T'u Shu Kuan Fa Chan Chou I 我國圖書館發展芻議 [The Proposal for Librariy Development of Our Country], "in *Chien Li T'u Shu Kuan Kuan Li Chih Tu Chih Yen Chiu 建立圖書館管理制度之研究 [Study on the Establishment of the Library Management System]* (Taipei: RDEC, 1985), 138-143.
28. Hsing Cheng Yuan Yen Chiu Fa Chan K'ao He Wei Yuan Hui Pien 行政院研究發展考核委員會 編[Research, Development and Evaluation Commission, Executive Yuan, ed.], *Tzu Hsun Li Fa Chih Yen Chiu 資訊立法之研究 [The Study on the Information Legislation]* (Taipei: RDEC, 1985), 407.

Thanks to Mrs. Bie-hwa Chen Ma, RECON Project Work Leader, East Asian Library, U.C. Berkeley, USA for citation verification.

Paper presented at the Library Cooperation and Development Seminar, Taipei, Taiwan, R.O.C., 17-18 August 1986.

Reprinted with permission from *圖書館學與資訊科學 [Journal of Library & Information Science]* 13, no. 1 (April 1987): 17-28.

2

The Development of National Library/Information Policy for the R.O.C.

ABSTRACT

The development of library and information services all over the world has greatly been influenced by the impact of information and communication technology, the contents and format of library/information services are thus confronted with tremendous changes. In responses to such changes, colleagues in the ROC reached a consensus that a national library/information policy is urgently needed. *White Paper on Library Development* has thus been prepared in response to the call for a national library/information policy. This paper first identifies the definitions and scope of information policy; it describes the pressing demands for a national library/information policy for the ROC. The environment and impetus occurred during our continuous efforts paid to national development are stated. These include our economic, social, and political developments, the impacts of educational reform, the promotion of life-long learning, reformation of communities, and the establishment of Taiwan to be the Asian Pacific Operations Center, etc. with special description of the National Information Infrastructure's (NII) effects upon library/information service policy. It then delineates the contents of the national information policy which is treated as a guide for the navigation of library and information services in the ROC for the 21st century. A review of current library services, and analysis on problems confronting library development, identification of the new functions of libraries and their servicing objectives, and action conspectus are presented with proposals for future strategies.

INTRODUCTION

Information policy, according to Weingarten, is a set of public laws, regulations, and policies that encourage, discourage, or regulate the creation, use, storage, and communication of information.[1] It is a set of interrelated principles, laws, guideline rules, regulations, procedures, and judicial interpretations that guides the oversight and management of the information life-cycle: the production, collection, distribution/dissemination, retrieval and retirement of information. It also embraces access to and use of information.[2]

Rowlands suggests that the fundamental role of policy is to provide the legal and institutional frameworks within which formal information exchange can take place. He further suggests that information policy should be flexible, dynamic and responsive to changing circumstances.[3]

As we know, a national information policy is required by every country to ensure harmonious implementation and operation of information resources, services and systems. Such a policy enables coordination of national information systems with legislation and the implementation of new technical and information developments.[4]

ENVIRONMENT AND IMPETUS

In the past five decades, dynamic economic, social and political progresses have been demonstrated and evidenced by "Taiwan Miracle." Economically, per capita income has reached US$10,918; our foreign reserve has reached US$930 billions.[5]

Politically, Taiwan has enjoyed complete democracy – with

direct election of president/vice president, mayors, magistrates, the existence of multiple political parties, and the revision of ROC Constitution. All these endeavors have accelerated a new horizon of government infrastructure and will move toward more efficient performances. Socially, the society tends to be more liberated, to be able to accommodate multiple cultures and cope with the ideas of globalization.

The above mentioned successes have largely been credited to the availability of quality and knowledgeable human resources. The popularization of education and upgrading of educational system are recognized as the cause of the successful "Taiwan Experience."

While we are stepping into the 21st century, the ROC strives to implement the NII programs, to initiate government reinvention, to upgrade our national competitiveness, to reform our educational system, to promote life-long learning, and to make Taiwan the Asian Pacific Operations Center. In the age of knowledge and innovation-based information networking, learning becomes a life-long challenge. The educational and learning opportunity readily available from the worldwide information network would raise the knowledge level of people and germane to national competitiveness. All these planning and implementations demand fine organization of information, timely supply of library/information service and easy access to library/information service through the use of modern technology. The recent abolition of Publication Laws, the processing of Library Laws by the Legislative Yuan, the proclamation of Government Information Public Laws have exerted great influence upon library services. As early as 1986, during the Seminar on Library Cooperation Development in Taipei, colleagues in the library profession have already realized the importance of the formation of a national information policy.[6]

Many efforts have since been made, such as the proposals made by Dr. Kaser and Dr. Becker.[7] Actual actions started from 1994 when Library Association of China made a resolution to draft the *White Paper on Library Development* with the guidelines given by Dr. C. K. Wang.[8] Being a policy in nature, it is drafted for the purpose of providing a blueprint for the development of library and information services in the ROC.

EFFECTS OF NII UPON THE DEVELOPMENT OF LIBRARY/ INFORMATION SERVICE POLICY

NII is considered to be a crucial index in evaluating the competitiveness of a nation. The following description of the nature of NII and the current status of NII of the ROC will give us a clear picture of the relationship with library/information service policy. The NII requires government agencies to consider, develop, and implement policies that assist them in the management of digital resources.

These policies include, but are not limited to the following:

1. Information management,
2. Information technology (IT) management,
3. Security,
4. Intellectual property/copyright,
5. Universal service, and
6. Privacy.[9]

At the present stage, our NII development is aiming at the following five goals:

1. Promoting the use of Internet: To promote pervasive use of network applications.
2. Putting every middle school and every primary school on Internet. In the year of 2000, we shall attain the ratio of 20 students to one networking-multimedia computer at the minimum.
3. Developing Taiwan into an Internet hub in the Asia-Pacific area: The purpose is to fully liberalize our communication market from monopoly, and to expedite up our network

connection to all other Asia-Pacific countries as well as all continents. By the superior technology and high quality of services employed along with free market offering, it will provide excellent incentives to attract the international Information Service Providers (ISP) and major network users.

4. Establishing "Global Chinese Content Center" : One fifth of the world population speak Chinese. Taiwan inherited profound Chinese culture, and Chinese heritage is deeply rooted. It is our duty to share it with the world by developing Taiwan to be the "Global Chinese Content Center."
5. Developing the new industry of network multimedia: It collectively includes computer, telecommunication and multimedia. This industry will be one of the most important driving industries in the 21st century with fast growth rate. In the Republic of China, this industry will grow very fast from our current information industry. It will be our key industry. The goal is that by the turn of the century, Internet will affect every aspect of our people's life: from industrial production, marketing and operational management, to government administration and services to the people. Till then, network applications will be widely developed and deployed for information access and retrieval. An 'Information Society' will thus be formed.[10]

The success of information highway depends on content. It is the content that makes all hardware and software meaningful. Therefore, we should realize that it is the information circulating on the information highway deciding our national infrastructure and cultural development.

In reaching this ambitious goal, further efforts must be placed upon network construction, education and training, information contents development, and regulatorial environment improvement through effective policy. NII does play an important role in the birth of our information policy.

LIBRARY/INFORMATION POLICY DRAFT

The Library Association of China (LAC) has prepared a *White Paper* to serve as a guideline for the future direction of library/information services development in Taiwan. This document delineates the missions and goals of library/information services, describes the current status of library/information services in Taiwan, identifies the dilemmas confronting library development, and finally, suggests the action/strategies to achieve future missions and goals. The main points are summarized as follows:

Goals and Missions of Library/Information Services

Library Association of China has identified the following missions and goals:

1. To preserve all forms of information: Libraries should preserve human knowledge and cultural heritage from generation to generation. In the digital era, libraries also need to create and preserve information in digitized form.
2. Equal access to information: Only with well-informed citizens, can a real democratic society exist. Being major institutions of social education, libraries should assure people the right to be thoroughly informed. Libraries, therefore, should provide equal opportunities for citizens to get access to information.
3. Organization of information: Libraries should organize information for individual and community users to get access to library and information with ease.
4. Fulfillment of information needs : Libraries should collect information on all subjects to meet the different needs of users at all levels.
5. Support to life-long learning: Libraries should support citi-

zens' life-long learning by building up learning resources and imparting information literacy skills.

Library Status in Taiwan

According to the most current statistics reported by the National Central Library, 4,815 libraries were in existence in Taiwan and Fukien Areas in 1997, including one national library, 434 public libraries, 150 college/university libraries, 440 high school and vocational high school libraries, 719 junior high school libraries, 2,540 primary school libraries and 512 special libraries, etc. The total amount of library collection were 91,534,682 volumes; among which 2,183,438 volumes were held by the National Central Library; 16,700,466 were held by the public libraries. College/university libraries held 36,392,587 volumes; school libraries had a total of 28,392,738 volumes and the special libraries held 7,865,453 volumes. Besides more than two-million-volume collection of NCL, the average public library holdings yielded only forty-five thousand volumes; average college/university libraries held approximately 263.4 thousand volumes; average school library holdings yielded 10 thousand volumes, and average 25 thousand volumes for special libraries.[12]

The seemingly low library holding was caused by budget constrains. Taking public libraries as an example: of 434 public libraries, a total budget for library acquisition was NT$1,432,110,000 in 1997. If every resident was to have one book available, with a total of more than 21 million population and 16 million volumes of collections in the public libraries, we would need to add more than 5 million volumes to the library collections. At an average and minimum cost of NT$250 per volume, we would need at least more than NT$1.25 billion for acquisition!

The total number of full-time staff were 8,637 as reported by 1,997 libraries, including 233 staff members in the National Central Library, 1,901 librarians in 242 public libraries, 2,562 librarians in 136 college/university libraries, 2,927 in 1,446 school libraries, and 1,014 librarians in 168 special libraries. The 1997 NCL statistics showed that there were only 4.3 librarians in each library, with an average of 7.8 full-time staff in the public libraries, 2.0 staff in school libraries (Table 1). Approximately one professional public librarian serves 6,183 registered patrons in Taiwan. College/university libraries were known to have better collections, better-qualified staff and better facilities; school libraries were somewhat limited as far as space, collection and staff were concerned. Shortage of professional staff in public and school libraries was the common phenomenon in Taiwan.

Table 1 Statistical Analysis of Taiwan & Fukien Areas Library Survey, 1997[13]

	Square meter(m2)		Amount of Collection		Number of Patrons Registered		Number of Full-time Staff	
	Total/Libraries	Average	Total/Libs	Average	Total/Libs	Average	Total/Libs	Average
NCL	42,155/1		2,183,438/1		597,565/1		233	
Public Libs.	2,085,446/374	5,576	16,700,466/372	44,893	16,927,821/351	48,227	1,901/242	7.8
College Libs.	861,296/145	5,939	36,392,587/138	263,714	12,500,798/132	94,703	2,562/136	18.8
School Libs.	1,803,129/2,731	660	28,392,738/2784	10,198	4,418,666/2,726	1,620	2,927/1,446	2.0
Special Libs.	423,558/317	1,336	7,865,453/313	25,129	1,019,161/296	3,443	1,014/168	6.0
Total	5,215,584/3,568	1,461	91,534,682/3608	25,369	35,464,398/3,506	10,115	8,637/1,993	4.3

Regarding library users and use, the total number of library users registered were 35,464,398. Just to highlight two types of libraries – public libraries and college/university libraries: 16,927,821 in 351 public libraries responded to the survey, and 12,500,798 in 132 college/university libraries that responded to the survey. A total of 28,145,365 users borrowed books from all types of libraries in the 1996-1997 fiscal year. Total volumes circulated in the same year were 58,791,054, approximately, an average of two volumes for each checkout.[14]

Besides the regular library users, increasingly demands of the Internet users are also the main concern of library management. Internet users in Taiwan numbered 3.17 million at the end of January

1999, increasing by about 160,000 or 5.3% from the 3.01 million recorded in December of 1998, According to Institute for the Information Industry (III), there are about 520,000 computers hooked up with the Internet in Taiwan, putting it the ninth in the world as well as the third in the Asia-Pacific region next to Japan and Australia in this respect. At the same time, Taiwan's Internet user population is the world's eighth largest.[15]

Problems Confronting Library Development

After thorough literature review, group discussions, and a public hearing held in May 1998, twelve major dilemmas confronting library development are identified as follows:

1. Inadequate public understanding of library services and functions: Most citizens view libraries as places to borrow books and/or read newspapers. The role of libraries as institutions to obtain information needed for daily life is not recognized. Without such public understanding, little progress can be expected of libraries.
2. Inflexible school curricula discourage the active use of libraries: Due to the inflexible design and heavy load of school curricula, students are not encouraged to use libraries actively. Current curricula design for K-12 students does not support a constructive approach to learning by exploring new knowledge independently or with the assistance of librarians. In colleges, not many faculties encourage students to use libraries effectively for self-paced learning. The younger generation, therefore, is unable to realize that the libraries' essential function of providing resources for life-long learning.
3. Underqualified library staff: Professionally trained staff is crucial to the quality of library service. At the present time, many public and school libraries are not staffed with qualified professional librarians. Up to now, there is no

law enforcement upon this important issue.

4. Insufficient funding for library collections: Budgets for library collections are limited. Total collections in public libraries stood at 16,700,466 volumes in 1997.[16] With a population of approximately twenty-one million people, acquiring one volume per citizen at NT$250 per volume would require a collection budget totaling NT$1.25 billion! (250x5,000,000=1,250,000,000)
5. Lack of overall planning and coordinating administrative mechanism: Different types of library report to different administration. College/university libraries and school libraries are under the supervision of the Ministry of Education and local governments. Public libraries are either administered by the provincial government and/or by cultural department of the central government. Poor coordination and cooperation among university, school and public libraries are thus evident.
6. Ineffective mechanisms for public libraries administration: The same problems not only occur in the different types of library systems, but also in the same type of libraries at different levels. County cultural centers and libraries are supervised and funded by the provincial government. Township libraries are supervised by the cultural centers but are funded by the towns themselves. Such administrative system indeed restricts the development of local small libraries.
7. Inadequacy of standards formulation: For some thirty years, in spite of the devoted efforts of the Library Association of China, library related laws and regulations to assure effective library infrastructure (funding, staffing and building), and for library operation (collection management and information services) are not yet comprehensively stipulated.

8. Missing management skills for library operation: Little planning and/or evaluation skills are applied to library management by libraries. Without application of these important skills, libraries' efficiency and attractiveness to user are lessened.
9. Inadequate mechanisms for effective resource sharing: Resource sharing is pivotal to quality information service. Inter-library cooperation is not satisfactorily implemented due to the lack of understanding and legal basis. Resource sharing, up to now, is a concept to which lip service is paid without efficient actions taken.
10. Imbalance in the provision of facilities for different types of libraries: Most facilities and resources are focused on college and national libraries. School and public libraries, particularly the township libraries that are closeset to the public, obtain the most limited resources, funding and staffing.
11. Imbalance in the provision of library facilities in rural and suburban areas: A similar imbalance also exists between rural and urban areas. Facilities are focused on urban areas. If information support systems can be made equally available in both rural and urban areas, this might help alleviating rural population drain.
12. Inadequate supply of knowledge-based and value-added information systems for all subject areas and disciplines: Value-added information systems, which organize knowledge, are the foundation for an information-rich and knowledge-based society. Good national bibliographic utilities, indexing and abstracting service, thesauri and encyclopedia compiling, etc. are major elements of knowledge infrastructure. It will not be possible to achieve the so-called information society without the creation of these knowledge-based, value-added information systems for all

subject areas and disciplines.

Action Strategies

Problems hampering library development are identified. In order to achieve the mission and the goals for future library development, the following action strategies, including policy issues, resource issues, management issues, and professional issues are recommended by the *White Paper*.

Policy Issues: Policy issues illuminate the urgent requirements for national information services policies, including the legislative process for the Library Law and the Government Information Access Law, etc. The following action strategies relating to policy issues that are highly recommended to decision makers in the government:

1. To enhance the legal foundation for library development: Library Law proposed by the Ministry of Education is now in the legislative process at the Legislative Yuan after thirty-three years of efforts made by the Library Association of China. The enactment of the law is pivotal to the sound development of library operation. Library community should generate public support to this set of laws and expedite its enactment with speedy and timely efforts. And in order to promote the overall information service environment, information related policies and laws need to be formulated and enacted, such as Archival Law Government Information Access Law, Privacy Law, and intellectual property legislation are all vital to build an information-rich society. Both librarians and the public at large should pay attention to these legislative actions.
2. To establish a nationwide administrative mechanism for library services: A nationwide administrative body would function as a national planning and coordinating agency for the betterment of overall library development

information services and the enhancement cooperation among different types of libraries. A centralized administrative mechanism, such as the National Commission on Library/Information Services is to be set up for better coordination and cooperation of all libraries.

3. To form library committees for public libraries at all levels: Each local government needs to establish its own library committee involving governors, administrators, representatives, educators and professional librarians in the supervision of its libraries. The committee can evaluate the performance of libraries based on the objectives and activities stated in their annual plans.
4. To promote the formulation of national library/information service standards: Service standards for library operations are the foundation of good and quality service providing. All types of libraries need service standards for the profession with constant timely updating to meet the challenges caused by change of circumstances and/or environments.
5. To establish a R&D fund for librarianship: Librarianship is a profession related to knowledge management, reader guidance, user information instruction and customer services, etc. Research and development funding is needed to encourage librarians/libraries to conduct empirical research to build up collections for life-long learning and to implement other meaningful projects. A unique foundation should be established with supports from government and the private sectors are encouraged to allocate such funds for these purposes.
6. To plan a comprehensive, value-added, decision support information system: A nation needs to accumulate and share its local history and knowledge by collecting, organizing, and publicizing such materials and information. Special disciplines related knowledge-based systems such as agri-

cultural information system; legislative information system and education resource systems are of utmost importance to national development. Such subject-oriented, value-added, decision-support information systems should be fully planned and generously supported by the government.

Resource issues: Resource issues require administrative support for human resources and collection development and funding. The following action strategies relating to resource issues are strongly recommended to library administrators and supervisors:

1. To strengthen human/financial resources, collections and library buildings: Library administrators and supervisors can strengthen human/financial resources, collections and library buildings by strategic planning and proposals writing for fiscal budgets. Only with well-equipped collections, good staff and good facilities can quality service be expected of libraries.
2. To connect library systems nationwide to the Internet: Libraries of all types can hope to meet the needs of the information society only if they are connected to the Internet. Administrative agencies need to plan and request budgets to do so.
3. To provide continuing education for librarians and information workers: Administrators should create and offer in-service training opportunities for librarians to improve their information technological, human communication and research skills. Incentive systems to encourage librarians to take up in-service training and to participate in continuing education are to be devised.

Management Issues: Management issues suggest the use of modern management skills to facilitate and improve information services for the individual library. The following action strategies relating to the management issues are strongly recommended to library managers for immediate action:

1. Planning, operating, and evaluating library performance: Librarians need skills in management, planning, supervising, operating, and evaluation to improve day-to-day performance and thereby attract citizens to use libraries. It is recommended that all libraries conduct annual planning exercises, and evaluate their own performance at the end of each year as a basis for formulating new plans for the subsequent year.
2. To formulate library service policies: To formulate and publish all kinds of library service policies is the foundation for quality service to the public. Library service policies include collection development policies, reference service policies, audio/video service policies, document delivery policies, etc. Each library needs to formulate its own service policy that meets the circumstances and needs of local patrons.
3. To join library networks to render better and more comprehensive library information services to local users: Libraries and librarians need to work together to provide better services to the public. Libraries are encouraged to join local as well as national consortia to better serve their patrons.
4. To promote information literacy education to the public: Libraries need to provide information literacy training programs to the public in order to equip the citizens with life-long learning skills. Librarians need to view themselves as educators in their community. They need take the lead in influencing the public to learn in the information age.

Professional Support: Professional issues suggests building a consensus among librarians by issuing a library bill of rights and a statement of ethics for librarians, and by conducting continuous research and study for the improvements of library/information services, theories and library/information science education. The following action strategies relating to professional issues are strongly recommended to library professional associations:

1. To program overall library and information science education/curricula: Professional societies such as the Library Association of China and the Chinese Association of Library and Information Science Education need to review and reform the overall library and information science education/curricula to meet the needs of the information society. Professional knowledge, skills, and ethics issues are the essential concerns. Formal education courses, in-service training programs to upgrade the skills of current librarians, need to be deliberated, studied and designed.
2. To formulate professional ethics for librarians and information workers: Librarians' professional associations need to issue codes of ethics for librarians to guide their professional behavior.
3. To issue a Library Bill of Rights: Librarians' professional associations need to issue a library bill of rights to encourage reading and to support intellectual freedom. This document should highlight the role and mission of libraries in a democratic society.

FUTURE OUTLOOK

Karl Popper, the famous philosopher of science, has emphasized the importance of objective knowledge which includes all types of products produced by human thinking, such as theories, artistic objects, periodicals, books and other materials collected by libraries. He further indicated that if all the tools, equipment and their use instructions are all destroyed, if the relevant objective knowledge collected by libraries and the learning abilities of human beings are still in existence, the human society can still operate without much difficulty. But if libraries are also destroyed, human beings will have to return to the barbarian age. Popper further stressed that subjective knowledge stored by human minds is limited, it would disappear at the time of death, but the objective knowledge is an accumulation of human civilization. Once it is stored in libraries, it is available to people for ages.[17]

That is why, well-developed countries pay special attention to libraries. No matter how good a person's memory is, he cannot possess all the knowledge that human beings generate. Library collections of cultural remains and of knowledge are the remedies to this drawback. That is also the reason why all renowned universities have to own a sizable library to start with. All universities need to collect comprehensive information resources to meet the information needs of faculties and students in teaching, research, and learning.

Information is considered as an indispensable element in enhancing human progress, advancing scientific and technological developments and upgrading national competitiveness. Libraries are the major institutions, which preserve, process, and disseminate information. From the perspectives of meeting the information needs of life-long learning, of promoting democratic system or of developing national information infrastructure or of establishing Asian Pacific Operations Center, government should pay utmost concerns to libraries development. This *White Paper* is presented to the government with concrete suggestions on actions to be taken on legislation, policies, budgets, and staffing. At the turn point of information age, it is necessary for all supervising agencies to realize the importance of the betterment of library and information services by giving adequate support. This is the time for librarianship to pursue far-sighted development, to correct what were improperly implemented. For better library/information services, libraries are advised to plan and implement training and continuing education programs to upgrade the professional quality of librarians.

The development of library and information services should proceed from the facets of policy, resources and management. It calls the attention to be paid by government agencies, all libraries and professional library/information workers with constant evaluation of library development objectives. Only with such efforts and commitments, can we expect a more satisfactory information service system to head for the promising information society in the 21st century.

NOTES

1. Fred W Weingarten, "Federal Information Policy Development: The Congressional Perspective," in *United States Government Information Policies*, ed. McClure, Charles R., Hernon, Peter, and Harold C. Relyea. (Norwood, N.J.: Ablex Publishing Company, 1989), 77.
2. Peter Hernon and Charles R. McClure, *United States Information Policies* (Philadelphia, PA: The National Federation of Abstracting and Information Services, 1991), 2.
3. Ian Rowlands, "Understanding Information Policy: Concepts, Frameworks and Research Tools," *Journal of Information Science* 22, no. 1 (1996): 13-35.
4. Athanasios Priftis and Charles Oppenheim, "Development of a National Information Policy in Greece," *Information Development* 15, no. 1 (March 1999): 32.
5. Data provided by the Hsing Cheng Yuan Chu Chi Ch'u 行政院主計處 [Directorate General of Budget and Statistics, Executive Yuan, ROC] in May 1999.
6. Margaret C. Fung, "National Information Policy – Some Basic Considerations," *T'u Shu Kuan Hsueh Yu Tzu Hsun K'o Hsueh 圖書館學與資訊科學 [Journal of Library & Information Science]* 13, no. 1 (April 1987): 17-28.
7. David Kaser and Joseph Becker. Proposal to the National Central Library for the Development of a ROC Information Policy, 1983.
8. Chung Kuo T'u Shu Kuan Hsueh Hui Pien 中國圖書館學會 編 [Library Association of China, ed.], *T'u Shu Kuan Shih Yeh Fa Chan Pai P'i Shu 圖書館事業發展白皮書 [The White Paper on Library Development]* (Taipei: Library Association of China, 1999), II, III.
9. Patricia D. Fletcher and John Carlo Bertot, "Introduction," *Journal of*

American Society for Information Science 50, no. 4 (1 April 1999): 295.

10. The National Information Infrastructure (NII) of R.O.C.: Abstract. (August 1997). http://www.nii.gov.tw/niieng/y1997/nii.htm
11. Chung Kuo T'u Shu Kuan Hsueh Hui Pien 中國圖書館學會 編 [Library Association of China, ed.], *T'u Shu Kuan Shih Yeh Fa Chan Pai P'i Shu 圖書館事業發展白皮書 [The White Paper on Library Development]* (Taipei: Library Association of China, 2000).
12. *T'ai Min Ti Ch'u T'u Shu Kuan Tiao Ch'a (Min Kuo Pa Shih Liu Nien) 臺閩地區圖書館調查(民國86年) [Library Survey of Taiwan & Fukien Areas, 1997]*, Unpublished progressing statistical report. National Central Library, 1999. Table 1.
13. Ibid., Table 1.
14. Ibid.
15. Shu-fen Li 李淑芬, "Kung Yuan Liang Ch'ien Nien Wo Wang Lu To Mei T'i Ch'an Chih Ta Ssu Ch'ien I, Juan T'i Ch'an Chih Tse Ta I Ch'ien Pai I Yuan. Li Wei Ts'u Cheng Fu Chia Su Shu Wei Ch'ien Chang Fa, Chu Tso Ch'uan Fa, So Te Shui Fa Teng Li Fa Kung Tso 公元兩千年我網路多媒體產值達四千億軟體產值則達一千百億元。立委促政府加速數位簽章法、著作權法、所得稅法等立法工作〔Government Speeding Up Legislation for Network Communication〕," *Kung Shang Shih Pao 工商時報*, 25 March 1998, 25.
16. *T'ai Min Ti Ch'u T'u Shu Kuan Tiao Ch'a (Min Kuo Pa Shih Liu Nien) 臺閩地區圖書館調查(民國86年) [Library Survey of Taiwan & Fukien Areas, 1997]*, Unpublished progressing statistical report. National Central Library, 1999. Table 1.
17. Karl Popper; trans. Cheng Shih-ting 程實定 譯, *K'o Kuan Chih Shih: I Ke Chin Hua Lun Te Yen Chiu 客觀知識：一個進化論的研究 [Objective Knowledge: An Evolutionary Approach]* (Taipei: Chieh Kou Ch'un, 1989), 141.

Thanks to Ms. Sonia Chen, Information Specialist, Ginzton Technology Center, CA, USA for citation verification.

Co-authored with Mei-mei Wu 吳美美 (Professor, Department of Social Education, National Taiwan Normal University), and Chia-ning Chiang 蔣嘉寧 (Editor, Information and Computing Library, National Central Library).

Reprinted with permission from *The IT and Global Digital Library Development.* Edited by Ching-chih Chen. Newton, MA: MicroUse Information, 1999. (pp. 127-138). This book includes *the Proceedings of NIT '99: 11th International Conference on New Information Technology for Library & Information Professionals, Educational Media Specialists & Technologists*, 18-20 August 1999, Taipei, Taiwan.

3

The First Four Decades of the National Central Library 1928-1966

ABSTRACT

National Central Library (NCL), being the national library of the Republic of China, was established during a unique period of Chinese history. Its developments during its first four decades of existence are considered to be of great importance to national development, to the development of Chinese librarianship and to the subsequent development of the National Central Library.

This paper explores the factors conducive to the establishment of the National Central Library and significant to its developments with analysis of its functions during the first four decades of its existence under the administration of its founding director - Dr. Chiang Fu-ts'ung.

INTRODUCTION

National library is well recognized as an instrument of national policy, essential to the development of the nation.[1] Sir Frank Francis further pointed out that a national library must be the "mind" of its society.[2] Godfrey Burston also thought that the library service of a state is the product of its geography, history, tradition, political, social and economic conditions.[3] The importance of national library, therefore, cannot be overlooked.

From a thorough study conducted on the National Central Library during the early 1980s, it has been discovered that the National Central Library of China was formed and developed under the following five significant factors.[4]

FACTORS SHAPING THE DEVELOPMENT OF THE NATIONAL CENTRAL LIBRARY

Political Factors and National Consciousness

UNESCO indicated in its Regional Seminar on the Development of National Libraries in the Asia and Pacific Area in 1964: "There are many countries with an ancient cultural and library tradition. Though the cultural tradition has survived, modern national libraries have not grown directly from it, but perhaps more from an awakening national consciousness."[5] The immediate impetus to the formation of the National Central Library was undoubtedly caused by an awakening national consciousness under the political circumstances described as follows:

At the end of 19th century and in the first decade of the 20th century, Chinese people came into close contact with the modern democratic thoughts. Under the leadership of Dr. Sun Yat-sen, the founder of the Republic of China, a new sense of national consciousness inspired the Chinese people to want to become rulers themselves rather than to be ruled by others.

The formation of a constitutional government in China ushered the need for well-informed and better-educated citizens. Each citizen was expected to play an active part to promote public welfare and to govern the nation.

After the successful revolution in China and the founding of the Republic, her internal problems, such as the occupation of various parts of China by warloads prohibited the Republic from immediately becoming a government guided by the Three Principles of the People, China was finally made into a united nation after the Northern Expedition of 1926-28, the capital was installed in Nanking.

Due to the general conviction that the capital city is the political, social, and cultural center of a country, National Central Library was recommended to be established in Nanking.[6]

For years, China suffered from foreign occupation and aggressions. Many foreign powers fought for the access to her enormous natural resources. As a result, the China was humiliated by losing fertile lands and ceding extra-territorial rights to foreign invaders.

It was under such circumstances, national consciousness emerged and prevailed in the Chinese society that called for independence and strength through education. The May Fourth Movement of 1919 clearly indicated the people's longing for democracy and scientific knowledge. This new national consciousness demanded national policy of having mass education, of acquiring subject specialization and of learning scientific/technological know-how. National libraries especially were considered to be one of the major means to meet these objectives. The National Central Library was thus evolved.

The World War II made such a national consciousness more evident. As Chinese people became more aware of the benefits of democracy, they became more interested in participating in national policy making which basically needed well-informed and educated citizens. National policy had its focus on mass education and attention was paid to acquiring knowledge for keeping alive under the constant fear of air-raids. These resulted in the need to make many pertinent publications available. Libraries became both the cause and the effect of these efforts.

In 1945, upon the termination of World War II, the government returned to its official capital-Nanking and immediately wanted to revive all activities with the hope to rebuild a strong nation. The government strongly supported the National Central Library's restoration and expansion through the repair of old premises, the planning of a new library building and the enrichment of its collection and additions of branches.[7] Before all these could begin, the internal dispute between the Nationalists and Communists forced the government to move to Taiwan. While the influence of Japanese occupation was still dominant. In Taiwan, the government tried to re-educate the inhabitants to be genuine Chinese. Japanese was replaced by Chinese in schools and in publications. Anti-Communism through democratic practices was advocated. Many countries ceased their diplomatic relationships with the Republic of China on Taiwan. The National Central Library was one of the effective educational means through its collection and various services. Through its international exchange of publications, it managed to keep in contact with other nations.

Cultural and Social Factors

Traditionally, the Chinese have always had a profound respect for learning and scholarship and have made attainment in education synonymous with prestige. Ability to read, originally a privilege reserved for the elites, suddenly became a necessity advocated by both the people and the government. The promotion of the colloquial language so as to extend literacy quickly resulted in the rapid spread of literacy and a large increase in the number of publications published. It also further encouraged the pursuit of education and enhanced the prestige of libraries as well. The traditional love of books prompted the establishment of private, public, and imperial collections throughout Chinese history, provided an environment conducive to the flourishing of all types of library in the twentieth century at the founding of the Republic.

The Chinese people treasure our culture and are proud of our civilization. The library function of preserving, perpetuating, and disseminating culture is thus much valued. This was a contributing factor to the development of the National Central Library, especially during the war years.

Limited recreational facilities in Chungking made the use of library extension services a popular pastime and a valuable means of self-education. The desire for more educational as well as recreational facilities encourage the NCL to provide more effective library services. Under the continuing influence of the New Life Movement, which was promoted before the war, the Chinese people were particularly industrious and conscientious during the war years, this helped stimulating the rapid growth of the NCL.[8]

Although the Japanese policy of colonization in Taiwan was exploitative, it nevertheless helped cultivating the reading habit of the islanders. Their demand for a diversity of reading materials gave added impetus to the development of national library services in Taiwan after its return to China in 1945.

Personal Supports

Through the efforts of Mary Elizabeth Wood, the Chinese people were introduced to modern libraries and librarianship. This appreciation of librarianship cultivated the seedling concept of a national library that would serve as a public library as well as a research facility.

Wang Yun-wu, a self-educated man and dedicated advocate of librarianship, was also instrumental to the development of the NCL. At the first nationwide conference on education, he presented a proposal for the establishment of the National Central Library. He assisted Chinese librarianship in general and the NCL in particular with his indexing method and his publishing facility – the Commercial Press.[9]

Leaders such as Ts'ai Yuan-p'ei, once Minister of Education, and Chu Chia-hua, once Minister of Education and of Communication, as well as Director of the Board for the Sino-British Educational and Cultural Endowment Fund, realized the importance of education through effective modern library services.[10] Their assistances given to Chiang Fu-ts'ung in building up the National Central Library were most influential.

Subsequent Ministers of Education, Wang Shih-chieh, Chen Li-fu, and Hang Li-wu all supported the National Central Library in various ways, especially in its funding, promoting the use of the British Boxer Indemnity Fund for the purpose of building construction and collection development, and permitting the removal of its rarities from China mainland to Taiwan.[11] During his tenure as the Minister of Education, Chang Ch'i-yun, ordered the reinstallation of the National Central Library in 1954 at the instruction of the late President Chiang Kai-shek.[12] Both of them were convinced of the significance of social educational programs and gave these programs national priority. The NCL thus was restored with priority.

Other influential supporters of the NCL included Hu Shih, once Ambassador to the United States, and Yuan T'ung-li, Director of the National Peking Library.[13] Their advice was of great use in the development and safekeeping of the NCL collections.

Chiang Fu-ts'ung was the single most important figure in the establishment and development of the National Central Library. Because of his expertise obtained in Germany, his dedication, his administrative and planning abilities, the NCL became an internationally recognized research facility. Following and motivated by the example set by Dr. Chiang, the NCL staff members made great contributions to the development of the library's collections and services. It is therefore fair to state that far-sighted personal supports and concerns exerted vital influences upon the National Central Library in its formative years.

Economic Conditions

With limited financial resources, deprived of sufficient revenues as the result of unequal treaties with foreign countries, and confronted by new societal pressures, the Chinese government was unable to adequately fund the vast number of new social and educational institutions including libraries. Ts'ai Yuan-p'ei's suggestion of utilizing the Boxer Indemnity Fund, the timely return of the United States Boxer Indemnity Fund, and subsequent appropriations from the British Boxer Indemnity Fund to the National Central Library, did relieve some of the economic difficulties affecting this particular educational institution.[14]

Philanthropic efforts and international book campaigns in the late 1930's also alleviated some of the financial constraints of the libraries during the war.[15] The increase of the National Social Education Fund from 1940 onward and the United States aid received in the 1950's also benefited the National Central Library. [16]

Technological Impacts

When China found herself exposed to Western civilization and became motivated to adopt modernization in the 20th century, she acquired a large amount of technological instruments and machinery for all types of activities. For the NCL, the most beneficial technological advances acquired during these four decades were chemical insecticides, modern photographic equipment, and printing facilities.[17] New chemical components enabled the NCL to preserve rare books and relics more efficiently and effectively, and new equipment facilitated the production of catalog cards and the reproduction of ancient books. Modern steel bookshelves introduced for open-shelf arrangement also facilitated easy access to its collections.

Motivated by an urgent national need for modernization, the NCL was expected to supply scientific and technological information and materials, as well as to hold special exhibits of scientific and technical materials. It even made an unsuccessful attempt to establish a scientific and technological information center. New technology, therefore, aided the NCL in improving its services and administration on one hand; and on the other hand, it provoked new societal demands on the NCL for provision of scientific and technical materials which were considered important to national advancements.

THE FUNCTIONS OF THE NATIONAL CENTRAL LIBRARY

It has generally been recognized that national libraries should serve as the permanent repository for all publications issued in the country, the national bibliographic control and information service center, the center for international publication exchange and the leader in planning and coordinating overall national library services. Among its many other functions, the National Central Library considered dissemination of knowledge, collection development, bibliographic control and leadership in librarianship as its major responsibilities.

Dissemination of Knowledge

The preservation and dissemination of national literature and a wide range of other records are the pivotal concerns of the national library. The National Central Library has always considered the preservation and propagation of Chinese culture to be one of its essential responsibilities, and its effort to disseminate knowledge has been evident in all of its programs. The most effective methods for accomplishing this mission were the reproduction of ancient and rare Chinese books, the international exchange of publications, and the preparation of exhibitions.[18]

Reproduction of Ancient and Rare Books

To make knowledge more accessible to researchers and the general public, the National Central Library reproduced scarce or precious ancient Chinese books ever since its inception. 231 rarest titles of *Ssu K'u Ch'uan Shu Chen Pen* in 2,000 volumes were reproduced in November 1933 by the order of the Ministry of Education issued on April 21, 1933.[19] *Hsuan Lan T'ang Ts'ung Shu*, the rarest Ming Dynasty historiographical work, acquired in the Japanese-occupied territories, was also reproduced. After its revival in Taiwan, the National Central Library devoted more efforts in reproducing valuable Chinese books. In 1966, long range plan for reproduction was drawn and a set of photo-reproduction rules was formulated in 1967.[20]

Exhibitions

The exhibitions of subject collection, new books and rare books were also means of promoting social education at home and of exchange abroad. The National Central Library has employed exhibitions of new books as a continuous and uninterrupted process of advertising its new acquisitions. Rare books exhibitions were held to provide the public with a better understanding of Chinese printing and books-making. The enormous amount of information in texts which were locked in cases were made available to readers. Exhibitions for special occasions, such as the one for the first National Assembly showed how a national library can participate in events of national significance.

International book shows were important in the dissemination of Chinese culture and in the promotion of international understanding through flow of information. During the years of 1954 and 1966, the NCL held 67 international exhibitions of a wide range of materials which included materials in Chinese studies, children's books, etc.[21] Most books exhibited abroad were donated to some interested libraries for wide dissemination of publications published in China.

International Exchange of Publications

With the purpose of acquiring foreign publications and sharing of knowledge, NCL's efforts in both the international and domestic exchange of publications have been successful. During the early years, incoming exchange items exceeded outgoing ones in a 2:1 ratio; outgoing ones exceeded the incoming ones from 1955 on.[22]

Collection Development

The quality of library services is based on the quality of library collection. Chiang believed that a national library should be the center of national culture, world knowledge, and scholarly research which made the NCL's collection to fall into three categories: publications of China, foreign publications, and scholarly works. The NCL acquired its collections through deposit, exchange, purchase, and gifts. Beginning with a meager collection of government documents, examination papers and books donated by the Archives Management Office of the Ministry of Education, the collection grew from 46,000 volumes in 1933 to 180,000 volumes in 1937.[23] Creative ways of acquiring publications included: 1) Hu Shih's suggestion to acquire foreign materials by exchanging government documents and reproductions of rare books;[24] 2) Chiang's advocacy of publication law which required one copy of trade publications and thirty copies of government publications to be deposited with the national libraries.[25] In addition, the acquisition of rare and ancient collections in the Japanese-occupied areas from 1940 to 1943, and the book campaign for Western language materials initiated in 1938.[26]

The dramatic recovery of rare Chinese books from Japan, the government allocation of the Tze-ts'un rare book collection and the production of copies of the rare books deposited in the Library of Congress not only added assets to the NCL rare book collection but also increased the utility and accessibility of the NCL collections.

The government's policy to protect the products of Chinese culture and heritage was evident in evacuating rare books to safe places prior to potential threat. The great pride of Chinese in their heritage as symbolized by these irresplaceable intellectual pieces was indeed well served by the efforts of the NCL to acquire and protect them.

Bibliographic Control

With sound technical principles, the NCL was able to organize its collections in a systematic manner and to provide quality public services. The concept to cooperate with other libraries has helped it to make more efficient use of its bibliographic, financial and human resources.

The NCL carried out its bibliographic control functions through the following processes: by producing card catalogs, books catalogs, union catalogs and various bibliographies. The drafting and standardization of cataloging rules were the most important task which helped making its bibliographic control programs successful.

In 1933, the NCL's first attempt to meet its bibliographic control obligations was to take over the Kuo Hsueh Shu Chu, a publishing company. The NCL printed cards with the modern printing facilities donated by the Ministry of Communication on September 11, 1936.[27] It began the centralized and cooperative cataloging venture which was later halted by the Sino-Japanese War in 1937. The publication of the *Catalogue of New Publications Submitted to the National Central Library* on February 15, 1935 marked the beginning of modern Chinese national bibliography.[28]

The bibliographic control efforts of the NCL were evidenced by the proliferation of bibliographic tools compiled and published by the Library during the war. Following its reactivation in 1954, the National Central Library implemented its bibliographic control program even more vigorously. It started to compile the Chinese section of *Index Translationum* in 1958.[29] This endeavor had a tremendous impact upon international bibliographic use and control. Such numerous bibliographic tools also served as keys to the enormous intellectual resources, as basis for interlibrary cooperation, and as foundation for successful library public services.

Chiang Fu-ts'ung paid great attention to standardization which is the basis of consistency conducive to effective library performances. The NCL observed Anglo-American practices for Western books, he started the study of the Interim and Experimental Cataloging for Serials and Books in 1935. Constant revisions and evaluations done in 1940, 1946, 1959 and 1965 indicated his understanding of the complexity of rules for cataloging Chinese and Western materials in Chinese libraries.[30] All these undertakings showed the NCL's firm intention of implementing bibliographic control.

Professional Leadership

The professional leadership expressed by the operations of the National Central Library prevailed throughout these four decades. Major accounts are discussed as follows:[31]

Library Education

Professional training is essential to the development of any profession. In China, librarianship was not considered as a profession in need of special education until Mary Elizabeth Wood introduced the American practice. While formal education for librarians was the responsibility of library schools, continuing education and in-service training were made available by the National Central Library. At its suggestions, five library schools were to be established in various parts of China on a regional basis. National Taiwan Normal University established a division of library science in the Department of Social Education at the suggestion made by the NCL.[32]

Research and Development

From the beginning, the NCL had a committee to study various libraries under the name of Counseling and Guidance Committee which was renamed into the Research Committee on Nationwide Librarianship with the responsibility to play the role of library leadership in China.

Library System Planning

The NCL made a proposal for China to establish five national libraries for the purpose of preserving regional resources and meeting local needs and it was directly involved in the planning of the National Lanchow Library, the National Sian Library, and the National Roosevelt Library.

Throughout its first four decades, the NCL was active in planning for the establishments of many local and provincial libraries during and after the war. In 1962, at the Fourth National Conference on Education, the NCL presented a detailed development plan for library services in Taiwan.[33]

Laws and Regulations

The National Central Library demonstrated its leadership role in the formulation of government policies pertaining to library-related activities. This could be proved by the various laws and regulations drafted by the National Central Library including Publication Laws, Library Regulations, Facility Standards for County and Municipal Social Education Centers, Guidelines Regarding Libraries' Assistance to Local Social Educational Institutions in Rendering Library Education, and Stipulations Regarding the Lowering of Book Prices.

Library Management and Services

The professional leadership assumed by the National Central Library in library management and services is demonstrated by its library operating manuals, organizational stipulations, cataloging rules, interlibrary loan terms and centralized cataloging which were adopted by other libraries in the nation for the provision of library management and services.

CONCLUSION

This presentation attempts to show how the National Central

Library was formed because of a wide range of political, social, economic, cultural, technological and personal factors. National Central Library was conceived, organized and developed under the dual influences of a historical heritage and a new national consciousness. Its very existence, its services, and its endeavors in education, bibliographic control, and librarianship leadership practiced in its first forty years have been and will remain vital to the wholesome development of Chinese society as well as to the preservation and dissemination of Chinese culture.

Due to time limitation of this presetation, it is impossible to narrate detailed developments of the National Central Library and some of its exciting undertakings in the chronological order of : the origin and conceptualization years, 1928-1933; preparatory stage and formative periods, 1933-1937; war-stricken days, 1937-1945; recovery period, 1946-1953; the development era, 1954-1966. Only the very important events were highlighted in this paper.[34]

Summarized by Chiang Fu-ts'ung, the most important functions of the National Central Library were: to offer more comprehensive, effective efficient and quality library services and to provide leadership in the attainment of overall excellence in Chinese librarianship and information services.

In 1966 when Chiang Fu-ts'ung retired from the National Central Library, it was clear that the convictions that he had for the Library and the foundations that he laid for the Library would be the directions for the NCL to fulfill its functions in the subsequent years and years to come.

In the frequent changes happened to the National Central Library, the characteristics pointed out by Sir Francis, Humphrey and Burston seemed to have all been reflected in the functions, formation and developments of the NCL.[35] Dynamic as the National Central Library was in its first forty years, its future achievements in the advancement of scholarship, in the popularization of education, in national policy-making, in the preservation and dissemination of

Chinese culture, and in national development are likely to be even greater. The continuation and strengthening of its efforts will help China to march into a more advanced and united future in full harmony with the family of nation.

NOTES

1 David C. Mearns, "Current Trends in National Libraries," *Library Trends* 4 (July 1955): 96.

2. Cliff Lashley, "West Indian National Libraries and the Challenges of Change," in *National Libraries*, ed. Maurice B. Line and Joyce Line (London: ASLIB, 1979), 306 – citing F. C. Francis.

3. Godfrey Burston, "*National Libraries*: An Analysis," in *National Libraries*, ed. Maurice B. Line and Joyce Line (London: ASLIB, 1979), 97.

4. Margaret C. Fung, *The Evolving Social Mission of the National Central Library in China 1928-1966* (Taipei: National Institute for Compilation and Translation, 1994), 197-204.

5. "Regional Seminar on the Development of National Central in Asia and Pacific Area, Manila, Philippines, 3-15 February 1964," in *UNESCO Bulletin for Libraries* 18, no. 3 (May-June 1964): 150.

6. "Peking" is used throughout the text to identify the city's name which is also known as "Peiping" after 1928 when it was designated as a city directly under the control of the Executive Yuan (the Cabinet). The date of 1928 is identified by Hsi-ying Ni, *Peiping* (Shanghai: Chung Hua Shu Chu, 1936), 13. It is also known as "Beijing" in Pin-yin system.

7. Kuo Li Chung Yang T'u Shu Kuan Pien 國立中央圖書館 編 [National Central Library, ed.], "Kuo Li Chung Yang T'u Shu Kuan I Nien Lai *Chung Hsin Kung Tso Kai K'uang 國立中央圖書館一年來中心工作概況 [The Past Year's Work at the National Central Library]*," Chung Kuo T' u Shu Kuan Hsueh Hui Pao *中國圖書館學會會報 [Bulletin of the Library Association of China]* 20 (15 June 1946): 8; National Central Library, [Administration Chronological File], 17 April 1946, Taipei, ROC; Peter Ch'ang 昌彼得, "Kuo Li Chung Yang T'u Shu Kuan Chien Shih 國立中央圖書館簡史 [Brief History of the National Central Library]," *Chiao Yu Yu Wen Hua 教育與文化 [Education and Culture]* 351/352 (March 1967): 5; Fu-ts'ung Chiang 蔣復璁, "Wo Yu Chung Yang T'u Shu Kuan 我與中央圖書館 [My Life with the National Central Library]," recorded by Ching Chiang 蔣京 記錄, *Chin Tai Chung Kuoru 近代中國 [Contemporary*

China] 11 (June 1979): 169; Ching Su 蘇精, "K'ang Chan Shih Ch'i Mi Mi Sou Kou Lun Hsien Ch'u Ku Chi Shih Mo 抗戰時期秘密搜購淪陷區古籍始末 [An Account of Purchasing Ancient Books in the Japanese Occupied Area]," *Chuan Chi Wen Hsueh 傳記文學 [Biographical Literature]* 35, no. 5 (November 1979): 109-114.

8. Arif Dirlik, "The Ideological Foundations of the New Life Movement: A Study in Counterrevolution," *Journal of Asian Studies* 34 (August 1975): 945-80.
9. *Chung Kuo T'u Shu Kuan Hsueh Hui Pao 中國圖書館學會會報 [Bulletin of the Library Association of China]* 3 (June 1928): 17, 164.
10. Fu-ts'ung Chiang 蔣復璁, "Wo Yu Chung Yang T'u Shu Kuan 我與中央圖書館 [My Life with the National Central Library]," recorded by Ching Chiang 蔣京 記錄, *Chin Tai Chung Kuo 近代中國 [Contemporary China]* 11 (June 1979): 162.
11. K'aiming Ch'iu, "Modern Library Movement in China," in *Library in China* (Peking: Library Association of China, 1935), 1-17.
12. Kuo Li Chung Yang T'u Shu Kuan 國立中央圖書館 [National Central Library], Kuo Li Chung Yang T'u Shu Kuan Pien Nien Cheng Shih Lu 國立中央圖書館編年政事錄 [Administration Chronological File], August 1954, Taipei, ROC; Peter Ch'ang 昌彼得, "Chiang Wei-t'ang Hsien Sheng Ch'i Shih Nien Paio 蔣慰堂先生七十年表 [Seventy Years of Chronology of Dr. Chiang Fu-ts'ung]," *in Ching Chu Chiang Fu-ts'ung Hsien Sheng Ch'i Shih Sui Lun Wen Chi 慶祝蔣復璁先生七十歲論文集 [Symposium in Honor of Dr. Chiang Fu-ts'ung on His 70th Birthday]* (Taipei: National Palace Museum, 1969), 284.
13. Tsuen-hsuin Tsien 錢存訓, "Kuo Li Peiping T'u Shu Kuan Shan Pen T'u Shu Yun Lai Ching Kuo 國立北平圖書館善本圖書運來經過 [An Account of the Shipping of the National Peiping Library's Rare Books to the United States]," *Chuan Chi Wen Hsueh 傳記文學 [Biographical Literature]* 10 (February 1967): 55-57; Fu-ts'ung Chiang 蔣復璁, "Wo Yu Chung Yang T'u Shu Kuan 我與中央圖書館 [My Life with the National Central Library]," 162; Interview with Fu-ts'ung Chiang 蔣復璁, National Palace Museum, Taipei, Taiwan, 22 February 1983.
14. Fu-ts'ung Chiang 蔣復璁, "K'an Chan Ssu Nien Lai Chih T'u Shu Kuan Shih Yeh 抗戰四年來之圖書館事業 [Librarianship During Four Years of the Sino-Japanese War]," *Kuo Li Chung Yang T'u Shu Kuan Kuan K'an 國立中央圖書館館刊 [Nationl Central Library Bulletin]* New 7 (September 1974): 3.

15. Margaret C. Fung, *The Evolving Social Mission of the National Central Library in China 1928-1966* (Taipei: National Institute for Compilation and Translation, 1994), 92-93.
16. Kuo Li Chung Yang T'u Shu Kuan 國立中央圖書館 [National Central Library], Kuo Li Chung Yang T'u Shu Kuan Pien Nien Cheng Shih Lu 國立中央圖書館編年政事錄 [Administration Chronological File], 6 December 1938; 16 May 1940, Taipei, ROC.; Fu-ts'ung Chiang 蔣復璁, "Kuo Li Chung Yang T'u Shu Kuan Te I I Yu Hui Ku 國立中央圖書館的意義與回顧 [The Significance and Recollections of the National Central Library]," *Ta Lu Tsa Chih 大陸雜誌 [The Continent Magazine]* 56, no. 6 (June 1967): 253; Interview with Fu-ts'ung Chiang 蔣復璁, National Palace Museum, Shihlin, Taipei, Taiwan, ROC, 21 February 1982.
17. Kuo Li Chung Yang T'u Shu Kuan Pien 國立中央圖書館 編 [National Central Library, ed.], "Fa Chan Chung Kuo T'u Shu Kuan Shih Yeh Fang An Chi Shuo Ming — Ti Ssu Tz'u Ch'uan Kuo Chiao Yu Hui I T'i An 發展中國圖書館事業方案暨說明 — 第四次全國教育會議提案 [An Explanation on the Program for Developing Librarianship]," *Chung Kuo T'u Shu Kuan Hsueh Hui Hui Pao 中國圖書館學會會報 [Bulletin of the Library Association of China]* 14 (December 1962): 10-15.
18. Margaret C. Fung, *The Evolving Social Mission of the National Central Library in China 1928-1966* (Taipei: National Institute for Compilation and Translation, 1994), 207-210.
19. Chiao Yu Pu Ling Kuo Li Chung Yang T'u Shu Kuan Yu Chiang Fu-ts'ung 教育部令國立中央圖書館與蔣復璁 [MOE to NCL and Fu-ts'ung Chiang], Hsun Ling San Ssu Ssu Pa Hao Hsun Ling 訓令三四四八號訓令 ["Instructions #3448"], 21 April 1933, Ch'eng Li Tang An 成立檔案 [Inaugural File], NCL, Taipei, ROC; *Chiao Yu Pu Kung Pao 教育部公報 [MOE Gazette]* 5 (April 1933): 7.
20. The Management Regulation of the Application of Reproduction and Photographing of the Rare Books of the National Central Library. Min Kuo Wu Shih Ch'i Nien Hsing Cheng Yuan Tai Wu Shih Ch'i She Tzu Ti Liu I Ling Ling Hao 民國五十七年行政院台五十七社字第6100號 [Executive Order no. 57 She Tzu 6100 dated 1968].
21. Margaret C. Fung, *The Evolving Social Mission of the National Central Library in China 1928-1966* (Taipei: National Institute for Compilation and Translation, 1994), 197-205.
22. Rui-lan Ku Wu 辜瑞蘭, " Kuo Li Chung Yang T'u Shu Kuan Te Ch'u Pan Pin Kuo Chi Chieh Huan Kuan Tso 國立中央圖書館的出版品國際交換

工作 [The International Exchange of Publications Work at the National Central Library]," *Chiao Yu Yu Wen Hua 教育與文化 [Education and Culture]* 351/352 (30 March 1967): 31-35.

23. Kuo Li Chung Yang T'u Shu Kuan Ch'eng Chiao Yu Pu Pao Kao 國立中央圖書館呈教育部報告 [NCL Report to MOE], December 1939-40, Kuo Li Chung Yang T'u Shu Kuan Pien Nien Cheng Shih Lu 國立中央圖書館編年政事錄 [Administration Chronological File], NCL, Taipei, ROC.
24. Margaret C. Fung, *The Evolving Social Mission of the National Central Library in China 1928-1966* (Taipei: National Institute for Compilation and Translation, 1994), 59.
25. Margaret C. Fung, *The Evolving Social Mission of the National Central Library in China 1928-1966* (Taipei: National Institute for Compilation and Translation, 1994), 44.
26. T'ung-li Yuan, "Grateful for Gifts to China," *ALA Bulletin* 33 (May 1939): 352; "Appeal from China," Library Journal 63 (1 June 1938): 439.
27. Ching Yu 淨雨, "Ch'ing Tai Yin Shua Shih Hsiao Chi 清代印刷史小記 [Brief Description of the History of Printing in the Ch'ing Dynasty]," in *Shu Lin Ch'ing Hua 書林清話 [Comments on Books and Book Trades]* by Teh-hui Yeh 葉德輝 (Taipei: Shih Chieh Shu Chu, 1968); Peter Ch'ang 昌彼得, "Kuo Li Chung Yang T'u Shu Kuan Chien Shih 國立中央圖書館簡史 [Brief History of the National Central Library]," 6.
28. Kuo Li Chung Yang T'u Shu Kuan 國立中央圖書館 [National Central Library], Kuo Li Chung Yang T'u Shu Kuan Pien Nien Cheng Shih Lu 國立中央圖書館編年政事錄 [Administration Chronological File], 11 September 1936, Taipei, ROC.
29. Kuo Li Chung Yang T'u Shu Kuan Pien 國立中央圖書館 編 [National Central Library, ed.], *Kuo Li Chung Yang T'u Shu Kuan Kai K'uang 國立中央圖書館概況 [Status of the National Central Library]* (Taipei: National Central Library, 1974), 13-14.
30. Kuo Li Chung Yang T'u Shu Kuan 國立中央圖書館 [National Central Library], Kuo Li Chung Yang T'u Shu Kuan Pien Nien Cheng Shih Lu 國立中央圖書館編年政事錄 [Administration Chronological File], 1 April and 5 May, 1936, Taipei, ROC.
31. Margaret C. Fung, *The Evolving Social Mission of the National Central Library in China 1928-1966* (Taipei: National Institute for Compilation and Translation,1994), 247-251.
32. Chiao Yu Pu Chiao Yu Nien Chien Pien Tsuan Wei Yuan Hui Pien 教育部教育年鑑編纂委員會 編 [Committee of the Chinese Education

Yearbook, Ministry of Education, ed., *Ti San Tz'u Chung Kuo Chiao Yu Nien Chien 第三次中國教育年鑑 [The Third Chinese Education Yearbook]* (Taipei: Chen Chung Shu Chu, 1957), 822.; Fu-ts'ung Chiang 蔣復璁 "Kuo Li Chung Yang T'u shu Kuan Kai K'uang 國立中央圖書館概況 [The Past Year's Work at the National Central Library]," Chung Kuo T'u Shu Kuan Hsueh Hui Hui Pao *中國圖書館學會會報 [Bulletin of the Library Association of China]* 8 (October 1957): 9.

33. "Fa Chan Chung Kuo T'u Shu Kuan Shih Yeh Fang An Chi Shuo Ming — Ti Ssu Tz'u Ch'uan Kuo Chiao Yu Hui I T'i An 發展中國圖書館事業方案暨說明 — 第四次全國教育會議提案 [An Explanation on the Program for Developing Librarianship]," 10-15.
34. Margaret C. Fung, *The Evolving Social Mission of the National Central Library in China 1928-1966* (Taipei: National Institute for Compilation and Translation,1994), 36-213.
35. F. C. Francis, "The Organization of National Libraries," in *National Libraries: Their Problems and Prospects* (Paris: UNESCO, 1960), 21-26; Humphreys, "Role of the National Library," in *National Libraries*, ed. Maurice B. Line and Joyce Line (London: ASLIB, 1979), 362-68; Godfrey Burston, "National Libraries: An Analysis," in *National Libraries*, ed. Maurice B. Line and Joyce Line (London: ASLIB, 1979), 97.

Published with thanks to the National Institute for Compilation and Translation for granting permission to use part of materials contained in *The Evolving Social Mission of National Central Library in China 1928-1966.*

Reprinted with permission from National Central Library. *The Proceedings of the International Conference on National Libraries – Towards the 21st Century*. Taipei, Taiwan: National Central Library, 1993. (pp. 59-70).

4

Safekeeping of the National Peiping Library's Rare Chinese Books at the Library of Congress 1941-1965

ABSTRACT

This article reports the history, contents and safekeeping of the National Peiping Library's rare Chinese books at the Library of Congress. The historical setting, LC's acceptance, preservation, cataloging/microfilming and return of this collection are thoroughly studied and presented. The unfolding of this event shows that at times of crisis require such extraordinary safety measures as depositing library rarities in the custody of another nation. Such an international joint effort in safekeeping rarities, however, can be adopted only by countries that enjoy common aspirations and congenial relations.

"Books are the foundation on which the entire service structure of the library rests."[1]

INTRODUCTION

Safekeeping and preservation of a library's materials comprise an important aspect of collection management. In times of large-scale emergency, this work can require drastic measures, sometimes involving high adventure and international intrigue. Several such cases arose during the cataclysmic times of World War II.

One well-known case involved the Lincoln Cathedral exemplar of the Magna Carta, the cornerstone of Western democracy, dated 1215 A.D. The best of the four originals, and a priceless memorial of the heritage of the English-speaking people, this document was sent to the United States for exhibition at the New York World's Fair in 1939. At the conclusion of the Fair, however, as a precaution against the risks associated with submarine warfare, it was deposited at the Library of Congress, for safekeeping, where it remained from 27 December 1940 to 11 January 1946.[2]

A second case concerned fourteen suitcases of wooden slips, dating back to the first century B.C., which had been excavated in North China by the Sino-Swedish Expedition in 1930.[3] Being the direct ancestors of Chinese books, these wooden slips are bibliographic rarities of great significance. On behalf of the Sinological Research Department of the National Peking University, Dr. Hu Shih, former Chinese Ambassador to the United States, arranged for the deposit of this collection in the Rare Book Room of the Library of Congress during the period from 1940 to 1965.[4] The present article, however, addresses the fate for a quarter of a century of 102 boxes of selected Chinese rare books owned by the National Peiping Library.[5] Consisting of approximately 75 Sung editions (960-1279 A.D.), 4 Chin editions (1115-1234 A.D.) and the succeeding Ch'ing period, 131 Yuan editions (1260-1368 A.D.), 2,000 Ming editions (1368-1644 A.D.), manuscripts, movable-type incunabula, handwritten, and annotated copies, these treasures were shipped in disguise from Shanghai to the Library of Congress for safekeeping in 1941.[6]

THE SETTING

The Japanese intention to occupy China was made evident by their support of Yuan Shih-kai in 1915, the subsequent Manchurian Incident on 18 September 1931, and the Shanghai Incident on 28 January 1932.[7] Their invasion continued with the initiation of the Sino-Japanese War on 7 July 1937.[8] Japan's swift occupation of

Tientsin and Shanghai in 1937 caused the evacuation of the Chinese government and people from the northern and southeastern coastal provinces to the southwestern mountain areas in China. Only parts of the universities, faculties, books, equipments, invaluable cultural treasures, and factory facilities, however, were able to move with the government.[9]

A modern library movement had been promoted by the work of Mary Elizabeth Wood since 1909, and the legal foundation for libraries had been laid by the promulgation of library laws during the subsequent two decades.[10] According to a survey conducted by the Ministry of Education in 1936, there were then 4,032 libraries in the country.[11] This blooming library scene, however, was shattered by the Japanese invasion, when literally millions of volumes were dispersed or destroyed by the War, and nearly 2,000 libraries were lost.[12] In Japanese-occupied areas, the looting of books went far, and it was reported by Schultheis that: "most of the pillaged books...[were] sold to Japanese collectors."[13] Even though some libraries moved with their parent organizations to the interior of the country, many others were left behind. Those that did move had to do so in a great hurry, and it was usually impossible for them to move all of their collections.[14]

THE PROBLEM

After the Manchurian Incident of 1931 and the Shanghai Incident in 1932, the Chinese government took immediate precautions, for the Library, against possible future wars. An order was given to the National Palace Museum, National Peiping Library (NPL), and National Central Library (NCL) to move their selected rarities to foreign concessions in Shanghai for protection against damage. Dr. Tung-li Yuan, the NPL Director, was so concerned about the collection that he sent for his assistant, Dr. Tsien Tsuen-hsuin, who was then the Librarian of NPL Nanking Branch, to go to Shanghai to take charge of this project in 1938.[15]

Five thousand titles of rare Chinese books (in sixty thousand volumes), nine thousand scrolls of Tun Huang Buddhist Sutras manuscripts, and hundreds of bronze and stone tablet rubbings were selected from the NPL collection and removed, first to the International Settlement in Shanghai, later to the French Concession, then to civilian housing, and eventually back again to the International Settlement.[16]

When the Sino-Japanese War broke out in 1937, making it impossible to evacuate in haste, Dr. Yuan became very much concerned about the safety of the NPL collection, and deliberated on ways for its safekeeping. Among the options available to him was one that had been pioneered a bit earlier by Dr. Hu Shih, the Chinese Ambassador to the United States.

On 31 October 1939, Dr. Archibald MacLeish, the Librarian of Congress, had responded favorably to a suggestion made by Dr. Hu Shih, expressing the Library of Congress's interest in increasing its Chinese holdings.[17] As a result of this correspondence, Dr. Hu deposited a small collection of the manuscripts of his father (Hu Chuan) at the Library of Congress in the following year. In October 1940 the aforementioned fourteen sealed suitcases of ancient Chinese inscribed woodslips were also deposited by Dr. Hu Shih at the Library of Congress for safekeeping.[18]

It was immediately after this second deposit by Dr. Hu that Dr. Tung-li Yuan approached the American Ambassador in Chungking to ask if the Library of Congress would also be willing to give the NPL'S rare Chinese books and manuscripts temporary safekeeping. Before the formal request was made, however, Dr. Hu Shih discussed the matter personally with Dr. Arthur Hummel, Chief of the Orientalia Division at the Library of Congress, and obtained his support.[19] The formal request, accompanied by permission for the LC to make microfilm copies of the rare books to be deposited, was officially conveyed to the LC through the Department of State on 27 November 1940.[20]

ENTHUSIASTIC ACCEPTANCE BY THE LIBRARY OF CONGRESS

The Library of Congress welcomed this deposit with enthusiasm. Dr. Hummel regarded the matter as very important, "both from an international point of view and for the benefit that would accrue to the Library of Congress."[21] Since the materials were considered "the rarest records of Chinese culture now existing,"[22] not only was temporary storage recommended but a speedy reply was also urged. Dr. Hummel emphasized: "Everyday's delay is hazardous, and ultimate loss of the materials for China would be disastrous."[23] Dr. MacLeish wrote to Mr. Adolf A. Berle, Assistant Secretary of State, to assure the value of this collection as "one of the greatest treasures of world literature," and urged the U.S. Consul in Shanghai to accept the collection on behalf of the LC.[24] Despite the eagerness of the Library of Congress to receive the collection, however, the Consul in Shanghai responded with little enthusiasm. When Dr. Yuan realized the lack of interest in the U.S. Consulate, he requested the LC to send a representative to China for direct negotiation and assistance instead.[25] As a result, an expert in Chinese bibliography, Chung-min Wang, was sent to Shanghai in March 1941, and Dr. Yuan, risking his own life, went back to Shanghai from Hong Kong to handle the case in person.[26]

PREPARATION AND ARRANGEMENTS FOR SHIPMENT

Their original proposal was to have these books shipped out of Shanghai by U.S. naval vessel.[27] After discussing its feasibility with the State Department, however, that was found to be impossible under the circumstances. Instead, the Chinese government would arrange for commercial shipment of the books to Manila first, whence it might be possible for a U.S. naval vessel to transport them to the United States at a later date.[28]

Because Shanghai was at that time occupied by the Japanese, the negotiators concluded that large shipments would be too conspicuous, although on 4 February 1941, Dr. Yuan, as a trial, sent two boxes through the United States Consulate.[29] With the help of the U.S. Consulate, 360 cases of the rarities were removed from storage in the French Concession to a safer place in the International Settlement in March 1941.[30] A month later, a grant to cover the transportation charges was secured from the Chinese government, and re-selection was done to reduce the quantity for shipment. Sheng-yu Hsu and Chung-min Wang, both experts in Chinese bibliography, made the re-selection, reducing the quantity to 100 boxes.[31] Although instructions were given by the National Chinese government authorizing the inspector general of customs to issue the necessary export permit,[32] the customs officer felt that his actions were being too closely scrutinized by Japanese occupation authorities to permit him to issue the export license.[33] Nelson T. Johnson, then U.S. Ambassador, suggested that it might help to have some kind of contract or agreement between the National Peiping Library and the Library of Congress, so Dr. Yuan proposed an agreement reading: "We [the NPL] are willing to lend these books to the Library of Congress for a period of five years with the understanding that they would be made available to scholars who come to Washington for research."[34] It was concluded, however, that this would not resolve the problem of Japanese surveillance.

Dr. Tsien was also trying at the same time to find ways to ship this collection. By accident it was discovered that the brother of his wife's former schoolmate worked as a customs inspector in Shanghai under Japanese supervision. Because of this Chinese inspector's patriotism, he was prevailed upon to issue the necessary custom clearance for these books during his duty hours but without the knowledge of the Japanese. In October 1941 these books were sent to customs disguised as new books purchased by the Library of Congress, complete with faked invoices issued by one Chung Kuo Shu Pao She (China Publishing Company), a phony company invented specifically for the purpose.[35] Thus the formality of shipment clearance was completed in ten batches without being noticed by the Japanese.

Actual shipment to the United States was made on three separate occasions. The first shipment of two boxes was sent via the U.S. Consulate, arriving at the LC on 26 May 1941; the second shipment containing twenty-five boxes, arrived at the LC on 18 December 1941; and the last shipment of seventy-five boxes was shipped aboard the "President Harrison" on 5 December 1941, two days before the Japanese attack on Pearl Harbor.[36] This last shipment was later held in the care of the University of California Library at Berkeley for some time before it finally arrived at the LC on 16 March 1942.[37]

The Library of Congress was greatly concerned about these shipments. On 1 December 1941, Dr. Luther H. Evans, the acting Librarian, alerted Samuel H. Croft, Chief of the Mail and Delivery Services, of these shipments and anthorized him to pay for any unpaid balance of the shipping charge against the appropriation "Increase of the Library of Congress, General, 1941-1942."[38]

PRESERVATION

The boxes used for storing these books in Shanghai were lined with zinc, which is best suited for preservation, and after they arrived in the United States, the Library of Congress paid close attention to their maintenance and safety. In the beginning the first two boxes were kept in a locked enclosure in the Asiatic Division and the next twenty-five were placed in the Auditorium.[39] Between December 1942 and March 1943, Alvin A. Kremer, keeper of the collections, suggested several alternative ways to store them.[40] When he and Verner Clapp, then Administrative Assistant, could not reach any consensus regarding this issue, Kremer even wrote to Dr. Evans for instruction.[41] Protection from loss and from pests were taken into consideration.

CATALOGING AND MICROFILMING

Official permission had been given to the LC by the NPL to microfilm this collection both for the LC itself and for any other library that might desire to have copies of it. Negatives were to be kept at the LC, and three copies were to be given to China.[42] "This microfilming alone would compensate for any inconvenience to us," observed Hummel.[43]

The microfilming began in early 1942 and was completed in 1946.[44] Mr. Chung-min Wang, who had worked at the LC since coming for the NPL in 1939,[45] was put in charge of this task. Building upon both his own knowledge of Chinese bibliography and the experience in handling Chinese manuscripts in the Bibliotheque Nationale and the British Museum, Wang cataloged the collection, determining the authenticity, date, authorship, and uniqueness of each work selected for microfilming. These were recorded as "Descriptive Notices." Fully 2,720 titles were microfilmed, whereas "600 titles already represented in the Library's collection were not filmed."[46] The resulting 1,070 reels of microfilm in 101,920 feet contained the works themselves, as well as the notices, catalog, shelf list, and packing list.[47] By 1 November 1945, they covered approximately two and half million pages.[48]

Many libraries expressed interest in obtaining the microfilm even before the work was completed, and copies were sold to Harvard, Columbia, and UC Berkeley.[49] Permission to send the first two copies of the microfilm to the NPL and the NCL was acquired from Dr. Tung-li Yuan either by letter or by telegram.[50] The set for the National Peiping Library was taken back by Chung-min Wang when he returned to China in 1947.[51] The second copy was sent to the NCL in Nanking on 18 August 1948 at the LC's expense.[52] A third copy, originally intended for the National Peiping University Library, was held at the Orientalia Division because of Dr. Hummel's instruction that it "not be sent, however, until we hear from Dr. Hu."[53] This last set was finally sent when Dr. Hu Shih, then serving as Director of the Academia Sinica, requested it on 14 February1959.[54] After carefully checking past correspondences on this issue, and to assure having an official record that the LC had discharged its duty, Dr. L. Quincy Mumford, Librarian of Congress, asked Dr. Hu Shih to submit his request through official channels — the Chinese Embassy and the U.S. State Department.[55] The request was then channeled through the Chinese Embassy and LaRue R. Lutkins, Deputy Director for the Chinese Affairs Section at the Department of State.[56] In his letter of 1 August 1959 to Dr. Mumford, Lutkins wrote, "I will appreciate whatever you may be able to do to expedite transmission of the microfilms to the Department of State for transmission to the Government of the Republic of China."[57] The Chinese Embassy picked up the microfilm, and Ambassador George Yeh officially acknowledged its receipt with appreciation on 19 August 1959.[58] In January 1960 the set finally reached the Library of the Institute of History and Philology of the Academia Sinica in Taipei,[59] seat of the government of the Republic of China.

RETURN OF THE COLLECTION

In spite of a severe space problem at the Library of Congress and Kremer's suggestion, Dr. Hummel was reluctant to see the rare books returned to China immediately after World War II, as had been planned, because at that time it was considered unsafe to do so with China under such unsettled civil conditions.[60] Dr. Hummel felt that "They should not now be sent back to China. No request has been made for its return, nor is it wise to raise the question now with the Chinese Embassy."[61] His view prevailed, and the case was not brought up again for review until 1955.[62] At that time Dr. Hummel's successor, Horace I. Poleman, held the same opinion that this collection should continue its "status quo."[63]

In 1957, Dr. Tung-li Yuan joined the LC staff, as consultant in Chinese bibliography, a position he held until a few days before his death on 6 February 1965.[64] In this position he was close to the deposited NPL collections. After Yuan's passing, Dr. Fu-ts'ung Chiang, Director of the re-established NCL, which with some of the rarest treasures from Nanking was now located in Taipei, became very much concerned over the maintenance of the collection at the LC. The NCL had resumed full operation ten years earlier, and it was now fully ready and able to take responsibility for its custody. Since there were also growing research programs in Taipei, this collection was increasingly in demand there. Dr. Chiang therefore approached the authorities both in Taipei and in the United States to request the return of the collection.[65] Speaking for his government, Ambassador Ting-fu Tsiang wrote to Dr. Mumford on 1 April 1965 requesting the return of the collection.[66] At the LC's suggestion, this request was channeled through the State Department on 4 May 1965, and on 24 May, it was transmitted to the LC by William B. Bundy, Assistant Secretary of State.[67] After careful review of its files on this case and hearing the opinions of its Orientalia Division,[68] the LC complied with this request.

SHIPPING METHOD

In 1965, the Republic of China on Taiwan had a pavilion at the New York World's Fair, and rarities from the NCL were on exhibit there under the supervision of Daniel Chang, a librarian at the NCL. When the LC consented to return the NPL rare books to Taiwan and designated Dr. Jennings Wood of the Gift and Exchange Division to be in charge of the transaction. Dr. Chiang ordered Daniel Chang to ship back the NPL rare books along with the NCL rarities that were on exhibit at the Fair.[69] Dr. Chiang also requested that the contents of the 102 boxes be checked and insurance be purchased at the value of US$50 per volume for a total premium of US$7,000.[70] After several exchanges of correspondence, however, it was decided that a complete inventory would not be conducted in the United States, so as to express Chinese confidence and good faith in the maintenance of this collection at the LC. It was pointed out that the LC had not checked the collection at the time of deposit. The final instruction was to check only those boxes that were open.[71] Since all had been boxed and sealed with zinc before the actual time of transaction, none was checked before return.[72] Since they were to be shipped with the NCL's rarities on display in the China Pavilion at the World's Fair, all the parties concerned were consulted - the Chinese Embassy in Washington, D.C., the head of the China Pavilion, the Chinese Ministry of Economic Affairs, and the Ministry of Education.[73]

Daniel Chang was ordered to ship the collection directly to San Francisco and place it on board a U.S. naval vessel with freight costs to be advanced by the Embassy and later reimbursed by the NCL.[74] On 21 October 1965, Mr. Chang accepted the 102 boxes from the LC, which was represented by Dr. Arthur Hummel (former Chief of the Orientalia Division) and his successor Dr. Edwin Beal.[75] Double zinc seals were put on the boxes in the presence of Dr. Y. Y. Bao, representing the Chinese Embassy, Cheng-che Chang, representing the China Pavilion of the World's Fair, and Dainel Chang, representing the NCL.[76] They were crated and sealed with another numbered label prior to loading onto trucks for shipment to the West Coast. When the North American Van Line discovered that there was no "Box 82" on its manifest,[77] Mr. Chang requested that the crate be reopened and checked, at which time the total number of boxes proved to be correct. They were double checked on route under the supervision of John H. Sle and Thomas R. Wolfe, sheriff and deputy sheriff, respectively, of Osceola, Iowa.[78] Upon its arrival in San Francisco, the shipment was handed over to Captain George Smith of the United States Naval Supply Center in Oakland, California.[79] They were then checked again at the Center on 2 November 1965 before being loaded onto the USNS "General H. Gaffey," which arrived in Keelung, Taiwan, on 23 November 1965.[80]

HOMECOMING

After Mr. Yen-kuan Ch'iao, rare book bibliographer at the National Central Library, received the shipment at the dock, they were transported to the NCL in Taipei. The Ministry of Education administered an inventory between 5 and 19 January, 1966. The crates were opened, and an item-by-item check was made under the supervision of representatives form the Legislative Yuan, Control Yuan, Ministry of Foreign Affairs, Ministry of Economic Affairs, and Academia Sinica.[81] At this time several inconsistencies were found, as follows:[82]

1. Some books not on the original packing list were found in the shipment (59 titles in 397 volumes);
2. Some books on the original packing list were not found in the shipment (11 titles in 49 volumes);
3. Some books that had been microfilmed were not found in the shipment (24 titles in 126 volues); and
4. Some non-rare books were found in the shipment.

Mr. Peter Ch'ang, an authority on rare Chinese books, examined and checked the entire collection against the original packing list, the microfilm descriptive notes, the "Rare Book Catalogs of the National Peiping Library" published in 1933 and 1959, and the list of NPL rare books remaining in Shanghai that had been shipped back to Peiping in 1941. His findings on the total missing titles of the National Peiping Library rare Chinese books were published in 1970 as the "Catalog of Missing NPL Rare Chinese Books."[83]

CONCLUSIONS

This great collection in Sinology is thus once again available for use by Chinese scholars after an itinerary that extended over three decades on two sides of the earth and involved the most extensive kind of international bibliothecal cooperation. The NCL does not claim ownership to the books; all are properly listed as

NPL property only temporarily housed in Taipei, implying that their long odyssey is indeed not yet concluded.

It is difficult to speculate what would have been the fate of these books if these extraordinary steps had not been taken. Certainly millions of Chinese books disappeared during World War II. Millions more have disappeared in China since the War, especially during the Great Proletarian Cultural Revolution between 1966 and 1975. As it is, however, only a small handful of these particular volumes have disappeared, and these may perhaps yet turn up.

Hindsight suggests that closer inventorying of the books comprised in this collection would have been prudent. Yet the conditions of Japanese occupation precluded that from happening at the time of their departure from China, and nice considerations of protocol seemed to militate against it at the time of their return.

The unfolding of this event supports the hypotheses that times of crisis sometimes require such extraordinary safety measures as depositing library rarities in the custody of another nation. Such an international joint effort in safekeeping rarities, however, can be adopted only by countries that enjoy common aspirations and congenial relations.

NOTES

1. Francis K. W. Drury, *The Selection and Acquisition of Books for Libraries* (Chicago: ALA, 1928), 2.
2. U.S. Llibrary of Congress, ed., *Annual Report of the Librarian of Congress* (Washington D.C.: Library of Congress, 1940), 115.
3. Tsuen-hsuin Tsien 錢存訓, *Chung Kuo Ku Tai Shu Shih 中國古代書史 [A History of Writing and Written Materials in Ancient China]* (Hong Kong: The Chinese University of Hong Kong, 1975), 91.
4. Hu Shih to Arthur A. Houghton, Jr., 23 October 1940, Central Service Office File, Library of Congress, Washington, D.C.
5. Founded by reorganizing the Imperial Palace Library in 1928 and merged with Peking Library in August 1929, the Chinese national library in Peiping retained its name as the National Peiping Library (also known as National Library of Peiping) until it changed its name to National Peking

(Beijing) Library in 1949 when the city's name was changed to Beijing (Peking) - cf. Wen-yu Yen 嚴文郁, "Liang Chi-ch'ao and the Peking Library 梁啟超與北京圖書館," in *Yen Wen-yu Hsien Sen T'u Shu Kuan Hsueh Lun Wen Chi 嚴文郁先生圖書館學論文集 [A Collection of Papers by Mr. Wen-yu Yen]* (Taipei: Catholic Fu Jen University Press, 1983); National Library of Peiping, ed., *The National Library of Peiping and Its Activities* (Peiping: NPL, 1931); Allen Kent, *Encyclopedia of Library and Information Science*, vol. 4 (New York: Marcel Dekker, 1970), 634.

6. Varying title and volume numbers of this collection have been reported by the following sources: Ching-lang Chang 張錦郎, "K'an Chan Ch'i Chien Te T'u Shu Kuan Shih Yeh 抗戰期間的圖書館事業 [Librarianship during the War], " *Kuo Li Chung Yang T'u Shu Kuan Kuan K'an 國立中央圖書館館刊 [National Central Library Bulletin]* New 7 (September 1974): 8-26; Peter Ch'ang 昌彼得, "Kuo Li Pei P'ing T'u Shu Kuan Shan Pen Ch'ueh Shu Mu 國立北平圖書館善本缺書目 [Catalog of Missing Titles of the Rare Chinese Books of the National Peiping Library]," *Kuo Li Chung Yang T'u Shu Kuan Kuan K'an 國立中央圖書館館刊 [National Central Library Bulletin]* New 3 (April 1970): 68-82; idem, "Kuan Yu Pei P'ing T'u Shu Kuan Chi Ts'un Mei Kuo Te Shan Pen Shu 關於北平圖書館寄存美國的善本書 [Regarding the Rare Chinese Books Deposited at the Library of Congress by the National Peiping Library]," *Shu Mu Chi K'an 書目季刊 [Bibliography Quarterly]* 4 (December 1969): 3-11; Fu-ts'ung Chiang 蔣復璁, "Yun Kuei Kuo Li Pei P'ing T'u Shu Kuan Ts'un Mei Shan Pen T'u Shu 運歸國立北平圖書館存美善本圖書 [The Shipping of the National Peiping Library's Rare Books Back to Taiwan]," *Chung Mei Yueh K'an 中美月刊 [West and East]* 11 (March 1966): 5-7; Yen-kuan Ch'iao 喬衍琯, "Kuo Li Chung Yang T'u Shu Kuan Te Shan Pen Shu 國立中央圖書館的善本書 [Rare Books of the National Central Library]," *Chiao Yu Yu Wen Hua 教育與文化 [Education and Culture]* 351/352 (March 1967): 7-10; Lien Chuan 莊練, "Tsung Shan Pen Shu Chan Lan Tan Ku Tai Shu Yen Pien 從善本書展覽談古代書演變 [Discussion on the Development of Ancient Chinese Books from the Rare Book Exhibit]," *Chung Mei Yueh K'an 中美月刊 [West and East]* 11 (April 1966): 4-5; Kuo Li Chung Yang T'u Shu Kuan Pien 國立中央圖書館 編 [National Central Library, ed.], *Kuo Li Chung Yang T'u Shu Kuan Tien Ts'ang Kuo Li Pei P'ing T'u Shu Kuan Shan Pen Shu Mu 國立中央圖書館典藏國立北平圖書館善本書目 [Catalog of Rare Books of the National Central Library]* (Taipei, National Central Library, 1969), Preface; James Chu-yul Soong, *Chinese Materials*

on Microfilm Available from the Library of Congress (Washington, D.C.: Center for Chinese Research Materials, Association of Research Libraries, 1974); Tingfu F. Tsiang to L. Quincy Mumford, 1 April 1965, Library of Congress, Washington, D.C.; *Ssu I Lu 思憶錄 [T. L. Yuan: A Tribute by Pearl S. Buck, et al.]* (Taipei: Commercial Press, n.d.); U.S. Library of Congress, ed., *Library of Congress Information Bulletin* 24, no.29 (6 December 1965): 649-650. The number of titles varied from 2,720 to 2,883, and the volume numbers varied from 20,500 to 30,000 as reported by different sources. Further investigation into this should be conducted in the future.

7. Hollington K. Tong, ed., *China Handbook, 1937-1945: A Comprehensive Survey of Major Developments in China in Eight Years of War* (N.Y.: Macmillan, 1947), 18; Yun-han Li, "The Origins of the War: Lurkouchiao Incident July 7, 1937," in *Nationalist China During the Sino-Japanese War, 1937-1945* (Hicksville, N.Y: Exposition Press, 1977), 14.
8. *China Handbook, 1937-194*5 (N.Y.: Macmillan, 1947), 299.
9. Tsuin-chen Ou, "Education in Wartime China, *Nationalist China," in Nationalist China during the Sino-Japanese War, 1937-1945*, ed. Paul K. T. Sih. (Hicksville, N.Y.: Exposition Press, 1977), 94.
10. Ching-1ang Chang 張錦郎, "K'an Chan Ch'i Chien Te T'u Shu Kuan Shih Yeh 抗戰期間的圖書館事業 [Librarianship during the War]," 9-10.
11. Fu-t'sung Chiang 蔣復璁, "K'an Chan Ssu Nien Lai Chi T'u Shu Kuan Shih Yeh 抗戰四年來之圖書館事業 [Librarianship During the Four Years of the Sino-Japanese War]," in *Kuo Li Chung Yang T'u Shu Kuan Kuan K'an 國立中央圖書館館刊 [National Central Library Bulletin]* New 7 (September 1974): 1.
12. Fu-ts'ung Chiang 蔣復璁, "Chung Kuo T'u Shu Kuan Shih Yeh Te Hui K'u Yu Ch'an Wang 中國圖書館事業的回顧與展望 [The Recollection and Future Outlook of Chinese Librarianship]," *Kuo Li Chung Yang T'u Shu Kuan Kuan K'an 國立中央圖書館館刊 [National Central Library Bulletin]* New 7, no.2 (September 1974): 4.
13. Frederic D. Schultheis, "Chinese Libraries and the Sino Japanese Conflict," *Pacific Northwest Library Association Quarterly* 3 (January 1939): 108.
14. Ding-u Doo, "A Librarian in Wartime," *ALA Bulletin* 38 (January 1944): 4-5.
15. Tsuen-hsuin Tsien 錢存訓, "Pei P'ing T'u Shu Kuan Shan Pen Shu Chi Yun Mei Ching Kuo 北平圖書館善本書籍運美經過 [An Account of the Shipping of the National Peiping Library's Rare Books to the United States], " *Chuan Chi Wen Hsueh 傳記文學 [Biographical Literature]* 10

(February 1967): 55-57.

16. Ibid.
17. Archibald MacLeish to Hu Shih, 31 October 1939, Executive File, Library of Congress, Washington, D.C.
18. Hu Shih to Arthur A. Houghton, Jr., 23 October 1940, Executive File.
19. A.W. Hummel to Archibald MacLeish, 27 November 1940, Asiatica File, Library of Congress, Washington, D.C.
20. E. Wilder Spaulding to Archibald MacLeish, 27 November 1940, Asiatica File.
21. A.W. Hummel to Archibald MacLeish, 27 November 1940, Asiatica File.
22. Archibald MacLeish to E. Wilder Spaulding, 30 November 1940, Asiatica File.
23. A.W. Hummel to Archibald MacLeish, 27 November 1940, Asiatica File.
24. Archibald MacLeish to Adolf A. Berle, 4 January 1941, Asiatica File.
25. C. L. Senn to Library of Congress, Telegram, 25 January 1941, Asiatica File.
26. Tsuen-hsuin Tsien 錢存訓, "Pei P'ing T'u Shu Kuan Shan Pen Shu Chi Yun Mei Ching Kuo 北平圖書館善本書籍運美經過 [An Account of the Shipping of the National Peiping Library's Rare Books to the United States], " 55-57.
27. E. Wilder Spaulding to Archibald MacLeish, 27 November 1940, Asiatica File.
28. Ibid.
29. T. L.Yuan to Archibald MacLeish, 4 February 1941, Asiatica File.
30. T. L. Yuan to Archibald MacLeish, 20 May 1941, Asiatica File.
31. Tsuen-hsuin Tsien 錢存訓, "Pei P'ing T'u Shu Kuan Shan Pen Shu Chi Yun Mei Ching Kuo 北平圖書館善本書籍運美經過 [An Account of the Shipping of the National Peiping Library's Rare Books to the United States], " 56.
32. T. L. Yuan to Archibald MacLeish, 20 May 1941, Asiatica File.
33. A.W. Hummel, Memorandum on Peking National Library Books in Shanghai, 29 May 1941, Asiatica File.
34. T. L. Yuan to Archibald MacLeish, 20 May 1941, Asiatica File; A. W. Hummel to Archibald MacLeish Memorandum on Peking National Library Books in Shanghai, 29 May 1941, Asiatica File.
35. Tsuen-hsuin Tsien 錢存訓, "Pei P'ing T'u Shu Kuan Shan Pen Shu Chi Yun Mei Ching Kuo 北平圖書館善本書籍運美經過 [An Account of the Shipping of the National Peiping Library's Rare Books to the United States], " 56.
36. U.S. Library of Congress, ed., *Library of Congress Information Bulletin* 24, no.29 (6 December 1965): 649 (written by Dr. Edwin G. Beal); Tsuen-

hsuin Tsien 錢存訓, "Pei P'ing T'u Shu Kuan Shan Pen Shu Chi Yun Mei Ching Kuo 北平圖書館善本書籍運美經過 [An Account of the Shipping of the National Peiping Library's Rare Books to the United States], " 56.

37. U.S. Library of Congress, ed., *Library of Congress Information Bulletin* 24, no.29 (6 December 1965): 649 (written by Dr. Edwin G. Beal); Harold L. Leupp to Luther H. Evans, 18 May 1945, Asiatica File.
38. Luther H. Evans to Samuel M.Croft, 1 December 1941, Asiatica File.
39. Alvin W. Kremer to Verner Clapp, 7 December 1942, Asiatica File.
40. Ibid.
41. Alvin W. Kremer to Luther Evans, 9 March 1943, Asiatica File.
42. U.S. Library of Congress, ed., *Annual Report of the Librarian of Congress* (Washington, D.C.: Library of Congress, 1943), 161.
43. E.Wilder Spaulding to Archibald MacLeish, 27 November 1940, Asiatica File.
44. U.S. Library of Congress, ed., *Library of Congress Information Bulletin* 24, no.29 (6 December 1965): 650 (written by Dr. Edwin G. Beal).
45. "Annual Reports on Acquisitions," *The Library of Congress Quarterly Journal of Current Acquisition* 3 (February 1946): 992.
46. James Chu-yul Soong, *Chinese Materials on Microfilm Available from the Library of Congress*, 6. (Date Varied: 1945 stated by Soong, 1946 by Edwin G. Beal in the *Library of Congrass Information Bulletin* 24, no.29) (6 December 1965), 6.
47. Ibid.
48. "Annual Reports on Acquisitions," 992.
49. Harold L. Leupp to Luther H. Evans, 18 May 1945, Asiatica File; Luther H. Evans to Harold L. Leupp, 28 may 1945, Asiatica File.
50. Luther H. Evans to T. L. Yuan, 10 January 1947, Asiatica File.
51. T. L. Yuan to Luther Evans, 29 April 1947, Asiatica File.
52. Assistant Director for Acquisition to Luther H. Evans, 9 March 1949, Library of Congress.
53. Arthur Hummel to Verner Clapp, 2 June 1948, Library of Congress.
54. Hu Shih to L. Quincy Mumford, 14 February 1959, Asiatica File.
55. L. Quincy Mumford to Hu Shih, 15 May 1959, Asiatica File.
56. Hu Shih to L. Quincy Mumford, 9 June 1959, Asiatica File.
57. LaRue R. Lutkins to L. Quincy Mumford, 1 August 1959, Asiatica File.
58. George K. C. Yeh to L. Quincy Mumford, 19 August 1959, Asiatica File.
59. Han-sheng Chuan to L. Quincy Mumford, 30 March 1961, Asiatica File.
60. Alvin W. Kremer to Luther Evans, "Chinese National Library Rarities," 31 October 1946, Library of Congress; Luther H. Evans to T. L. Yuan, 10

January 1947, Asiatica File.

61. Arthur W. Hummel to Jennings Wood, 3 April 1951, Tickler File, Library of Congress, Washington, D.C.
62. Frances F. Page to Keller, 22 April 1955, Tickler File.
63. Horace I. Poleman to Keller, 28 September 1955, Tickler File.
64. *Ssu I Lu* 思憶錄 *[T. L. Yuan: A Tribute by Pearl S. Buck, et al.]* (Taipei: Commercial Press, n.d.), 48.
65. Fu-ts'ung Chiang 蔣復璁, "Yun Kuei Kuo Li Pei P'ing T'u Shu Kuan Ts'un Mei Shan Pen T'u Shu 運歸國立北平圖書館存美善本圖書 [The Shipping of the National Peiping Library's Rare Books Back to Taiwan]," 5-7.
66. Tingfu F. Tsiang to L. Quincy Mumford, 1 April 1965, Asiatica File.
67. L. Quincy Mumford to Tingfu F. Tsiang, 16 April 1965, Asiatica File; William P. Bundy to L. Quincy Mumford, 24 May 1965, Asiatica File.
68. L. Quincy Mumford to William P. Bundy, 24 June 1965, Asiatica File.
69. L. Quincy Mumford to Tingfu F. Tsiang, 16 April 1965, Asiatica File; Fu-ts'ung Chiang to Daniel T. C. Chang, 7 July 1965, cited by Daniel T. C. Chang in his notes.
70. Fu-ts'ung Chiang to Nai-wei Chang, 20 July 1965, cited by Daniel T. C. Chang in his notes.
71. Fu-ts'ung Chiang to Daniel T. C. Chang, 20 August 1965, cited by Daniel T. C. Chang in his notes.
72. Fu-ts'ung Chiang to Daniel T. C. Chang, 23 September 1965, cited by Daniel T. C. Chang in his notes.
73. China Pavilion, New York World's Fair to Cultural Attache, Chinese Embassy, 26 August 1965.
74. Ibid.; Daniel T. C. Chang, Report, 31 December 1965, National Central Library Files, NCL, Taipei.
75. U.S. Library of Congress, ed., *Library of Congress Information Bulletin* 24, no.29 (written by Dr. Edwin G. Beal), 649.
76. Daniel T. C. Chang, Report, 31 December 1965, National Central Library Files, National Central Library, Taipei.
77. Ibid .
78. Ibid.
79. Ibid.
80. Ibid.; Fu-ts'ung Chiang 蔣復璁, "Yun Kuei Kuo Li Pei P'ing T'u Shu Kuan Ts'un Mei Shan Pen T'u Shu 運歸國立北平圖書館存美善本圖書 [The Shipping of the National Peiping Library's Rare Books Back to Taiwan]," 5-7.
81. Kuo Li Chung Yang T'u Shu Kuan Pien 國立中央圖書館 編 [National

Central Library, ed.], *Kuo Li Chung Yang T'u Shu Kuan Tien Ts'ang Kuo Li Pei P'ing T'u Shu Kuan Shu Mu 國立中央圖書館典藏國立北平圖書館書目*, Preface.

82. Peter Ch'ang 昌彼得, "Kuan Yu Pei P'ing T'u Shu Kuan Chi Ts'un Mei Kuo Te Shan Pen Shu 關於北平圖書館寄存美國的善本書 [Regarding the Rare Chinese Books Deposited at the Library of Congress by the National Peiping Library]," 3-11.
83. Peter Ch'ang 昌彼得, "Kuo Li Pei P'ing T'u Shu Kuan Shan Pen Ch'ueh Shu Mu 國立北平圖書館善本缺書目 [Catalog of Missing Titles of the Rare Chinese Books of the National Peiping Library]," 56-82.

Thanks to Dr. M. Chu Wiens, Area Specialist, Chinese Section, Asian Division, Library of Congress, USA, for varifying the references cited in this paper.

Reprinted with permission from *The Journal of Library History* 19, no. 3: 359-372.

5

Dr. Chiang Fu-ts'ung: A Giant in the Preservation and Dissemination of Chinese Culture

ABSTRACT

Dr. Chiang Fu-ts'ung's (the recognized giant in the preservation and dissemination of Chinese culture) biography is presented basing on reliable documents and interviews. His family background and childhood, college education, debut into librarianship, study tour in Europe, association with the National Central Library, professional contribution to librarianship, his work during the war, devotion to duty, and efforts and dedicated endeavors in his administration of the National Palace Museum, research interests, religion, hobbies, and honors are faithfully recorded.

FAMILY BACKGROUND AND CHILDHOOD

Chiang Fu-ts'ung was born on November 12, 1898 (September 29, 1898, according to the Chinese lunar calendar). His family, which was originally engaged in business, lived in the town of Hsia Shih, county of Hai Ning in the province of Chekiang.[1] Chiang Fu-ts'ung grew up in a Confucian environment because in his great grandfather's generation, his family had become associated with the academic sphere. His great grandfather, Chiang Kuang-hsu, a typical Confucian scholar who enjoyed music and calligraphy as well as books, stone rubbings, and the collecting of antiquities, was very hospitable to other people. His family library, known as Pei Hsia Chai, and his collection of antiquities known as "Shang Ku Chou Ting, Ch'in Chin, Han Pi Chih Chai" (Room for utensils from the Shang, Chou, and Han Dynasties and for the Mirror from the Ch'in Dynasty) were both very valuable. A series of Chinese rare books entitled the *Pei Hsia Chai* series, which covered some fifty titles, was printed by his family. Several other works on painting, calligraphy, and poetry were also published.[2] Chiang Kuang-hsu's second son, Chiang Hsueh-chi, was Chiang Fu-ts'ung's grandfather. Chiang Fu-ts'ung's father, Chiang Chi-en, who was the first son of Chiang Hsueh-chi, earned a Kung Sheng degree (licentiate in the Imperial Examination).[3] When his family found itself in financial trouble following T'ai P'ing T'ien Kuo, Chiang Chi-en changed his profession to teaching. It was in this bibliophilic environment that Chiang Fu-ts'ung was raised and educated.

Not physically strong when he was young, Chiang Fu-ts'ung had to remain at home to be taught personally by his father. At the age of six, however, he was exposed both to such classical works as *Ch'ien Tzu Wen* (Thousand Characters), the *Four Books*, and the *Tso Chuan* (Tso's Commentary on the *Spring and Autumn Annals* by Ts'o Ch'iu Ming), and to modern history textbooks as well. His formal education began at the age of twelve when he was enrolled in the Ch'ien T'ang County Senior Primary School. He received instruction from his cousin Chiang Fu-ching (also known as Chiang Kung-ku), from Wang Ch'in (also known as Wang Man-feng), an advocate of popular education, and from a famous teacher of the Chinese language, Ch'eng Tsung-ch'i (also known as Ch'eng Yu-fu). These scholars imparted to him an education both in knowledge and in personality refinement.[4]

In 1913, before he completed primary education, he took an examination at a Sino-German school named Tsing-tao Special Senior College and was admitted to its lower class. When the Japanese attacked Tsingtao in August of 1914, he was forced to continue his education in Tientsin, where he was enrolled in Te Hua (Sino-German) Middle School, which was run by German businessmen. When China broke off relations with Germany in 1917, the school was taken over by the Chinese authorities. At that time, he decided to seek higher education at the National Peking University.

COLLEGE EDUCATION AND DEBUT INTO LIBRARIANSHIP

Chiang took the entrance examination for the College Preparatory Class of the College of Arts at the National Peking University and was admitted in 1917. Majoring in German in the Preparatory Class, he participated actively in the May Fourth Movement, and supported programs for the modernization of China. In the fall of 1919, he formally entered the University as a freshman majoring in philosophy and involved himself actively in the extra-curricular activities of the music club.

His association with librarianship started during his college years, when his uncle Chiang Po-li formed a reading club together with Liang Ch'i-ch'ao in 1920.[5] At the club he worked as a cataloger, cataloging German language books mostly brought back from Europe by Liang Ch'i-ch'ao. Unfortunately, in the summer of 1921, affliction with typhoid and pneumonia almost killed him and forced him to quit school for a year of recuperation. In February 1922, he married Sun Chia-yi through family arrangement. Later, in the summer of 1922, he was able to return to the National Peking University to complete his college education.[6]

In February 1923, six months before graduation from the University, Chiang Fu-ts'ung began employment as an editor with the Sung P'o Library in charge of acquisition, cataloging and readers' services. This Library, originating from the reading club that his uncle and Liang Ch'i-ch'ao had founded, was reorganized in 1922, in memory of Ts'ai O (1882-1916), with the courtesy name of Ts'ai Sung-p'o, under the direction of the head librarian, Liang

Ch'i-ch'ao.[7] During this initial year, he cataloged 10,000 volumes, set up service rules and regulations, drafted and promoted a plan for compiling a dictionary of library science.[8] Being also involved in professional activities in the Peking Library Association, he was recruited as its secretary. In that capacity, he contributed greatly to Chinese librarianship. Two years later, when the Library Association of China was established in Shanghai on April 25, 1925, he was elected at the inaugural convention to serve as its executive staff.[9]

As soon as the National Peking Library began operation in 1926, Liang Ch'i-ch'ao, the director and Yuan T'ung-li, the head of the Department of Books, invited Chiang to work there as a cataloger in charge of Chinese books. His work there as a cataloger provided him with such valuable experiences and such deep understanding of classification principles and practices that he soon decided to try to improve the traditional scheme of Chinese classification.

In 1929, he chaired the Committee on Classification at the Peking Library Association, playing a leading role in its various projects.[10] He analyzed the Chinese classification schemes, and discovered that neither the traditional four-division system of classifying Chinese books into Ching (classics), Shih (history), Tzu (philosophy), and Chi (collections) nor the modern decimal systems were suitable for the Chinese books. He then designed a system which was quite similar to that of the Library of Congress Classification Scheme, dividing knowledge into thirty-two categories.[11] Instead of English alphabets and numerals used as notations, however, he suggested that the first Chinese word of a subject or of its subheading be used as the class number. The author number, according to his concept, was to be abolished. Instead, books should be arranged in chronological order by author.

In 1929, Chiang Fu-ts'ung was invited to be a lecturer in Peiping College (Pei Ta Hsueh Yuan) teaching Chinese and classics.

STUDY TOUR IN EUROPE

Having demonstrated great potential in librarianship, Chiang was immediately sent to Germany by the Chekiang Provincial Department of Education to study librarianship in preparation for future services at the Chekiang Provincial Library upon completion of its building.

Chiang arrived in Berlin in August 1931, and entered the Preussische Staats Bibliothek as a visiting librarian. There he was awarded the Humboldt scholarship and was admitted by the Philosophy Department of the Berlin University.[12] In addition to his full-time course work, he continued his internship at the library, and worked successively in its Oriental Collection Department, Union Catalog Department, and Reference Services Department. During the summer vacation he worked in the National Austrian Library in Vienna for a short period of time and visited Swiss library facilities. Following two years' internship, he worked in the exchange division of a German scholarly association.

A three-month intensive library science course, co-sponsored by the Berlin University and the Preussische Staats Bibliothek in 1932, provided him with the knowledge of modern library technical and public services.[13] Upon completion of the course in September of that year, he made a trip to England and France and benefited greatly from this extensive study tour. He was particularly interested in the European practices of union catalog, international publication exchange, and reference services.

ASSOCIATION WITH THE NATIONAL CENTRAL LIBRARY

Upon Chiang's return from Europe in the winter of 1932, Chu Chia-hua, then Minister of Education (MOE), gave him the assignment to start planning the National Central Library, and within the year he had accomplished the preparation work for this social institution.[14] By accomplishing the following major tasks, he laid a solid foundation for the National Central Library:

1. He personally went to Peking and inspected the archival materials of the Ch'ing Dynasty, especially the files of the Departments of Protocol and Education which were held there by the Ministry of Education. He managed to transport these archival materials together with some 40,000 volumes of books to Nanking, where they became the founding collection of the National Central Library.[15]
2. He established NCL's repository of national literature system through copyright deposit as stipulated by publication laws.[16]
3. He negotiated with the Commercial Press in Shanghai regarding the reproduction of the *Ssu K'u Ch'uan Shu* (Wen Yuan Ko edition), and was successful in this endeavor to have its best editions (2,000 volumes of 231 titles) reproduced under a descriptive title of *Ssu K'u Ch'uan Shu Chen Pen.*[17]
4. He managed to initiate the preparation work by renting quarters at Sha T'ang Yuan with limited governmental financial support in April 1933.[18]
5. He purchased from the Meng Family in Tientsin a fine collection of stone rubbings which became the foundation of the NCL valuable rubbing collection.
6. He took over the printing facilities of the Sinology Publishing Company for producing publications for exchange and cataloging cards for distribution.[19]

In the following year, when the National Central Library took over the international publication exchange activities from the Academia Sinica, Chiang Fu-ts'ung was able to make additions to the NCL collection by exchanging the reproduced *Ssu K'u Ch'uan Shu Chen Pen* and government documents for foreign publications. By means of reproduced ancient Chinese books and through this international exchange channel, he was able to disseminate Chinese culture to the four corners of the world. It was typical of his administrative practice to have written rules and regulations for whatever tasks he embarked upon, so as to assure consistency of actions and to provide a uniform basis of performance evaluation.

PROFESSIONAL CONTRIBUTIONS TO LIBRARIANSHIP

Chiang Fu-ts'ung's participation in the Executive Yuan conference in 1935 on revising Publication Laws and his appointment by the MOE in 1936 to the Committee on the Rehabilitation of Cultural Treasures of the Old Capital by the Executive Yuan were both noteworthy indications of the cultural impact and leadership status of the new National Central Library.[20]

It was through his efforts and those of Chu Chia-hua that the NCL received an appropriation of $1,500,000 from the Sino-British Educational and Cultural Endowment Fund for the construction of new NCL quarters in June 1934.[21] Chiang's excellent building programs and his key role on an ad hoc committee of the NCL building all indicated his remarkable administrative ability. Following the Lukouch'iao Incident, the government in September 1937 organized a group headed by Chiang Po-li to visit Europe, and Chiang was appointed to go along as a secretary.[22]

WORK DURING THE WAR

Upon his return from this trip in 1938, and immediately after reporting to Chiang Kai-shek, he went to Wu Ch'ang to take charge of the NCL's evacuation of 131 crates of precious library materials.[23] It was through his efforts that the vessels necessary for transportation to Chungking were acquired and that the NCL operations were established there so promptly in May 1938.[24] With only limited resources, he nonetheless quickly began rendering reader services there and operating the international exchange of publications.

When Japanese air-raids threatened the NCL's safety in Chungking, the Library was again moved to nearly Pai-sha across the Yangtze River, although its international exchange of publications remained in Chungking. Large quantities of books were transported between Chungking and Pai-sha despite dangers of air-raids and hazards in the Yangtze River. Whenever the NCL transported rare books to Chungking for exhibition, Chiang would personally be on board supervising the shipment. Recalling this era later he remarked: "Should something happen to the books on the way, I would also die with them."[25] For books and his work, he thus risked his life.

The preparatory work for the National Central Library was finally completed, and on August 1, the central government appointed Chiang the first director of the National Central Library. At that time the NCL organizational stipulations were also announced. Using assumed names and again at the risk of his life, he went in the early 1940s to Japanese-occupied Shanghai and Hongkong to acquire valuable rare Chinese books which came onto the market there.[26] As a result of this dramatic, adventurous, yet highly fruitful trip, the NCL was able to acquire the cream of Chinese rare books and many of the most valuable Chinese cultural remains. His personal life always came second in priority, as he gave up opportunities to be with his family on many occasions because of his dedications to his work.

Chiang Fu-ts'ung experienced great personal grief during this time, not only when his father passed away in 1938, but also when his cousin and former teacher Chiang Fu-ching died of a heart attack in 1942.[27] Chiang Fu-ching was actually his own brother, but was adopted by his uncle in accord with old Chinese family practice. He mourned the passing of this brother not only as kin but also as his student. In China, the high esteem of one's teacher is indicated by the maxim: "Once a person has been your teacher, treat him as a father forever."

Dedicated as he was to librarianship, social education and scholarship, Chiang Fu-ts'ung planned and directed all of the wartime activities of the Library. In addition to his duties at the NCL, he also involved himself constantly in research. As a result, the

National Central University invited him, in 1944, to teach bibliography of history as a part-time professor.[28]

When the Japanese surrendered to the Allies at the end of the World War II, the Ministry of Education appointed Chiang Fu-ts'ung to take charge of its post-war educational rehabilitation activities in the Nanking and Shanghai areas in 1945. To accomplish this work he was made chairman of the MOE's Committee on Guidance in Education in charge of the recovery work of educational institutions in the provinces of Chiangsu, Chekiang, Chiangsi, and Anhui, where he personally handled the transfer of universities.[29] As a result of careful planning and outstanding administrative ability, he handled this assignment with his usual efficiency. Through the use of detailed instructions, he was able to delegate some of the tasks and complete the mission in three months, an accomplishment felt by many to be the single most efficient and rapid job of this kind assigned to individuals after the war.

A far-sighted person, who had a full understanding of China's past heritage, her current local conditions, and her future needs, Chiang Fu-ts'ung envisioned a network of libraries to fulfill various local information needs throughout the nation, and he advocated a diversified and multi-library national system in China.[30]

Based on his suggestions in the mid 1930s, the government decided to establish the National Lanchow, Sian, and Roosevelt Libraries in the 1940s.[31] After the war, he handed over the NCL building and part of its collection in Chungking to the Roosevelt Library and returned to Nanking where his NCL rehabilitation work went to full speed. As top priority, he repaired the building, and he sought out the collections bought during the war in the Japanese-occupied areas of Shanghai and Hongkong.

As a result of his persistence, many of the missing items were located and successfully recovered from Japan. He was, of course, instrumental in the drafting and promulgation of many library-related laws and regulations. Significant among them were the revised NCL Organizational Stipulations of 1940 and of 1945, as well as the 1946 organizational stipulations for the Bureau of the International Exchange of Publications, all of which were matters of great importance to Chinese librarianship in general and to the NCL in particular.[32]

In observance of traditional Chinese practice, a person should eventually return to his roots (his native place), and Chiang Fu-ts'ung honored this tradition when he moved his cousin Chiang Fu-ching's coffin back to Chekiang in 1946.[33] His respect for Chinese tradition has been obvious in all of his behavior, both at work and at home. Work, moreover, has always gained more of his attentions than personal family life. Out of his entire married life, he spent only five years at home.[34] He treated his offices as homes and his colleagues as families.

CONTINUOUS DEVOTION TO DUTY

In the spring of 1947, Chiang Fu-ts'ung traveled to the county of Wu Hsing to acquire for the NCL the calendar collection of the Chang Family. During this trip he experienced an accident when his pedicab turned over, and he was serious injured with a broken right arm. It took him three months to recover from this injury, although he managed to continue working and writing poems in his hospital bed.[35]

In March 1948, for the purpose of disseminating and encouraging the restoration of Chinese culture in Taiwan, the Ministry of Education formed a Cultural Propagation Group with delegates from the National Central Library, the Preparatory Office of the National Central Museum, and famous collectors in Shanghai. His group was assigned to go to Taiwan for an exhibition of Chinese cultural artifacts, and as the Group's leader, Chiang was chiefly responsible for conducting a series of successful displays of antiquities there. Four months later, the MOE sent him on still another trip, this time to the United States for observation of modern librarianship. This trip was both hastened and shortened, however, by the conflicts between the Nationalists and Communists. In December of that year, the MOE ordered him to select and transport the NCL's rarest Chinese books to Taiwan. The books where shipped in three shipments aboard naval or commercial vessels, and Chiang personally went to Taiwan to supervise their receipt. Upon completion of this work, he went to Canton for the purpose of establishing a NCL liaison office there. This proposal did not meet with the government's approval, due to budget constraints.[36]

In April 1949, UNESCO invited this experienced librarian to visit Europe again and to spend six months touring libraries in France, England, Denmark, Germany, and Switzerland. While in Paris, he attended the fifth UNESCO Conference as a delegate representing China.[37]

CONTINUING EFFORTS

He was revived from his depression by the reactivation of the National Central Library in August 1954.[38] He immediately launched again upon all the significant tasks which facilitated the functions of a national library, such as planning for building construction, collections development, international publication exchange activities, and reader services. In the same year, the Executive Yuan appointed him a director on the Joint Board of the National Palace and the Central Museums.

At the invitation of the Taiwan Provincial Department of Education in the spring of 1955, he served concurrently as the Director of the Taiwan Provincial Taipei Library. As soon as he was in charge of that Library, the administration was put to order. However, he resigned from the post and recommended Wang Sheng-wu to be his successor.[39] Cooperation between the national library and the local library has since been enhanced.

In borrowed quarters in the Botanic Garden in Taipei in February 1956, Chiang first remodeled two rooms to serve as the Chinese and the Western Reference Rooms for the revitalized NCL, with continuing efforts thereafter to either make repairs or construct new additions to the structure. He added quarters for the Periodical Room in October 1957; a rare book room and rare book stacks in May 1960; a large central reading room and offices on the second floor in April 1962; their additions in 1963; and finally a five-level stack in 1964.[40] His continuous striving for additional financial assistance from various sources made the building possible.

Chiang always held that library construction should never interfere with public services. In order to make materials more accessible to readers, he managed in 1960 to move 1,600 duplicate volumes of rare Chinese books from Pei-kou-ts'un storage to Taipei quarters.[41]

It was through his efforts that the collection of rare Chinese books safe-deposited at the U.S. Library of Congress by the National Peking Library was returned to Taipei in 1965, and since have been deposited at the National Palace Museum on behalf of the NCL.[42] His continuous care, concern and support for the National Central Library have greatly assisted the completion of its new building in 1986. When the new NCL building was completed in 1986, he fought hard to get the above mentioned collection returned to the custody of the National Central Library. When his efforts were in vain, he claimed that he could never close his eyes at the time of his passing if the collection was not eventually returned to the NCL custody.[43]

DEDICATED ENDEAVORS IN HIS ADMINISTRATION OF THE NATIONAL PALACE MUSEUM

In September 1965, the government ordered the reinstallation of the National Palace Museum in Taiwan, and appointed Chiang Fu-ts'ung to act as its advisor on November 13, 1965.[44] He concurrently administered the National Palace Museum and the National Central Library for one year. In order to cope with the numerous responsibilities assigned to the Museum administrator, he resigned from the directorship of the National Central Library on September

21st of 1966 after thirty-three years of service.[45]

The late President Chiang Kai-shek named November 12th as the National Cultural Renaissance Day since 1966 and also named the Museum after Dr. Sun Yat-sen (Chung Shan Po Wu Yuan). The Museum has thus been identified with the important mission of preserving, organizing, and disseminating Chinese culture.

On August 26, 1967, the Executive Yuan appointed Dr. Chiang to be a member of the National Palace Museum Administrative Committee and on September 12, 1967, Dr. Chiang was formally appointed to head the Museum.[46]

During his tenure at the National Palace Museum, from November 13, 1965 to January 15, 1983, he again designed a magnificent building equipped with modern technological facilities (i.e., computer and security devices), established a sound administrative system, and developed excellent service policies for these great national cultural treasures. For eighteen years, he devoted himself to the enterprise of National Palace Museum, another dimension of the nation's cultural efforts.

His contributions to the National Palace Museum can be summarized under five categories:[47]

Acquisitions

In addition to the 605,770 items shipped from mainland China in 1949, Dr. Chiang acquired 15,223 exquisite items through purchase or gifts.

The Museum's collection reached 620,993 pieces at the time of Dr. Chiang's retirement in January of 1983. This invaluable collection, aside from its significance in artistic value, is a living testimony to the wealth of Chinese history and culture.

His innovative administration and preservation work at the Museum have attracted many generous donations and/or deposits of personal collections. 7,130 items of ancient bronzeware, chinaware, jadeware, paintings and calligraphy, rare books and rubbings donated by individuals are items of millions and billions in value. For example, Shen Chung-tao's donation of books printed in the Sung and Yuan dynasties would value up to a billion dollars. Such a valuable collection is beyond the acquisition budget of the Museum but is now possessed by the Museum without any cost. Prominent collectors like Chang Chun, Wang Shih-chien, Lo Chih-shih, Yeh Kung-chao, Chiang Meng-shan, Tan Pai-yu all donated rare items to the Museum collection.

Preservation

Dr. Chiang strove for preservation in two dimensions: safekeeping and repairing. To safeguard the collection against deterioration and earthquakes, wooden cases were replaced by iron cases with chemicals added for safety.

Due to the fragile nature of the collection or the poor storage facilities, many items were damaged. Local gazetteers and archival materials handed down from Ch'ing Dynasty suffered destructions caused by worms. In 1965, Dr. Chiang installed a Repair Unit under the Division for Books and Archival Materials with a major purpose to mend defective pages. During his tenure, many items were mended and restored to their original conditions: 2,971 pieces of calligraphy, 500 titles in 4,439 volumes of rare books and local gazetteers, 1,101 documents, 7,344 portfolios of *Ssu K'u Ch'uan Shu* and *Ssu K'u Hui Yao*.

With a far-sighted vision to use modern technology for preservation, Dr. Chiang established a Scientific Preservation Room in which 68 pieces of bronzeware and 268 pieces of porcelain were successfully repaired.

Such fine new technical preservation techniques also won people's confidence and attracted many valuable deposits or donations of priceless antiquities, books and rubbings.

Collection Organization and Publications

It was hard to use the rich collection because the original inventory list was in a very primitive and unclear state. In order to best facilitate the use of the collection, Dr. Chiang took two steps of collection organization: First he attempted to do a complete inventory and cataloging by the establishment of the Registration Department. He started numbering system for the collection. Each item has a unique number for easy and clear identification.

Secondly, he published detailed catalogs of rare books, old books, and historical data including reports, orders, and official documents. The rare book collection consists of *Ssu K'u Ch'uan Shu* and rare editions printed in Sung/Yuan Dynasties.

These catalogs are of great value to historians and scholars in various disciplines. In addition, catalogs of artifacts have also been published, such as *Illustrative Catalog of Bronzeware at the Palace Museum, Catalog of Chinaware* (5 volumes), *Catalog of Porcelains of the Sung Dynasty, Illustrative Catalog of Porcelains in the Ming Dynasty* (2 volumes), *Illustrative Catalog of Porcelains in the Ch'ing Dynasty and Illustrative Catalog of Ancient Jade.* Under his administration, the Museum was able to publish *the Collection of National Palace Museum Calligraphy and Paintings, Collection of Silk Products, 300 Famous Paintings of the Palace Museum* (6 volumes), *Cream of the Sung Dynasty Paintings* (3 volumes), *Cream of the Yuan Dynasty Paintings* (2 volumes). *Calligraphy Collection of the Palace Museum* (22 series in 35 volumes), *Complete Collection of Calligraphy in the National Palace Museum* (30 volumes).[48]

Dissemination

Dr. Chiang employed three methods to publicize and disseminate these cultural remains of great importance: (1) Display of artifacts, books, and paintings through domestic and international exhibitions; (2) Public access of books and documents; and (3) Publication and reproduction of selected items.

Two billion Chinese and foreign visitors visited the Museum during the period of November, 1965 and December, 1983. In line with the government's effort in promoting tourism and in educating the general public through recreation, Dr. Chiang attempted to make innovative improvements upon various administrative practices in order to better serve the public. Efforts have especially been directed toward continuing staff education, training of tour-guides, the updating of exhibition facilities, and the modernization of display methods.

In addition to the above mentioned publications, the National Palace Museum also published serials, such as *Ku K'ung Chi' K'an (National Palace Museum Quarterly), National Palace Museum Bulletin* (Bi-monthly in English), *Exhibition Newsletters* (in English), and *Ku K'ung Chien Hsuan (Brief News of the National Palace Museum)*, etc.[49]

Subsequent to many unsuccessful attempts in the past, the recent reproduction of *Ssu K'u Ch'uan Shu* (Wen Yuan K'o edition) by the Commercial Press highlighted Dr. Chiang's efforts is support of the preservation and dissemination of scholarship and Chinese culture.[50]

Research and Development

These cultural remains can best be disseminated and interpreted through continuous research efforts. The continuously undertook two projects: (1) reinforcement of resources, and (2) betterment of human resources. The former has been achieved by increasing acquisitions of materials. The latter aimed at systematical on-the-job training of new employees, cooperative educational endeavors with the National Taiwan University in establishing a graduate school of art history, international exchange of personnel through foundation and fellowship support. He not only provided his staff with opportunities to receive advanced education in European and North American academic institutions but also facilitated many foreign scholars such as Beatrice Bartlett and Susan Naquin to complete their studies/research projects at the Museum.[51]

Many of the workshops on artifacts and continuing educational lectures were instrumental in the successful accomplishment of the Museum in its endeavors in research and development. Outreach programs in the forms of lectures were instrumental to the popularization of understanding toward Chinese culture and to the enhancement of social education. He only not was instrumental to the establishment of Social Education Department and Children's Library at the National Taiwan Normal University but also responsible for conducting Chinese Cultural Public Speech Series at the National Taiwan Normal University for a year.[52] This is another dimension of his contribution to social education for which he has been highly regarded.

RESEARCH INTERESTS, RELIGION, AND HOBBIES

While Chiang Fu-ts'ung was enroute back from Paris in October 1949, the Nationalist Government lost Canton to the Communists, and the National Central Library was ordered to merge with two other institutions into a joint organization. Feeling quite depressed, Chiang stayed in Hongkong for approximately a year and half teaching at Chu Hai College.[53] In May 1951, he was invited to National Taiwan University to teach Chinese. During his tenure as a professor at the National Taiwan University, he spent much of his time doing research on the history of the Sung Dynasty and on Catholicism.

In October 1950 Rev. Kung Shih-jung, a colleague at National Taiwan University, converted Chiang to Roman Catholicism, and since that time except during periods of hospitalization, he has not missed a single daily Mass.[54] In his mid-fifties, he gained recognition as an authority in Sung Dynasty History when his paper on national policy of the Sung Dynasty was published in *the Continent Magazine*, winning him wide acclaim by scholars. For many years, he taught courses of Sung History at Catholic Fu-jen University and Chinese Culture College/University. The lectures that he gave on Chinese Bibliography at the National Taiwan Normal University were comprehensive and influential and they can never be duplicated.

The depth and breadth of his professional and religious knowledge, as well as of scholarly disciplines are evidenced by the diversity and proliferation of his writings, speeches, and translations which, for example, included: *The Significance of the Exhibition of Local History* in November 1954,[55] *The Mission of the Library Association of China* in November 1955,[56] *Su Hsin Lu* (A Testimony in Religious Belief) in June 1958,[57] *Books and Libraries* in September 1959,[58] *The Origin and Mission of National Libraries* in December 1963,[59] *A New Inquiry into the Sung Dynasty History* in January 1965,[60] and the Collections entitled *Chen Chou Chi* in August 1965.[61] After his retirement from the National Palace Museum, he was able to concentrate his efforts on research and complete a collection of his works entitled: *Chen Chou Chai Wen Chi* in 1985.[62]

Being a person of versatility and creativity, he has preserved and promoted the art of Kun Ch'u, which is a local opera of Kun Shan, a town in Chiangsu province of China. Not only is he actively participating in the singing and performance of Kun Ch'u, he is the leader in a club which meets regularly for this type of artistic appreciation.[63]

HONORS

His religious devotion and scholarly accomplishments have earned him various recognitions and appointments in addition to professional competence. He has been and is extremely active in professional, civic, religious, and cultural activities that his numerous assignments, as indicated in the appendix, are testimonies to his numerous contributions to Chinese culture and scholarship.

Deeply involved in professional activities, Chiang Fu-ts'ung was always more interested in deeds than in titles and honors. When he was elected to the Board of the Library Association of China in 1934, he declined; the LAC, however, continued to invite his participation as an honorary director of the Board.[64]

His outstanding performance before, during, and after the war attracted nationwide attention. In appreciation of his manifold contributions, the government in 1947 awarded him its "Victory Citation and Award."[65]

Upon his return from the Conference on Sino-American Scholarly Cooperation in Seattle in August 1960, Chiang was invited to Korea in March of 1961 to receive an honorary doctorate degree of literature from Sungkyun Kwan University for his contribution to Sino-Korean scholarly and cultural exchange.[66] Chiang completed the conversion of the old temple at Nanhai Road into a palatial library building with limited resources. At the twenty-fifty anniversary of Chiang's service at the NCL, Chang Ch'i-yun, then Minister of Education, expressed the nation's appreciation by presenting "Chung Shu Hsuan Lan (Central administration supervises from afar) ." He praised Chiang saying that his "outstanding accomplishment is highly admirable."[67]

As a result of his strong support of Catholicism, the Holy See in the Vatican awarded him the title of "Knight" in June 1962. Upon the thirtieth anniversary of the National Central Library in 1963, Huang Chi-lu, then Minister of Education, awarded him a gold medal in appreciation of his extensive contributions to the Library.[68] In 1971, he was awarded an honorary doctoral degree of literature by St. John's University. After his retirement from the Palace Museum, on January 1983, he was honored with the awards of "Order of Brilliant Star with Grand Cordon" in recognition of his life-long contribution to Chinese culture.[69]

At the ages of 88 and 90, he was and is still mentally and physically strong to take up new endeavors among which are his potential global travel plans in addition to his extensive travels to

Japan in 1981, to European countries and to the United States in 1985. In each of these trips, he propogated the blessings of Chinese culture to these places by delivering speeches. In his lectures tour at the Preussische Staats Bibliothek in Germany and Harvard-Yenching Library in the United States in 1985 were inspiring and well-attended.[70] As a person, he has been well-liked and honored by his associates at home and abroad.

RECOGNIZED GIANT

Chiang's concern for easy access to materials, centralized bibliographic control, and the preservation and dissemination of Chinese culture has inspired him to secure publications through publication laws, to prepare and distribute various bibliographies, indexes, and cataloging cards, to mount exhibitions, to promote inter-organizational cooperative ventures, to acquire and reproduce valuable materials, to secure rare Chinese books/artifacts and to conduct international publication exchange.

This is Chiang Fu-ts'ung, the man who built the National Central Library and the National Palace Museum, despite innumerable hardships over six decades. He is an acknowledged giant not only in Chinese but also in world librarianship as well as museumology. It is this remarkable person who has made both the National Central Library and the National Palace Museum the foremost centers of Chinese culture, nuclei of universal scholarship, and vaults of human knowledge. It is this dedicated individual who helped preservation and propagation of Chinese culture possible in the last seven decades.

NOTES:

1. Peter Ch'ang 昌彼得, "Chiang Wei-t'ang Hsien Sheng Ch'i Shih Nien Piao 蔣慰堂先生七十年表 [Seventy Years of Chronology of Dr. Chiang Fu-ts'ung]," in *Ching Chu Chiang Fu-ts'ung Hsien Sheng Ch'i Shih Sui Lun Wen Chi 慶祝蔣復璁先生七十歲論文集 [Symposium in Honor of Dr. Chiang Fu-ts'ung on His 70th Birthday]* (Taipei: National Palace Museum, 1969), 273-276.
2. Ibid.
3. Ibid.
4. Fu-ts'ung Chiang 蔣復璁, "Introduction," in *Chen Chou Chi 珍帚集 [Collections]* (Taipei: T'ai Ping Yang Wen Hua Shih Yeh Kung Ssu, 1965), 1.
5. Fu-ts'ung Chiang 蔣復璁, "Wo Yu Chung Kuo Te T'u Shu Kuan Shih Yeh 我與中國的圖書館事業 [My life in Chinese Librarianship]," *Hsin Shih Tai 新時代 [New Epoch]* 1, no. 3 (March 1961): 50.
6. Peter Ch'ang 昌彼得, "Chiang Wei-t'ang Hsien Sheng Ch'i Shih Nien Piao 蔣慰堂先生七十年表 [Seventy Years of Chronology of Dr. Chiang Fu-ts'ung]," 275.
7. Ching-lang Chang and Yuan Ch'uan Huang 張錦郎，黃淵泉, *Chin Liu Shih Nien Chung Kuo T'u Shu Kuan Tai Shih Chi 近六十年中國圖書館大事記 [A Chronology of Chinese Librarianship in the Past Sixty Years]* (Taipei: The Taiwan Commercial Press, 1974), 36.
8. Peter Ch'ang 昌彼得, "Chiang Wei-t'ang Hsien Sheng Ch'i Shih Nien Paio 蔣慰堂先生七十年表 [Seventy Years of Chronology of Dr. Chiang Fu-ts'ung]," 277; Fu-ts'ung Chiang 蔣復璁, "*T'u Shu Hsueh Ta Tz'u Tien Hsu 圖書學大辭典序 ["Preface" to Library Science Dictionay]," in T'u Shu Hsueh Ta Tz'u Tien 圖書學大辭典 [Library Science Dictionary]*, comp. Cheng-ching Lu 盧震京 (Taipei: Taiwan Commercial Press, 1971); The Library Science Dictionary was inspired by a project led by Erwin Ackerknecht in Germany during Chiang's visit there.
9. Chien-cheng Sung 宋建成, "Chung Kuo T'u Shu Kuan Hsueh Hui Tsu Chih 中國圖書館學會組織 [Library Association of China]," in *Chung Hua Min Kuo T'u Shu Kuan Nien Chien 中華民國圖書館年鑑 [Library Yearbook of the Republic of China]* (Taipei: National Central Library, 1981), 317.
10. Peter Ch'ang 昌彼得, "Chiang Wei-t'ang Hsien Sheng Ch'i Shih Nien Piao 蔣慰堂先生七十年表 [Seventy Years of Chronology of Dr. Chiang Fu-ts'ung]," 277.

11. Fu-ts'ung Chiang 蔣復璁, "Chung Kuo T'u Shu Fen Lei Wen T'i Chih Shang Ch'ueh 中國圖書分類問題之商榷 [A Discussion on the Issues of Classification for Chinese Books]," *T'u Shu Kuan Hsueh Chi K'an 圖書館學季刊 [Library Science Quarterly]* 3, no. 12 (June 1929): 1-42.
12. Interview with Fu-ts'ung Chiang, National Palace Museum, Taipei, Taiwan, ROC, 7 December, 1981.
13. Ibid.
14. Ministry of Education (MOE) to NCL, Chiao Yu Pu P'ai Ling 教育部派令 ["Appointment #565"] 23 January 1933, [Inaugural File], NCL, Taipei, ROC.
15. Fu-ts'ung Chiang 蔣復璁, "Wo Yu Chung Yang T'u Shu Kuan 我與中央圖書館 [My Life with the National Central Library]," recorded by Ching Chiang 蔣京 記錄, *Chin Tai Chung Kuo 近代中國 [Contemporary China]* 11 (June 1979): 162; Interview with Chiang, 22 February 1982.
16. Ibid., 166-167.
17. Chiao Yu Pu Ling Kuo Li Chung Yang T'u Shu Kuan Yu Chiang Fu-ts'ung 教育部令國立中央圖書館與蔣復璁 [MOE to NCL and Fu-ts'ung Chiang], Hsun Ling San Ssu Ssu Pa Hao Hsun Ling 訓令三四四八號訓令 ["Instructions #3448"], 21 April 1933, Ch'eng Li Tang An 成立檔案 [Inaugural File], NCL, Taipei, ROC; *Chiao Yu Pu Kung Pao 教育部公報 [MOE Gazette]* 5 (April 1933): 7.
18. Kuo Li Chung Yang T'u Shu Kuan 國立中央圖書館 [National Central Library], Kuo Li Chung Yang T'u Shu Kuan Pien Nien Cheng Shih Lu 國立中央圖書館編年政事錄 [Administration Chronological File], 21 April 1933, Taipei, ROC.
19. Kuo Li Chung Yang T'u Shu Kuan Ch'eng Chiao Yu Pu Pao Kao 國立中央圖書館呈教育部報告 [NCL to MOE], "Pao Kao Ch'ou Pei Ching Kuo 報告籌備經過 [Report on the Preparation and Plans for the National Central Library]," 14 July 1933, Ch'eng Li Tang An 成立檔案 [Inaugural File], NCL, Taipei, ROC; NCL, "Kuan Shih Shih Liao Hsuan Chi 館史史料選輯 [Selected Historical Resources]," *Kuo Li Chun Yang T'u Shu Kuan Kuan K'an 國立中央圖書館館刊 [National Central Library Bulletin]* New 16, no. 1 (April 1983): 61-62.
20. Tan-yin 蟫隱, "Chiang Wei-t'ang Hsien Sheng Yu Kuo Li Chung Yang T'u Shu Kuan 蔣慰堂先生與國立中央圖書館 [Mr.Wei-t'ang Chiang and the National Central Library]," *Chung Kuo T'u Shu Kuan Hsueh Hui Hui Pao 中國圖書館學會會報 [Bulletin of the Library Association of China]* 18 (December 1966): 1.
21. Ibid., 2.

22. Fu-ts'ung Chiang 蔣復璁, "Wo Yu Chung Kuo Te T'u Shu Kuan Shih Yeh 我與中國的圖書館事業 [My life in Chinese Librarianship]," *Hsin Shih Tai 新時代 [New Epoch]* 1, no. 3 (March 1961): 51.
23. Ibid.
24. Kuo Li Chung Yang T'u Shu Kuan Pien 國立中央圖書館 編 [National Central Library, ed.], "Kuo Li Chung Yang T'u Shu Kuan Hsien K'uang 國立中央圖書館現況 [Status of the National Central Library]," *Kuo Li Chung Yang T'u Shu Kuan Kuan K'an Fu K'an Ti I Hao 國立中央圖書館館刊* 復刊第一號 *[National Central Library Bulletin]* 1 (Nanking: National Central Library, 1947): 51.
25. Fu-ts'ung Chiang 蔣復璁, "Wo Yu Chung Yang T'u Shu Kuan 我與中央圖書館 [My Life with the National Central Library]," 168; Cheng-pang Wang 王震邦, "Chiang Fu-ts'ung Shih Chung Hua Kuo Pao Te Shou Hu Shen 蔣復璁是中華國寶的守護神 [Fu-ts'ung Chiang, the Guardian of the Chinese National Treasuries]," *Min Sheng Pao 民生報 [Min Sheng Daily News]*, 7 March 1983.
26. Fu-ts'ung Chiang 蔣復璁, "I Ch'a No Te Chueh Ting 一剎那的決定 [Decisions That Affected My Life]," *Chuan Chi Wen Hsueh 傳記文學 [Biographical Literature]* 3 (July 1963): 29-30.
27. Fu-ts'ung Chiang 蔣復璁, "Hsien Chung Hsiung Kung Ku Hsien Sheng Hsing Lueh 先仲兄公穀先生行略 [Biographical Sketch of My Brother, Mr. Kung-ku]," in *Hsien Ching San Yueh Chi 陷京三月記 [Three Months in the Occupied Capital by Kung Ku Chiang]* (Taipei: The Author, 1981), 1-17.
28. Peter Ch'ang 昌彼得, "Chiang Wei-t'ang Hsien Sheng Ch'i Shih Nien Piao 蔣慰堂先生七十年表 [Seventy Years of Chronology of Dr. Chiang Fu-ts'ung]," 281.
29. Fu-ts'ung Chiang 蔣復璁, "Wo Yu Chung Kuo Te T'u Shu Kuan Shih Yeh 我與中國的圖書館事業 [My life in Chinese Librarianship]," 52.
30. Fu-ts'ung Chiang 蔣復璁, "Hsi Wang Chung Te T'u Shu Kuan Hsin Chien She 希望中的圖書館新建設 [Hopes for the New Development of Librarianship]," *Chung Yang Jih Pao 中央日報 [Central Daily News (Taiwan, ROC)]*, 3 January 1946.
31. Ibid., 52.
32. Chao-sheng Cheng 鄭肇陞, "Kuo Li Chung Yang T'u Shu Kuan Wu Shih Nien 國立中央圖書館五十年 [Fifty Years of the National Central Library]," *Kuo Li Chung Yang T'u Shu Kuan Kuan Hsun 國立中央圖書館館刊 [National Central Library Bulletin]* New 16, no. 1 (April 1983): 17.
33. Peter Ch'ang 昌彼得, "Chiang Wei-t'ang Hsien Sheng Ch'i Shih Nien

Piao 蔣慰堂先生七十年表 [Seventy Years of Chronology of Dr. Chiang Fu-ts'ung]"

34. Lin-ling Chang 張菱舲, "T'u Shu Sheng Ya Ssu Shih Nien Ch'un — Fang Chung Yang T'u Shu Kuan T'ui Hsiu Kuan Chang Chiang Fu-ts'ung 圖書生涯四十年春 — 訪中央圖書館退休館長蔣復璁 [Forty Years in Library: A Special Report on Dr. Chiang Fu-ts'ung, Retired Head of the National Central Library]," *Chung Hua Jih Pao 中華日報 [Chung Hua Daily News]*, 28 January 1965, 11.
35. Peter Ch'ang 昌彼得, "Chiang Wei-t'ang Hsien Sheng Ch'i Shih Nien Piao 蔣慰堂先生七十年表 [Seventy Years of Chronology of Dr. Chiang Fu-ts'ung]."
36. Ibid., 281.
37. Interview with Chiang, 21 February 1982.
38. Tsung-peng Bao 包遵彭, "Chiang Fu-ts'ung Chueh Shih Yu Kuo Li Chung Yang T'u Shu Kuan 蔣復璁爵士與國立中央圖書館 [Sir Chiang Fu-ts'ung and the National Central Library]," *Chung Kuo I Chou 中國一周 [China Newsweek]* 678 (April 1963): 10; Fu-ts'ung Chiang 蔣復璁, "Wo Yu Chung Kuo Te T'u Shu Kuan Shih Yeh 我與中國的圖書館事業 [My life in Chinese Librarianship]," 170.
39. Taiwan Sheng Li Taipei T'u Shu Kuan Pien 台灣省立台北圖書館 編 [Taiwan Provincial Taipei Library, ed.], "Sheng Li Taipei T'u Shu Kuan Shih 省立台北圖書館史 [Taiwan Provincial Taipei Library History]," *T'ai Wan Sheng Li T'ai Pei T'u Shu Kuan Kuan K'an 台灣省立臺北圖書館館刊 [Bulletin of Taiwan Provincial Taipei Library]* 2 (September 1965): 6-7.
40. Fu-ts'ung Chiang 蔣復璁, "I Nien Lai Te Kuo Li Chung Yang T'u Shu Kuan 一年來的國立中央圖書館[Past Year at the National Central Library]," *Chiao Yu Yu Wen Hua 教育與文化 [Education and Culture]* 260 (May 1961): 8; Fu-ts'ung Chiang 蔣復璁, "Kuo Li Chung Yang T'u Shu Kuan I Nien Lai Kung Tso Kai K'uang 國立中央圖書館一年來工作概況 [Past Year at the National Central Library]," *She Hui Chiao Yu Nien K'an 社會教育年刊 [Social Education Annual]* 16 (January 1963): 41; Fu-ts'ung Chiang 蔣復璁, "Kuo Li Chung Yang T'u Shu Kuan Te I I Yu Hui Ku 國立中央圖書館的意義與回顧 [The Significance and Recollections of the National Central Library]" *Ta Lu Tsa Chih 大陸雜誌 [The Continent Magazine]* 56, no. 6 (June 1967): 253.
41. Peter Ch'ang 昌彼得, "Chiang Wei-t'ang Hsien Sheng Ch'i Shih Nien Piao 蔣慰堂先生七十年表 [Seventy Years of Chronology of Dr. Chiang Fu-ts'ung]," 286.

42. Fu-ts'ung Chiang 蔣復璁, "Yun Kuei Kuo Li Pei P'ing T'u Shu Kuan Ts'un Mei Shan Pen T'u Shu 運歸國立北平圖書館存美善本圖書 [The Shipping of the National Peiping Library's Rare Books Back to Taiwan]," 5-7.
43. Interview with Chiang, 31 October 1987.
44. Exeutive Yuan, P'ai Ling 派令 [Appointment], Tai Wu Shih Ssu Jen Tzu Pa Erh Liu Chiu 台伍拾肆人字 8269, 13 November 1965.
45. Lin-ling Chang 張菱舲, "T'u Shu Sheng Ya Ssu Shih Nien Ch'un — Fang Chung Yang T'u Shu Kuan T'ui Hsiu Kuan Chang Chiang Fu-ts'ung 圖書生涯四十年春 — 訪中央圖書館退休館長蔣復璁 [Forty Years in Library: A Special Report on Dr. Chiang Fu-ts'ung, Retired Head of the National Central Library]."
46. Executive Yuan, P'ai Ling 派令 [Appointment], Tai Wu Liu Jen Tzu Ch'i I Erh San 台伍拾陸人字 7123, 12 September 1963.
47. Fu-ts'ung Chiang 蔣復璁, "Kuo Li Ku Kung Po Wu Yuan Shih Pa Nien Kung Tso Chien Pao 國立故宮博物院十八年工作簡報 [Brief Report on 18 Years' Work at the National Palace Museum]," *Hua Hsueh Ch'i K'an 華學季刊* 5, no. 4 (December 1984): 70-75.
48. Kuo Li Ku Kung Po Wu Yuan Pien 國立故宮博物院 編 [National Palace Museum, ed.], *Ku K'ung Li Tai Fa Shu Ch'uan Chi 故宮歷代法書全集*, 30 vols. (Taipei: National Palace Museum, 1979).
49. Kuo Li Ku Kung Po Wu Yuan Pien 國立故宮博物院 編 [National Palace Museum, ed.], *Kuo Li Ku Kung Po Wu Yuan Ch'u Pan P'in Mu Lu 國立故宮博物院出版品目錄 [Catalogue of Publications in the National Palace Museum]* (Taipei: National Palace Museum, 1982).
50. Fu-ts'ung Chiang 蔣復璁, "Ssu Ku Ch'uan Shu Te Hsing Chih Yu Pien Tsuan Chi Ying Yin Te Ching Kuo 四庫全書的性質與編纂及影印的經過 [The Nature, Editing, and Reproduction of Ssu K'u Ch'uan Shu]," *Tung Fang Tsa Chih 東方雜誌* 17, no. 11 (May 1984): 12-20.
51. Chiang, "Kuo Li Ku Kung Po Wu Yuan Shih Pa Nien Kung Tso Chien Pao 國立故宮博物院十八年工作簡報 [Brief Report on 18 Years' Work at the National Palace Museum]," *Hua Hsueh Ch'i K'an 華學季刊* 5, no. 4 (December 1984): 73.
52. "T'u Shu Kuan Chin Jih Tung T'ai 圖書館近日動態," *Shih Ta Chiao K'an 師大校刊* 231 (January 1979): 12.
53. Fu-ts'ung Chiang 蔣復璁, "Wo Yu Chung Yang T'u Shu Kuan 我與中央圖書館 [My Life with the National Central Library]," 170.
54. Interview with Chiang, 21 February 1982; Ch'ang, 283-284.

55. Fu-ts'ung Chiang 蔣復璁, "Fang Chih Chan Lan Te I I 方志展覽的意義 [The Significance of Exhibitions on Local History]," *Chung Kuo T'u Shu Kuan Hsueh Hui Hui Pao 中國圖書館學會會報 [Bulletin of the Library Association of China]* 4 (March 1955):1-4.
56. Fu-ts'ung Chiang 蔣復璁, "T'u Shu Kuan Tsai Chin Jih Taiwan Te Chung Yao Hsing 圖書館在今日台灣的重要性 [The Mission of the Library Association of China]," in *T'u Shu Yu T'u Shu Kuan 圖書與圖書館 [Books and Libraries]* (Taipei: Chinese Cultural Publishing Company, 1959), 40-57.
57. Fu-ts'ung Chiang 蔣復璁, *Su Hsin Lu 訴信錄 [A Testimony in Religious Belief]* (Taipei: Kuang Ch'i She, 1958).
58. Fu-ts'ung Chiang 蔣復璁, *T'u Shu Yu T'u Shu Kuan 圖書與圖書館 [Books and Libraries]* (Taipei: Chinese Cultural Publishing Company, 1959).
59. Fu-ts'ung Chiang 蔣復璁, "Kuo Li Chung Yang T'u Shu Kuan Te Ch'i Yuan Yu Shih Ming 國立中央圖書館的起源與使命 [The Origin and Mission of the National Libraries]," *Chung Kuo T'u shu Kuan Hsueh Hui Hui Pao 中國圖書館學會會報 [Bulletin of the Library Association of China]* 15 (December 1963): 1-3.
60. Fu-ts'ung Chiang 蔣復璁, *Sung Shih Hsin T'an 宋史新探 [A New Inquiry into the Sung Dynasty History]* (Taipei: Cheng Chung Shu Chu, 1965).
61. Fu-ts'ung Chiang 蔣復璁, *Chen Chou Chi 珍帚集 [Collections]* (Taipei: Tai P'ing Yang Wen Hua Shih Yeh Wei Yuan Hui, 1965).
62. Fu-ts'ung Chiang 蔣復璁, *Chen Chou Chai Wen Chi 珍帚齋文集* (Taipei: Taiwan Commercial Press, 1985).
63. Interview with Chiang, 21 February 1982.
64. Peter Ch'ang 昌彼得, "Chiang Wei-t'ang Hsien Sheng Ch'i Shih Nien Piao 蔣慰堂先生七十年表 [Seventy Years of Chronology of Dr. Chiang Fu-ts'ung]," 284.
65. Ibid.
66. Tsung-peng Bao 包遵彭, "Chiang Fu-ts'ung Chueh Shih Tsui Hsin Shu Ch'eng — Chu Kuo Li Chung Yang T'u Shu Kuan Chien Kuan San Shih Chou Nien 蔣復璁爵士醉心書城 — 祝國立中央圖書館建館三十週年 [Sir Chinag Fu-ts'ung is in Love with Books]," *Taiwan Hsin Sheng Pao 台灣新生報 [Taiwan Hsin Sheng Daily News]*, 20 April 1963, 4.
67. Tsung-peng Bao 包遵彭, "Chiang Fu-ts'ung Chueh Shih Yu Kuo Li Chung Yang T'u Shu Kuan 蔣復璁爵士與國立中央圖書館 [Sir Chiang Fu-ts'ung and the National Central Library]."
68. Lin-ling Chang 張菱舲, "T'u Shu Sheng Ya Ssu Shih Nien Ch'un — Fang Chung Yang T'u Shu Kuan T'ui Hsiu Kuan Chang Chiang Fu-ts'ung

圖書生涯四十年春 — 訪中央圖書館退休館長蔣復璁 [Forty Years in Library: A Special Report on Dr. Chiang Fu-ts'ung, Retired Head of the National Central Library]."

69. *Chung Yang Jih Pao 中央日報 [Central Daily News (Taiwan, ROC)]*, 14 January 1983.
70. Yen-ch'iu Wang 汪雁秋, "Ch'u His Mei Kuo T'u Shu Kuan Hsieh Hui Ti I Ling Ssu Chieh Nien Hui Pao Kao出席美國圖館協會第104屆年會報告 [A Report of the Chinese Delegation to the 104th Annual Conference of the American Library Association]," *Chung Kuo T'u shu Kuan Hsueh Hui Hui Pao 中國圖書館學會會報 [Bulletin of the Library Association of China]* 37 (December 1985): 169-178.

Reprinted with permission from The *Collection of Papers in Honor of Dr. Chiang Fu-ts'ung on His 90th Birthday*. Taipei: Library Association of China, 1987. (pp. 73-106).

APPENDIX

LIST OF APPOINTMENTS*

Despatching Organization	Position	Date
Executive Yuan	Advisor	November 13, 1954
Catholic Church, Taipei	Preaching Committee	August 15, 1966
Committee on Scholarly Cooperation with the U.S. Academic Sinica	Member, Committee on Humanistic and Social Sciences	August, 1966
Presidential Office	Commissioner, Civil Service Examination Commission	August 29, 1966
Taipei Catholic Archdioses	Member, Archdioses Cultural Committee	January 21, 1967
Library Association of China	Member & Chair Committee on Education	February 4, 1967
Chiao-yu Sheng-Ho Weekly	Editor-in-Chief	February 1, 1967
Presidential Office	Member, Planning Committee of the National Development Seminar	March 8, 1967
Chinese Culture Univ.	Member, Committee of Chen Cheng-chen, Graduate Student	May 10, 1967
Catholic Fu-jen University	Member, Dissertation and Examination Committee on Master Degree Program of Philosophy	May 23, 1967
Executive Yuan	Member, National Palace Museum Administrative Committee	August 26, 1967
Executive Yuan	Director, National Palace Museum	September 12, 1967
Council on Chinese Cultural Renaissance	Member	August 23, 1967

*Collected from National Palace Museum files.

Council on Chinese Cultural Renaissance	Member, Committee on Scholarly Research & Publications	December 26, 1967
Chinese Culture College	Professor, Ph. D. Program in History	January 8, 1968
Council on Chinese Cultural Renaissance	Member, Guidance Committee on Citizens' Living	March 28, 1968
Central Committee,Democratic Club of Japan	Advisor	March 1, 1968
Chinese Culture College	Part-time Professor Institute of History	July 7, 1968
Taipei Subcommittee, Council on Chinese Cultural Renaissance	Standing Member of the Subcommittee	September 23, 1968
Chekiang T'ung Hsiang Hui	Advisor	October 25, 1968
Committee on Scholarly Research and Publications	Member, Editorial Committee	October, 1968
China Academy	Advisor, Institute of Study on Catholicism	October, 1968
Committee on Scholarly Cooperation with the U.S.	Member	January 30, 1969
Ministry of Foreign Affairs	Lecturer, Training Class for Consular Personnel	January 9, 1969
Presidential Office	Member, Civil Service Examination Committee	August 28, 1968
Catholic Diacesean Headquarters, Taipei	Member, Editorial Board, Catholic University and College Professors Association Journal	February 1969
Committee on the Reproduction of Huang-Ho Wan-Li-Tu	Preparatory Committee Member	April 1, 1969
Chinese Culture College	Professor, Institute of History (August 1, 1969-July 31, 1970)	August, 1969

Council for Chinese Cultural Renaissance	Member	September 10, 1969
Chinese Culture College	Professor, Institute of History (August 1, 1972-July 31, 1973)	August, 1972
Executive Yuan	Advisor	June 28, 1972
Executive Yuan	Member, National Palace Museum 14th Administrative Committee	October 8, 1972
Taipei Municipal Government	Member, Taipei Municipal Documents Committee	January 7, 1969
Committee on Scholarly Cooperation with the U.S.	Special Advisor to the Delegation. Second Joint Conference on Sino-American Cooperation in the Humanities and Social Sciences	May 14, 1969
China Academy	Honorary Chair, Committee on Exhibition of Korean Artifacts, Second International Conference on Sinology	July, 1969
Commission on Sino-Japanese Cooperation	Member	November 3, 1969
Executive Yuan	Member, National Palace Museum Administrative Committee	September 12, 1969
I Shu Kuan	Advisor, Chinese Music Orchestra	November 1, 1969
Council on Chinese Cultural Renaissance	Member, Committee on Scholarly Research and Publications	October 11, 1969
Preparatory Committee of Dr. Sun Yat-sen's 80th Birthday Celebration	Member, Fundraising Committee	April, 1970
National Chengchi University	Member, Committee on Masters' Program	May 1970
Department of Public Construction, Taiwan Provincial Government	Member, Planning Committee of Antiquities and Resorts in Tainan Area	May 26, 1970

Bureau of Cultural Affairs Ministry of Education	Honorary Chair, Chinese Music Society	June 17, 1970
6th National Fine Arts Exhibition	Member, Committee on Exhibition	July 1, 1970
China Academy	Advisor, Institute of Korean Studies (July 1, 1970-June 30, 1971)	July 1, 1970
Catholic Fu-jen University	Professor	September 1, 1970
Sino-Iranian Cultural and Economical Association	Member, Preparatory Committee in Celebration of the Founding of Iran	November 1970
Presidential Office	Member, Civil Service Examination Committee	August 17, 1970
Bureau of Cultural Affairs Ministry of Education	Advisor, Chinese Music Society	December 12, 1970
Catholic Fu-jen University	Member, Examination Committee on Master's Degree Program of History	1971
Catholic Fu-jen University	Member, Examination Committee on Master's Degree Program of Philosophy	May 1971
Chinese Arts Society	Advisor	August 1971
Chinese Culture College	Professor	July 1971
Council on Chinese Cultural Renaissance	Member	August 23, 1971
Executive Yuan	Director, National Palace Museum	October 30, 1969
Chinese Culture College	Professor, Doctoral Program, Institute of History	November 8, 1971
Executive Yuan	Director, National Palace Museum	November 19, 1971
Personnel Department, Executive Yuan	Advisor	June 29, 1972

Catholic Fu-jen University	Professor	September 1, 1972
Yangmingshan Administration Bureau	Member, Advisory Committee on Development	August 15, 1972
Committee on Social Work KMT Central Committee	Member, Liason Committee on Religion	July 30, 1972
Taipei Municipal Government	Member, Taipei Confucius Temple Management Committee	August 19, 1971
Presidential Office	Member, 1972 Civil Service Examination Committee	August 26, 1972
Ministry of Education	Member, Evaluation Committee of Chao Ya-shu, Doctoral degree candidate	October 16, 1972
Chung-kuo Chuan-shan Society	Honorary Director	October 31, 1972
Ministry of Education	Member, Evaluation Committee of Ma Hsien-hsin, Doctoral Degree candidate	November 5, 1972
Chinese National Musical Society	Honorary Advisor, Chinese Orchestra	November 1972
Yangmingshan Administration Bureau	Member, Committee on Yangmingshan Development	March 10, 1973
Chinese Culture College	Member, Committee of Kuo Feng-ming, Doctoral candidate	March 27, 1973
Provincial Taichung Library	Advisor, PreparatoryCommittee on Exhibition of Chinese Artifacts	February 1974
China Academy	Director, Research Institute on Kun-chu (September 1, 1973-August 31, 1941)	September 1973
Chinese Culture College	Member, Examination Committee on Doctoral candidate, Ling Lin-huang	April 25, 1973

Ministry of Education	Member, Evaluation Committee on Doctoral candidate,Tan Su-cheng	May 14, 1973
National Cheng-chih University	Member, Doctoral Program Committee	June 1973
Social Work Committee, KMT Central Committee	Member, Religion Liason Committee	July 1, 1973
Ministry of Education	Member, Evaluation Committee on Doctoral Candidate, Sun Tzu-ho	July 1, 1973
Catholic Fu-jen University	Professor	September 1, 1973
Council on Chinese Cultural Renaissance	Member	August 16, 1973
National Central Library	Advisor	September 10, 1973
Presidential Office	Member, 1973 Civil Service Examination Committee	August 16, 1973
Association for Japanese Calligraphy	Honorary Advisor	August 1, 1973
Executive Yuan	Member, National Palace Museum Administrative Committee	October 2, 1973
Confucius-Mencius Society	Member, Committee on the Construction of Chinese Cultural Park in San Jose, CA.	October 5, 1973
China Academy	Honorary Director, Institute of Kun-chu (August 1, 1973-July 31, 1974)	August, 1973
Council on Chinese Cultural Renaissance	Member, Committee on Scholarly Research and Publications	September 26, 1973
Executive Yuan	Director, National Palace Museum	November 5, 1973
7th National Art Exhibition of the Republic of China	Member	November 10, 1973

Cardinal Lo-kuang	Advisor, Association of Asian Cardinals	January 16, 1974
Catholic Fu-jen University	Member, Examination Committee on Doctoral Program, Institute of Philosophy	January 16, 1974
Society of Oriental Calligraphy	Advisor	June 15, 1974
Committee on Social Work, KMT Central Committee	Member, Religion Liason Committee	June 15, 1974
Catholic Fu-jen University	Professor	September 1, 1974
Chinese Culture College	Member, Examination Committee of Chao Cheng-chi, Doctoral candidate	September 1, 1974
Chinese Culture College	Member and Chair Oral Examination Committee Doctoral Degree Program Institute of History	July 24, 1974
Presidential Office	Member, Committee on 1974 Civil Service Examination	August 18, 1974
Ministry of Education	Member, Examination Committee of Shih Wen-yuan, Doctoral degree candidate	October 19, 1974
Academia Sinica	Member Committee on Scholarly Cooperation with the U.S.A.	October 1, 1974
Chinese Culture College`	Professor	February 1975
Ministry of Economic Affairs	Founder, Sino-Arabian Cultural and Economical Association	February 28, 1975
Library Association ofChina	Member, Editorial Board, Chinese Art and Literary Records	January 1975
Presidential Office	Evaluation Commissioner, Academia Sinica	May 9, 1975

Hsu-hui Middle School	Director of the 14th Board	June 1975
Social Work Committee, KMT Central Committee	Member, Religion Liason Committee	July 1, 1975
Catholic Fu-jen University	Professor	September 1, 1975
Sino-Arab Cultural and Economic Association	Member, Cultural Interchange Committee	October 13, 1975
Council on Chinese Cultural Renaissance	Member, Committee on Scholarly Research and Publications	October 13, 1975
Council on Chinese Cultural Renaissance	Member	October 27, 1975
Executive Yuan	Director, National Palace Museum	October 29, 1975
Presidential Office	Member, Committee on 1975 Civil Service Examination	August 18, 1975
Chiang Kai-shek Memorial	Member, Evaluation Committee on Building Design for the Chiang Kai-shek Memorial	May 5, 1976
The 8th National Art Exhibition of the Republic of China	Member	June 10, 1976
Chinese Culture College	Member, Evaluation Committee on Doctoral Program in Literature	June 1976
1976 Summer Northern Area Institute for Taiwanese Historical Remains	Professor	July 1, 1976
Social Work Committee, KMT Central Committee	Member, Religion Liason Committee (July 1, 1976-June 30, 1977)	July 1, 1976

6

David Kaser and Sino-American Librarianship

ABSTRACT

This article reports the valuable assistance rendered by American library professionals to the establishment of Chinese professional librarianship and the enhancement of Chinese librarianship services which in turn were instrumental to China's development and modernization. The first phase of Sino-American library activity (1910-1950) is briefly described. Dr. David Kaser's significant contibution to the development in the Republic of China on Taiwan in the second phase (1960-the present) is noteworthy in:

1. Education and training of librarians,
2. Library building planning,
3. Sino-American joint understanding of books and libraries,
4. The establishment of national information policy.

This article concludes with Dr. Kaser's own comments on his efforts in support of Sino-American librarianship which well illustrates his professional dedication to international librarianship to an extent that no one can surpass.

INTRODUCTION

The establishment of professional librarianship and the enhancement of library service in China since the turn of the century have been instrumental to that nation's development and modernization. From the beginning, one of the principal factors contributing to the improvement of Chinese librarianship has been the involvement of foreign librarians, including American experts. This Sino-American library activity occurred largely in two phases: the first extended approximately from 1910 to 1950, and the second phase began around 1960 and continues today.

No record indicates that any individual has been more involved in the second phase of Sino-American librarianship in the last quarter of a century than David Kaser. In doing so, however, he was following in the footsteps of a number of others who had been active in its first phase, which concentrated on education for librarianship.

FIRST PHASE OF SINO-AMERICAN LIBRARY ACTIVITY

As early as 1913, Harry Clemons, a graduate and librarian of Wesleyan University and Princeton University, introduced library science courses into China at the University of Nanking.[1] Six years later, Mary Elizabeth Wood founded China's first library school, the Boone Library School in Wuhan. Established by an American librarian, this school was supported financially either by Christian missions or American foundations, and its courses were taught by American or American-trained graduates.[2] The Boone Library School aimed at transplanting American systems, methods, and ideas into Chinese library practice.

Many Chinese were also sent on scholarships to the United States for advanced professional training during this period. They either brought back American systems for Chinese rooting or exerted a great impact upon Chinese collections in the United States. These individuals included Hsiu Cha, Kai-ming Ch'iu, Chia-pi Hsu, Chin-shen Hu, Hsing-hui Huang, Yu-feng Hung, Chih-ber

Kwei, Fang-fu Li, Siao-yuan Li, Kuo-chuin Liu, Ming-hing Mok, Tsu-yung Seng, Tze-chien Tai, Hung-tu Tien, Vi-line Wong, Wen-yu Yen, and Tung-li Yuan.[3]

In December 1947, Charles Harvey Brown, Chairman of the American Library Association's (ALA's) Committee on the Orient and Southwest Pacific, and Verner Warren Clapp, Deputy Librarian of Congress, recommended that China should have four additional library schools - at West Union University in Chengtu, at the University of Nanking in Nanking, at National Sun Yat-sen University in Canton, and at National Peking University in Peiping.[4] Their recommendation resulted in the establishment of a library school at the National Peking University.

One of the most profound influences introduced into Chinese librarianship embraced the modern principles of book classification schemes: flexibility, expandability and inclusiveness. Dewey Decimal Classification and Relative Index, Library of Congress Classification, Cutter's Expansive Classification, and Brown's Subject Classification were either used as foundations for the revision of Chinese classification or were employed by libraries in classifying their books. Several classification schemes were produced as a result: Tsu-yung Seng's *A System of Classification of Chinese Books Based on Dewey's Classification*, Ding-u Doo's *Universal Classification*, Jih-chang Ho and Yung-chin Yuan's *Decimal Classification for Chinese Books*, Kuo-chuin Liu's *A System of Book Classification for Chinese Libraries*, and Kai-ming Ch'iu's *A Classification Scheme for Chinese and Japanese Books*[5].

American cataloging rules, such as *ALA Catalog Rules: Author and Title Entries*, Jennie D. Fellows' *Cataloging Rules with Explanation and Illustrations*, Susan G. Akers' *Simple Library Cataloging*, and Theresa Hitchler's *Cataloging for Small Libraries*, were either adopted by Chinese libraries or were used as bases for developing Chinese cataloging rules[6]. The use of subject headings and author numbers can also be attributed to American influence.[7]

Insofar as public services in libraries were concerned, the Boone Library began to introduce such innovations as open shelves, free access, home use, reading guidance, and traveling libraries in 1910.[8] Arthur Elmore Bostwich's visit to China in 1925 inspired the Chinese government with the ideas of modern public libraries and led to the founding of the National Library in Peiping.[9] His visit to fifty libraries in China and his suggestions for practical ways to establish free public libraries in China were instrumental to the development of the Chinese public library system. Many other services, such as interlibrary cooperation and a national union catalog for bibliographic control, were also patterned after American practices.[10]

With the establishment of the China Foundation for Promotion of Education and Culture, and thanks to Mary Elizabeth Wood's efforts, a portion of the Boxer Indemnity Fund was remitted by the United States to China beginning in 1924. This fund would establish and maintain public libraries in China and develop professional librarianship by providing scholarships and professorships to the Boone Library School. In addition, Christian missionary organizations, foundations, and other private donors were major financial supporters.[11]

Regrettably, the library movement in China was halted by the Sino-Japanese war during the period 1937-1945, when many libraries were destroyed.[12] In response to an appeal in 1938 from Tung-li Yuan, Chairman of the Executive Committee of the Library Association of China, ALA launched a Books-for-China campaign on June 12, 1938. The Association collected 20,000 books, as well as microfilms of selected periodicals and these to offset the damages.[13] By the end of the 1940s, however, civil war had ended the first phase of Sino-American librarianship.

KASER'S INVOLVEMENT IN THE SECOND PHASE

The above brief historical account exemplifies some of the American efforts that had exerted a significant impact upon the modernization of librarianship in China before 1950. Subsequently, David Kaser's contribution to the development of librarianship in Taiwan has been noteworthy in the following areas:

1. Education and training of librarians,
2. Planning for library buildings,
3. Sino-American joint understanding of books and libraries.

Education and Training of Librarians

David Kaser's personal impact upon Sino-American librarianship began in 1960 when he was appointed Director of the Joint University Libraries at Vanderbilt University and Professor of Library Science at Peabody College in Nashville, Tennessee.[14] At that time, several libraries in Taiwan sent young Chinese librarians to study in the master's program at Peabody, where they came into close contact with Kaser and were influenced by his teaching.

Most of these Peabody graduates subsequently became leaders of the Chinese library community, and their efforts toward the advancement of Chinese librarianship since 1960 have been paramount. Yung-hsiang Lai returned to Taiwan to initiate and head the library school at National Taiwan University, which has become the best library school on the island. Lai-lung Chau became the director of the third largest university library, the National Chengchi University Library, and built there a modern modular library building. William Chia-chun Ju served as Director of the National Central Library, which is now directed by Chen-ku Wang. The National Central Library is charged with providing overall leadership in the development of librarianship, library policies, services, and systems throughout the Republic of China (ROC) on Taiwan. The achievements of Peabody graduates in strengthening the professional associations, promoting professional publications, formulating library standards and legislation, enhancing professional education, and advocating interlibrary cooperation in Taiwan must be partly attributed to the education, guidance, and inspiration those graduates acquired in Kaser's lectures.

Dr. Chiang Fu-ts'ung, who devoted his entire life to the collection, preservation, and dissemination of Chinese culture through his directorship of the National Central Library (1933-1966) and of the National Palace Museum (1966-1982), visited Kaser in Nashville during the fall of 1960.[15] This brief visit resulted in a lasting professional friendship between Chiang and Kaser that has extended over almost three decades. These two dedicated professionals spoke the same professional language and shared the same professional aspirations, even though they were unable to speak each other's native tongue. Some of Chiang's proposals, ideas, and endeavors for the blueprints and policies of library services in Taiwan coincided with the long-range planning and administrative efforts advocated by Kaser. It was partly Chiang's dedication to Chinese librarianship that earned Kaser's constant support for library professionalism in China. Chiang respected Kaser as a scholar and a librarian of vision and wisdom: "It is commendable," he remarked recently, "that Dr. Kaser devotes much effort to the promotion of international understanding through librarianship with his keen observation, far-sightedness and wisdom. Chinese librarians have benefited greatly from his various endeavors in the field."[16]

Between 1968 and 1973, Kaser was the Director of Libraries at Cornell University. His duties, his interactions with faculty members and students, and his oversight of the important Wason Collection of Sinology put him into constant contact with Chinese librarians, students, and scholars in many parts of the world.

During his teaching career at the School of Library and Information Science at Indiana University since 1973, David Kaser taught and advised many Chinese students from both sides of the Taiwan Straits, as well as from Hong Kong, Singapore, Malaysia, and other parts of the Orient. Several Chinese are among Kaser's doctoral graduates: Robert Pin-chuan Chen, currently professor/coordinator of Documents Services at Eastern Illinois

University; Mei-hua Yang, librarian of Feng Chia University in Taichung; and Margaret C. Fung, currently conducting research under the affiliation of a research associateship at Harvard University and serving as advisor to several cultural and library projects in Taiwan and in the United States. Robert Pin-chuan Chen's project, "Library Resources for American Studies in Taiwan: An Evaluation," Mei-hua Yang's dissertation on Chinese education for librarianship entitled "Library Educational Personnel Planning in ROC on Taiwan," and Margaret C. Fung's research on the topic "Evolving Social Mission of the National Central Library 1928-1966" all received Kaser's undivided attention and guidance from beginning to end.[17] All of them have expressed gratitude for his guidance, patience, support, care, enthusiasm, and encouragement.[18] He was never too busy for his students or turned any of them away, but rather he treated their projects as if they were his very own and literally labored with them during the course of research. This professional integrity and dedication served them as examples to follow throughout their careers. With Kaser's advice and support, they, too, have been continuously working for the betterment of Sino-American librarianship since their graduation.

As a historian, David Kaser has long been interested in the evolution of Chinese libraries. He became especially interested in the efforts of Dr. Tung-li Yuan to develop librarianship in China during the middle of this century. With the encouragement of Yuan's family, Kaser was instrumental in establishing the Yuan Tung-li Memorial Scholarship Fund in the School of Library and Information Science at Indiana University. Since 1983 Kuo-chun Chen, Lily Wee, and Hsiu-ying Chiang have received this scholarship.[19] Since this scholarship is an endowed fund, Chinese librarianship will benefit from it in perpetuity, in recognition of Yuan Tung-li's contributions to the Chinese library profession. Already the above-mentioned recipients have successfully completed their studies at Indiana University; Chen and Chiang returned to

Taipei to serve the library community at the National Institute of the Arts and National Central Library, while Wee devotes herself to the academic library profession in the United States.

In addition to the students David Kaser taught in the United States, librarians in Taiwan and other parts of the world have learned a great deal from his lectures and publications on Chinese libraries. His first lecture at National Taiwan University in 1967 exerted a profound influence upon faculty members and students of that newly established library school.[20] Also at National Taiwan University, in November 1969, Kaser lectured on some of the persistent problems of international librarianship.[21] Meanwhile his speech entitled "Humanism, the Library and Quality of Life," delivered at the Chinese-American Librarians Association meeting in River Forest, Illinois on May 10, 1975, inspired Chinese librarians in the United States and they responded to his talk with enthusiasm.[22]

In November 1979 Kaser was invited to participate in a continuing education workshop, "Library Planning and Media Technology" at National Taiwan Normal University.[23] More than 200 practicing librarians from all parts of Taiwan participated in the workshop and were inspired by the principles of participatory management, the importance of identifying goals, missions, and objectives for library services, and the planning guidelines for modern library buildings. The series of lectures opened up a new horizon to Chinese library administrators and practitioners and greatly enriched many of the planning efforts of libraries in Taiwan. When the proceedings were published in 1980, they were in great demand and were widely distributed.

On December 2, 1979, Kaser addressed the Library Association of China Annual Conference at Taipei in a speech entitled "Why Libraries Indeed?" He emphasized the importance of knowing the why of library services and librarians' duties rather than the traditional how.[24] In another lecture at National Central Library in Taipei three years later, he also stressed the impact of modern technology upon library services and the ways in which librarians must prepare themselves for the twenty-first century.[25] On these occasions, in recognition of his contributions to Sino-American librarianship, he was presented with plaques by the National Taiwan Normal University, the Library Association of China, and the National Central Library.

As part of the observance of Captive Nations Week in 1982, Kaser was invited by the World Anti-Communist League to present a talk at National Taiwan Normal University on July 20. In his address, "Free Knowledge or Fettered Minds," he outlined the importance of intellectual freedom, especially with regard to books and libraries, citing historical examples that illustrated the reasons why attempts to suppress ideas are inevitably self-defeating.[26] Here, as on many other occasions, his audience was not limited to practitioners in the field of library and information science. His talks at the Institute of Chinese Architects at National Taiwan Normal University on December 1, 1979, and at the ROC Chapter of the Indiana University Alumni Association on March 25, 1982, reached a large and varied audience.[27]

David Kaser has continuously paid attention to the promotion of professional understanding among American and Chinese librarians on both the professional and personal level. Most of the Chinese librarians who have attended conferences of professional associations in the United States have had the pleasure of meeting him because he makes an effort to become acquainted with foreign librarians. One particular case deserves recording. In October 1982, after the American Society for Information Science Conference in Ohio, Harries B.H. Seng (Professor of Library Science, National Taiwan University), Jack Kai-tung Huang (Ming Chuan College), and Margaret C. Fung (Professor of Library Science, National Taiwan Normal University) went to visit Indiana University. Kaser drove back and forth four times between Indianapolis and Bloomington (a total of more than 200 miles) within twelve hours to meet these foreign friends. He and Mrs. Kaser showed them the warmest American hospitality by inviting all the faculty members of the library school, university faculty members of Chinese descent, and Chinese students in the library school to meet them in their home. "This meeting was most impressive and beneficial to faculty members," Seng observed later. "It furthered cooperation and understanding between Chinese and American librarians and information scientists."[28]

Planning for Library Buildings

David Kaser also has exerted an important influence upon the planning of library buildings in Taiwan. In 1979. His address to the Institute of Chinese Architects on planning for modern library buildings helped architects there to understand the special specifications, criteria, and needs of an academic library building. The timing of this lecture was particularly opportune because the Taiwan area's economy was then expanding and the ROC was implementing an extensive Cultural Planning and Development Program. As a result, there was a great need for constructing functional library buildings. When Kaser was invited to consult on the design of a new library building at the National Taiwan Normal University in the same year, he pointed out to the university administrators and to Ying-hsuan Peng, the architect, both the desirable and undesirable features of modern academic library structures.[29]

The ROC government's efforts to launch a wide range of cultural and educational projects resulted in the establishment of the new National Institute of the Arts in 1982. As a new Institution of higher learning, this Institute's faculty and staff members, under the preparatory guidance of its director, Yao-yu Bao, realized the importance of a library to meet the educational, informational, and instructional needs of its four departments. At the invitation of the Institute, Kaser made a special trip to Taipei in March 1982 for consultation with the well-known Chinese architect C.Y. Lee.

Their meetings on the design of a new library building for that institution produced a functional library blueprint. Yao-yu Bao particularly appreciated Kaser's assistance and stated:

"Dr. Kaser's insights into the importance of the close relationship between culture and the library have been extremely valuable to us in designing our new library. He always takes the cultural uniqueness of each institution and country into consideration when he is asked to consult on the library buildings. I have been greatly impressed by this concern. We have adapted his ideas of a functional library and we also added additional quarters for an art museum behind the library. This hybrid building was resulted from his strong advocacy for the close relationship between culture and library building."[30]

Lee thought that Kaser's practical principles set for the academic library building were indeed helpful: "Dr. Kaser insisted on air-conditioning, carpets, and a mixture of books and readers in order best to preserve the library collection and to provide easy accessibility and comfort to the users."[31]

When construction was just begun on the fine new National Central Library (NCL) building, the architect, Pau-sen Chen, and his associates went to Bloomington, Indiana on December 17, 1983. Their specific purpose was to discuss the project and the plans with Kaser. Chen-ku Wang, Director of the NCL, and Pau-sen Chen recalled Kaser's concern over the relationship of cultural assets and national heritage. This idea about the library building reinforced their conviction that the NCL's new library building plans should indeed reflect the close relationship between the Chinese cultural heritage and the future development of the library. The NCL building is designed for people – the readers, staff, and other users – as well as for the book collection. Its rich 858,158-volume collection and spacious 443,000-square-foot building strive to : (1) achieve coordination and integrity between the parts and the entirety, (2) provide abundant information through the use of modern technological facilities, and (3) present the inner cultural heritage through the symbolic subtlety of the new building layouts.[32]

In addition, NCL Director Chen-ku Wang expressed appreciation for Kaser's publications on library buildings, including his draft of a library building program for the National Institute of the Arts, which is required reading for library building seminar courses taught in graduate library schools in Taipei. Kaser's article on academic library buildings published in *College and Research Libraries* (July 1984) was translated into Chinese and the Chinese translation was published in Taipei in the *T'u Shu Kuan Hsueh Yu Tzu Hsun K'o Hsueh (Journal of Library & Information Science)*.[33] It is likely that it too will assist in solidifying Kaser's influence on library building planning in the ROC.

Sino-American Joint Understanding of Books and Libraries

Doubtlessly, David Kaser's most substantive contribution to Sino-American understanding came when he brought his expertise in publishing history to bear upon a serious problem in book trade relations between the two countries. The unauthorized reprinting, usually called "piracy," of English-language books in the ROC had aroused international attention and dispute since the early 1950s.

In 1966 Kaser, then Director of the Vanderbilt University Libraries, stopped in Taipei en route from a tour of duty in Korea with the United States Agency for International Development's contract studying the needs and capabilities of the Korean book industry. During this visit to Taiwan, he encountered modern book piracy for the first time and immediately became impressed with its similarities to the American pirates of British publications in the nineteenth century.[34] Accordingly, he returned to Taiwan twice in 1967 as a Guggenheim Fellow to investigate this phenomenon. In 1969 the University of Pennsylvania Press published Kaser's report entitled *Book Pirating in Taiwan*.[35] This research turned out to be important to both the book trade and government circles in the United States and in Taiwan.

Through access to both American and Chinese private and governmental files, and through interviews with publishers, booksellers, government officials, educators, and others in the United States, Taiwan, Hong Kong, Japan, Macao, Korea, and the Philippines, Kaser documented the entire issue and pinpointed its problems. His report was viewed as a systematic, unbiased, scholarly investigation, and it won instant popularity and exerted its due impact. Two weeks after its appearance in Philadelphia, it was legally reprinted by the Mei Ya Publishing Company of Taipei. This work expedited remedial measures taken by the governments and book industries of both countries.

In a book review article, Chi-wu Wang, a renowned social scientist, commented on Kaser's work. "This book is not only important to the study of contemporary Chinese cultural history but is also a pivotal resource for the study of Sino-American relations."[36] Kaser pointed out that psychological and behavioral problems prevented a resolution of the American and Chinese publishers' dispute. No political, economic, or legal difficulties were involved. This book provided the foundation for understanding and mutual trust.

Sueling Li, the Chinese who has been more diligent than anyone else in seeking a resolution to the problem, commented on the significance of Kaser's work as follows:

> "Dr. Kaser, in 1967, researched and vividly authored *Book Pirating in Taiwan* – a masterpiece of documentary recording never seen before on the English-language book industry in Taiwan, as opposed to the Chinese-language industry there.
>
> He examined the governmental aspects, like the Republic of China on Taiwan not being a member of a world copyright convention; local laws not being able to protect a foreign work against piracy until the work is copyrighted and licensed in Taiwan; local customs

> not being able to curb smugglers from smuggling books out; the 1903 U.S./China Treaty giving… to the Chinese people free rights to translate any English-language work of American authorship, and so forth."

> "Dr. Kaser discreetly used such terms as "unauthorized reprinting" instead of "literary piracy," in view of the local circumstances. He urged the local trade to apply for authorization and to pay royalties. He urged U.S. copyright proprietors to grant rights to requests and locally register copyright for local protection. He knew that this educational process to recognize and respect intellectual property rights would take time. Through Dr. Kaser's enlightening disclosure, governments' new actions, and the incessant practice of authorized publishing… by Mei Ya Publishing Company, there is definite evidence of improvements towards eliminating book pirating in Taiwan, even though a handful of unscrupulous and incorrigible business people still operate in the market. The cure may be faster if Dr. Kaser would update his work again soon."[37]

Tun-sheng Hsiung, President of Chung Hwa Book Company, who was directly involved in the dispute, recently made the following comments:

> "Dr. Kaser's book collected detailed information and provides [an] in-depth description of the actual status of the problem of intellectual property in Taiwan. It presents factual information on how and what [the] U.S. and Chinese government[s] did in helping to stop illegal reprinting. It is not only the most comprehensive and accurate report but also serves as an inspiration to the

> Chinese government as well as Chinese academicians. It enhances the Chinese government's [and] civilians' understanding...[of] the importance of intellectual property. Through Dr. Kaser's work, they have been led to understand that the protection of intellectual property is essential to the nation's development. As a result, laws have been revised for the purpose of building up the protection of intellectual property. Dr. Kaser's work was completed twenty years ago, but its influence and contribution to the solution of illegal reprints have indeed been tremendous and should be recognized."[38]

Basil Dandison, former Senior Vice President of the McGraw-Hill Company, commented in a recent interview on Kaser's work as follows:

> "He gave a well-balanced view to the subject. His comprehensive treatment of the problem not only has given guidance to the United States of America and Taiwanese publishers but also has given recognition to the protection of authors. His thoughtful contribution has alerted all the parties involved in the matter to rethink the long-range needs and work toward the establishment of a reasonable solution. We all are deeply indebted to David Kaser for his work."[39]

This remark was also supported by Leo Albert, President of Prentice-Hall International.[40] After thirty year's dispute, revision of the copyright laws was announced by then ROC President Chiang Ching-kuo on July 10,1985.[41] To the degree that there is law and order in the book reprinting business in Taipei today, Kaser's effort must be credited.

In addition to his important work on book pirating in Taiwan,

David Kaser also wrote and lectured extensively on both sides of the Pacific, seeking better mutual understanding. Important to both the American and Chinese library communities are his presentation "Books and Libraries in the Far East," given to the ALA Armed Forces Librarians meeting on June 24, 1968;[42] his article "Books for International Studies";[43] his report "Library Development in the Republic of China";[44] his talk, "Organizing an Oriental Collection," at an ALA gathering on July 1, 1970 in Detroit;[45] his article "Library Development in Asia," published in the 1972 edition of *Encyclopedia Americana*;[46] and his work on the significance of libraries, published in *Journal of Library & Information Science* in 1980.[47]

Kaser's effort in reporting the status of Chinese libraries to an American audience deserves special recognition. His book entitled *Library Development in Eight Asian Countries* (1969) , in which the ROC was thoroughly presented, was for a long time considered the best survey of the topic available in English.[48]

CONCLUSION

All enterprises in the world are interdependent and librarianship is no exception. Like other professionals preceding him, David Kaser's efforts are deeply rooted in Chinese-American librarianship; their legacy is impressive and their impact is lasting.

Kaser's most recent contribution to Sino-American librarianship is expressed through his concern over the need for the ROC to establish a well-balanced national information policy. This concern indeed reflects his enduring care for China.[49]

This discussion has given a bird's-eye view of one scholar-librarian's contribution to international librarianship through the documentation of his efforts in support of Sino-American librarianship. In these labors, Kaser has always emphasized the importance of "adaptation," rather than "adoption," of library practices when they are introduced from one country to another. This is sage advice for librarian working on the international front.

David Kaser's own comments on his endeavors in Sino-American librarianship well illustrate his professional dedication to international librarianship, which few people can surpass:

> "There were great differences in the library principles and practices of East and West a century ago when Kipling opined that "Never the twain shall meet." Time, however, has proved him to be wrong. Thanks to extensive trans-Pacific bibliothecal contact and mutual exploration over the decades, there are today many remarkable library similarities and a strong sense of professional community binding together the librarians of the United States and the Republic of China on Taiwan. The experience, I believe, provides compelling evidence of the universal brotherhood of man."[50]

NOTES

1. Fu-ts'ung Chiang 蔣復璁, "Chung Kuo T'u Shu Kuan Kuan Yuan Te Chiao Yu Wen T'i 中國圖書館館員的教育問題 [The Education lProblems of Chinese Librarians]," *Chung Kuo T'u Shu Kuan Hsueh Hui Hui Pao 中國圖書館學會會報 [Bulletin of the Library Association of China]* 1 (December 1960): 1.
2. Tsu-yung Seng, "Professional Training of Librarianship in China," in *Libraries in China* (Peiping: Library Association of China, 1935), 60; *Ti I Tz'u Chung Kuo Chiao Yu Nien Chien 第一次中國教育年鑑 [The Education Yearbook, First Issue]* (Shanghai: Kaiming Shu Chu, 1934), 786; *Ti Erh Tz'u Chung Kuo Chiao Yu Nien Chien 第二次中國教育年鑑 [The Education Yearbook, Second Issue]* (Shanghai: Commercial Press, 1948), 1114; George Huang, "Miss Elizabeth Wood: Pioneer of the Library Movement in China," *T'u Shu Kuan Hsueh Yu Tzu Hsun K'o Hsueh 圖書館學與資訊科學 [Journal of Library & Information Science]* 1 (April 1979): 72.
3. Chih-chun Tien Au, "American Impact on Modern Chinese Library Development" (master's thesis, University of Chicago, 1964), 27-40.
4. Verner Warren Clapp, "Visit to China," *Library of Congress Information*

Bulletin (March 1948): 7.

5. Tsuen-hsuin Tsien, "A History of Bibliographic Classification in China," *Library Quarterly* 22 (October 1952): 318, 321-22; Yuan-ch'ing Chiang 蔣元卿, *Chung Kuo T'u Shu Fen Lei Chih Yen Ko 中國圖書分類之沿革 [History of Chinese Book Classification]* (Shanghai: Chung Hua Shu Chu, 1937), 207-8, 214-21; K'aiming Ch'iu, "Classification in China," *T'u Shu Kuan Tsa Chih 圖書館雜誌 [Library Journal]* 52 (April 1927): 409-14.
6. Kuang-tsing Wu, "Ten Years of Classification and Cataloging in China," in *Libraries in China* (Peiping: Library Association of China, 1935), 47-48.
7. Hsiu Cha, "Chung Wen Shu Chi Pien Mu Wen T'i 中文書籍編目問題," *Hsin Chiao Yu 新教育 [New Education]* 9 (September 1924): 191-207.
8. Tsung-yung Seng, "Can the American Library System Be Adopted to China?" *T'u Shu Kuan Tsa Chih 圖書館雜誌 [Library Journal]* 41 (June 1916): 388.
9. Arthur Bostwick, "Report of Arthur E. Bostwick's Mission to China as ALA Delegate," *American Library Association Bulletin* 11(October 1926): 41.
10. Chih-chun Tien Au, "American Impact on Modern Chinese Library Development" 27-40.
11. Ibid., 49-52.
12. *Ti Erh Tz'u Chung Kuo Chiao Yu Nien Chien 第二次中國教育年鑑 [The Education Yearbook, Second Issue]* (Shanghai: Commercial Press, 1948), 1115; Tung-li Yuan, "Library Situation in China," *T'u Shu Kuan Tsa Chih 圖書館雜誌 [Library Journal]* 69 (March 1944): 235-38.
13. J. P. Danton, "Books for China," *T'u Shu Kuan Tsa Chih 圖書館雜誌 [Library Journal]* 63 (October 1938): 714; Tung-li Yuan, "Library Situation in China," *T'u Shu Kuan Tsa Chih 圖書館雜誌 [Library Journal]* 69 (March 1944): 237.
14. David Kaser, notes to author, 6 December 1986.
15. Ibid.
16. Fu-ts'ung Chiang, interview with author, Taipei, Taiwan, 13 August 1987.
17. Robert Pin-chuan Chen, *Library Resources for American Studies in Taiwan: An Evaluation* (Taipei: The American Studies Association of the Republic of China, 1979); Mei-hua Yang, "Library Educational Personnel Planning in ROC on Taiwan" (Ph. D. diss., Indiana University, 1986); Margaret C. Fung, *The Evolving Social Mission of the National Central Library 1928-1966* (Ann Arbor, Mich.: University Microfilms, 1983).
18. Robert Pin-chuan Chen to Herbert S. White, letter, 17 June 1985; Margaret C. Fung to Herbert S. White, letter, 5 June 1985, in support of Dr. Kaser's

nomination for the title of Distinguished Professor.

19. Barbara Dewey, letter to author, 24 July 1987.
20. David Kaser, notes to author, 6 December 1986.
21. David Kaser, "Problems in International Librarianship," *National Taiwan University Library Science Circular* 18 (November 1969): 1-7; reprinted in Library Progress 3 (1970): 77-82.
22. David Kaser, "Humanism, the Library and the Quality of Life," *T'u Shu Kuan Hsueh Yu Tzu Hsun K'o Hsueh 圖書館學與資訊科學 [Journal of Library & Information Science]* 1 (October 1975): 25-35.
23. *Library Workshop Proceedings*, 28-30 December 1979 (Taipei: National Taiwan Normal University, 1980).
24. David Kaser, "Why Libraries Indeed?" *Chung Kuo T'u Shu Kuan Hsueh Hui Hui Pao 中國圖書館學會會報 [Bulletin of the Library Association of China]* 31 (December 1979): 110-12; David Kaser, "Why Libraries Indeed?" *National Central Library Newsletter* 11 (January 1980): 86-91.
25. David Kaser, "Preparing for the 21st Century Library," *Chung Kuo T'u Shu Kuan Hsueh Hui Hui Wu T'ung Hsun 中國圖書館學會會務通訊 [Library Association of China Newsletter]* 30 (July 1982): 9-12.
26. David Kaser, "Free Knowledge or Fettered Minds," *T'u Shu Kuan Hsueh Yu Tzu Hsun K'o Hsueh 圖書館學與資訊科學 [Journal of Library & Information Science]* 9 (April 1983): 19-26.
27. "Dr. Kaser Lectures before Librarians," *China Post*, 25 March 1982; Institute of Chinese Architects Announcement, November 1979.
28. Harris B.H. Seng, interview with author, Taipei, Taiwan, 17 August 1987.
29. National Taiwan Normal University Library Files, 26 November 1979.
30. Yao-yu Bao, interview with author, Taipei Taiwan, 13 August 1987.
31. C.Y. Lee, interview with author, Taipei, Taiwan, 18 August 1987.
32. Chen-ku Wang, interview with author, Taipei, Taiwan, 12 August 1987; Pau-sen Chen, interview with author, Taipei, Taiwan, 18 August 1987.
33. Chen-ku Wang, interview with author, Taipei, Taiwan, 12 August 1987; David Kaser, "Erh Shi Wu Nien Lai Mei Kuo Hsueh Shu T'u Shu Kuan Kuan She Chih Kwei Hua 二十五年來美國學術圖書館館舍之規劃 [Twenty Five Years of American Academic Library Building Planning]," originally published in *College & Research Libraries* 45 (July 1984): 268-281; translated into Chinese by Margaret C. Fung 張鼎鍾, published in *T'u Shu Kuan Hsueh Yu Tzu Hsun K'o Hsueh 圖書館學與資訊科學 [Journal of Library & Information Science]* 12 (October 1986): 240-51.
34. David Kaser, *Messrs. Carey and Lea of Philadelphia: A Study in the History*

of the Book Trade (Philadelphia: University of Pennsylvania Press, 1957).
35. David Kaser, *Book Pirating in Taiwan* (Philadelphia: University of Pennsylvania Press, 1969).
36. Chi-wu Wang 王紀五, "Fan Ying Yang Shu Te Lai Lung Chu Mo 翻印洋書的來龍去脈 [The Accounts of Foreign Book Reprints]," *Tsung Ho Yueh K'an 綜合月刊* (October 1969): 85.
37. Sueling Li, letter to author, 1 August 1987.
38. Tun-shen Hsiung's comments made at the request of Sueling Li on July 24, 1987, during Hsiung's visit to Chicago, Illinois.
39. Basil Dandison, letter to author, 11 July 1987.
40. Leo Alpert, telephone interview with author, 9 July 1987.
41. *Tsung T'ung Fu Kung Pao 總統府公報 [Presidential Office Gazette]* 4475 (10 July 1985): 1-6.
42. David Kaser, "Books and Libraries in the Far East," *Wilson Library Bulletin* 43 (June 1969): 974-79.
43. David Kaser, "Books for International Studies," *Cornell University International Studies Bulletin* 2 (May 1971): 1-2; (Alumni Issue, 1971):2-3.
44. David Kaser, "Library Development in the Republic of China," *National Taiwan University Library Science Circular* 14 (May 1969):1-14.
45. David Kaser, "Organizing an Oriental Collection," *Foreign Acquisitions Newsletter* 33 (Spring 1971):2-5.
46. *Encyclopedia Americana*, international ed., s.v. "Library Development in Asia," by David Kaser.
47. David Kaser, "Significance of Libraries: Four Cases," *T'u Shu Kuan Hsueh Yu Tzu Hsun K'o Hsueh 圖書館學與資訊科學 [Journal of Library & Information Science]* 6 (October 1980): 131-39.
48. David Kaser, C. Walter Stone, and Cecil K. Byrd, *Library Development in Eight Asian Countries* (Metuchen, N.J.: Scarecrow Press, 1969), 72-88.
49. Hui-hsing Lu 盧蕙馨, "Yu Ying T'i, Yu Juan T'i, Wo Men Hai Hsu Hsiang I Hsiang, Wei She Mo Yao Wei T'u Shu Kuan Fei Hsin Fei Li 有硬體，有軟體，我們還需想一想，為什麼要為圖書館費心費力 [When We Have Hardware and Software, We Have to Think What Efforts We Have to Contribute to Librarianship]," *Min Sheng Pao 民生報 [Min Sheng Daily News]*, 3 September 1983, 9.
50. David Kaser, note to author, 31 July 1987.

Reprinted with permission from *The Academic Librarianship: Past, Present, and Futures: A Festschrift in Honor of David Kaser*. Colorado: Libraries Unlimited, 1989. (pp. 115-128).

Part II

LIBRARY AUTOMATION
INFORMATION TECHNOLOGY

7

Library Automation in the Republic of China

ABSTRACT

This paper reports the history, development, and present status of library automation in Taiwan, R.O.C. Examples of computer applications for libraries and the essentials required for the processing of Chinese library materials are given.

INTRODUCTION

Computer applications for libraries and information centers in the Republic of China were initiated in the early 1970s, first in the area of processing Roman alphabet materials and later in the processing of Chinese vernacular materials. (Figure 1)

Efforts have been directed to the compilation of union lists, lists of new accessions, and the production of catalog cards. Serials were the first materials to be processed with a computer. The first library automation attempt in the ROC was made in 1973, when the third edition of the *Union List of Scientific Serials in the Libraries of the Republic of China* (in Western languages) was computer-processed. It was eventually published in 1975.[1]

THE PROCESSING OF CHINESE VERNACULAR MATERIALS

Chinese I / O

The 15x18, 16x18, 24x20, 24x24, 32x32, and 64x64 dot matrix representations of Chinese characters, the input devices of the number-code method, phonetic code system, and component code mode (also called radical method), in addition to the various output devices (such as the screen display of 42 Chinese characters (two lines), 192 characters, 210 characters, 300 characters, and 384 characters (scroll)) and various line printers (such as dot matrix plotter mode, electrostatic, and laser printers) have all made the processing of Chinese vernacular materials possible.[2]

Early Experiments

The idea of using Chinese computer devices to process library materials has been advocated since 1974. The input device available then was the large keyboard type developed jointly by Professor Te-yao Chiang and Wang Laboratories. The component type was used.[3] A 64-key keyboard was constructed to include all the radicals and bases.

The first integrated system of cataloging, acquisition, and circulation was tested on the Wang 2200 mini computer with soft-ware developed by Mr. Ching-chin Su in Taipei in 1975. The experiment was quite successful.[4]

Using Prof. Chiang's keyboard with the Wang computer, the National Taiwan University demonstrated the storage and retrieval technique for Chinese library reference materials during Chinese National Library Week in December 1975.[5] This input method calls for the operator to be proficient in Chinese. Since the library profession emphasizes the interflow of information at an international level, we are constantly searching for devices which should be convenient for the Chinese as well as non-Chinese to comprehend and operate with ease. In other words, we are concerned over the needs of East Asian collections all over the world where computer operators are not necessarily Chinese and most likely do not know the language. What we adopt, we hope, will be accessible to the entire library community, regardless of country. When the Three Corner Coding Method was developed by Professor K.T. Huang[6], we tried this method for several projects.

The Three Corner Coding Method is a coding, indexing, and retrieving system which logically assigns an identification number to the corresponding Chinese character or Kanji. The primary objective is to provide a more consistent means of digitalization in order to significantly reduce the problems associated with the input of Chinese and Japanese data. Basically, Chinese ideographs are analyzed into 309 fundamental symbols (210 minor and 99 major) which are arranged on a 10x10 matrix with a two-digit code number. The chart on figure 2 known as the fundamental chart illustrates the tabulation of symbols which are represented at the lower right corner. Only three parts of any one character (upper left, upper right, and lower left parts) are used in the convertion from ideograph to symbols.

Present Projects

Chinese Educational Resources Information System (CERIS) developed by the National Taiwan Normal University in collaboration with the MiTAC. Inc. (Agent for Perkin Elmer) in 1978 is a large educational periodical database consisting of 1,115 periodicals which has been designed by using a database management system called TOTAL. Multi-key retrieval method is used. Both Chinese vernacular and English alphabets can be presented on the Chinese CRT terminals.[7] Hard copies are produced by the plotter mode dot matrix type of line printer at a speed of 100 LPM. (Figure 3) It is implemented on Perkin Elmer 3220 computer which is based on microprocessor with functions of inserting, verifying and editing the Chinese characters, skipping and protecting the field.

The *National Union List of Chinese Periodicals* – A joint venture with Wang Laboratories, National Central Library has completed the compilation of the list in December, 1979.

This first computer-processed Chinese union list covers the entire Chinese serial holdings of 136 private and public libraries, with a total of 6,543 journal titles.[8] (Figure 4)

The following information – entry number, journal title, frequency, publishing place, publishing year, publisher, distributor, holdings and locations, ISSN and classification number – can be retrieved by using single key or multikeys. The complete union list is formatted by computer in the sequence of number of strokes with additional subject index and classification number index.

The package is written in COBOL Language with functions of updating, skipping, editing, modifying, and deleting. 32 special-function keys can be used for the most commonly-used information such as the frequency of a journal.

Two hundred and ten Chinese characters are available on each screen display. Both Chinese and English characters or mixed characters can be displayed on the CRT at the same time with hard copy printed by the dot matrix line printer at a speed of 100 LMP. The hardware used is Wang VS 2200 which is compatible with IBM 370/135.

The Management Information System in Agriculture Science and Technology (MISAST) is a complete information system in the field of agriculture set up by the Agriculture Science Information Center with TOTAL Database Management System. The system, implemented on the Perkin Elmer 3220 computer, is designed to include six databases:[9]

FASTEP: Files on Agricultural Science and Technology Personnel.

FASTER: Files on Agricultural Science and Technology Research Reports.

FASTEL and FASTCL: Files on Agricultural Science and

Technology Literature.

FASTEA: Databases of Agricultural Terms in English-Japanese-Chinese Language.

FASTCA: Library Catalogs of English and Chinese Materials.

FASTEJ : Files on Agricultural Science and Technology Project.

The Freedom Council Information Abstracts (FCIA) – As a project sponsored by the Freedom Council in its information center, this non-profit private organization provides abstracts of articles and reports from various international publications (*New York Times, Japanese Times, Department of State Bulletin, etc.*) which analyze or discuss the ROC. Along with identifying the title, publisher, author's names, date of publication, and etc., each abstract contains a Chinese and an English synopsis. The access points are title, author's name, entry number (computer number), abstractors' names, classification number, publisher, and series. It is again input and retrieved by using the Three Corner Coding Method on Wang 2200 MVP which is an interactive system. Both on-line retrieving and off-line hard copy are available. (Figure 5)

THE PROCESSING OF LIBRARY MATERIALS IN ROMAN ALPHABETS

The Periodicals Information Service System – The Science and Technology Information Center of the National Science Council completed the *Union List of Scientific Serials* by using IBM 370/135, CICS (Customers' Information Control System), DOS/VS and DL/1. The first computer printout listed 7,578 journals. It is updated annually, and the 7th ed. (1979) covers 11,416 periodicals.[10] The functions include updating, retrieving, printing a union list, printing periodical holding lists of individual libraries, and producing analytic reports or statistics.

The Management Information System (MIS) – The Information Center is currently working on management information system of science and technology with the idea of building up a national automated scientific and technical network which has been planned to include six databases.[11] The Scientists and Technological Personnel and Research Reports Databases are to be completed soon.

The Chung Shan Library Information System (CLIS), implemented on IBM 370/138,[12] is a package written in COBOL covering information retrieval, serials control, acquisition, circulation, and cataloging systems. This package is especially tailored to the needs of Chung Shan Institute of Science and Technology. It started to produce catalog cards with computers as early as 1974 and has also subscribed to LC MARC tapes for many years.

The Browsing MARK III Database Generation System – It has been completed in June, 1979 by the Academia Sinica's Institute of Information Science as a research project. The updating function was somewhat slighted and will revised to be useful.

The Telebrowsing system contains a large number of document descriptions. These descriptions are separated into categories. Each category is then divided into subcategories. It begins searching by comparing the query to each of the major categories. Each category is assigned a numerical rating. The higher the rating, the more likely the category is to contain information related to the reader's interest. Telebrowsing will select the category having the highest rating for further examination.

Tamkang University has also developed sets of serial control and acquisition packages to be implemented on IBM 370/148. They have also been designed exclusively to meet their own needs and have proven effective and efficient for that particular library. It is one of the pioneers in the processing of Roman script library materials among the libraries in the ROC.

The Chinese systems are developed and tried out on the hardwares of Wang Laboratories and Perkin Elmer. The Three Corner Coding System has been proven efficient when it is used as the input device for library data entry. Researches have been continued in developing better hardwares, more handy softwares, and more efficient and effective input methods. The following are examples:

In 1977, Mr. Ta-jen Liu's *Chinese-English Dictionary* introduced the Left-Top Radical System of 251 radicals. It is a modified version of the Kang Hsi Radical System (214 radicals). Employing a binary code of 16x16 to 64/64 dot matrix, it feeds the characters into the computer via keyboards or tape, based on a pattern-recognition technique: the Chinese characters are analyzed into shapes, and codes are derived from the shapes of the characters. It is actually a combination of the component and number code methods. The same author also introduced Liu's Tonal Build-In System, a revised and much improved version of the Pinyin system with indication of four tones to present accurate pronunciations.[13]

Chinese Data Processing System (CDPS-2) – This is the first Chinese/English data processing terminal which has been domestically designed and manufactured by the Electronics Research and Service Organization of the Industrial Technology Research Institute. It can serve as an intelligent terminal to any mini or mainframe computer via RS232 ASCII interface. It can also work as a stand-alone Chinese file management system when optional disk drives are added. There are plans to connect this standard terminal to other popular main frame or mini computers and to develop a Chinese data-processing software package. At the present time, it takes 8 seconds to display a 300 Chinese character screen page. The terminal has been connected to HP 3000 and PDP 11/34 and has proven to be successful in using existing softwares.[14]

Another feature of this terminal is the character generator which consists of 150K bytes solid state memory to store nine thousand Chinese characters. The character generator can also be used with other keyboard input systems through simple interface modification.

The above-mentioned endeavors in processing Chinese data have assured us that the difficulties of data processing caused by the complexity of the Chinese language have been solved and the vernacular character can be successfully processed with computers. However, in the past few years, library automation in Taiwan has always been developed by individual libraries to meet their particular needs. No overall plan was proposed until the recent organization of the Library Automation Working Group which consists of computer scientists, information scientists, and librarians. This Working Group is to study, explore, plan, and implement the national computerized information system.[15]

BASIC WORK IN PREPARATION FOR LIBRARY AUTOMATION

1. Revision of Chinese cataloging rules to be consistent with ISBD and AACR 2 principles.
2. Compilation of Chinese subject headings to facilitate access point and effective use of materials.
3. Chinese Character Code for Information Interchange (CCCII): With the aim of facilitating the interchange of information among data processing systems and message transmission systems, following the ISO Escape Sequence, we have developed a set of interchange code for Chinese characters. The first level consists of the 4,808 most frequently-used characters which were announced by the Ministry of Education in 1979 as a result of a study done on the Chinese language at National Taiwan Normal University (NTNU).[16] Many more levels will follow until a total number of 50,000 Chinese characters is include. A working group of 15 people, including linguists, computer scientists, is working on it. This is an effort not only to standardize coding for Chinese characters, but also to develop a systematic method of learning the Chinese language. (Figure 6)
4. Chinese MARC Format: Following in principle the Format for Bibliographic Information Interchange on Magnetic

Tape, the record labels stipulated by ISO 2709-1973, and the Universal MARC format (UNIMARC), with additions made to meet our unique requirements, we are working on the Chinese MARC Format which should be completed in the near future. Thesauri used by different fields are to be built up gradually to facilitate the use of databases.

These basic preparatory tasks are to be in full operation in May 1980 for the overall, unified, and centralized implementation of library automation in Taiwan, R.O.C.

NOTES

1. Hsing Cheng Yuan Kuo Chia K'o Hsueh Wei Yuan Hui K'o Hsueh Chi Shu Tzu Liao Chung Hsin Pien 行政院國家科學委員會科學技術資料中心 編 [Science and Technology Information Center, National Science Council, Executive Yuan, ed.], *Kuo Hsueh Ch'i K'an Lien He Mu Lu 科學期刊聯合目錄 [Union List of Scientific Serials in Libraries of the Republic of China]* (Nankang, Taipei: Science and Technology Information Center, National Science Council, 1975), 2-3.
2. Ching-chun Hsieh, *Chinese Data Processing in Taiwan, ROC* (Taipei, 11 November 1979), 5-6.
3. Te-yao Kiang, *A Chinese Billing System Implemented on WANG 2200B Mini Computer System*, conducted by Graduate Institute of Electrical Engineering (Taipei: National Taiwan University, 1975), 7.
4. Margaret C. Fung 張鼎鍾, *T'u Shu Kuan Hsueh Yu Tzu Hsun K'o Hsueh Chih T'an T'ao 圖書館學與資訊科學之探討 [On library and Information Science]* (Taipei: Feng Ch'en Publishing, 1979), 62.
5. Ju-hsiang, Jung-Ch'in Chin 蔡如湘，金蓉琴, "T'u Shu Kuan Tzu Tung Hua Chan Lan Shih K'uang 圖書館自動化展覽實況," *T'u Shu Kuan Hsueh K'an (T'ai Ta)) 圖書館學刊（台大）[National Taiwan University Journal of Library Science]* 3 (June 1976): 338-41.
6. Jack Kai-tung Huang, Yuan-wei Chang, and Li-ren Hu, *The Digitalized Chinese Dictionary: "Three Corner Coding Method"* (Taipei: Ming Chuan College, 1978).
7. Kuo Li Taiwan Shih Fan Ta Hsueh T'u Shu Kuan, Shen T'ung Tien Nao Kung Ssu Pien 國立台灣師範大學圖書館，神通電腦公司 編

[National Taiwan Normal University Library and MiTAC. Inc., ed.], *T'u Shu Kuan Ch'i K'an Chung Wen Hsien Shang Ch'a Hsun Hsi T'ung 圖書館期刊中文線上查詢系統 [On-Line Chinese Searching System of Library Periodicals]* (Taipei, 1977). (Brochure).

8. Kuo Li Chung Yang T'u Shu Kuan, Wang An Tien Nao Kung Ssu Pien 國立中央圖書館，王安電腦公司編 [National Central Library and Wang Labortories, ed.], *Chung Hua Min Kuo Chung Wen Ch'i K'an Lien Ho Mu Lu Tien Nao Tso Yeh 中華民國中文期刊聯合目錄電腦作業 [The Computer Processing of the ROC Chinese Periodicals Union Catalog]* (Taipei, 1977). (Brochure).
9. Nung Yeh K'o Hsueh Tzu Liao Fu Wu Chung Hsin Pien 農業科學資料服務中心 編 [Agriculture Science Information Service Center, ed.], *Nung Yeh K'o Chi Jen Tsai Tzu Liao Tang Hsi Tung Kung Nung 農業科技人才資料檔系統功能 [The Function of Files of the Agricultural Scientists and Technological Personnel]* (Taipei: Agriculture Science Information Service Center, 1977). (Brochure).
10. Hsing Cheng Yuan Kuo Chia K'o Hsueh Wei Yuan Hui K'o Hsueh Chi Shu Tzu Liao Chung Hsin Pien 行政院國家科學委員會科學技術資料中心 編 [Science and Technology Information Center, National Science Council, Executive Yuan, ed.], *K'o Hsueh Ch'i K'an Lien He Mu Lu 科學期刊聯合目錄 [Union List of Scientific Serials in Libraries of the Republic of China]* (Nankang, Taipei: Science and Technology Information Center, National Science Council, 1979), 11.
11. Hsing Cheng Yuan Kuo Chia K'o Hsueh Wei Yuan Hui K'o Hsueh Chi Shu Tzu Liao Chung Hsin Pien 行政院國家科學委員會科學技術資料中心 編 [Science and Technology Information Center, National Science Council, Executive Yuan, ed.], *Ch'uan Kuo Hsing K'o Chi Kuan Li Tzu Hsun Hsi T'ung Tso Yeh Chi Hua 全國性科技管理資訊系統作業計畫 [National Technology Management Information System Plan]* (Taipei: Science and Technology Information Center, 1978). (Brochure).
12. Lin-chin Huang, *The Requirements of Serials Control System* (Lungtan, Taoyuan: Chung Shan Institute of Sciene and Technology, 1978). (Brochure)
13. Ta-jen Liu, *Linguistic Analysis of the Chinese Radical and Pinyin Problem* (Taipei, 1980), 7, 30.
14. Kung Yeh Chi Shu Yen Chiu Yuan Pien 工業技術研究院 編 [Industrial Technology Research Institute, ed.], *Chung Wen Erh Hao Tzu Liao Chu Li Hsi Tung 中文二號資料處理系統 [Chniese Data Processing System No. 2]* (Hsinchu: Industrial Technology Research Institute, 1979). (Brochure).

15. Kuo Li Chung Yang T'u Shu Kuan Pien 國立中央圖書館 編 [National Central Library, ed.], *Ch'uan Kuo Tzu Hsun Fu Wu Hsi Tung Chi Hua 全國資訊服務系統計畫 [The Plan of National Information Service System]* (Taipei: National Central Library, 1980), 1-7.
16. Kuo Li Taiwan Shih Fan Ta Hsueh Kuo Wen Yen Chiu So Pien 國立台灣師範大學國文研究所 編 [National Taiwan Normal University. Graduate Institute of Chinese Literature, ed.], *Ch'ang Yung Tzu Kuo Tzu Piao Chun Tzu T'i Piao 常用字國字標準字體表 [The Most-Used Chinese Standard Characters Chart]*, revised ed. (Taipei: Ministry of Education, 1979).

Reprinted with permission from *圖書館學與資訊科學 [Journal of Library & Information Science]* 6, no. 1 (April 1980): 1-6.

Figure 1 DEVELOPMENT OF LIBRARY AUTOMATION IN ROC

Organization	System name	Nature	Hardware	Year
		Chinese Systems		
Agriculture Science Information Center	MISAST	Personnel Data Base	Perkin Elmer 3220	Fall 1979
Freedom Council Information Center	FCIA	ROC Information Data Base	Wang 220 MVP	Spring 1980
National Central Library	National Union List of Serials	Bibliographic Data Base	Wang VS2200	Fall 1979
National Taiwan Normal University	CERIS	Educational Information Data Base	Perkin Elmer 3220	1978
National Taiwan Normal University	ACCI (prototype)	Bibliographic Data Base (acquisition, cataloging and circulation)	Wang 2200 MVP	Summer 1975
National Taiwan University	Demonstration	Storage & Retrieving	Wang MVP	Dec. 1975
		English Systems		
Chung-Shan Institute of Science	CLIS	Serial Control	IBM 370/138	1979
		Cataloging Cards		1975
		New Accession List		1975
Information Science Research Institute	Browsing MARK III Data Base Generation System	Data Base	PDP 11/34	1979
Scientific and Technology Information Center of National Science Council	PISS	Bibliographic Data Base	IBM 370/135	1973
	MIS	Data Base	IBM 370/135 IBM 3031	1980
		Acquisition Control	IBM 370/135	1979
Tamkang College of Arts and Sciences		Serial Control and Acquisition	IBM 370/148	1977

Figure 2 FUNDAMENTAL SYMBOL CHART
OF THREE CORNER CODING METHOD

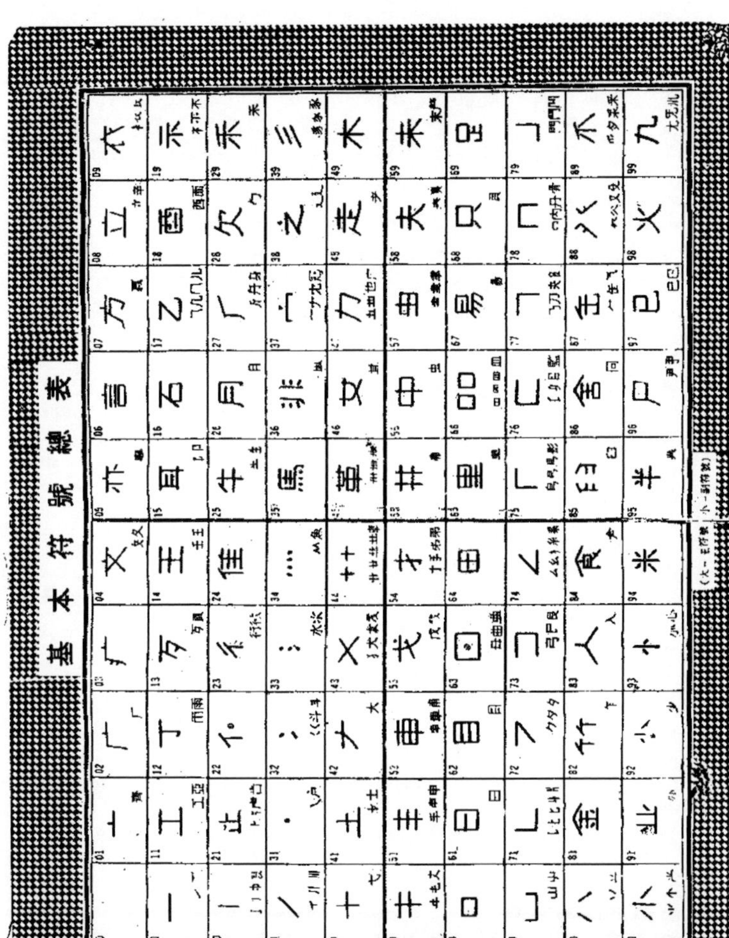

Figure 3 SAMPLE OF CERIS PRINTOUT

0930
我國西書採購電腦化作業之探討
黃鴻珠 圖書館學與資訊科學 5卷1期 第104頁至110頁 68年10月 有圖
▲簡述我國私立大學圖書館的西書採購程序，詳細探討採購作業電腦化的可能性及其問題。

0931
社會學與圖書
彭歌 中央日報 第十一版 68年1月3日
▲本文首先闡述社會學之定義和特性，然後說明社會學與圖書館和各種出版品關係密切，社會學圖書之出版，在世界各國都在不斷增加中。最後列出二十種由西方社會學者和教授多人所評鑑選出之社會學的重要期刊。

0932
兒童及青年圖書館的重要性
蔣復璁 中央日報 第十一版 68年12月19日
▲本文述及：一．設置兒童及青少年圖書館的重要性，二．讀物之缺乏及建議補救之辦法，三．認為教育部規定各級學校兼辦社區社會教育的法令不當。

0933
兒童圖書館的重要性
李波特 中央日報 第十一版 68年9月19日
▲簡介國內幾所比較著名的兒童圖書館概況以及這些圖書館努力的目標和有待改進的問題等。

0934
兒童圖書館的發展與文化建設
張鼎鍾 社教系刊 7期 第87頁至98頁 68年6月
▲文化建設是一切建設的源頭，而文化建設之一的公共圖書館若缺乏兒童圖書服務，則不能成其為完整的公共圖書館，兩者的關係異常的密切。由此為出發點，本文依次介紹兒童圖書館的定義，類型，功能，建立要素以及中美兒童圖書館發展史，並說明發展兒童圖書館服務應做的幾件工作，期能使文化建設由「點」而「線」而「面」，真正發揮其深遠的影響。

0935
兒童圖書館的意義
蔣復璁 中央日報 第十版 68年4月16日
▲闡述兒童圖書館之意義，經營方式和源起。

Figure 4-1 SAMPLE OF NATIONAL UNION LIST OF CHINESE PERIODICALS

一劃一二劃一一二十力

總藏 1-22: (49-66)
中圖 1:4-6, 2:1-2, 4-6, 3:1, 3-4, 4-22: (49-66)
中圖分館 14:9-12, 15:1-12, 16:2-12, 17:1-12, 18:1-8, 19-22: (58-66)
中研經濟 3-22: (51-66)
政大 12:2, 4, 6-12, 13:1, 3, 5-7, 9, 11-12, 18-22: (56-66)
淡水工商 11-12:, 15:8, 16:3-12, 17-22: (55-66)
國大會 8-13: (53-57)
逢甲 10-12:, 21:9-12, 22:1-7 (54-66)
實踐家專 7:2-12, 8-22: (52-66)
台大 8-22: (53-66)
台銀 1-22: (49-66)
商檢局 17-20: (61-64)

二劃

0007 二十世紀 不定期 上海 二十世紀雜誌社
(050)
總藏 1:8 (21)
中圖分館 1:8 (21)

0008 十字論壇週刊 半月刊 台北市 十字論壇社
(050)
總藏 5-6, 8-9: (49-53)
省中 5-6: (49-50)
國大會 8-9: (52-53)

0009 力生 月刊 6 4年 4月 台北縣 力生電子股份有限公司管理部編輯
(480)
總藏 :1-4 (64)
中圖 :1-4 (64)

0010 力行 半月刊 4 5年 新竹市 經濟部
(550)
總藏 1-8: (45-50)
中油研訓 1-5: (45-48)
中委會 1-3: (45-46)
金屬中心 1-8: (45-50)

0011 力餘 月刊 4 1年 7月 台北市 中國力餘學社
(050)
總藏 1:, 2:1-7, 3:1, 8:1, 9:1 (41-60), SP(60)11, (62)1, (64)1

Figure 4-2 SAMPLE OF NATIONAL UNION LISE
CHINESE PERIODICALS

	Title	No.
	圖書集刊	5862
	圖書與圖書館	5863
	圖書雜誌	5871
	學文	6142
	聯合國出版品目錄	6231
	聯經書訊	6245
	雜誌資料索引	6276
	讀書人	6458
	讀書月刊	6459
	讀書通訊	6461
	讀書與出版	6462
	讀書雜誌	6464
(020)	圖書館學	
	上海市立圖書館館刊	0278
	山東省圖書館季刊	0305
	文華圖書館專科學校季刊	0382
	中央大學國學圖書館年刊	0554
	中央軍校圖書館月報	0559
	中法漢學研究所圖書館館刊	0635
	中國文化學院圖書博物館館刊	0679
	中國圖書館學會出版委員會	0859
	中國圖書館學會會務通訊	0860
	中國圖書館學會會報	0861
	中華圖書館協會會報	1116
	北平北海圖書館月刊	1563
	北京圖書館月刊	1571
	冊府	1681
	台灣省立台北圖書館館刊	2011
	江蘇省立國學圖書館年刊	2384
	江蘇省立蘇州圖書館館刊	2385
	全國學術工作諮詢處月刊	2682
	孟氏圖書館館刊	3175
	省立台北圖書館館刊	3589
	浙江省立圖書館館刊	3775
	浙江圖書館報	3780
	拼書集	4085
	國立中央圖書館通訊	4479
	國立中央圖書館館刊	4482
	國立北平圖書館月刊	4487

	Title	No.
	國立北平圖書館館刊	4488
	國立北平圖書館館集	4489
	厦門圖書館聲	5264
	廣州大學圖書館季刊	5712
	廣東國民大學圖書館館刊	5763
	圖風	5852
	圖書季刊	5858
	圖書館季刊	5864
	圖書館週刊	5865
	圖書館學刊	5866
	圖書館學刊	5867
	圖書館學季刊	5868
	圖書館學報	5869
	燕京大學圖書館報	6077
	遼寧省立圖書館館刊	6109
	學風	6161
(050)	普通期刊	
	一般	0003
	一週大事分析	0004
	一週大事報導	0005
	二十世紀	0007
	十字論壇週刊	0008
	力餘	0011
	九陽雜誌	0013
	人人畫刊	0015
	人人週刊	0016
	人人週報	0017
	人文	0020
	人文月刊	0021
	人文世界	0022
	人民世紀	0029
	人生	0031
	人間世	0042
	人間世	0043
	人道	0044
	人鏡畫報	0047
	三六九小報	0051
	工作競賽月報	0075
	大千快訊	016_
	大中華	0182

Figure 5 SAMPLE OF FCIA COMPUTER PRINTOUT

FC INFORMATION ABSTRACTS RECORDS

```
RECORD  TYPE    : 03
TITLE           : EAST ASIA : TAIWAN RELATIONS ACT
CLASSFICATION   : 230.3
PUBLICATION     : DEPT. OF STATE BULLETIN, U.S.A.
PUBLISHER       :
AUTHOR          : PRESIDENT'S STMT.
ABSTRACTOR      : Y.K. YEH
COMPUTER CODE   : 200-79-06-00-0 -C
DATE (YY/MM/DD) : 68/06/00
```

台灣關係的立法將使美國人民與台灣人民．在沒有官方代表及外交關係的基礎上．能夠維持商業．文化及其它關係．台灣關係法授權給在台協會——一個在哥倫比亞特區的法律下組成的非官方的法人組織．來執行這些關係．同樣的．台灣人民將經由非官方的組織—北美事務協調委員會．來執行這些關係．

THE LEGISLATION OF THE TAIWAN RELATIONS ACT WILL ENABLE THE AMERICAN PEOPLE AND THE PEOPLE ON TAIWAN TO MAINTAIN COMMERICAL, CULTURAL, AND OTHER RELATIONS WITHOUT OFFICIAL GOUERNMENT REPRESENTATION AND WITHOUT DIPLOMATIC RELATIONS. IT AUTHORIZES THE AMERICAN INSTITUTE IN TAIWAN, A NONGOUERNMENTAL ENTITY INCORPORATED UNDER THE LAWS OF THE DISTRICT OF COLUMBIA, TO CONDUCT THESE RELATIONS. SIMILARLY, THE PEOPLE ON TAIWAN WILL CONDUCT RELATIONS THROUGH A NONGOUERNMENTAL ORGANIZATION - THE COORDINATION COUNCIL FOR NORTH AMERICAN AFFAIRS.

COMPILED BY FREEDOM COUNCIL	DATA PROCESSED BY R.P.T.I
自由基金會製作	榮電公司電腦處理

Figure 6 SAMPLE OF CCCII

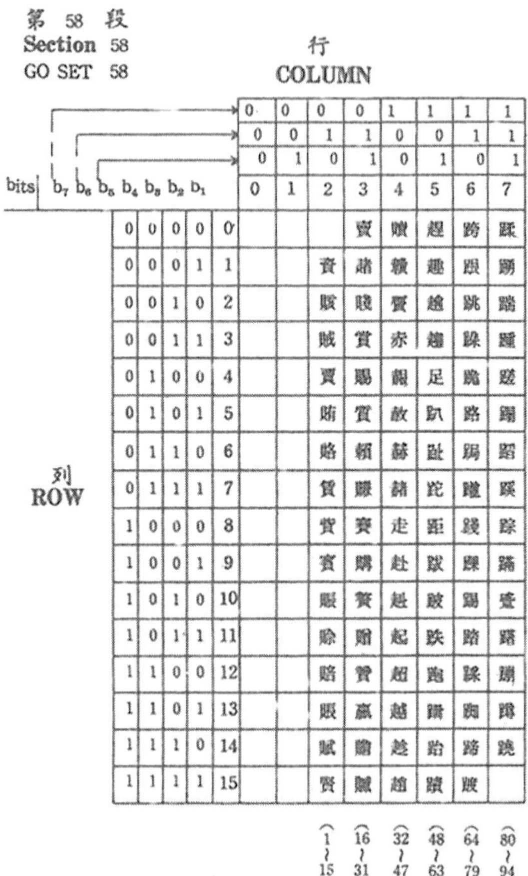

第 58 段
Section 58
GO SET 58

行
COLUMN

列
ROW

bits b7 b6 b5					0 0 0	0 0 1	0 1 0	0 1 1	1 0 0	1 0 1	1 1 0	1 1 1
b4	b3	b2	b1		0	1	2	3	4	5	6	7
0	0	0	0	0				賨	贖	趕	跨	踩
0	0	0	1	1			資	賭	贛	趣	跟	踴
0	0	1	0	2			賅	賤	贗	趨	跳	蹈
0	0	1	1	3			賊	賞	赤	趯	跺	躍
0	1	0	0	4			賈	賜	赧	足	跪	蹉
0	1	0	1	5			賄	質	赦	趴	路	蹋
0	1	1	0	6			賂	賴	赫	趾	跼	蹓
0	1	1	1	7			貿	賺	赭	跎	踵	蹊
1	0	0	0	8			賁	賽	走	距	踐	蹤
1	0	0	1	9			賓	購	赴	跋	踝	蹣
1	0	1	0	10			賑	贅	赳	跛	踢	蹩
1	0	1	1	11			賒	贈	起	跌	踏	蹠
1	1	0	0	12			賠	贊	超	跑	踩	蹦
1	1	0	1	13			賬	贏	越	跚	踘	蹲
1	1	1	0	14			賦	贍	趁	跆	踣	蹺
1	1	1	1	15			賢	贓	趙	跡	踱	
							(1～15)	(16～31)	(32～47)	(48～63)	(64～79)	(80～94)

8

Development in the Computerization of Non-Roman Scripts

ABSTRACT

This presentation reports the development of non-Roman scripts computerization. Current status of Chinese computers, I/O devices for Chinese data processing, prerequisites for library application and automatic library systems of vernacular materials are presented with examples. Several important issues are identified: 1) The preliminary plans on a national network should be drawn, 2) The need of an integrated system is necessary, 3) Various standards such as interchange codes and machine readable cataloging format should be devised.

INTRODUCTION

In the past decade, computer facilities have been widely utilized in Taiwan for many purposes by a variety of users. As of 1982, 638 organizations had installed computers for efficiency, better service, and accuracy. Almost one-fourth of the organizations (149) use computers for personnel administration; eighty-four organizations use them for inventory. Private enterprises are the big users of this new product, numbering 343 organizations which amount to more than half of the total user population. Educational and research institutions rank second place (101) and public enterprises (80) rank third as seen in Table 1.[1]

Table 1. List of Chinese Data Processing Utilization

Organization Uses	Total	Private Sector	Information Industry	Government	Public Admin	Education & Research
Total Number of Organizations with Data Processing	638	343	49	65	80	101
Personnel	149	101	12	9	11	16
Inventory	84	62	13	2	3	4
Accounting	82	58	12	3	6	3
Financial Management	58	38	10	4	4	2
Statistics	48	29	2	8	5	4
Accounts Processing	72	50	11	4	6	1
Education & Training	23	3	6	4	0	10
Engineering	13	3	2	3	2	3
Science	6	0	3	0	1	2
Service Industries	51	31	13	0	4	3
Manufacturing	41	30	9	2	0	0
Shipping	7	5	2	0	0	0
Taxes	30	14	4	9	1	2
Others	86	42	3	31	4	6

A library application initiated by the Science and Technology Information Center in 1973 was to process a union list of Western language serials and was followed by several other organizations' projects. Experiments in processing vernacular materials in 1978 ushered the subsequent efforts in building up Chinese Educational Resources Information System (CERIS), in forming the

Library Automation Planning Committee, in formulating various required standards for automation (e.g. the Chinese MARC Formats, cataloging rules, subject headings, etc), and in building up MARC databases.[2]

Computer installations have grown steadily until 1982. Installations grew in 1978 by 43%, in 1979 by 49%, in 1980 by 40%, and in 1981 it had the highest growth rate of 53%. In 1982, the growth rate dropped to 31%.[3] The reason for the drop was caused by an evidence of insufficient use of some of these facilities. Evaluations were conducted on the need for additional installations in order to avoid possible waste. The use of Chinese data processing prevails in the following applications:[4]

1. Personnel administration,
2. Business management and production management (including inventory control, accounting, billing, etc.),
3. Educational use (computer-assisted instruction and library application),
4. Tax processing,
5. Stock management and banking operations,
6. Telecommunication and transportation management, and
7. Hotel, supermarket, and hospital management, etc.

The vernacular language usually is used only to indicate Chinese names, addresses, captions of tables and charts.[5] The only large amount of vernacular Chinese language processing rests with the library automation applications. Its historical background was briefly reported earlier and its current status will be discussed later.

CURRENT STATUS OF CHINESE COMPUTERS

Studies made on computer processing of Chinese data were initiated in 1971 by the National Science Council and some research institutions. According to a recent survey, forty-four vendors/manufacturers and research organizations (excluding universities and academic programs) are developing Chinese data processing techniques,[6] Most of them have either developed commercially available Chinese data processing systems or have designed special equipment which can be attached to existing computer equipment to process Chinese data. Basically, these efforts only bring some solutions to the input and output of Chinese characters. Processing of Chinese data with computers must address four elements: input, internal processing and storage, output, and the exchange of data. All these elements involve certain computer software for control and processing. The Chinese computer facilities at the present time, therefore, are synonymous with input/output devices to be attached to the main hardware which is completely or partially imported. Engineering interface efforts and software control have been the major objects under development even though the intention to design a complete Chinese computer has been advocated.[7]

I/O DEVICES FOR CHINESE DATA PROCESSING

As indicated earlier, the major components needed to process Chinese scripts are the input device, internal processing and storage, output devices, and data communications. Due to the length limitation of this chapter, only a few most related items – the I/O devices – are to be briefly discussed.

Input

Due to the complexity of the Chinese language, indexing of the Chinese character has always been complicated.[8] There is not yet a perfect solution to this problem. However, twenty-four different input methods are available out of which fourteen methods to be used interchangeably are now under development at the National Taiwan Institute of Technology for a text processing project. The following describes the major available ones:

Telegraphic Code

Containing 10,000 characters, it is based on the telegraphic code stipulated by the Department of Telecommunication. Each character is represented by an assigned code ranging from 000 to 999.[9]

Three Corner Coding Method

Invented by Jack K. T. Huang, each Chinese character is represented by a six-digit code which is derived by examining the upper left-hand corner, then the upper right-hand corner, then the lower left corner, proceeding in a Z fashion when analyzing the shape of the character. A total of 300 fundamental symbols categorized into 99 units, comprising 99 major and their related 201 minor fundamental symbols, are used.[10]

Four Corner Coding Method

Twenty-nine separate patterns of Chinese characters are represented by ten fundamental numerical symbols. Each character is identified by a four-number code comprising the appropriate numerical symbols that correspond to each of its four corners and was invented by Yun-wu Wang in compiling his Chinese dictionary.[11]

Revised Four Corner Coding and Phonetic Symbols Method devised by Chun-liang Chou

A character's code is derived by determining the shape of the character first and then supplementing it with the character's phonetic symbol.[12]

Fixed Position Method

A position is assigned to a Chinese character according to its frequency of use. It is arranged in one or several different registers which holds 1,000 Chinese characters each.

Phonetic Symbol Method

Each character is indexed according to its phonetic pronunciation. There are thirty-seven phonetics and four tone marks available in this system.[13]

Root or Radical Method

Chinese characters are formed by breaking a Chinese character into its basic parts according to its various roots or radicals.[14]

Chuang-chieh Method (also called T'ien-lung or Dragon System or the Chinese Character Alphabet Method)

Invented by P'ang-fu Chu, it is based on an analysis of the principles of the structure and organization of the Chinese language. Letters of the English alphabet used as symbols are given to the basic components of the Chinese character, e.g. 'H' stands for bamboo and 'B' stands for moon, etc. The most significant aspect of this method does not lie in its symbols, rather in the vector type of the storage of Chinese characters.[15]

A method similar in principle, devised by S. C. Chen for Control Data Corporation, is called the Chung Kuo Tzu Shou Tzu Wei San Ma and Chung Kuo Shou Wei Chien I Shu Ju Fa (Chinese Character's Beginning, Middle and Ending Three-Component Coding Method, and the Beginning and Ending Five-Component Coding Method). This system separates the strokes for Chinese characters into 123 types and organizes them into twenty-six component categories. Each component corresponds to one English letter. A total of three letters comprises each character's code.[16]

In summary, these methods, each with its distinct advantages and disadvantages, must be carefully considered when choosing a system. It has been found that for library operations the Three Corner Coding system is efficient because it does not require linguistic knowledge and the input speed (42 words per minute) is fairly satisfactory.[17]

Input keyboards can be categorized into the following types:

1. Standard ASCII keyboard with English keys: They are used for the Telegraphic Coding method.
2. Modified standard keyboard: A regular standard keyboard which is given new and/or different functions is used for the Phonetic Symbol method, Three Corner system and several Chinese character component methods.
3. Large keyboard: Used for inputting individual characters.

Output

Since the image of Chinese characters are stored in the form of dot matrix, the output devices then also must be able to produce dot matrix images. Two types of output devices are available:

1. Hard copy produced by impact printers. The density of the character and the ability to create complex character forms in various styles are determined by the resolution of the dot matrix, i.e. the number of dots per inch. Various resolutions are available from different manufacturers: 14 ×15, 16×14, 24×24, 24×48, 32×24, 32×32, and 28×28, etc. (Figure 1).
2. The CRT display of Chinese characters follows the same principle as the printing. The display unit must be dot addressable, meaning it should have graphics capability. The number of characters displayable on a screen is determined by the resolution of the screen and the size of the character dot matrix, for example: a 256×256 dot screen can display 12 lines with 12 characters per line, each character having the size of 16×18 dots and including the spacing between characters and lines.

PREREQUISITES FOR LIBRARY APPLICATION

The revision of Chinese cataloging rules to meet the needs of library automation, the development of Chinese Character Code for Information Interchange, the MARC formats for non-book and book materials and the compilation of Chinese subject headings have served as a solid foundation for the standardization of data processing for libraries.

Revised Chinese Cataloging Rules

Based on ISBD (G) and AACR2, the Cataloging Rules Working Group of the Library Automation Planning Committee, the Library Association of China began preparing a new code for the bibliographic description of library materials in June 1980. This new code not only retains the essence of traditional Chinese bibliographic description, especially suitable for Chinese graphic materials, but also complies with the international codes. While compiling these new rules, the following guidelines were observed: (a) applicable to all types of publications including print and non-print materials for use in book, card, and machine readable catalogues; (b) adaptation of AACR2's merits as the framework of the rules; and (c) consulting UNIMARC for its application to machine readable cataloguing.[18]

Chinese Character Code for Information Interchange (CCCII)

As a tool of absolute necessity for information interchange, CCCII has been designed in accordance with ISO standards in a three-dimensional 94×94×94 structure which will be adequate to cover 80,000 characters of the following types: (a) The 4,807 most frequently used characters, (b) 16,198 less frequently used ones, and (c) 10,793 various forms including those corresponding to the characters listed in (a) and (b), ancient forms, simplified forms (including those used in ancient China, China mainland, Singapore, etc.) and characters used by minority groups such as Tibetan, Mongolian and Manchurian.[19]

Figure 1 Samples of Various Printer Dot Matrix Resolutions

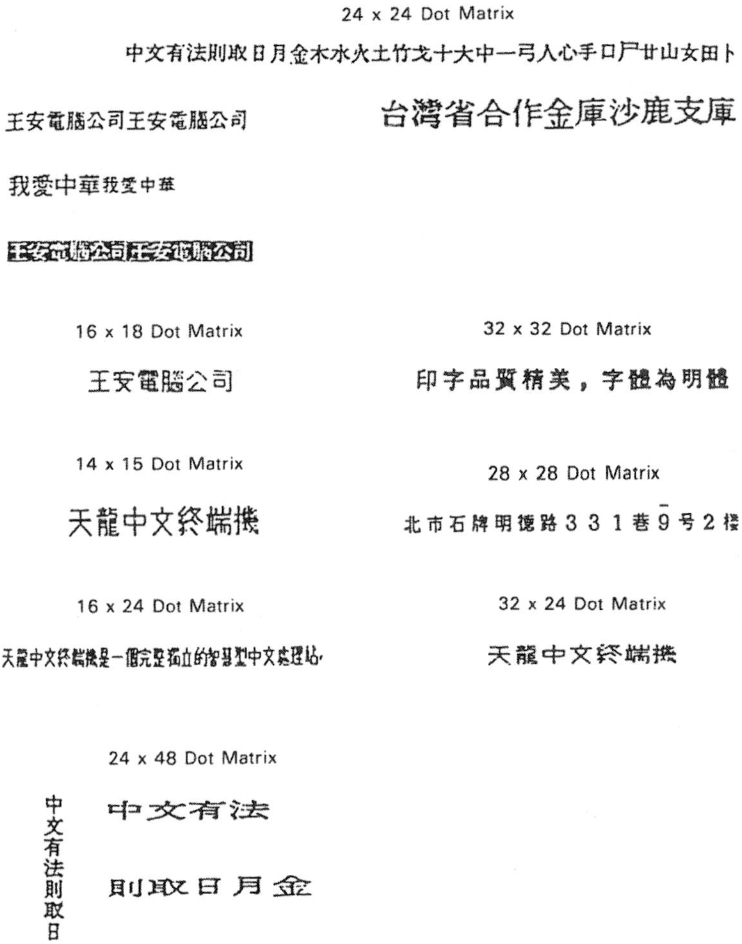

24 x 24 Dot Matrix

中文有法則取日月金木水火土竹戈十大中一弓人心手口尸廿山女田卜

王安電腦公司王安電腦公司

台灣省合作金庫沙鹿支庫

我愛中華我愛中華

王安電腦公司王安電腦公司

16 x 18 Dot Matrix

王安電腦公司

32 x 32 Dot Matrix

印字品質精美，字體為明體

14 x 15 Dot Matrix

天龍中文終端機

28 x 28 Dot Matrix

北市石牌明德路331巷9号2樓

16 x 24 Dot Matrix

天龍中文終端機是一個完整獨立的智慧型中文處理站,

32 x 24 Dot Matrix

天龍中文終端機

24 x 48 Dot Matrix

中文有法則取日

中文有法

則取日月金

Chinese MARC format

After the completion of Chinese MARC format for books in 1981, an integrated Chinese MARC format for books and non-books (including AV materials, maps, music, and serials, etc.) was published in October 1982. Based on UNIMARC and in consideration of LC MARC II format, this integrated Chinese MARC format incorporates the uniqueness of Chinese materials and the necessary aspects of handling Chinese materials in a non-Chinese enviroment.[20] In comparison with the UNIMARC, the following are the major differences:

1. Undefined indicators in UNIMARC for Fields, 010, 011, 204, 215, and 225 are assigned new functions,
2. Field 501 (collective uniform title) and 503 (Uniform conventional headings) are not used in Chinese MARC because of Chinese cataloging rules requirements,
3. Fields 432, 433, 442, 443 of UNIMARC are not included by Chinese MARC format because they are not compatible with ISBD (S) and AACR2,
4. Subfield identifiers are added to Field 805 to record agency, location, accession number, etc.,
5. Additions for Chinese music compositions and instruments are recorded in Field 125,
6. Addition of Tag 550 for series titles,
7. Fields 770-792 are added to record names in Roman scripts and 700-722 are used for names in Chinese characters,
8. Subfield identifier '$r' is added to Fields 200, 225, and 5xx for Romanized title proper and other variant titles,
9. Subfield identifier '$s' is assigned to Fields 600, 700, 701, and 702 for identification of a dynastic era in which a Chinese person is involved,
10. Subfield identifier '$u' is added to Field 3xx for libraries using cataloging rules other than the Chinese Cataloguing

Rules to record notes in Chinese, English, and in Romanized forms.[21]

Research that has been conducted on Chinese subject headings for the purpose to facilitate better use and accession of materials will be published in the near future.

AUTOMATED LIBRARY SYSTEMS OF VERNACULAR MATERIAL

The development of computerized library systems in Taiwan was carried out in two distinct directions: The processing of Roman script materials and the processing of Chinese vernacular materials. Since the topic under discussion is computer applications for vernacular library materials, only the vernacular systems will be discussed.

Agriculture Science Information Center (ASIC)

ASIC has set up the Agricultural Science and Technology Information Management System (ASTIMS). This system that previously was implemented on a Perkin Elmer 3220 super mini was switched in June 1982 to the PRIME 750 because of operating system and hardware performance considerations and is equipped with eighteen Multitech 75 terminals which use the Chuang-chieh Coding method. At the present time, this system includes the following four databases that have incorporated the previous files of FASTCL (Files on Agricultural Science and Technology Literature in Chinese), FASTER (Files on Agricultural Science and Technology Research Reports), and FASTEL (Files on Agricultural Science and Technology Literature).[22]

FASTEP

Files containing information on agricultural scientists has a target completion date in May 1983. All fields will be searchable, e.g. name, education, present occupation, past occupation, training, etc.

FASTEJ

Files on Agricultural Science and Technology Research Project is in a development stage with partial retrieving operations possible. Input for the database, which began in 1982 and will include four years' retrospective files in addition to current data, is expected to be completed by June 1983.

ASIC MARC Bibliographic Database

This is a Chinese and Western language bibliographic database of agricultural science and technology reports, monographs and journal articles based on the modified UNIMARC format and LC format for authority file.

AGRI-THESAURUS

Being a Chinese and English indexing and retrieving tool for ASTIMS, it is fully developed and currently contains over 10,000 keywords which are completely retrievable.[23]

The different databases are not interactive and must be accessed separately. Continuous efforts are consistently made to improve file designs and to modify indexing terms. At present, the greatest problem does not lie with Chinese character input but rather with lack of indexing standards. Due to the existing inadequacy in AACR2 and Chinese Cataloging Rules for Serials, ASIC has set up its own guidelines which undergo constant revision in response to new problems encountered during indexing. It is anticipated that an additional year of revisions and changes will be needed for completion. For the sake of accurate feedback, immediate problem identification, and rapid problem analysis, indexers are performing their own input keying, and will continue to do so throughout the testing and development stages and perhaps later unless it is determined that it slows down their indexing speed too much. The extensive in-house training that uses the Library of Congress subject specialists training method is very impressive.

Future plans include: development of a serials control subsystem of the ASIC MARC bibliographic database, its design was to be begun in 1983; an interlibrary loan system to be designed in 1984; microfilming capabilities to be made available by the end of 1983; possible production of printed serials index and union catalogues for other libraries; development of a dual data retrieval system, similar to the US National Library of Medicine's System, which will offer retrieval functions geared to both technically skilled indexing specialists and less technically trained persons, e.g. reference librarian; and establishing a network of agricultural libraries by 1984. When the network is established, ASIC will develop other library management software packages, e.g. acquisitions, circulation, etc.

National Central Library (NCL)

NCL is developing the National Union Catalog Bibliographic Database by using Wang facilities with ten terminals and two printers, one for catalog card production and the other for other printed outputs (see Figures 2 and 3). The Three Corner Coding Method for Chinese character input and retrieving is used. Software written in COBOL is developed jointly with the RPT Intergroups International Ltd. following the Chinese MARC format. Development of the cataloging subsystem began in 1981, and on-line use in NCL commenced in December 1982. At the present time, data will be keyed in by library staff themselves from prepared data input worksheets. As a joint venture with seven academic institutions, a database of six thousand records has been built up with immediate plans to start retrospective conversion.

The access points for books are: (a) Subject, (b) System ID, (c) ISBN, (d) ISSN, (e) CODEN, (f) CCS (Chinese Classification Scheme), (g) Author (Chinese/English), (h)Title (Chinese/English), (I) Author & Title (Chinese/English), and (j) Corporate Author. The system will produce printed products such as author indexes,

Figure 2

(a) Book Catalog Card (for domestic libraries),
(b) Book Catalog Card (for domestic and foreign),
(c) Serial Catalog Card (for domestic libraries).

a

898.092　七十年中國報業史/賴光臨著。--台北市：
8364　中央日報社，民70[1981]
409面：地圖；19公分
附錄：1.我國報紙調查；2.文獻；3.出版法與報業道德規範
611048　新台幣120元(平裝)

1.報業-中國-歷史 I.賴光臨

b

PN5364　Lai, Kuang-Lin.
.L3　(Ch'i shih nien Chung-kuo pao yeh shih)
七十年中國報業史/賴光臨著。--台北市：
中央日報社，民70[1981]
409p.：maps；19cm.

Appendices：1.我國報紙調查；2.文獻；
3.出版法與報業道德規範
NT$120(pbk)
1.Chinese newspapers-History. I. Title.

c

期
570　政論週刊＝China critic weekly.--第78期
8749　(民45年5月)-第185期(民47年1月)。--台北市：
中國新聞出版公司，民45-47【1956-1958】
冊：圖；26公分
ISSN 0528-9688 (平裝)

1.政治-中國-期刊

Figure 3 Computer-Produced National Bibliography

00001-0010
第1頁

005.121/8749

FORTRAN程式語言 / 劉振漢著。--台北市：三
民，民70【1981】
【8】278面：圖：21公分
大學用書
附：附錄及索引
基價3.11圓(平裝)
I. 劉振漢

001.642/8776

POP-11組合語言/劉振漢著。--台北市：三
民，民70【1981】
【10】，274面：圖：21公分
大學用書
附：附錄及索引
基價3.11
1. 劉振漢

001.642/8776

三民主義精編本/黎明文化事業公司編著。--
台北市：編著者，民70【1981】
【261】面：19公分
附錄：1.民生主義育樂兩篇補述；2.中國的光
明大道—三民主義
新台幣50元(平裝)
1. 黎明文化事業司

005.12/9556

三民主義之科學觀與特/陳士誠撰。--台北
市：世紀書局，民70【1981】
【5】，142面：圖：21公分
新台幣100元(平裝)
1.

005.121/8742

三民主義理論體系之研究/劉士傑。--台北
市：張月卿，民70【1981】
【16】，197面：圖表：21公分
附錄：論中國之轉變與知識份子應有的努力等
11種
新台幣100元(平裝)
1.劉士傑

三民主義統一中國論集 / 林桂國主編。--台北
市：東方文物出版社，民70？【1981？】
【4】，407面；21公分
附錄：台灣好詞百首，周士奎撰
新台幣300元(平裝)
I・林桂國

005.121/8745

三民主義統一中國座談紀實/中國大陸研究出
版社編。--台北市：編者：民70【1981】
47面：19公分
中國大陸問題研究中心座談紀實
新台幣20元(平裝)
1.中國大陸研究出版社。

005.121/8756

三民主義與民法/國立政治大學法律研究所編。
--台北市：國立編譯館，民70【1981】
[18]，218面；21公分，--(三民主義理論叢
書)
(平裝)
1.國立政治大學，法律研究所

005.121/8772

三民主義心物合一哲學的研究：兼批判共產主
義辯證唯物哲學/張全鋒著。--台北市：
撰者，民70【1981】
288面；26公分
陳士誠　　油印本
碩士論文—國立政治大學
(平裝)
1. 張全鋒

008.23/8767

七十年來教育雜誌展覽目錄/國立教育資料館
編。--台北市：編者，民70【1981】
2.42面：26公分
(平裝)
1.國立教育資料館。

title indexes, a monthly-updated bibliography for new books, catalog cards, proof sheets for verification and editing, etc.

NCL has also created the first computer-produced the *National Union List of Chinese Periodicals*, that covers the entire Chinese serial holdings of 136 private and public libraries.[24] First implemented in 1979 on a Wang VS 2200 computer, this union list contains records through the end of 1981, and it can also be used on the Wang VS100 computer. Entry number, journal title, frequency, publishing place, publishing year, publisher, distributor, holdings and locations, ISSN, and classification number can all be retrieved by using single key or multi-keys. With the exception of the '805' tag for local library holdings, record contents are compatible with Chinese MARC format for serials. Additions will be made that will conform to requirements for Chinese MARC format for serials. Plans are underway to interconnect the serials and union catalogue databases.

Upon completion of Chinese MARC format for rare books, the NCL's immediate project is to build a rare book database in June 1983. A consolidated bibliographic database of Chinese and English materials is being attempted by converting English bibliographic records of LC MARC tape into Chinese MARC tape and by inputting English data at the NCL. An integrated approach is definitely being followed. Bibliographic databases of journal article indexes and abstracts have been attempted and will be developed in the near future. A three-stage overall automated national library plan has been gradually carried out as scheduled.

National Taiwan Normal University

The Chinese Educational Resources Information System (CERIS), developed in 1978 in cooperation with the MiTAC. Inc., is a large educational periodical database consisting of 1,223 periodicals that was designed by using TOTAL Database Management System. Implemented on a Perkin Elmer 3220 computer with inserting, verifying, editing Chinese characters as well as skipping and protection capabilities, this system uses a multi-key retrieval method. Both Chinese and English vernacular scripts can be produced on the Chinese CRT terminals, and hard copies are produced by a plotter mode dot matrix line printer at a speed of 100 LPM.[25]

Science and Technology Information Center (STIC)

The major database system using Chinese vernacular processing is the On-line Retrieval System for Domestic Science & Technology Information which includes the Science and Technology Experts Database, Research Reports Database, and the Research Projects Database.[26] This system uses the Hewlett Packard 3000/IMAGE Database Management System implemented on a HP 3000/44 computer with one HP 2621 console and two HP 2648 display terminals for English language, and two HP 2648 display terminals with Chinese, English and graphics capabilities. STIC began using the Telegraphic Coding method for input in September 1982, but found that it was too slow and inconvenient, and changed to the Chuang-chieh Coding method on Multitech terminals in March 1983. The basic database designs all are completed, and are now undergoing testing and further development. The first stage of inputting data should be completed in June 1983, at which time the three systems can be officially used. The systems are interactive, and search procedures and query language used are similar to those used by DIALOG.

1. The Scientific and Technical Experts Database, in its on-line development since November 1982, contained 521 entries as of February 1983. Codes rather than the full data field are used for searching, e.g. education code "3" displays "Ph. D." Searchable items include Chinese name, English name, specialty, major subject, degree, position, etc. Six different output formats are available.
2. The Research Reports Database has been in an on-line

testing and development stage since the end of November 1982 and contains over 725 entries. Efforts currently are devoted to inputting English abstracts, and Chinese abstracts will be added in the future. There is no fixed record length. Searchable fields include: researcher's Chinese name, English name, sponsoring unit, type of research, keyword, etc.

3. The Research Projects Database which contains the same searchable fields as the Research Reports Database, is also in a data inputting and further developmental stage. Five data set formats for on-line output and four sets for reports output are available.

Future plans include the design of a national acquisition system for foreign publications, a possible database for STIC publication subscribers, and bibliographic databases for both its periodical and book holdings.

CONCLUSION

In conclusion, our experiences have revealed several important issues in developing Chinese library automation and in providing effective information service to the Chinese community.

1. Because information sharing is the ultimate goal for library automation, and library automation is in turn an essential tool to facilitate information sharing, a network serving the information seekers is vitally needed to support national development in this country. It is therefore absolutely necessary to have preliminary plans on a national network drawn and studies conducted with the aim to develop an efficient and effective system throughout the island. The problem confronting us is more of a technically-oriented telecommunication nature and the cooperative efforts among libraries.
2. An integrated system is definitely needed. It is therefore nec-

essary to have an overall, comprehensive and coordinated planning effort and to proceed accordingly.

3. For the purpose of information sharing, various standards such as interchange codes and a machine readable cataloging format should be devised, tested and practiced before embarking upon library automation.
4. Sufficient funding should be acquired prior to building up databases to avoid possible interruptions.
5. Selection of hardware is extremely important in library application because it is a long-term project forbidding constant changes of equipment.
6. Technical personnel training is instrumental to the success of the system.

Great strides have been taken in addressing these issues, such as the formulation of standards, creation of I/O devices, and other advancements made in computerized Chinese vernacular processing. We look forward to additional achievements in the near future that may result from current studies underway in Taipei on Chinese text processing which is hoped will lead to the eventual start of an electronic library.

NOTES

1. Tzu Hsun Kung Yeh Ts'e Chin Hui Pien 資訊工業策進會 編 [Institute for the Information Industry, ed.], "Table 1. List of Chinese Data Processing Utilization," in *Chung Hua Min Kuo Ch'i Shih I Nien Tsu Hsun Kung Yeh Nien Chien 中華民國七十一年資訊工業年鑑 [Information Industry Yearbook of the Republic of China, 1982]* (Taipei: Institute for the Information Industry, 1982), 22.
2. Margaret C. Fung, "Library Automation in the Republic of China," *T'u Shu Kuan Hsueh Yu Tzu Hsun K'o Hsueh 圖書館學與資訊科學 [Journal of Library & Information Science]* 6, no. 1 (April 1980): 1-16; Margaret C. Fung 張鼎鍾, "State of the Art: Library Automation in Taipei, ROC," in *T' u Shu Kuan Hsueh Yu Tzu Hsun K'o Hsueh Chih T'an T'ao 圖書館學與資訊科學之探討 [On library and Information Science]* (Taipei: Student Book Co, 1982), 131-147.

3. Tzu Hsun Kung Yeh Ts'e Chin Hui Pien 資訊工業策進會 編 [Institute for the Information Industry, ed.], *Chung Hua Min Kuo Ch'i Shih I Nien Tzu Hsun Kung Yeh Nien Chien 中華民國七十一年資訊工業年鑑 [Information Industry Yearbook of the Republic of China, 1982]* (Taipei: Institute for the Information Industry, 1982), 109-113.
4. C. C. Yang, C. C. Hsieh and D. T. Lin, "Chinese Computer Technology in Taiwan – An Overview," in *Symposium on Computer Processing of Chinese Library Materials and Computer-Assisted Chinese Language Instruction at ASIS-82: Proceedings*, Columbus, Ohio, 19 October 1982. (Taipei: ASIS Taipei Chapter, 1982), 3-1-13.
5. Tzu Hsun Kung Yeh Ts'e Chin Hui Pien 資訊工業策進會 編 [Institute for the Information Industry, ed.], *Chung Hua Min Kuo Ch'i Shih I Nien Tzu Hsun Kung Yeh Nien Chien 中華民國七十一年資訊工業年鑑 [Information Industry 1982 Yearbook of the Republic of China]* (Taipei: Institute for the Information Industry, 1982), 109-113.
6. Ibid.
7. Yung Wei, "Keynote Speech," in *Chiao Yu Tzu Liao Yen T'ao Hui Chi Lu 教育資料研討會紀錄 [Proceedings of Conference on Educational Materials Research at National Taiwan Normal University]* (Taipei: National Educational Materials, May 1970).
8. C. C. Yang, C. C. Hsieh and D. T. Lin, "Chinese Computer Technology in Taiwan – An Overview," 3-1-13.
9. Tzu Hsun Kung Yeh Ts'e Chin Hui Pien 資訊工業策進會 編 [Institute for the Information Industry, ed.], *Chung Hua Min Kuo Ch'i Shih I Nien Tzu Hsun Kung Yeh Nien Chien 中華民國七十一年資訊工業年鑑 [Information Industry Yearbook of the Republic of China, 1982]*, 45.
10. Li-ren Hu, Yuan-wei Chang, and Jack Kai-tung Huang 胡立人，張源渭，黃克東, *Chung Wen San Chiao Hao Fa Hsun Lien Shou Ts'e 中文三角編號法訓練手冊 [The Training Manual for the Three Corner Coding Method]* (Taipei: System Publications, 1979).
11. Yun-wu Wang 王雲五, *Wang Yun-wu Tsung Ho Tz'u Tien 王雲五綜合辭典*, 5th ed. (Taipei: Hua Kuo Ch'u Pan She, 1982).
12. Tzu Hsun Kung Yeh Ts'e Chin Hui Pien 資訊工業策進會 編 [Institute for the Information Industry, ed.], *Chung Hua Min Kuo Ch'i Shih I Nien Tzu Hsun Kung Yeh Nien Chien 中華民國七十一年資訊工業年鑑 [Information Industry Yearbook of the Republic of China, 1982]*, 109-113.
13. "Kuo Jen Yen Chiu Chung Wen Tien Nao, Ying Yung Kuang Fan I Tsou Ch'eng Hsiao 國人研究中文電腦，應用廣泛已奏成效 [National

Research into Chinese Vernacular Computers],” *Chung Yang Jih Pao 中央日報 [Central Daily News (Taiwan, ROC)]*, 4 February 1983, 4. Y. H. Chin et al., “An Automated Chinese Telephone Directory,” *IEEE Computer* 8 (May 1975):49-54.

14. Tzu Hsun Kung Yeh Ts’e Chin Hui Pien 資訊工業策進會 編 [Institute for the Information Industry, ed.], *Chung Hua Min Kuo Ch’i Shih I Nien Tzu Hsun Kung Yeh Nien Chien 中華民國七十一年資訊工業年鑑 [Information Industry Yearbook of the Republic of China, 1982]*, 109-113.
15. Ling I K’o Chi Ku Wen Kung Ssu 零壹科技顧問公司, *Ts’ang Chieh Chung Wen Tzu Hsun Ma 倉頡中文資訊碼 [Chang Chieh Chinese Information Code]* (Taipei: Ch’uan Hua K’o Chi T’u Shu Kung Szu, August 1982).
16. “Kuo Jen Yen Chiu Chung Wen Tien Nao, Ying Yung Kuang Fan I Tsou Ch’eng Hsiao 國人研究中文電腦，應用廣泛已奏成效 [National Research into Chinese Vernacular Computers],” 4. Y. H. Chin et al., “An Automated Chinese Telephone Directory,” 49-54.
17. Tzu Hsun Kung Yeh Ts’e Chin Hui Pien 資訊工業策進會 編 [Institute for the Information Industry, ed.], *Survey Report on Chinese Data Processing Computers* (in Chinese), Technical Note No. C12 (Taipei: Institute for the Information Industry, December 1981).
18. C. C. Lan and M. D. Wu, “The New Chinese Cataloging Rules as the Foundation of the Chinese MARC,” in *Symposium on Computer Processing of Chinese Library Materials and Computer-Assisted Chinese Language Instruction at ASIS-82: Proceedings*, Columbus, Ohio, 19 October 1982. (Taipei: ASIS Taipei Chapter, 1982), 4-1-5; T’u Shu Kuan Tzu Tung Hua Tso Yeh Kuei Hua Wei Yuan Hui Chung Kuo Pien Mu Kuei Tse Yen Ting Hsiao Tsu 圖書館自動化作業規劃委員會中國編規則研訂小組 [Cataloging Rules Working Group, Library Automation Planning Committee], *Chung Kuo Pien Mu Kuei T se 中國編目規則 [Chinese Cataloging Rules]* (Taipei: National Central Library, 1982), I.
19. Chung Wen Tzu Hsun Ch’u Li Yung Tzu Yen Chi Hsiao Tsu Pien 中文資訊處理用字小組 編 [The Chinese Character Analysis Group, ed.], Chung Wen Tzu Hsun Chiao Huan Ma 中文資訊交化換碼 [Chinese Character Code for Information Interchange], 1 vol. (Taipei: Library Association of China, 1980); Kuo Tzu Cheng Li Hsiao Tsu Pien 國字整理小組 編 [The Chinese Character Analysis Group, ed.], *Chung Wen Tzu Hsun Chiao Huan Ma I T’i Tzu Piao 中文資訊交換碼異體字表 [Variant Forms of Chinese Character Code for Information Interchange]*,

2nd ed., vol. 2 (Taipei: The Chinese Character Analysis Group, 1982); Hsing Cheng Yuan Kuo Tzu Cheng Li Hsiao Tsu Pien 行政院國字整理小組 編 [The Chinese Character Analysis Group, Executive Yuan, ed.], *Chung Wen Tzu Hsun Chiao Huan Ma Tzu Hsing Piao 中文資訊交換碼字形表 [Symbols and Character Tables of Chinese Character Code for Information Interchange]*, 1 vol. (Taipei: The Chinese Character Analysis Group, Executive Yuan, 1981); Ching-chun Hsieh et al., "The Design and Application of the Chinese Character Code for Infromation Interchange (CCCII)," in *Chung Wen T'u Shu Tzu Liao Tzu Tung Hua Kuo Chi Yeh T'ao Hui Lun Wen Chi 中文圖書資料自動化國際研討會論文集 [Papers of the International Workshop on Chinese Library Automation]*, Taipei, 14-19 February 1981 (Taipei: Library Association of China, 1981), 1-17.

20. T'u Shu Kuan Tzu Tung Hua Tso Yeh Kuei Hua Wei Yuan Hui, Chung Kuo Chi Tu Pien Mu Ke Shih Kung Tso Hsiao Tsu Pein 圖書館自動化作業規劃委員會中國機讀編目格式工作小組 編 [Chinese MARC Working Group, Library Automation Planning Committee, ed.], *Chung Kuo Chi Tu Pien Mu Ko Shih 中國機讀編目格式 [Chinese MARC Format]* (Taipei: National Central Library, 1982); Chinese MARC Working Group, Library Automation Planning Committee, ed., "Chinese MARC Format and Bibliographic Databases," in *Symposium on Computer Processing of Chinese Library Materials and Computer-Assisted Chinese Language Instruction at ASIS-82: Proceedings*, Columbus, Ohio, 19 October 1982. (Taipei: ASIS Taipei Chapter, 1982), 5-1-27.
21. Ibid.
22. Wan-jiun Wu, "The Agricultural Science and Technology Information Management System," in *Chung Wen T'u Shu Tzu Liao Tzu Tung Hua Kuo Chi Yeh T'ao Hui Lun Wen Chi 中文圖書資料自動化國際研討會論文集 [Papers of the International Workshop on Chinese Library Automation]*, Taipei, 14-19 February 1981 (Taipei: Library Association of China, 1981), D11-D46.
23. Wan–jiun Wu et al., "Agri-Thesaurus: A Chinese Thesaurus for the Agricultural Science and Technology Information Management System," in *Symposium on Computer Processing of Chinese Library Materials and Computer-Assisted Chinese Language Instruction at ASIS-82: Proceedings*, Columbus, Ohio, 19 October 1982. (Taipei: ASIS Taipei Chapter, 1982), 6-1-6.
24. Rui-lan Ku Wu, "The Union List of Chinese Serials in the Republic of China: A Case Report," in *Chung Wen T'u Shu Tzu Liao Tzu Tung Hua*

Kuo Chi Yeh T'ao Hui Lun Wen Chi 中文圖書資料自動化國際研討會論文集 [Papers of the International Workshop on Chinese Library Automation], Taipei, 14-19 February 1981 (Taipei: Library Association of China, 1981), D57-D82.

25. Kuo Li Taiwan Shih Fan Ta Hsueh Pien 國立台灣師範大學 編 [National Taiwan Normal University, ed.], *Chiao Yu Lun Wen Chai Yao 教育論文摘要 [Abstract of Chinese Educational Periodical Literature]*, Series V (Taipei: National Taiwan Normal University Library, 1982). (Brochure); Margaret C. Fung, "The Chinese Educational Resources Information System: A Case Report," in *Chung Wen T'u Shu Tzu Liao Tzu Tung Hua Kuo Chi Yeh T'ao Hui Lun Wen Chi 中文圖書資料自動化國際研討會論文集 [Papers of the International Workshop on Chinese Library Automation]*, Taipei, 14-19 February 1981 (Taipei: Library Association of China, 1981), D1-D10; Margaret C. Fung, "State of the Art: Library Automation in Taipei, ROC," in *T'u Shu Kuan Hsueh Yu Tzu Hsun K'o Hsueh Chih T'an T'ao 圖書館學與資訊科學之探討 [On Library and Information Science]* (Taipei: Student Book Co, 1982), 131-147.
26. Tung-sheng Fang, "The Establishment and Use of Information System on Science and Technology in ROC," in *Symposium on Computer Processing of Chinese Library Materials and Computer-Assisted Chinese Language Instruction at ASIS-82: Proceedings*, Columbus, Ohio, 19 October 1982. (Taipei: ASIS Taipei Chapter, 1982), 10-1-3.

Reprinted from *The Library in the Information Revolution: Proceedings of the Sixth Congress of Southeast Asian Librarians*, Singapore, 30 May–3 June 1983. Singapore: Published for Consal VI by Maruzen Asia, 1983. (pp. 280-292).

9

Productive Use of Information through New Technologies and Information Systems in Taiwan, ROC

ABSTRACT

The presentation covers the following topics:

1. General information of Taiwan,
2. Factors facilitating the production, processing, and use of information:
   (1) Publishing industry,
   (2) Development of computer technology and its applications;
3. Productive use of information through existing information systems:
   (1) Libraries and information systems,
   (2) Existing national management information system, and
4. Future outlook.

INTRODUCTION

Taiwan, ROC covers an area of 35,941 sq. km., has a population of 18,413,220 people (of which 25% are students), and is known for its high literacy rate (86%). The land reform program, the local self government, the ten construction projects, and the recent twelve construction projects in addition to the 9-year compulsory education have facilitated the continuous prosperity of the Island in spite of international constraints placed on it. The Chinese people on Taiwan enjoys an annual per capita national income of NT$91,553 (US$2,334) and the gross national product was US$46,163,000,000 in 1982. Under such an environment, the Island has been considered a marvel.

In a place where cultural heritage is greatly cherished, preserved, and disseminated, where the economy is booming, where academic research is emphasized, and where the people strive for freedom, national integrity, and prosperity, special efforts are required for collecting, handling, processing, producing and utilization of information. Information plays an important role in every sector of the Chinese society there, it ranges from national planning and policy making to daily operations. The industry there is changing from a labor intensive one to a technology intensive one. While the information industry has recently been designated as a national strategic industry, information science as a discipline has been well presented by institutions of higher education. Theoretical and applied researches are conducted in industrial, engineering, national, governmental, academic, and private institutions. Information needs and information technology have reciprocal effects on each other. Recent developments in new technology have facilitated the collecting, processing, and dissemination of information through information services.

FACTORS FACILITATING THE COLLECTING, HANDLING, PROCESSING, AND UTILIZATION OF INFORMATION

In addition to what are mentioned above regarding the need for effective use of information, the following factors facilitate the collecting, handling, processing, and utilization of information.

Publishing Scene

Upgraded living standard and high educational level of the people prompted environment for publishing. In 1982 more than ten thousand new titles were published that included the following categories:

Category	Titles
General	764
Philosophy	322
Religion	346
Social sciences	1,364
Natural and applied sciences	2,013
Literature and philology	2,396
Arts	356
History, biography, and geography	1,314
Government document	1,513
Total	10,378

International book trade is also active in this area:

Category	Import	Export
Chinese books	5,864,537	5,513,697
Chinese periodicals	4,681,066	1,518,697
Foreign language books	7,161,771	3,583,296
Foreign periodicals	12,942,349	3,616,734
AV materials	843,621	249,348

The booming publishing industry is the cause and effect of the increasing information needs.

Development of Chinese Computer Technology and Applications

Ever since information industry has been designated as a strategic one, computer industry is rapidly developed recently. A recent survey shows 44 vendors/manufacturers and research organizations (excluding universities and academic programs) are developing Chinese data processing techniques[1]. Most of them have either developed commercially-available Chinese data processing systems or have designed special equipment which can be attached to existing computer equipment to process Chinese data.

Studies made on computer processing of Chinese data were initiated in 1973 by the National Science Council and several research institutions. Basically these efforts only bring some solutions to the input and output of Chinese characters. Processing of Chinese data with computers must address four elements: (1) input, (2) internal processing and storage, (3) output, and (4) the exchange of data.

Input

Indexing of the Chinese character has always been complicated. While no perfect solution yet exists, twenty-four different input methods are available. As a project of Chinese Character Analysis Group, out of them fourteen methods will be used interchangeably known as the cross reference database. The major available methods are the: telegraphic code, three corner coding methods, fixed position method, phonetic symbol method, root and radical method, Chuang-chieh method (also called T'ien-lung or Dragon system or the Chinese character alphabet method, and Control Data Corporation's Chung Kuo Tzu Shou Tzu Wei San Ma and Chung Kuo Shou Wei Chien I Shu Ju Fa) (Chinese characters beginning, middle and ending three component coding method, and the beginning and ending five-component coding method). Input keyboard can be categorized into the following types: (1) Standard ASCII keyboard with English keys, used for telegraphic coding method, (2) Modified standard keyboard, a standard keyboard that is given new and/or different functions and used for Phonetic Symbol Method and Three Corner Coding Method, (3) Large keyboard for individual characters.

Output

The image of Chinese characters are stored in the form of dot matrix, the output devices must also be able to create matrix images. Two ways of output are available: (1) Hard copy produced by impact printers, e.g. 14x15, 16x14, 14x24, 24x24, 24x28, 32x24, and 28x28 and the CRT which is determined by the resolution of the screen and the size of the character dot matrix, e.g. a 256x256 dot screen can display 12 lines with 12 characters per line if each character has 16x18 dots.

The growth rate of the installation of computer facilities was 30% (998 systems in 1981 and 1,298 in June 1982). Private industries constitute the largest users of computer facilities, educational institutions rank the second place, public enterprises the third, information organizations the fourth, and government agencies the fifth. The use of Chinese data processing prevails in the following applications:

1. Business management and production management (including inventory control, accounting, billings, etc.),
2. Educational use (library and computer-assisted instruction),
3. Hotel, supermarket, and hospital management,
4. Personnel administration,
5. Stock management and banking operations,
6. Tax processing,
7. Telecommunication.

Library automation is one single area that uses the full capacity of Chinese computer technology. Special success evident in the areas of improved input/output devices, softwares, and standards enhanced the development of library automation in recent years. Such productive response to the processing of information is the direct result of the recent breakthrough made by the computer technology in Taiwan and the urgent need for adequate, speedy and accurate information.

PRODUCTIVE USE OF INFORMATION THROUGH EXISTING INFORMATION SYSTEMS

Libraries and Information Systems

Library and information service points for the entire population prevail throughout the Island with 207 public libraries (one national and one branch of the national library, 22 provincial and municipal libraries, 27 city and county libraries, 101 village libraries, 7 social educational centers, and 47 private libraries (including temple libraries), 135 academic libraries (34 college and research libraries, 77 junior college libraries, 10 military academy libraries, and 14 religious college libraries,) 2,456 school and children libraries (370 high school libraries, 358 junior high school libraries, and 1,728 grade school libraries) 219 special libraries (44 institutions libraries, 29 business libraries, 55 government libraries, 29 industrial libraries, 25 military libraries, 18 medical libraries, 6 news agency libraries, and 13 information centers). Under the promotion of the Cultural Development Program, cultural center libraries are to be prolifically established in the next few years.

Automated Library/Information Systems

Automated library services have been initiated since 1973 with full speed advancement in processing Chinese language materials since 1978:

Development and Current Status of Automated Library Systems in Taipei, ROC

Organization	Nature or System Name		Hardware	Date
National Science Council Information Center	Union List of Serials (R)	Periodical Information Service System	IBM 370/135	1973
Chung-shan Institute of Technology Library	Producing catalog cards and new accessions list (R)	CLIS	CYBER 170/730	1975
National Taiwan Univ. Library School	Bibliographic Database	Information Retrieval	WANG MVP	1975
Tamkang University Lib.	Serial Control and Acquisition (R)		IBM 370/148	1977
National Taiwan Normal Univ. Library	Educational Information database	CERIS	Perkin-Elmer	1978
Chung-shan Institute of Technology Library	Serial Control (R)	CLIS	IBM 370/138	1979
Institute of Information Science, Academia Sinica	Bibliographic Database (R)	Browsing MARC III Database generation system	PDP 11-34	1979

National Central Library	*National Union List of Serials*		WANG VS	1979
Agriculture Science Information Center	Files on Agricultural Literature Personnel information Research Project Research Reports Agri. Literature in Chinese	FASTEL *FASTEP *FASTEJ FASTER FASTCL	Perkin Elmer & Prime	1979 1982
*Renamed as Agriculture Science and Technology Information Management System (ASTIMS) which includes 1) FASTER, 2) FASTEJ, 3) ASIC MARC Bibliographic Database, and AGRU-Thesaurus.				
Chung-shan Institute of Technology Library	Acquisition and Circulation (R)	CLIS	IBM/370	1980
NSC Scientific & Technical Information Center	Scientific and Technical Experts Database, ST Research Projects, ST Research Projects Database	**MIS	IBM/370/ 135 & HP3000/44	1980 1982
**Renamed as On-line Retrieval System for Domestic Science and Technology Information.				
Freedom Council Information Center	ROC Information Database	FCIA	WANG MVP	1980
National Central Library	National Union Catalog of Books		WANG VS100	1980
National Taiwan Univ. Lib.	Serial Control (R)		UNIVAC	1981
National Taiwan Normal Univ. Library	Serial Control of English Language Journals (R)		Perkin-Elmer 830	1981
National Central Library	*National Union List of Chinese Periodicals*		VS100	1981
National Taiwan Institute of Technology	Circulation		Tien-lung	1981
National Chengchi University Library	Circulation		Perkin	1982
National Central Library	National Union Catalog of Rare Chinese Books		WANG VS100	1983
National Central Library	Acquisition		WANG VS100	1983

Note: (R) = processing of Roman characters only.

Some of the above projects were experiments and are no longer in existence. Their efforts in designing the systems are beneficial to the development of library automation in Taiwan, ROC. However, the successful on-going projects are represented by the following systems:

1. Agriculture Science Information Center (ASIC)'s ASTIMS including FASTEP, FASTEJ, ASIC MARC Bibliographic Database (a Chinese and Western language bibliographic

database of agriculture science and technology reports, monographs and journal articles based on the modified UNIMARC format and LC format), and Agri-Thesaurus (a Chinese and English indexing and retrieving tool for ASTIMS) originally implemented on a Perkin Elmer 3220 super mini, has been converted in June 1982 to a Prime 750 due to operation system and performance consideration.

2. National Central Library's National Union Catalog Bibliographic Database (as a joint venture with seven academic institutions, a database has been created with 1982 new publications and with plans to add those of the 1983 publications and to start retrospective conversion immediately) and *National Union List of Chinese Periodicals* (covers the entire Chinese serial holdings of 136 private and public libraries through the end of 1981), originally installed on a Wang VS 2200, has been implemented on the Wang VS 100 system with Three corner system as the input device. Facilitated with ten terminals and two printers, the system is developed jointly with the R.P.T. Intergroups International, LTD.

National Taiwan Normal University's (NTNU) Chinese Educational Resources Information System (CERIS), pioneered the computer processing of Chinese library materials, developed in 1978, is an educational periodicals database designed with TOTAL Database Management System. Implemented on a Perkin Elmer 3220 computer with mult-key retrieval method, it searches both Chinese and English scripts (alphabetically in English and by using Three corner system for the Chinese) online in addition to the production of hard copies in a plotter mode dot matrix line printer at a speed of 100 LPM.

Both National Taiwan University (NTU) and NTNU have in-house serial control systems for accounting purposes.

The Science and Technology Information Center (STIC) of the National Science Council, now implemented on Hewlett Packard HP 3000/44 computer, uses a HP 3000/IMAGE Database Management System for developing its software. STIC began using the Telegraphic Coding Method for input on HP terminals in September 1982, but has changed to the Chuang-chieh Coding Method on Ultitech terminals in March 1983.

National Management Information Systems

Management information system is recognized to be pivotal to national development program. Six management information systems are being planned by Research, Development and Evaluation Commission (RDEC), Executive Yuan to meet the various management information needs:

1. General administration information system,
2. Economic development information system,
3. Scientific and technological information system,
4. National defense and security information system,
5. Communication development information system,
6. National status or facts information system.

These six information systems are further composed of fifty-three branch systems and twenty-four subsystems. They are expected to provide management information to different levels by different organizations that are overseen by Research, Development and Evaluation Commission, Executive Yuan.

FUTURE OUTLOOK

Several important issues must be addressed in developing effective information services to the Chinese community: (1) A network to serve information seekers is needed to support national development and it requires preliminary planning to develop an efficient and effective system throughout the Island. Problems to be confronted are more of a technically-oriented telecommunication nature and the cooperative efforts among institutions. (2) An integrated system for library/information services is needed, with overall, comprehensive and coordinated planning efforts. (3) To facilitate information interchange, various standards such as interchange codes and a machine readable cataloging format, thesauri, commands, and protocols are of absolute necessity. (4) Selection of proper hardware is extremely important in order to avoid constant change of equipment, and finally, (5) Technical personnel training is crucial to the success of systems. Measures have been taken in this regard already such as the newly-formed Working Group on Networking, the study on national information policy, the adoption of Chinese Character Code for information Interchange (CCCII) as national standard, the consolidation of MARC formats, and the restructuring of library/information educational curricula and system.

NOTE

1. Tzu Hsun Kung Yeh Ts'e Chin Hui Pien 資訊工業策進會 編 [Institute for the Information Industry, ed.], *Chung Hua Min Kuo Ch'i Shih I Nien Tzu Hsun Kung Yeh Nien Chien 中華民國七十一年資訊工業年鑑 [Information Industry Yearbook of the Republic of China, 1982]* (Taipei: Institute for the Information Industry, 1982).

Reprint of the paper presented at the 46th ASIS annual meeting, Washington, D.C. U.S.A., October 2, 1983.

10

The Challenges of Library Automation

ABSTRACT

This paper outlines the challenges of library automation in general and those confronting the libraries in the East Asian countries in particular by tracing the causes that accelerated library automation. The challenges elicitied by human (sociological), technological, policy and standards issues are presented with concluding remarks for deliberations. National information policies and some international guidelines are suggested to be the foundation on which efficient and effective library automation should be built.

INTRODUCTION

The factors accelerating library automation are usually attributed to the following:

1. The needs generated by information explosion,
2. Increasing availability, sophistication, and price declination of computers,
3. Demand for better information services, and
4. The need for resources sharing, e.g. information resources, financial resources, and human resources.

In the mid 70's, libraries in the Far East also saw a real need for computer application for libraries due to these causes. However, in this area, some of these factors have played more important roles than others. All developing or under-developed countries are eager to build up and reinforce their national power by being fully and efficiently informed. East Asian countries, though some of them are already developed, are even more conscious of the power of information.

The need to improve library services in the Orient is more evident than in countries in the West, because most libraries were inadequate in organizing materials and in providing services. The old misconception of the library as a warehouse of books and a study hall or a place to read, in addition to the inefficient bibliographic tools and unindexed publications, have handicapped the proper development of libraries.

When education is popularized in the East Asian countries, new ways of learning, self-education, continuing-education, and independent studies have led people to feel the importance of library resources and to appreciate the efficient services that libraries should provide. All of these invite people to explore the best and the fastest possible ways to solve the above mentioned problems. Computers thus come into the scene.

In addition to the above factors, the built-in complexities of the East Asian languages, especially in the case of the Chinese language, have been a real challenge confronting computer technology and its application for libraries. The complexity and heterogeneity of the Chinese library materials and operations were used as a means for experimentation on the processing of non-Roman scripts. With the magnitude of characters that the Chinese libraries need in order to process data, librarians, linguists, and computer scientists in China attempted to find some answers through computer applications for Chinese libraries.

Library automation has thus been elicited in this part of the world. However, there are numerous challenges confronting us. Some of the observations on this topic that I am going to share with you may be no longer true in some countries, but they are still evident in many cases.

CHALLENGES OF LIBRARY AUTOMATION

Human Factors

1. Librarians' insufficiency in technical know-how and system concept:
   Most librarians, being oriented in the humanities and social sciences, have little background in computer technology. Librarians are usually not knowledgeable enough to illustrate or quantify their needs in order to make the system analysis and specification writing feasible. Our needs and requirements must be identified in order to utilize computer application for any type of operation. Regretfully, most librarians are unable to do that very well.
2. The fear of replacement:
   Certain librarians resist library automation because of a false conception they are afraid of being replaced by machines and as a result they are resisting against it.
3. The technique to find out the information seekers' needs, how the readers express their needs, and the ways to fulfill their needs through "user-friendly" products.

Reference service has always been a weakness of the libraries in the Eastern hemisphere. In the past the automated systems were merely mechanization of manual process, or rather, they were designed chiefly for bibliographic and/or management purposes.

In recent years, more emphasis is placed on how to cater to readers' informational needs; library automation is to provide the substance of information itself in addition to bibliographic information.

Library automation aims at "user-friendly" products. For example, the best on-line catalog is designed to be in a dialogue mode. It depends on the librarians to master the skill of question negotiating in order to ascertain what the readers really want and how they want it so that enough materials can be documented for the production of a real "user-friendly" facility. How to get the real essence of the inquiry, how to analyze the real needs of the inquirers, and how to present "user-friendly" systems seem to be a real challenge as well.

Issues of Standards

In processing library materials, we need standards such as cataloging rules, thesauri, subject headings, standard terminologies or names in the form of authority file. To process library materials with computers, there are more standards with which to be concerned: the MARC formats, character set, and indexing methodologies, etc. Not only should we think in terms of national use but also in terms of conforming with international standards. Fortunately, most of these have already been established. However, certain concerns of inconsistencies still exist: a) within one country, there are instances of several different character sets and different MARC formats; b) the failure to register with national and international standards organizations; and c) the magnitude of Chinese indexing methods.

Technological Factors

1. In the East Asian countries, not only should we think how we handle materials of our own languages, we have to incorporate resources of Roman-language as well. The magnitude of library materials in various different languages and the various library operational needs call for a piece of all-purpose hardware and a multi-function software package which are hard to find.
   (1) The developed packages for Western library automation, such as DOBIS and various other commercial packages developed by vendors, cannot be readily adopted by libraries in the East Asian countries. As a result, we cannot avoid wheel inventing; individual libraries try

to explore on their own to devise some systems by cooperating with computer companies or venders.

Because library and information centers are the minor computer users, none of such cooperative ventures have successfully produced any "all-purpose" hardware with "multi-function" software packages yet. None of the commercial firms would want to cater to a relatively smaller-user group with large investments.

(2) When libraries develop software on an existing piece of equipment for their own use, these packages are usually developed by programmers who have little knowledge of library requirements, standards, operations, and services. Librarians are not knowledgeable enough to convey to them all the library needs. As a result, the hardware they use and software they produce are usually neither free of problems nor practical.

2. While we are concentrating on the possibility of an integrated system (integrating methods to handle all languages materials and all operations of the library) in an efficient networking setting for the purpose of economics, efficiency and resources sharing, we are confronted with a new challenge of the advancement of computer technology.

   For the past decade, the libraries in East Asian countries hope to develop some kind of networking, similar to that of OCLC, RLIN or WLN. Before we are able to implement this, new technological products are announced every day. Before an application is fully developed, new computer technology appears again. For example, the super main-frame computer is in the threshold; a revolutionary class of microcomputer rises. Microcomputers are much cheaper, yet they tend to be increasingly more powerful everyday. However, they have to depend on a network for communication purposes. A microcomputer can be used as an intelligent terminal of the main computing facilities for networking and sharing purposes. At the same time, some of the library functions can be implemented on micro-computers to keep its autonomy.

The individualized micro-computer application undoubtedly can be designed to gear to the unique needs of the libraries. Such individuality will also lead to heterogeneous applications with a possible danger of too much individuality. Being relatively low in price, it is a more cost-effective means for library automation.

Library automation is not an inexpensive venture. In comparison with the performance and end result, it may be cost effective. However, the investment is high, the maintenance is also an overhead. Assessing the needs, planning, and evaluation are undoubtedly necessary to make library automation a blessing instead of a disaster.

3. Some kind of workable national and international information policies might help us to meet these challenges. Most of the countries have not yet explored the importance of this basic document.

Concluding Remarks

In view of the many challenges confronting us, I believe that for the East Asian countries, the basic solution lies in a workable national information policy and some international information guidelines which should address all important information issues.

Some of these issues are brought to your attention here for your consideration for the purpose of developing some necessary mechanisms to meet the above mentioned challenges:

1. Due to the fact that libraries belong to a small-user group of computer facilities, and little effort can be expected of the computer or software manufacturers to meet our needs, should library automation be a government-sponsored,

non-profit project in the East Asian countries? Should the government invest in the development of a more flexible and total system to be adoptable by all users? Or should the national library be responsible for bibliographic control only, and let the individual libraries pursue their individual management applications by using microcomputers? In other words, how should we proceed to achieve "... a state of dynaimc equilibrium between these two seemingly disparate sets of circumstances," as suggested by Dr. Davis and Dr. Lundeen?

2. Ways to advocate computer literacy through formal school education or continuing education? Ways to provide librarians with basic knowledge or computers by systematic retraining?
3. How can a better integrated library and information science curriculum be designed for librarians and information providers? Should such courses as library automation be integrated into all courses of technical and public services in library schools?
4. In preparing to provide better library services through automation, should some basic problems inherent in our publications be solved first? Should there be a national effort in indexing all important past reference materials and in requiring all publications to provide indexes and abstracts?
5. Should there be a special effort in standardizing terms, translations, and use of words, and in compling them into thesauri as basic tools for automation?
6. Cross references of indexing methods have been provided by the CCCII Working Group. Should there be continuous effort in this respect?
7. How can such issues of copyright and the protection of intellectual property be properly addressed?
8. Should we establish a regional professional association to

coordinate matters and enhance communication concerning library automation in this ares? Ultimately, how can libraries in the East Asian countries which share the same problems and have the same aspirations to cooperate efficiently in facing the challenges of library automation?

REFERENCES

1. Gullman, Peter, and Peniston, Silvina. *Library Automation: A Current Review*. London: ASLIB, 1984.
2. International Cooperation in Chinese Bibliographic Automation: Papers Presented at a Conference Held at the Australian National University, 29 August – 1 September 1982, Challenges.
3. Lanham, Richard. "The Library of the Future." In *Library Automation Handbook*. Chicago: ALA, 1982.
4. National Academy of Sciences, Washington, D.C. Computer Science and Engineering Board. Information Systems Panel ed. *Libraries and Information Technology: A National System Challenges*. Washington, D.C.: National Academy of Sciences, 1972.
5. Lundeen, Gerald W. and Davis, Charles H. "Library Automation." In *Annual Review of Information Sciences and Technology*, vol. 19. Edited by Williams, Martha. White Plains, N.Y.: Knowledge Industry Publications, 1983. (pp. 161-186).
6. Matthews, Joseph R., Lawrence, Gary S. and Ferguson, Douglas K. *Using On-line Catalogs*. N.Y.: Neal-Schuman Publishers, 1983.
7. The Staff of the Domestic Council Committee on the Right of Privacy, ed. *National Information Policy: Report to the President of the United States.* Washington D.C.: National Commission on Libraries and Information Science, 1976.
8. Overmyer, LaVahn. "Deus Ex Machina." In *Introduction to Library Science*, edited by Jesse Shera. Littleton, Colorado: Libraries Unlimited, 1976. (pp. 80-106).
9. Salton G. "On the Development of Libraries and Information Centers." *Library Journal* (15 October 1980): 3433-3442.

Reprinted with permission from *The Proceedings of the Second Asian-Pacific Conference on Library Science*, 20-24 May 1985, Seoul. Seoul, Korea: Cultural and Social Center for the Asian and Pacific Region, and Central National Library, Republic of Korea, c1985. (pp. 218-223).

11

New Technology and Information Services in Taiwan, ROC

ABSTRACT

This paper presents the state-of-art on the technological applications for library and information services in the ROC on Taiwan. A brief description of the overall developments, pertinent standards, various computer-aided information services, and networks are reported. Certain issues and problems experienced by Chinese library/information practitioners are also pointed out.

INTRODUCTION

The importance of information industry and information services has been universally and unaminously recognized; information is considered indispensable for all endeavors. Information industry has become one of the major enterprises instrumental to the overall modernization and national development for the ROC on Taiwan in the last decade. It has been identified as one of the important strategies creating the "Taiwan Miracle."[1]

Increasing number of computer hardwares were manufactured and exported in the past ten years. In 1981, the export value of computer hardware here was US$110 million, in 1982, US$160 million, in 1985, US$1,222 million, US$2,071 million in 1986,

US$5,000 million's worth in 1988, US$5,245 million worth of products exported in 1989 and US$5,873 million worth of computer exported in 1990. A remarkable growth of 52 times in ten years. A total of 10,287 sets of computers were installed in various organizations in Taiwan by June of 1990, and in 1991 the total amount of computers installed reached 11,897 sets. A growth rate of 15.9% is seen.[2]

In the early 1960s, government agencies started using computers for data processing and office automation, such as tax administration, the national defense administration, and budgeting/auditing administration, etc. Information services have also been given due attention. With the purpose of integrating planning, the Government organized a special group to study various issues and completed a preliminary blueprint for national information system which include general administrative information system, economic information system, national security information system, communication information system and scientific and technological information system to be developed by the pertinent government agencies. Library information system has been incorporated into the scientific and technological information module to be coordinated and developed by the Ministry of Education and the National Science Council.

Several national development plans have exerted direct impacts upon the development of library/information services. The 12th National Development Projects announced in 1978 ushered the Cultural Construction Program which promoted the establishment of cultural centers, county and town libraries, and in turn enhanced library/information services all over the island. The recently inaugurated Six-year National Development Plan will further accelerate more programs for the development of computer applications for library/information services. For example, NT$1,800,000,000 (the equivalent of US$72,000,000) is approved for the National Central Library's various projects which includes almost NT$810,700,000 (US$32,500,000) for its computer application projects. Another NT$1,384,350,000 (equalivant of US$55,375,000) has been estimated for library automation at the Taiwan Branch of the National Central Library.[3]

EXPERIMENTS OF COMPUTER APPLICATIONS FOR LIBRARY IN INFORMATION SERVICES (1970 ~ 1980)

Computer applications for library/information services initiated in the early 1970s were experimented on the compilation of union lists, production of catalog cards, acquisition, serial control, and creation of bibliographic databases. Facilitated by better international communication system made available by the Universal Database Access Service (UDAS), National Taiwan Normal University Library introduced ORBIT and DIALOG into Taipei in 1979. Various applications made in the first decade are stated in the following table:[4]

Date	Organization	System Name	Contents	Hardware
1973	Science and Technology Information Center, NSC	PISS	Bibliographic database of periodical literature	IBM 370/135
1975	National Taiwan Normal University	ACCI	Acquisition, Cataloging & Circulation	Wang MVP 2200
1975	National Taiwan University	Demonstration	Information storage and retrieval	Wang MVP 2200
1975	Chung-shan Institute of Science	CLIS	Cataloging cards; new accession List	IBM 370/135
1977	Tamkang College of Arts and Science		Serial Control	IBM 370/148
1978	National Taiwan Normal University	CERIS	Database of Educational Information	Perkin Elmer 3220
1979	Agricultural Science Information Center	MISAST	Personnel Database	Perkin Elmer
1979	Chung-shan Institute of Science	CLIS	Serial Control Acquisition Control	IBM 370/138
1979	National Central Library	National Union List of Serials	Bibliographic database	Wang VS2200

1979	Industrial Technology Research Institute	Browsing MARK III Database Generation System	Bibliographic database	PDP11/34
1980	Industrial Technology Research Institute	MIS	Bibliographic Database	IBM 3031
1980	Freedom Council Information Center	FCIA	ROC Information database	Wang MVP2200

STANDARDS

In general, the above experiments of computer applications for library/information services have been successful. They were somewhat handicapped by lack of integrated planning, lack of standards and inadequate use of computer as a processing tool. Instead, in most cases, it was primarily used as a printing device. The effectiveness of library automation was not fully utilized at the time.

It came to my notice that unless we have the following tools completely ready, we could not fully be benefited by the expected efficiency of computer applications for library and information services – the efficient bibliographic control and the effective use of information resulting in the ultimate library objective of resources sharing. My proposal made to National Central Library and to the Library Association was kindly accepted and duly implemented. The proposal suggested the formulation of pertinent standards/rules to be consistent with pertinent international standards:

1. The formulation of Chinese MARC (Machine Readable Cataloging) Format,
2. The revision of Chinese Cataloging Rules to be consist with AACR2 (Anglo-American Cataloging Rules II),
3. The adoption of ISBN (International Standard Book Number) and ISSN (International Standard Serial Number),
4. The formulation of standard subject headings.

Chinese MARC Format

The Library Association of China and the National Central

Library jointly organized the Committee on Library Automation Planning in April 1980 to study, formulate, promote and execute the above proposed projects. The first edition of Chinese MARC format (using UNIMARC as reference) was published in January of 1982; Chinese MARC Format has been completed for monographs, analysis of periodical literature and authority files etc.[5] With the exception of the project of subject headings, all of the proposed standards have been completed. Some of them, such as Chinese MARC Format is under going revision and updating to meet the needs prevailed.

Standard Character Set

In addition to the above standards, the most important one was the standard Chinese Character Code for Information Interchange (CCCII). The need for such a character Code was first mentioned to me by Mrs. H. Avram of the Library of Congress and was again expressed by Dr. John Haeger who was sent by the American Council of Learned Societies to visit Taipei exploring the possibility of a standard character set for Chinese characters used by Chinese, Japanese and Korean. To meet the urgent national and international needs, Chinese Character Code for Information Interchange based on ISO 646 and ISO 2022 was devised since 1978.[6] Up to 1992, this set, covering 59,832 characters, has been successfully adopted by the Library of Congress and RLIN first under the name of REACC and later of EACC. Several international conferences and seminars, such as International Conference on Chinese Library Automation (February 1981), Conference on International Cooperation in Chinese Bibliographic Cooperation (August 1982). A symposium conducted at ASIS Annual conference (October 1982) have all been conducted specially to discuss Chinese library automation related issues. The structure of this character set is described in Figure 1.

AUTOMATED LIBRARY/INFORMATION SYSTEMS

Computer applications for library/information services have been proceeded with great interest on this island. This phenomenon is evidenced by the following statistics resulted from two surveys.

In 1988, a survey indicated that out of the sixty four libraries surveyed, forty six libraries responded. Certain operations of thirty five libraries have either been automated or planned to automate.[7]

The Ministry of Education reported in 1990 that out of two hundred sixty libraries surveyed, sixty nine libraries (26.54%) did not have plans for automation, one hundred ninety one libraries (73.64%) completed library automation or were in planning stage.[8]

MAJOR ENDEAVORS

National Central Library

In 1979, the National Central Library (NCL) experimented its first automated library system by building up the bibliographic database of national union list of serials with Wang VS 2200. It expanded the hardware and software to offer NCL Automated Information Service (NCLAIS). Up to June 1992, the following databases consisted a total of 644,899 bibliographic records:[9]

1. Index to Chinese periodical literature (273, 757 records),
2. Index to Chinese Gazettes (65,420 records),
3. Monographs (287,811 records),
4. Chinese rare books (17,911 records).

NCLAIS offers the following services

1. Computer-produced items including catalog cards, *Catalog of Books Published in the ROC*, *Index to Periodical Literature, Index to Chinese Official Gazattes, Catalog of Administrative Government Publications, National Union list of Chinese Periodicals, and the Union Catalog of Western Periodicals of*

the Humanities and Social Sciences.

2. Online information retrieval system for the above mentioned databases. All information is accessible through the following access points: title, author, subject headings, ISBN, ISSN, CODEN, Chinese Classification numbers and call numbers, etc.
3. Online information retrieval services to search databases provided by DIALOG, MDC, and OCLC.
4. CD-ROMs of databases.
5. Housekeeping functions of acquisition cataloging, serial control, readers control, statistics, etc.
6. OPAC for its collection.

The National Central Library, being the library of libraries in Taiwan, started its National Bibliographic Information Center which offers online cooperative cataloging – Chinese CATSS (Chinese Cataloging Support System) in 1988 by installing Tandem with the assistance of UTLAS and SYS COM Co. The online cooperative cataloging with sixteen university and college libraries was officially operated on October 30, 1981. Member libraries include National Chengchi University, National Cheng Kung University, National Chiao Tung University, National Chung Cheng University, National Chung Hsing University, National Chinghua University, National Kaohsiung Normal University, National Institute of Arts, National Taiwan Institute of Technology, National Taiwan Normal University, National Taiwan University, National Yangming Medical College, and National Ocean University, etc.

This database covers 170,449 pieces of CIP bibliographic records, 184,241 records of Chinese publications, and 3,949 bibliographic records provided by participating libraries.

It also provides CD-ROM for the 100,000 bibliographic records of books, serials, maps, and microforms collected during

1980 and December of 1989. the CD-ROM of the *Index to Chinese Periodical Literature* is also made available by a system designed by the Industrial Technology Research Institute which successfully presented the first Chinese CD-ROM on April 15, 1991. It covers 157,360 articles published in 1,161 Chinese periodicals from March 1972 to September 1980.[10]

The hardware used by NCL for library automation is rather diversified:

1. WANG VS 100, 1 CPU (16F), 4MB, Wang VS 2200, WANG VS 8460 – 32, 16MB, 3 (314 MB) disks, 3 (288 MB) disks, and 3 (629 MB) disks, 1 (1 GB) disk, 2 (1.3 GB) disks 23 sets of 5425C terminals, 5 sets of Wang (280) PC, 6 sets of Wang (8280) PC. 6 sets of Wang (8420) PC, 1 (9580) printer, 11 (M4024) printers and one Laser (0 : { -20) printer, 1 tape drive (WANG 2209V)
2. Tandem TXP system. 2 Tandem CPU with 4 MB memory each, 6 (512 MB) disks, 2 LP170 printers, 49 (6557) workstations, 27 (P70, 4023) printers and one tape driver.
3. PDP-11/73 CPU with 2MB memory 2 (140 MB) disks, 4 Japanese and Korean terminals and four line printers used for its Japanese and Korean Collections.
4. IBM PC/AT for CD-ROM (640 KB RAM; MS DOS 3.3; hard disk (40 MB).

In addition, personal computers are used for CD-ROMs to search the databases provided by STICNET, to use the video disk provided by Ministry of Communication on international trade, economic and financial news, and databases on news clippings provided by the Central News Agency.

Legislative Yuan

Being the Congress, Legislative Yuan pays attention to the prompt acquisition of accurate and up-to-date information as it is of great importance to the legislators in making legislative decisions. In 1981, at the Legislative Yuan's 68th session, the legislators expressed their strong desire for computer-based legislative information services. In January 1984, Committee on Computerized Information Management was organized to initiate feasibility studies and plans. After careful study and evaluation, in October of 1987, digital system was installed for the Legislative Information System (LEGISIS). During the past five years, great strides have been made; as of May 1992, six systems, having been completed and being made available through the use of WAN (Wide Area Network) are:[11]

1. Legislative Electronic Bulletin Board – providing information on meetings, important events in Taiwan, and decisions made by the Legislative Yuan.
2. Interpellation System – searchable with 14 access points such as date, subject, name, etc.
3. Chinese Legal Information Service – providing full text of the laws of the ROC. Titles, texts, subjects, related articles, enacting dates, amending dates, etc. are given.
4. Chinese Laws Amendments Information System – providing codes amended by the Legislative Yuan since 1970 which was the year when the Central Codes Standard was promulgated.
5. Legislative Literature Information System – database of periodical articles and research papers published since 1985 in the field of laws, politics, economics, finances, public administration and technical education, accessible with the following access points: subject, keywords, author, article title and journal title.

6. Legislative News Information System – providing new clippings of 16 local daily and newspapers pertaining to important news.

   The Legislative Information Services Center gets access to some 500 databases made available by DIALOG and LEXIS/NEXIS. It also provides DIAL ORDER downloading. Its cataloging, OPAC and serial control modules are also implemented on VAX. Its hardware configurations are as follows :

   VAX 8530 (one CPU, 80 MB memory)
   Micro VAXII (for backups)
   Hard disks: SA 600, SA 482, and three RASI.
   Tape drivers : TA 79 and TA 81
   Two intelligent disk controllers, HSC 70
   124 terminals and workstations

Microcomputers are used for the following two systems:

1. Congressional Diplomats Information System – Keeping a record of foreigners visiting the Legislative Yuan, providing information on the date of visit, number of visitors, and activities, etc.
2. LEGISIS Thesaurus System – providing both Chinese and English indexing terms.

Agricultural Science Information Center

With the mission to gather, organize and provide agricultural science and technology information, and to set up an agricultural information system for the promotion of research endearvors of the nation's agricultural community, the Agricultural Science Information Center, established in 1977, has devoted much efforts to computer applications. The Agricultural Science and Technology Information Management System (ASTIMS), including the following four databases is searchable on-line:[12]

1. Files on Agricultural Science and Technology Thesaurus (AGRI-THESAURUS) – consisting of 20,115 Chinese terms and 20,521 English terms, displaying synonyms, narrow terms, broad terms and related terms; being constantly updated.
2. Files on Agricultural Science and Technology Personnel (FASTEP) covers 16,073 professionals specializing in agriculture, forestry, fishery, husbandry and food science, working in various administrative, educational, research institutions, and public or private enterprises. There are fifty-nine access points: name, birth date, graduating year, degree, dissertation contents, major, office, position, job description, language, examinations taken, examination year, examination category, special professional training, memberships, patent content, patent year, honors, paper presentation and language used in conferences etc.
3. Files on Agricultural Science and Technology Project (FASTEJ) – providing information on 24,999 research projects supported by the Commission on Agricultural Development. The access points include project number, project leader, project executors, persons responsible for the project, experts, cooperating agency, keywords, budget category, file number, classification, year, and source of

budget. This database is useful in evaluation, project control, follow-ups and auditing, and research to be continued.

4. Files on Agricultural Science and Technology Literature (FASTEL) – covering all research reports. Periodical articles, conference papers, theses/dissertations, conference proceedings and papers since 1980. They are accessible by using database number, subjects, keywords, authors, publication source, dates, classification name and number, holding library/unit, research report number, serial number, project number, ISSN and ISBN. The system is implemented on Prime 750.

The Center also provides on line retrieving service to 589 databases provided by DIALOG, ORBIT, BRS, ESA-IRS, STN, DIMDI, FOODLINE.

The Center's Library Automation System, consisting of bibliographic subsystem, authority control subsystem, serial control system, and acquisition subsystem, provides excellent technical services.

In addition, the Center recently acquires an image processing system from Filenet for the purpose of storing in the optical disks the texts of the materials mentioned in the above databases. The new endeavor will provide even more efficient services to its patrons after it is hooked up with VAX 6420 with RS 232 port.

The Center is in the transition period at the moment, it tries to convert their hardware from Prime 750 (4 MB) to VAX 6420 (2 CPU, 96 MB).

National Science and Technology Information Center, National Science Council

Being one of the pioneers in computer applications for library and information services, it has created a unique service offering access to the following 12 domestic and 6 international databases through its STICNET (Science Technology Information Center

Network) since 1988:[13]

Union List of Non-Chinese Sci-Tech Serials in the ROC;
Union Catalog of Non-Chinese Sci-Tech Books in the ROC;
Sci-Tech Journal Articles of the ROC;
Humanities and Social Sciences Journal Articles of the ROC;
Ongoing Research Projects of the ROC;
Sci-Tech Research Reports of the ROC;
Sci-Tech Briefs;
National Science Council Awarded Research Papers Abstracts;
Conference Papers of Academic Societies in the ROC;
Abstracts of Doctoral Dissertations and Index of Masters' Theses;
Index of Domestic Sci-Tech Conferences and Seminars;
Technical Reports of the ITRI;
BIOSIS PREVIEWS; CA SEARCH; COMPENDEX; ERIC; INSPEC; NTIS; SPORT; DAO.

STICNET, based on a retrieving software named STATUS, was developed with Wang Laboratories and Computer Power Company. It is implemented on Wang 7150 computers (36 MB CPU; hard disk of 9 GB). Twenty-six workstations and 24 IPCs are available for input and retrieval at the Center. It is available to patrons in three different manners depending on user environment: PC dial up, Wang host computer facilities or through Taiwan Academic Network.

user environment	PC (Dial Up) PC	Wang PC	Host (Wang)	TANET
hardware	Serial port RS 282 Modem 1200bps+ Telephone	Serial port S282 Modem 1200bps+ telephone Wang Chinese card or WACO card	Modem leased line or X25 port 6650 communication control device	PC / AT compatible file server which contains Ethernet card
software	PCLink	Wang VS Link MS Dos 3.3 ET.COM V1.52+	WSN (Wang network) Transport Module	MS DOS V3.0 ET Chinese v1.60 Simulate software of Wang Terminal

Tamkang University

Based on the DOBIS/LIBIS, the Tamkang Automated Library Integrated System (TALIS), developed in cooperation with IBM, implemented on IBM 4381/M11 has been officially and efficiently in operation since November 1986.[14]

This integrated library automation system includes cataloging, OPAC, acquisition, serial control, circulation, interlibrary loan, etc. In addition to electronic mail system, it has recently added three other functions proven to be useful to the community: electronic bulletin board (announcements of new accessions, library hours, circulation regulations, etc.), ranking of books, and library statistics.

Academia Sinica

Being the highest ranking research institute in Taiwan, it has devoted much effort to the research on automated library services and on-line retrieving techniques. Dr. Hsieh Ching-chun has made great contributions to the design of CCCII and full-text databases-Full Text Database for Chinese History, Chinese Electronic Dictionary , Database of Ancient Tombs, Household Registers During the Period of 1906-1947, Land Reports, Classifications of

Chinese Verbs for Parsing, Masters' Theses Database, Ming/Ch'ing Dynasties Archival Materials Database, Academia Sinica Researchers' Biographical Materials and Works Database, etc.[15]

As far as library automation at the Academy is concerned, they tried URICA system for two years and five months.[16] It has decided to install a new system called INNOPAC which is developed by Innovative Interfaces Incorporated to be also installed by eight other college and university libraries: Chung Cheng University, National Kaoshiung Normal University, National Chengchi University, National Taiwan Normal University, National Taiwan University, National Yangming Medical College, and Pingtung Normal College. The Academy has also tried to transfer the computer multi-media technology from the Industrial Technology Research Institute to produce a multimedia presentation of its Computer Center in the near future.[17]

Recent survey indicated that academic and research libraries show much interest in applying new technologies to library/information services. News agencies and newspapers are particularly keen in exploring various means to upgrade their news collecting functions. Almost all the large newspaper publishers use computer facilities for production of their papers. The most sophisticated and modern facilities are used by United Daily News.

Central News Agency

Central News Agency has provided a special computer-aided information retrieving service with a database of news clippings collected from more than forty international and domestic Chinese newspapers[18]. The newsclippings database covers various subjects ranging from politics, foreign affairs, international relations, business, society, science and technology, etc. They are classified into 8,720 categories. In addition to news, special reports, editorials, special interviews, major events, and statistics are included. The system is made available with the following facilities: PC #80386 (8 MB/MM)

1.2 GB of hard disk, SCSI interface card, Novell network card.

For the purpose of supplying information on China mainland, the Central News Agency developed Mainland News Computer Information Retrieving System with image processing technique. There are sixty thousand pieces of newsclippings ready for retrieving with sixteen access points such as subjects, pagination, descriptors, events, names of person, geographic names, names of association/society, dates and keywords. Boolean logic is fully applied to information retrieval of this database.

DATABASES, CD-ROM AND NETWORKS

Reported by *Directory of Electronic Databases in the Republic of China 1992*, in addition to the database made available through tele-communication or CD-ROM, many databases of various subjects matters and of various nature (bibliographic, numerical, full text or directory) are either built or provided by various public or private organizations.[18]

Two hundred twenty-nine databases are available as follows :

Type	Domestic (Chinese)	Foreign (English)	Sub-total
Credit	1	1	2
Business	36	6	42
Market	31	2	33
News	6	4	10
Information	17	1	18
Real Estates	3	0	3
Transportation	5	2	7
Laws	10	0	10
Travel	18	0	18
Science	37	38	75
Others	11	0	11
Total	175	54	229

CD-ROM was officially introduced to this area in 1987 when Bibliofile was brought in to assist the cataloging work of books in Western languages. Within a year, Bibliofile was used by seventeen academic and research libraries. Out of the 43 universities subsidized by the National Science Council to purchase books and periodicals, 37 libraries have acquired CD-ROMs which covered 54 different subjects.[19] Some databases such as Dissertation Abstracts Ondisc, LISA, Sociofile, ERIC, Books in Print, MEDLINE, ABI/INFORM, Social Science Citation Index, Science Citation Index, OCLC CAT CD 450 and COMPENDEX available in CD-ROM format are popularly used. Facilitated by LAN, users find them very convenient even though some of the information retrieved may not be up-to-date. As mentioned above, National Central Library provides the first Chinese CD-ROM for its book collections and *Index to Chinese Periodical Literature* which is considered a big step forward in technological applications.[20]

Information accessibility is greatly enhanced by various networks developed. Networks are instrumental to resources sharing which is the ultimate objective of library automation.

Some of the above mentioned databases are searchable on line through tele-communication/networks. Tymnet and Telenet were connected to our telephone company in December 1979, the dial up service is called Universal Database Access Service (UDAS). DIALOG, ORBIT and BRS are available through them. Starting from 1984, packet switching equipments enabled us to be connected with the following:

AUSTPAC, MIDAS-Australia;	DSC-Brussels;
DATEX-P, RADIO -Austria;	DATAPAC, GLOBDAT, CNCP-Canada;
TRASPAC, NTI-France;	INTELPAK, DATAPAC-Hongkong;
VENUS-P, DDX-P -Japan;	DNS-Korea;
LUXPAC-Luxemburg;	DATANETI, DABAS-The Netherlands;
TELEPA-Singapore;	TIDA, IBERPAC-Spain;

DATAPAC, DATAC-Switzerland IPSS, PSS-United Kingdom;
UDTS, BBS, LSDS, Tymnet, Telnet, Autonet, Uninet and CNS-United States.

BITNET (Because It's Time Network), brought in by the Ministry of Education in 1987, laid a solid foundation for TANet (Taiwan Academic Network) which is also now connected with Internet (Figure 2). TANet, being an inter-campus network connecting colleges and universities domestically and communicating with more than 5,000 networks in 35 countries all over the world supports teaching and research, promotes information sharing, facilitates electronic mails and file transfer.[21] With such a fine communication environment created by this open systems, we look forward to much improved library/information service in the near future. The entire library and information community is very enthusiastic in developing efficient networks. Studies have been conducted with recommendations to set up National Library/Information Network.[22]

PROBLEMS AND ISSUES

In the past, we experienced the following problems:

1. Lack of overall planning, most libraries started individual planning. Each library planned independently on its own without seriously considering the objective of resources sharing aimed by library automation. Each module of computer application for library/information services within the library was planned as an independent unit by itself. Diversified equipments in one institution or in several institutions of the same nature handicapped coordinated efforts.
2. Lack of consensus and the will to cooperate among libraries. Each library wanted to have a system better or more unique than others.

3. Lack of adequate amount of trained staff. Most librarians do not have adequate training in handling computer applications for library/information services. Computer science graduates do not understand the professional work required for librarianship.
4. Lack of authorities in supervising operations and formulating policies.
5. Redundancy of databases. As an example, let us take a look at the numerous databases of dissertation and theses which could have been consolidated.

Fortunately, we learned the hard way early, it is not too late for remedies at the present time. Several recent plans for library automations made by several libraries, the newly developed networks, and the promotion of integrated network planning, and the adopting of the same software packages seem to have indicated general awareness of the existing problems and a strong will for correct directions of future endeavors.

NOTES

1. K. T. Li, "Policy Formulation in a Dynamic Economy: The Experience of the ROC on Taiwan," First Annual K. T. Li Lecture sponsored by the Center for International Affairs, Harvard University and Center for Continuing Education, National Taiwan University, 15 October 1990.
2. Tzu Hsun Kung Yeh Ts'e Chin Hui Pien 資訊工業策進會 編 [Institute for the Information Industry, ed.], *Chung Hua Min Kuo Ch'i Shih Pa Nien Tzu Hsun Kung Yeh Nien Chien 中華民國七十八年資訊工業年鑑 [Information Industry Yearbook of the Republic of China, 1989]* (Taipei: Institute for the Information Industry, 1989), 58; Tzu Hsun Kung Yeh Ts'e Chin Hui 資訊工業策進會 [Institute for the Information Industry], *Chung Hua Min Kuo Ch'i Shih Chiu Nien Tzu Hsun Kung Yeh Nien Chien 中華民國七十九年資訊工業年鑑 [Information Industry Yearbook of the Republic of China, 1990]* (Taipei: Institute for the Information Industry, 1990), 51.
3. Kuo Chia T'u Shu Kuan Pien 國家圖書館 編 [National Central Library, ed.], *Chia Ch'iang Kuo Li Chung Yang T'u Shu Kuan Chien She Liu Nien Chi Hua 加強國立中央圖書館建設六年計畫 [Strengthening National*

Library Development: 6-Year Plan] (Taipei: National Central Library, 1992), 28–29; Kuo Chia T'u Shu Kuan T'ai Wan Fen Kuan Pien 國家圖書館台灣分館 編 [National Central Library Taiwan Branch, ed.], *Chia Ch'iang Kung Kung T'u Shu Kuan Chien She Liu Nien Chi Hua 加強公共圖書館建設六年計畫 [Strengtenhing Public Libraries 6-Year Development Plan]* (Taipei: National Central Library Taiwan Branch, 1992), 16, 29.

4. Margaret C. Fung, "Library Automation in the Republic of China," *T'u Shu Kuan Hsueh Yu Tzu Hsun K'o Hsueh 圖書館學與資訊科學 [Journal of Library & Information Science]* 6, no. 1 (April 1980): 1-6.
5. Kuo Li Chung Yang T'u Shu Kuan Chung Kuo Chi Tu Pien Mu Ko Shih Hsiu Ting Hsiao Tsu Pien 國立中央圖書館中國機讀編目格式修訂小組 編 [National Central Library Chinese MARC Format, Revision Working Group, ed.], *Chung Kuo Chi Tu Pien Mu Ko Shih 中國機讀編目格式 [Chinese MARC Format]*, 3rd ed. (Taipei: National Central Library, 1989).
6. Tzu Hsun Ying Yung Kuo Tzu Cheng Li Hsiao Tsu Pien 資訊應用國字整理小組 編 [The Chinese Character Analysis Group, ed.], *Chung Wen Tzu Hsun Chiao Huan Ma Tzu Chi 中文資訊交換碼字集 [Chinese Character Code for Information Interchange]* (Taipei: Council for Cultural Affairs, 1987); Margaret C. Fung 張鼎鍾, "Chung Wen Tzu Hsun Chiao Huan Ma Yu Chung Wen T'u Shu Tzu Tung Hua Chih Hui Ku 中文資訊交換碼與中文圖書自動化之回顧 [A Recollection on CCCII and Chinese Library Automation]," in *Kuo Tzu Cheng Li Hsia Tsu Shih Nien 國字整理小組十年 [Ten Years of Chinese Character Analysis Group]* (Taipei: Chinese Character Analysis Group, 1989), 71-75.
7. Yu-ling Cheng (organized by) 鄭玉玲 整理, T'u Shu Kuan Tzu Tung Hua Tso Yeh Kuei Hua Wei Yuan Hui (provided by) 圖書館自動化作業規劃委員會 提供 [Yu-ling Cheng and Library Automation Planning Committee], ed., "Wo Kuo T'u Shu Kuan Hsien K'uang Tiao Ch'a 我國圖書館現況調查 [An Investigation of Present Status of Automated Library Systems in the R. O. C]," *Chung Kuo T'u Shu Kuan Hsueh Hui Hui Pao 中國圖書館學會會報 [Bulletin of the Library Association of China]* 45 (December 1989): 63-80.
8. Tzu Hsun Tieh Pao Pien Chi Pu Pien 資訊諜報編輯部 編 [Editorial Committee of Information Reports, ed.], "Kuo Nei T'u Shu Kuan Tzu Tung Hua Hsien K'uang 國內圖書館自動化現況 [Current Status of Domestic Library Automation]," *Tzu Hsun Tieh Pao 資訊諜報* 6 (5 March 1992): 17-21.
9. Heng-hsiung Cheng and Chien-cheng Sung 鄭恆雄，宋建成, "Kuo Li Chung Yang T'u Shu Kuan Tzu Tung Hua Chi Shu Mu Wang Lu

Hsien K'uang Pao Kao 國立中央圖書館自動化及書目網路現況報告 [Report on the Current Status of NCL Library Automation and Bibliographic Network]," in *Kuo Li Ta Hsueh Yuan Hsiao T'u Shu Kuan Tzu Tung Hua Kuei Hua Ti Liu Tz'u Yen T'ao Hui Hui Yi Tzu Liao 國立大學院校圖書館自動化規劃第六次研討會會議資料 [Proceeding of the 6th Seminar on the Library Automation of National University Libraries]* (Taipei: National Central Library, 1992), 15-26; Nancy Ou Lan Hu 胡歐蘭, "T'u Shu Kuan Tzu Tung Hua Tso Yeh 圖書館自動化作業 [Automated Library Operations]," in *Ti Erh Tz'u Chung Hua Min Kuo T'u Shu Kuan Nien Chien 第二次中華民國圖書館年鑑 [Second Library Yearbook of the Republic of China]* (Taipei: National Central Library, 1988), 81-117.

10. Pi-chuan Wu and Mei-chen Sung 吳碧娟，宋美珍, "Wo Kuo Chi K'an Wen Hsien Chien So Hsin Mei T'i: Kuo Li Chung Yang T'u Shu Kuan Ch'i K'an Lun Wen So Yin Kuang Tieh Hsi T'ung 我國期刊文獻檢索新媒體: 國立中央圖書館期刊論文索引光碟系統 [The New Media for Chinese Periodical Article Retrieving System]," *Kuo Li Chung Yang T'u Shu Kuan Kuan K'an 國立中央圖書館館刊 [National Central Library Bulletin]* New 24, no. 2 (December 1991): 13-30; Mei-yu Shih 石美玉, "Kung Tieh Wei Tu T'i (CD-ROM) Tsai Taiwan Ko Ta T'u Shu Kuan Chih Ying Yung 光碟唯讀體 (CD-ROM) 在台灣各大學圖書館之應用 [The Application of CD-ROM in University Libraries in Taiwan]," *Chiao Yu Tzu Liao Yu T'u Shu Kuan Hsueh 教育資料與圖書館學 [Journal of Education Media and Library Science]* 28, no. 3 (Spring 1991): 331-344.

11. Karl Min Ku, "Developmental Strategies of Computerized Legislative Information Services" (Paper presented at the 58th IFLA General Conference, New Delphi, India, August 3 – September 5, 1992); Chai–hsiung Cheng 郭介恆, "Chien Chu T'u Shu Kuan Fa Hsueh Tzu Hsun Hsi T'ung 建構圖書館法學資訊系統 [Building of Legal Information Systems]," *Kuo Li Chung Yang T'u Shu Kuan Taiwan Fen Kuan Kuan K'an 國立中央圖書館台灣分館館訊 [Bulletin of the National Central Library Taiwan Branch]* 8 (1 April 1992): 15-23; Li Fa Yuan T'u Shu Kuan Tzu Liao Shih 立法院圖書館資料室 [Library and Material Center, Legislative Yuan], ed., *Li Fa Yuan Tzu Hsun Fu Wu Chien Chieh 立法院資訊服務簡介 [Brief Introduction on Information Services of the Legislative Yuan]* (n. d.); Karl Min Ku 顧敏, "Li Fa Yuan T'u Shu Tzu Hsun Fu Wu 立法院圖書資訊服務 [Library and Information Services of the Legislative Yuan]," *Yen K'ao Yueh K'an 研考月刊 [Yen K'ao Monthly]* 12, no. 9 (1977): 31-40; Karl Min Ku 顧敏, "Li Fa Yuan Tzu Hsun Hsi T'ung Te Kai Fa Ts'e Lueh 立法院資訊系統的開

發策略 [Strategies Used in Developing the Legislative Information System]," *Kuo Li Chung Yang T'u Shu Kuan Taiwan Fen Kuan Kuan Hsun 國立中央圖書館台灣分館館訊 [Bulletin of the National Central Library Taiwan Branch]* (1 April 1991): 8-14.

12. Wan-jiun Wu 吳萬鈞, "Nung Yeh K'o Hsueh Tzu Hsun Fu Wu Chung Hsin Chien Chieh 農業科學資料服務中心簡介 [Brief Introduction on the Agricultural Science Information Center]," *T'u Shu Kuan Hsueh Yu Tzu Hsun K'o Hsueh 圖書館學與資訊科學 [Journal of Library & information Science]* 17, no.1 (April 1991): 82-104.
13. *K'o Chi Ch'uan Kuo Tzu Hsun Wang Lu Shen Ch'ing Yu Fu Wu Hsien K'uang 科技全國資訊網路申請與服務現況 [National Scientific and Technical Information Network: Application and the Current Status of Service].* (Brochure); Nancy Ou Lan Hu 胡歐蘭, "T'u Shu Kuan Tzu Tung Hua Tso Yeh 圖書館自動化作業 [Automated Library Operations]," in *Ti Erh T'zu Chung Hua Min Kuo T'u Shu Kuan Nien Chien 第二次中華民國圖書館年鑑 [Second Library Yearbook of the Republic of China]* (Taipei: National Central Library, 1988), 81-117.
14. DOBIS / LIBIS / TALIS *Tan Chiang T'u Shu Kuan Tzu Tung Hua Hsi T'ung DOBIS / LIBIS / TALIS 淡江圖書館自動化系統 [Tamkang Library Automated System]*, June 1988. (Brochure).
15. Margaret C. Fung, "The Use of Source Materials Enhanced by Modern Information Technology," *T'u Shu Kuan Hsueh Yu Tzu Hsun K'o Hsueh 圖書館學與資訊科學 [Journal of Library & Information Science]* 14, no. 2 (October 1988): 165-170.
16. Shih-hsiung Tseng 曾士熊, "Chien Chieh Pen Yuan T'u Shu Kuan Yeh Wu Tzu Tung Hua Chi Hua 簡介本院圖書館業務自動化計畫 [Brief Introduction of Library Automation Plans]," *Chi Suan Chung Hsin T'ung Hsun 計算中心通訊 [Newsletter of Computing Centre]* 7, no. 19 (23 September 1991): 146-148.
17. Ya-ning Chen 陳亞寧, "INNOPAC Chien Chieh [Introduction of INNOPAC]," *Chi Suan Chung Hsin T'ung Hsun 計算中心通訊 [Newsletter of Computing Centre]* 7, no. 19 (23 September 1991): 149-151.
18. Chung Yang T'ung Hsun She Chien Pao Tzu Liao Ch'a Hsun Fu Wu Ting Kao Pan Fa 中央通訊社簡報資料查詢服務訂購辦法 [Central News Agency Newsclipping Retrieving Services: Purchase Plans]; Chung Yang She Ta Lu Hsin Wen Chi Ko Hsin Wen Tien Nao Ch'a Hsun Hsi T'ung Fu Wu Pan Fa 中央社大陸新聞及各新聞電腦查詢系統服務辦法 [Central News Agency China Mainland News and All Newspaper Information

Retrieving System].

19. Tzu Hsun Kung Yeh Ts'e Chin Hui Pien 資訊工業策進會 編 [Institute for the Information Industry, ed.], *Ching Chi Pu K'o Chi Ku Wen Shih K'o Chi Chuan An Yen Chiu Ch'en Kuo, Pa Shih Yi Nien Chung Hua Min Kuo Tien Tzu Tzu Liao K'u Ts'ung Lan 經濟部科技顧問室科技專案研究成果，八十一年中華民國電子資料庫總覽 [Ministry of Economic Affairs' Scientific and Technical Advisors' Office Special Research Result, Directory of 1992 Electronic Databases in the ROC]* (Taipei: Institute for the Information Industry, 1992).
20. Hsiu-ying Chiang 江綉瑛, "Chung Wen Shu Mu Kuang Tieh Hsi T'ung Chih She Chi Yu Chan Wang kuo Li Chung Yang T'u Shu Kuan Ching Yen 中文書目光碟系統之設計與展望國立中央圖書館經驗 [The Design and Perspectives of Chinese Bibliographic CD-ROM – The Experience of National Central Library]," *Kuo Li Chung Yang T'u Shu Kuan Kuan K'an 國立中央圖書館館刊 [National Central Library Bulletin]* New 24, no. 2 (December 1991): 3-12.
21. Fei-li Tu 涂菲莉, "Taiwan Hsueh Shu Wang Lu (TANet) Yu Internet Chih Hsien K'uang Yu Chan Wang 台灣學術網路(TANet)與Internet之現況與展望 [Current Status and Future Perspectives of TANet and Internet]," *Kuo Li Chung Yang T'u Shu Kuan Kuan K'an 國立中央圖書館館刊 [National Central Library Bulletin]* New 24, no. 2 (December 1991): 31-48; Wen-shen Chen 陳文生, "Wo Kuo Hsueh Shu Wang Lu Hsien K'uang Yu Chan Wang 我國學術網路現況與展望 [Current Status and Future Perspectives of Taiwan Academic Network]," *Chiao Yu Pu Tien Tzu Chi Suan Chung Hsin Yen Chiu Fu Wu Chien Hsun 教育部電子計算中心研究服務簡訊 [Ministry of Education, Computer Center Research and Service Bulletin]* 8106 (1991): 7-17.
22. Te-chu Lee, Shih-hsion Huang Chi Hua Chu Ch'ih 李德竹，黃世雄 計劃主持, [Lucy Te-chu Lee and Shih-hsion Huang, Project Leaders], *Cheng T'i Kuei Hua Ch'uan Kuo T'u Shu Kuan Tau Hsun Wang Lu Hsi T' ung 整體規劃全國圖書館資訊網路系統 [Integrated Planning of National Library/Information network System]* (Taipei: Chiao Yu Pu T'u Shu Kuan Shih Yeh Wei Yuan Hui, 1991); Kuo Li Chung Yan T'u Shu Kuan Fu She Tzu Hsun T'u Shu Kuan Pien 國立中央圖書館附設資訊圖書館 編 [The Information and Computing Library of the National Central Library, ed.], *Tzu Hsun Wang Fu Wu Chuan T'i Chiang Tso 資訊網服務專題講座 [Special Lectures on the Service of Information Networks]* (Taipei: National Central Library, 1992).

Figure 1 Structure of the Three Dimensional 94×94×94 Coding Space

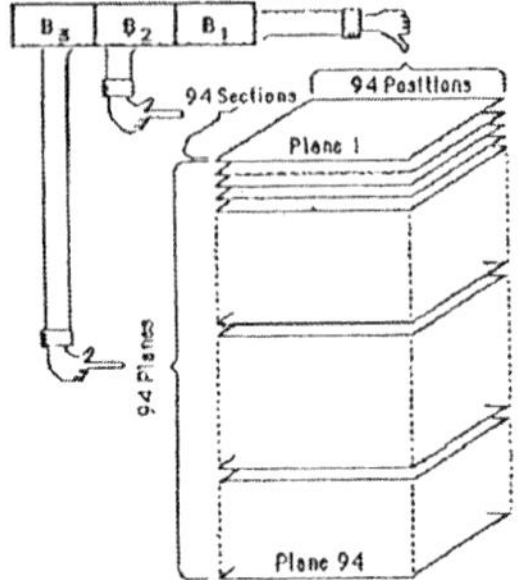

Figure 6-4 Structure and Allocation of *CCCII's* 16 *Layers*

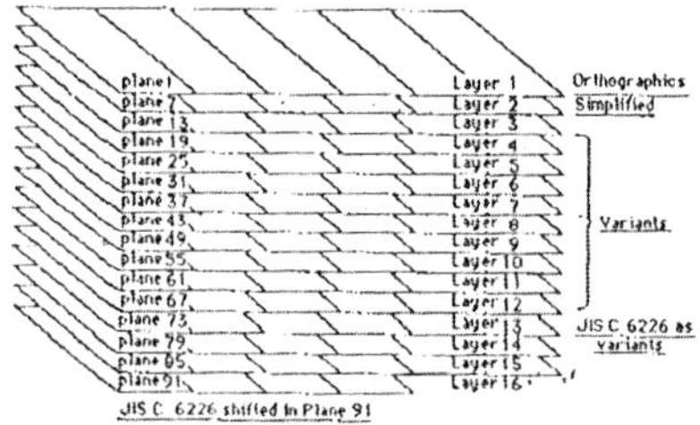

Figure 6-5 The Structure of the First 15 *Sections* in *Layer* 1

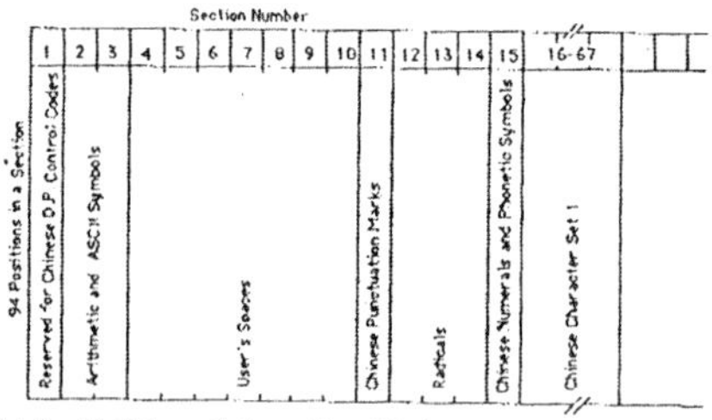

Figure 6-6 Relationship Between *Orthographic* and *Variants*

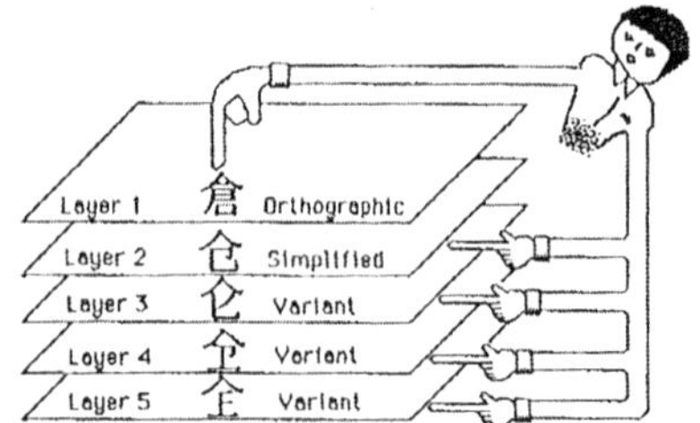

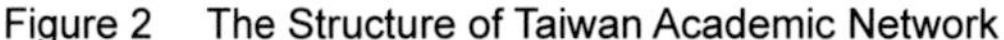
Figure 2 The Structure of Taiwan Academic Network

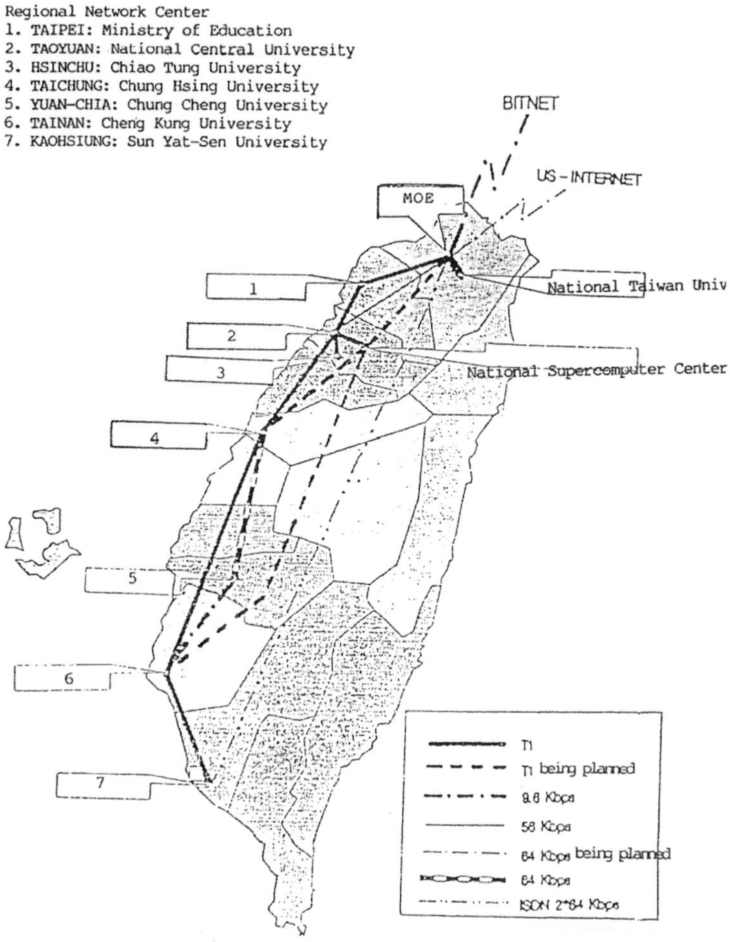

Reprinted with permission from *The Proceedings of NIT '92: 5th International Conference on New Information Technology for Library & Information Professionals, Educational Media Specialists & Technologists*, 30 November – 2 December 1992, Hong Kong University of Science & Technology, Kowloon, Hong Kong; edited by Ching-chih Chen. Newton, MA: MicroUse Information, 1992. (pp. 141-156).

Part III

DATABASES
INFORMATION SYSTEMS/
SERVICES

12

The Chinese Educational Resources Information System-A Case Report

ABSTRACT

This paper introduces the Chinese Educational Resources Information System – the first computerized Chinese bibliographic database and reference services developed by the National Taiwan Normal University Library in the Republic of China in 1978. This first attempt to render organized educational bibliographic information in printed and on-line modes in the ROC is discussed under the following headings:

1. The historical background,
2. The scope and function,
3. The methods used in compiling the Chinese Educational Abstracts,
4. The structure and retrieving system of the database,
5. Problems to be solved.

INTRODUCTION

In this information-rich and information-seeking era, information workers are constantly striving to maximize the utility of graphic records. With the assistance of technological innovations, the demand for accessibility, speed, efficiency, and effectiveness can be more easily fulfilled. Computerized bibliographic databases have been widely used in the States, and the number of databases has been doubled in the recent years. Bibliographic and numeric databases, amounting by a recent count of 518, have greatly benefited every facet of the society and especially the researchers and management. With the efforts of the ROC Telephone and Telegraph Organization, Chinese users have access since December 1979 to the databases offered by ORBIT (SDC) and DIALOG (Lockheed) through the National Taiwan Normal University Library which is the first educational institution offering such service to the public.

Building a databases of resources in Chinese has long been an emphasized research area at the National Taiwan Normal University Library. The first such venture was to index the Chinese educational periodicals, an index which has made great contributions in assisting library users to locate the exact information they need for bibliographic identification. Ever since the feasibility of the Chinese vernacular data processing was ascertained in 1974, efforts have been directed toward facilitating accessibility of resources through online interaction in addition to the printed bibliographic tool.

For purposes of sharing experiences and exploring possible improvements on the project, this paper presents the case very briefly in the following five different parts:

1. The historical background,
2. The scope and function,
3. The methods used in compiling the Chinese Educational Abstracts,
4. The structure and retrieving system of the computerized databases,
5. Problems to be solved.

HISTORICAL BACKGROUND

The Chinese Educational Resources Information System

(CERIS), developed in 1978 form the computerized database of the Chinese Educational Abstracts which is the outgrowth of *The Index to Educational Periodical Literature. The Index to Educational Periodical Literature* was first published in 1962 covering the period of 1957 to 1961.

Starting from 1963, an annual index covering literature on education published in the previous years was published annually to 1977. From 1978 on, abstracts have been added to the index entries, and the work was renamed as *Abstract of Chinese Educational Periodical Literature*. The Abstracts have been computerized, and the 1980 issue has been input and output in the Chinese language by using the Perkin Elmer 3220 hardware and TOTAL software package (Figure 1).

FUNCTION AND COVERAGE

Like the functions of the other bibliographic tools, the *Chinese Educational Abstracts* (CEA) and its computerized database are compiled and built up for the convenience of users in locating educational resources and information essential to their research, study, teaching, management and decision making. Its aim is to provide accurate, comprehensive, and fast bibliographic information, similar to what is offered by ERIC in the United States.

The first issue of CEA covers 3,000 scholarly educational articles published in Taiwan and Hongkong during the period of 1957 to 1961.

Book reviews, brief comments, correspondences, news items, and literary features are not indexed. Between 1963 and 1977 the annual index listed and average of 1,500 journal articles. From 1978 on the coverage has remained the same, indicating a static scholarly publishing mode.

ARRANGEMENT AND METHODS OF COMPILATION

Both the Index and the Abstracts are hierarchically arranged in accord with subject categories independent of any particular classification scheme used in libraries. It is a mixture of various classification principles and special needs raised by the users of the National Taiwan Normal University Library. Within each subject category, citations are arranged according to the number of strokes of the titles. Each citation includes entry number, title, author/translator, journal title, volume number, page number, publishing date, and abstract .

The first step in the actual compiling work is to select informative and research oriented educational articles from the pre-determined scholarly periodicals and newspapers. The choice of scholarly periodicals and newspapers to be indexed is based upon faculty recommendation. The second step is to record all pertinent information on the index card. The third step involves writing the abstract and sending a copy of it to the original author for verification. The fourth step is the sorting of citations according to subject category, assigning entry number, compiling author and title indexes, and preparing a list of periodicals from which articles are selected. Ample cross references are provided. The flow chart (figure 2) as shown now indicates the entire procedure taken.

STRUCTURE OF THE DATABASE

For the purpose of serving multi-users and distant users in the future, the network concept is used in designing the structure of the Chinese Educational Abstracts database. The network-structured TOTAL Database Management System is thus used. Its special features – "linkpath" and "randomizing" – facilitate the organization and updating of information. The bi-directional communication and multi-key access have made exact retrieving, freedom of choice, and easy communication possible. With Boolean logic, the items retrieved can be very exact. The items illustrated in figure 3 indicate the structure of the database. The rectangular block represents the "Master Dataset" which is also the access point, and the octagonal shape represent the storage of variable and detailed data. The subject, title, author, journal title, and date constitute the five master datasets. Variable data field 1 keeps article titles, journal titles, and the year; variable data field 2 stores article title and subject; and variable data field 3 lists article title and author. Information can be retrieved by using article title, subject, author, journal title, or year, or the combination of all these different elements.

From the subject category, one can locate a list of citations either by author's name (in stroke order) or in chronological sequence of the publication date. Any combination of the data elements can be used as searching keys.

Three Corner Coding System is used in inputting as well as retrieving data. One does not need to know the structure and etymology of the Chinese language to use this method. This relieves many problems caused by the complexity of Chinese language in the processing of Chinese materials. The output with dot-matrix-plotter line printer, in addition to online interactive input and output devices, have made the service a beneficial one to the library users. The format of the line printer output is different from the CRT output for sake of publication which is controlled by program. Both the network structure and the capacity of the hardware compatible to IBM 370/158 are adequate to handle such a huge and growing database. At the present time, the field and formats have been fixed ones. Improvements have to be made in this respect.

CONCLUSION (PROBLEMS TO BE SOLVED)

The preliminary attempt has been successful within the National Taiwan Normal University (NTNU) Library. This service will become available also in the NTNU Science Library once terminals are installed and cables are connected. It needs to be expanded to other libraries throughout the country as soon as the telecommunciation problem is solved. In the future, the need to save memory capacity should also be explored through improved design of formats. The possibility of computer-generated index and the need to include entry number in the online retrieval are matters of research on software. What CERIS has accomplished so far is to prove that Chinese language online databases are feasible even at this stage when only 10 Chinese devices are available. It is a potentially very promising area to be investigated with joint efforts and cooperation. A nationwide network will depend on standardization of machine-readable communication format and systematic retrieving methods. These await decentralized, but cooperative efforts in studies and researches both in the library profession and in subject specializations.

Figure 1 TOTAL DBMS

Network Database Structure — Permits automatic cross-referecing among data records

Two Types of Records (Files)
- * Master File — Single entry data set
- * Variable File — Variable entry data set

Called by host languages (FORTRAN, COBOL) to access the database

Using randomizing algorithm to calculate master record physical address based on the value of the control field

Bi-directional threads to establish data relationship

Figure 1-1 THE BASIC SYSTEM

Perkin Elmer 3220 processor

Disc storage 50 MB

Chinese CRT terminal

Dot-matrix type line printer

Multi-task operating system

Figure 1-2 CHINESE TERMINAL SYSTEM

A micorprocessor-based system using Intel SBC 80/30 to control the I/O of Chinese characters

Chinese characters repersentation

* 2 Byte internal code to represent a Chinese character
* 6 digits symbolic code to call a Chinese character
* Single key using large keyboard to call a Chinese character
* Pattern formed by 16 x 18 dot matrix
* 16,000 Chinese characters available

Chinese software system called by host language

Figure 2

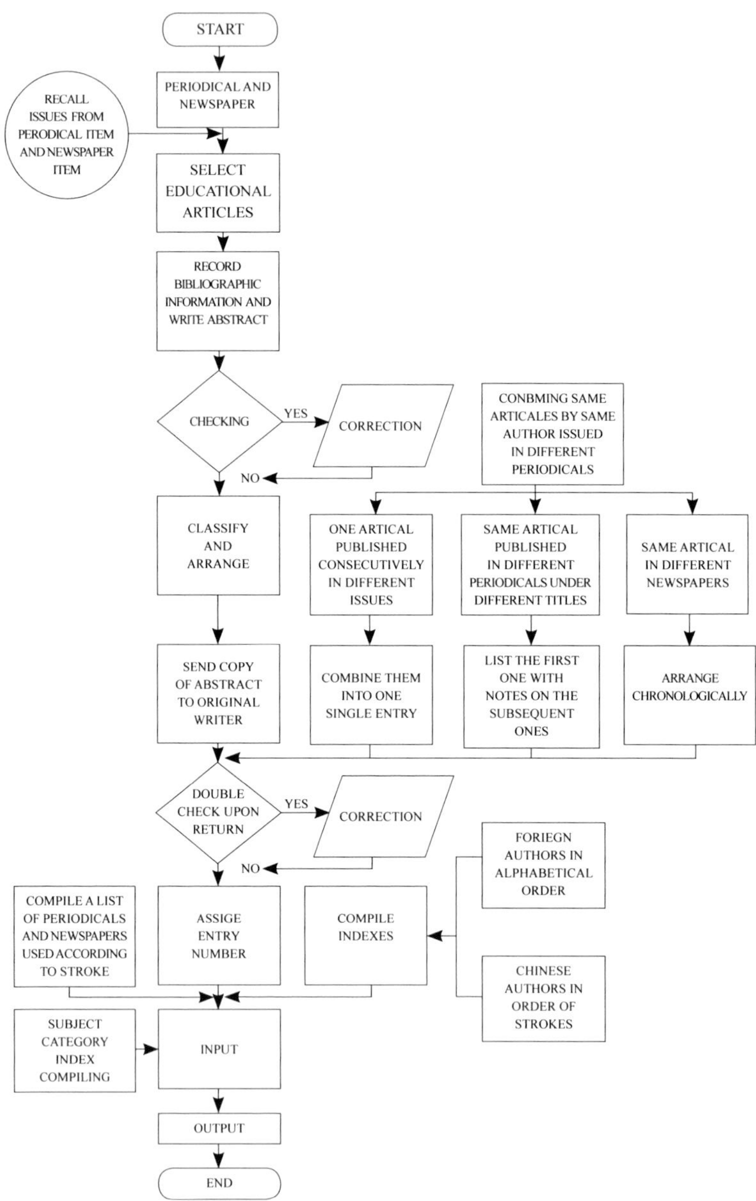
START
PERIODICAL AND NEWSPAPER
RECALL ISSUES FROM PERODICAL ITEM AND NEWSPAPER ITEM
SELECT EDUCATIONAL ARTICLES
RECORD BIBLIOGRAPHIC INFORMATION AND WRITE ABSTRACT
CHECKING
YES
CORRECTION
NO
CONBMING SAME ARTICALES BY SAME AUTHOR ISSUED IN DIFFERENT PERIODICALS
CLASSIFY AND ARRANGE
ONE ARTICAL PUBLISHED CONSECUTIVELY IN DIFFERENT ISSUES
SAME ARTICAL PUBLISHED IN DIFFERENT PERIODICALS UNDER DIFFERENT TITLES
SAME ARTICAL IN DIFFERENT NEWSPAPERS
SEND COPY OF ABSTRACT TO ORIGINAL WRITER
COMBINE THEM INTO ONE SINGLE ENTRY
LIST THE FIRST ONE WITH NOTES ON THE SUBSEQUENT ONES
ARRANGE CHRONOLOGICALLY
DOUBLE CHECK UPON RETURN
YES
CORRECTION
NO
FORIEGN AUTHORS IN ALPHABETICAL ORDER
COMPILE A LIST OF PERIODICALS AND NEWSPAPERS USED ACCORDING TO STROKE
ASSIGE ENTRY NUMBER
COMPILE INDEXES
CHINESE AUTHORS IN ORDER OF STROKES
SUBJECT CATEGORY INDEX COMPILING
INPUT
OUTPUT
END

Figure 3

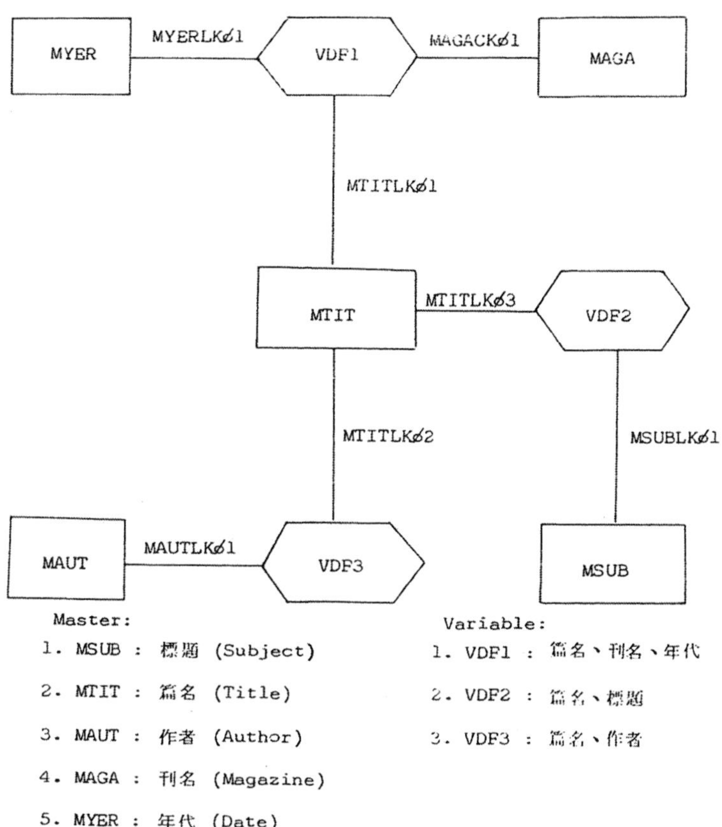

Reprinted with permission from *中文圖書資料自動化國際研討會論文集 [Papers of the International Workshop on Chinese Library Automation]*, Taipei, 14-19 February 1981 (Taipei: Library Association of China, 1981). (pp. D1-D10).

13

The Use of Source Materials Enhanced by Modern Information Technology

ABSTRACT

Following a general description of the increasing availability of source materials in Roman languages offered to social scientists and scholars in the humanities through online information retrieval services, this paper discusses recently-enhanced services rendered by bibliographic utilities to libraries and research projects on Chinese Studies supported by computer-based technology.

With a succinct account of computer-processing of Chinese vernacular materials in Taipei as background information, the author highlights some of the new resources and systems made available to the scholars of Chinese Studies through recent technological developments. The paper is concluded with suggestions for possible future developments and the role that China scholars may play in this endeavor.

INTRODUCTION

The success of research lies greatly in the effective and efficient use of source materials. The availability, accessibility and effective use of source materials determine the quality and fruitfulness of research endeavors. In the last two decades, with the advent of the information explosion, these factors effecting research have drawn much attention. Numerous efforts have been made to aid research by investigating and experimenting with modern technological products. Equipments, such as photocopying devices, microfilming, and computer/information technologies, have made remarkable and revolutionary contributions to research activities.

For decades, people associated the use of technological equipment with fields in basic sciences only. However, the use of such tools has gained increasing popularity in the fields of social sciences and the humanities since the 1970's as indicated by McGee and Trees :[1]

> The 1970's and early 1980's will probably be known to information specialists as the age of the machine-readable, numeric, social sciences data file. Public interest in social problems and the widespread use of computer based systems to administer, transfer programs and conduct evaluation research has resulted in an exponential increase in the amount of computer-readable data being generated.

In particular, the computer's data compilation, analytic and storage capabilities, statistical packages, and advent of bibliographic databases have greatly enhanced the efficiency of research in social sciences and the humanities. ERIC, Psychological Abstracts, Management Contents, ABI/INFORM, Social Scisearch, Sociological Abstracts, Social Science Citation Index, Comprehensive Dissertation Abstracts. New York Times Information Bank, Economic Abstracts International, MLA Bibliography International, Language and Language Behavior Abstracts, Exceptional Child Education Abstracts, Historical Abstracts, Public Affairs Information Service (PAIS) exemplify some of the available databases through BRS, DIALOG, INFORMATION BANK, and ORBIT.[2] However, these databases cover mostly materials in Roman languages. They can assist China scholars to locate materials in Roman languages, but they provide no data in vernacular languages, this gap is in need of immediate attention.[3]

Most of the equipment uses (photocopying, microfilming, etc.) make no difference as far as language of the research resources is concerned; however, they do make a difference when computer technology is employed, especially in the case of Chinese source materials. After many experiments in the 1970's, finally in the late 1980's, we can enjoy the assistance of computer and computer-related technological developments in the use of Chinese materials.

INITIAL EFFORTS IN COMPUTER PROCESSING OF CHINESE SOURCE MATERIALS

Current computer processing of Chinese vernacular materials is still in the stage of I/O devices, which enable people to input and output Chinese materials in vernacular form. The computer assisted use of Chinese source materials was first experimented by library automation projects in the mid 1970's with considerable success.[4]

The Agricultural Science and Technology Information Management System (ASTIMS), ROC Information Database (FICA), Chinese Education Information Database (CERIS), and the Acquisition, Cataloging and Circulation modules (ACCI) were respectively developed by the Agriculture Science Information Center, Freedom Council Information Center, National Taiwan Normal University, and National Taiwan University. They have proven to be successful prototypes in the 1970s. Unfortunately, some of them are now discontinued.

Subsequent projects on Chinese Character Code for Information Interchange (CCCII), Chinese MARC formats, the revision of Chinese Cataloging Rules, the adoption of ISSN and ISBN have made substantial contributions to standards essential to operation of Chinese library automation.[5] As a result, National Central Library's National Union List of Serials, National Bibliography and other automated modules have greatly improved both the technical and public services in Taiwan. These projects initiated in Taiwan, as described below, have also benefited programs in the United States.

INTERNATIONAL COOPERATION AND THE ENHANCEMENT OF THE USE OF CHINESE MATERIALS

In the East Asian library community in the United States, several projects using modern technological devices have been in existence for quite some time, such as the East Asian Microfilming Project, the Task Force on Rare Chinese Books, the East Asian Cataloging Subcommittee, and the East Asian Conspectus for Collection under the umbrella of the East Asian Program. The American Council of Learned Societies have also published a report written by the Joint Advisory Committee to the East Asian Library Program.[6] The report entitled, *Automation, Cooperation and Scholarship: East Asian Libraries* in the 1980's reflects that due attention is given to automation in the East Asian library community in North America. Thus, the need for better support of East Asian research and scholarship is not only a domestic concern in the East Asian countries, but has also become an international concern in the United States and Canada.

Aided by initial and successful efforts achieved in computer technology, and in information interchange codes by the Chinese library, computer, and linguistics communities in Taiwan in the early 1980's, two information networks in the United States were able to make breakthroughs enabling them to provide bibliographic control of Chinese vernacular materials and related services to libraries and readers in the United States. In addition, various recent technological developments such as personal computers, artificial intelligence, CD-ROM and interactive videodisc have greatly enhanced the use of source materials.

Research Libraries Group and Research Libraries Information Network[7]

The above mentioned East Asian Program guides the developments of the Research Libraries Information Network (RLIN). RLIN has supported the input, display, retrieval, storage, and transmission of bibliographic records containing Chinese, Japanese and Korean (CJK) scripts since 1983.

Currently, RLIN provides approximately one half million East Asian records to twenty-two participating East Asian libraries in the United States including major East Asian libraries such as Columbia, Cornell, Hoover Institution, Library of Congress, Princeton University, University of Chicago, University of Hawaii, University of Illinois, University of Michigan, and Yale University, etc. These collections represent 75% of the total East Asian library holdings. Even though RLIN is set-up for cataloging and bibliographic control purposes of libraries, its by-product online union catalog has been extremely helpful to researchers. The database covers books, serials, maps, recordings, scores, audio-visual materials, archival and manuscript materials which can be made available to patrons through its online interlibrary loan system. The LC Author Heading authority file and the Link System Project (LSP) greatly facilitate convenient searching.

The RLG CJK Thesaurus provides a resource file of 35,000 records, with each record representing an East Asian character. It is an online, multi-indexed, multi-lingual dictionary. Each character record shows such information as radical, stroke-count, reading in the three East Asian languages, and how to compose the character. It also shows all variant forms associated with a particular character. It is considered an "East Asian character authority file" for CJK bibliographic records, and it also serves as an useful dictionary as well.

With PC based equipments, fonts supplied by JHL, and key boards devised by Transtech International Corporation, the recently developed RLG Multi-script Workstation will help the Network to accomplish its multi-faceted objectives. It features CJK word-processing and CJK interface with other software as well as RLIN functions. Scholars are able to search the RLIN database for relevant materials; download the records to floppies on their PC; merge the data with bibliographies and text; and print multi-script document on a printer.

On-line Computer Library Center[8]

The largest bibliographic utility in the United States, OCLC, started to explore the possibility of automating East Asian vernacular materials in 1983. A pilot project with the participation of eleven libraries began in May of 1986. Its CJK membership has been increased rapidly with current participation of 65 users including three foreign libraries (National Central Library, University of Alberta Library, and Australia National Library), and other universities and public libraries. With some alterations on their PC/XT based terminal, it offers a variety of input and retrieving methods: Chuang-chieh Method. Wade-Giles and Pin-yin I/O devices have proven to be more user-friendly than other methods. Most scholars in the China field are familiar with both Wade-Giles and Pin-yin. In closer cooperation with National Central Library and other libraries in the Far East, the OCLC CJK database will soon have a large volume of records added to their 110,000 unique vernacular records – almost half of these records are pertaining to Chinese materials. Assisted by US$240,000.00 grant from the Henry Luce Foundation, 100,000 records of Chinese publications with 1911-1949 imprints will be merged into OCLC CJK database. The OCLC CJK program offers services to users with its online catalog and online interlibrary loan services. It will prove to be even more useful once subject search is made available to users in addition to its original fifteen access points.

The First Emperor of China – Project Emperor-I

Joseph Raben indicated that databases of humanistic materials are beginning to alter the way in which researchers interact with objects of their studies.[9] The videodisc's large storage, integration of multi-type information, high resolution and fast random access capabilities have made these interactions possible.[10]

For example, NEH sponsored the Project Emperor-I which presents and interprets a major historical/archaeological period of China past. Using the latest technology, the most spectacular discovery of 7,000 life-size terracotta figures of warriors and horses near Ching Shih-huang's tomb was stored, processed and made accessible to people who wanted to view and study the artifacts.

Dr. Ching-chih Chen and her team, under the sponsorship of NEH grants, were able to demonstrate the capabilities of the new technologies in supplying users with the improved and more efficient large-scale information processing, storage, access and delivery.

The visual information from two double-sided 12" NTSC CAV videodiscs (each side composed of 108,000 frames of visual images), the visual information is matched with appropriate bilingual narrations, the texts are divided into chapters, very similar to an electronic book. This format allows very speedy retrieval of both the audio and visual information on a thematic topic even though any one of the 108,000 frames of visual images can be retrieved randomly and easily in less than three seconds. Various related factual information stored in a micro-based system when used conjunctively with the videodisc, will enable the user to retrieve one will be able to retrieve specific textual, visual and audio data by means of a micro-based interactive videodisc system.

With the use of DEC's Interactive Video Information System (IVIS), the Project developed a variety of computer-assisted instructional courseware in order to meet the various needs of users who have different levels of knowledge of Chinese art history and archaeology. In addition to various topical choices of lessons, the main menu includes other options such as :

1. References – checking the glossary file or viewing the bibliography file. Items included in the bibliography can also be retrieved and viewed in full-text form.
2. Exploration – choosing to view three-dimensional pictures and to browse through the slide collection by going forward, backward, zooming in and out, etc.
3. In addition, electronic message is available to patrons.

Thus, the interactive videodisc has proved to be an effective wide-ranging educational and experimental tool in the new era of interactive learning and education. It can be used in any of the research projects for the humanities or social sciences.

DEVELOPMENTS OF INFORMATION TECHNOLOGY AND ENHANCEMENTS IN TAIWAN

As with other developed countries, many organizations in Taiwan have also devoted much attention to the improvement of information supply. Libraries and information centers, of course, consider information provisions their raison d'etre for existence. The following is a description of recent developments in Taiwan :

Academia Sinica

Academia Sinica, the highest research institution in Taiwan has fully used the new technologies and produced ten automated modules as follows:

Full Text Database for Chinese History[11]

This pioneering project of the Chinese electronic book was lunched in July of 1984, and aims at processing Chinese historical texts of the 25 dynasties which contain 60 million Chinese characters. As a prototype, *Shih Ho Chih* (*Treatise on Food and Money*) has been implemented on three different systems:

Location of Prototypes	Computing Center, Academia Sinica	East Asian Lib. Univ. of Wash.	Computing Center, Academia Sinica
Date of Installation	March 1985	March 1986	September 1987
Hardware	IBM 5550 16 bit PO	Micro-VAX II Dragon 570	AT & T 3B15 Dragon 580
Operating System	PC-DOS	VMS 4.1	UNIX V; BINIX 1.0
Query Form	Interactive	Interactive	Interactive
Access Method	Inverted list	Inverted list Full-text scan	Document-structure Full-text scan
No. of User	1	2 – 4	8 - 48

The databases soon to be completed *Shih Chi*, *Han Shu*, *Hou Han Shu*, *San Kuo Chih*, and *Shih Ho Chih*. It is expected that the entire database will be completed by June of 1990. Controlled vocabulary (keywords) and free-text searching are currently available. They are classified into six categories: names, places, time, official titles, references, and major events. Six inverted list files were built to include these keywords and the pointers of the corresponding basic text elements.

Materials sought and viewed on the terminal can be copied to the readers' own files and are to be used along with the readers own notes. Concordances can be generated as well. Statistical analysis for Chinese character/word usage is the most proper application and welcomed feature of this system.

Chinese Electronic Dictionary[12]

Based on *Kuo Yu Jih Pao Tzu Tien (Gwoyeu Ryhbaw Tsyrdean)*, the most popular Chinese dictionary in Taiwan, the Computing Center of the Academia Sinica developed a database of Chinese vocabulary and named it "Chinese Electronic Dictionary" (CED). CED is to be used as a machine readable tool for various Chinese information processing applications, especially for the study of Chinese computation linguistics.

This textual database, having 40,000 most-frequently-used

Chinese vocabulary words and related information expressed by 1.6 million Chinese characters, serves as an electronic dictionary on line. Each entry consists of Chinese character strings, pronunciation, definition, syntactic categories, and annexed attributes, all of which can be used with great ease and efficiency.

With a set of machine-readable files, index files, a number of management programs, and a user interface, CED can provide users with immediate access to the words and related information stored in 3.1M bytes AT & T computer facilities.

Database of Ancient Tombs[13]

Using AT & T 3B/2, UNIX, and informatics/SDL database management systems, data pertaining to 3,040 tombs of Han Dynasty have been processed. The database contains information on each individual tomb's date, structure, location, direction, path decoration, inscriptions, accompanying buried items, method of burial, and the structure of the coffin. Related statistics on dates, location, and buried items pertaining to any the above mentioned items can be generated.

Household Registers during the Period of 1906 – 1947[14]

Expert system technology is applied to automate the analysis of household registers for anthropological research. Embedded Structured Query Language C was applied to model an expert's knowledge of a physical process: The system organizes knowledge into three levels : data, knowledge base and control. The IBM PC database (with PASCAL Programming Language) covers intermediate file (several mega bytes for each district) of 10,338 families from three districts (Chu Pei, O Mei, Ta Nei). Records include marriage, family type, adoption, ethnicity, occupation, sibling, age, spouse, etc.

From these records one can reconstruct the marriage and adoption practices for the preceding sixty years. Anthropological research will greatly benefit from the massive amount of data stored and processed with expert. For example, with the manipulation of the household census records, they will be able to find out information, such as:

1. The effect of a person's birth order upon the change of family structure, upon family models, divorce rates, and birth rates.
2. The cultural difference and similarities between groups speaking Fukien and Keha dialects in Taiwan.
3. The relationship of mutual assistances among Chinese families.
4. The adaptability of Schachter and Caplow's theory on association in a Chinese society.

A Classification of Chinese Verbs for Language Parsing[15]

The Academia Sinica attempted to establish a better classification for parsing Chinese by adopting current theories of feature-based categorization. The new classification is based on the results of analyzing 16,824 verbs. It is found that both syntactic and semantic information have to be used in parsing Chinese sentences. The system provides three types of information about a verb:

1. Its case type with their semantic restrictions and syntactic representations.
2. All possible sentence patterns constructed by the verb and its required arguments.
3. Its syntactic and semantic features, such as dimension, control relations, complement and internal structure of verbal compounds.

Land Reports[16]

The collection of archival materials on Land Repots gathered in Hsinchu area by the Japanese government during its occupation of Taiwan is the source material used for the study on Taiwan's socio-economic history. This database, consisting of 472 volumes of 250,000 land reports, is essential to the study of Taiwan's economic history, the format of land developments, and the relationship between the land owners and tenants, etc. Pertinent statistics can be generated to verify various hypotheses.

Study on Formosan Languages[17]

With various data collected on the above subject, the following linguistics related research projects have been accomplished :

1. A comparative vocabulary of Formosan languages.
2. Five dialects thesauri (Atayal, Puyuma, Pazeh, Kavalan, and Tao Dialects).
3. Cognates database.
4. Bibliography of Formosan languages.
5. Male and female forms of speech in the Atayalic group.
6. The differences between affirmative and negative speeches of the MAGA dialect.
7. The development and the change of tones as affected by Formosan languages.

Masters' Theses Database[18]

This online database consists of some 23,111 masters' theses completed in the Republic of China during the years of 1974 to 1985. For each thesis the following information is included: author, title, adviser(s), degree granting university, college, and name of graduate institute, etc. They can be retrieved with one condition or the combination of multiple conditions.

Ming/Ch'ing Dynasties Archival Materials Database[19]

Containing approximately 200,000 official reports of Ming and Ch'ing Dynasties, this IBM PC/AT based database supplies information on dates, reigns, emperor names, types, and those responsible for drafting of reports.

Academia Sincia Researchers' Biographical Materials and Works Database:[20]

This database provides biographical materials and publications of 450 researchers at the Academy. The following information is made available on line: name of the researcher, institute and division of his affiliation, publication titles, dates of publications, scope of study, the researcher's field of specializations and pertinent keywords.

In addition, the Academy's note-card system for personal use has been successfully designed and implemented on its history document database. Its capacity of 1K bytes holds thirteen types of information including content, sequential number, source, subject classification, and keywords. It is, indeed, a welcomed tool for researchers.

National Central Library Bibliographic Databases

Subsequent to the successful formulation of all types of library automation standards as mentioned earlier, the Library Association of China and the National Central Library jointly developed the national plan for library automation in 1980. As part of the inauguration of the program, the National Central Library began to build up an online union catalog of its own monograph holdings and those of the following libraries: National Taiwan University Library, National Taiwan Normal University Library, National Chengchi University Library, Catholic Fu-jen University, and Tamkang University Library.

The following are also available in the NCL cluster of bibliographic databases:[21]

1. Automated National Bibliography including all Chinese publications published in Taiwan since 1981.
2. Periodical and Government Document Indices indexing 800 periodicals published in the Taiwan area and 19 official gazetters.

3. *National Union List of Chinese Periodicals* covering 8,000 periodicals held by 170 local libraries in Taiwan.
4. Chinese Rare Books (Shan Pen) On-line Catalog including some 15,000 titles of the printed editions and movable-type editions prior to the Ming Dynasty (1368-1644 A.D.), rare editions of the Ch'ing Dynasty (1644-1911 A.D.), manuscripts and editions revised by famous scholars, and hand-written editions, etc. Since 1983, those rare Chinese books in the categories of classics and history have already been inputted into the database. The remaining three categories are to be inputted into the database in the next two years.

The National Central Library has automated its acquisition, cataloging and serials control modules, through which the NCL is able to provide bibliographic services to its patrons with its online searching capabilities. At the National Central Library, the Center of Chinese Studies is planning an online guide covering biographical information of China scholars. When this database is completed, it should prove to be a useful tool in locating subject specialists and pertinent works in the field.

Other Endeavors in Taiwan

Most of the libraries in Taiwan have paid keen attention to the development of automated Chinese library services and have experimented with various projects in the last decade. Some have achieved moderate success; some have discontinued their individual planning and operations in order to wait for the results of united efforts among academic libraries; and some are taking new initiatives in planned networking.

The Tamkang Automated Library Integrated System (TALIS) designed cooperatively with IBM, based on DOBIS, is an integrated system capable of networking for acquisition, cataloging, circulation, serial control, electronic mail and public online catalog.

Implemented on IBM 4381/M11 system since 1986, it has great potential in networking with domestic and foreign libraries.[22]

NCTU LIAS developed by National Chiao Tung University since 1983 offers several modules which include on automated monograph system and a serial control system, etc. Each of these two systems has two components: technical service and public service. The public service portion would provide online cataloging and retrieving functions whereas the technical service portion aims at acquisition, accession, claiming, and shelving, etc.[23]

The Science and Technology Information Center (STIC) pioneered library automation with its *Union List of Scientific Serials* in Roman alphabets in the early 1970's. In addition to what it has accomplished in building databases for scientific/technical periodical literature and personnel data, the Center is now undertaking the following projects with the purpose of providing up-to-date online information retrieval service:[24]

1. Establishing the STICNET, a nationwide Sci-Tech information network.
2. Integrating domestic R & D information sources.
3. Importing selected international databases of great importance.

LEGISIS (Legislative Information System), developed by the Information Center of the Legislative Yuan on VAX 8530 system, offers three useful databases at the present time:[25]

1. Legislator Interpellation System covers more than eleven thousand interpellations made by legislators since September 1984. All interpellations raised by legislators concerning administration, proposals, and budgets can be retrieved via the name of the legislator , pertinent subjects, government organization's name, keywords, and session number of the interpellations.
2. The Full-text Database of Acts, Laws, and Codes of the Republic of China: It consists of 560 types of legal documents

(12,000 items), and each legal document is described in details regarding its contents and structure. Readers can get access to information with many accessible points such as dates, content summaries, categories and subjects.

3. LEGISIS THESAURUS online database serves as a tool to the above databases, and an online dictionary of legal terms.

Two additional databases on newspaper clippings and legal periodical literature index will be available within the next two years.

CONCLUSION

The systems briefly described above, illustrate some of the computer-assisted research aids and library services which are already available to scholars in the China field. It indicates that bibliographic information is easily made available through bibliographic utilities in a network mode or through individual library services. What is available is mostly pertaining to bibliographic information; people share resources by using an online network bibliographic union catalog.

What will aid the researchers the most in the next decade probably will be full-text databases. As the basis of electronic books, full-text databases will become more useful and effective, if they employ various types of technologies including CD-ROM and videodisc, made available internationally through telecommunication devices. Furthermore, these fill-text databases need subject analyses made by subject specialists. Such analyses can best be made if those conducting the research have basic knowledge of computer applications and tools.

More vernacular full-text databases, or databases consisting of vernacular Chinese periodical indexes should be incorporated into existing databases for universal use. Automated Union Catalog of Chinese Rare Books planned cooperatively by the RLG and the National Central Library should be implemented as soon as possible.[26]

Standardized database structures, software packages, indexing methodologies, and closely cooperative and coordinated efforts among scholars (users), librarians and computer scientists (suppliers) are areas to be encouraged. A clearing house of computerized source materials perhaps is an area to be explored by professional associations. Since supply and demand are closely related, no sophisticated tools and resources can be provided unless the researchers make these demands. It is up to the scholars to use these tools, which can be improved with repeated use.

It is the most opportune time for scholars in the China field to look into this important development, and for professional associations to take appropriate initiatives in coordinating such meaningful efforts.

NOTES

1. Jacqueline M. McGee and Donald P. Trees, "Major Available Social Science Machine-Readable Database," *Drexel Library Quarterly* 18 (Summer / Fall, 1982): 107-134.
2. Robert Donati, "Selective Survey of On-line Access to Social Science Databases," *Special Libraries* (November 1977): 396-406.
3. Lucinda D. Conger, "International Resources Online in the Social Science: The Holes in the Swiss Cheese," *Behavior & Social Sciences Librarians* 1, no. 4 (Summer 1980): 275-279.
4. Margaret C. Fung, "Development in the Computerization of Non-Roman Scripts," in *The Library in the Information Revolution (Singapore: Maruzen Asia*, 1983), 280-292.
5. Margaret C. Fung, "Library Automation in the Republic of China," *T'u Shu Kuan Hsueh Yu Tzu Hsun K'o Hsueh 圖書館學與資訊科學 [Journal of Library & Information Science]* 6, no. 1 (April 1980): 1-16.
6. Warren Tsuneishi, "East Asian Collections in North American Libraries: Some Recent Development in Cooperation," *International Association of Orientalist Librarians Bulletin* 28-29 (1986): 3-11.
7. John Haeger, "RLIN CJK: A Review of the First Four Years" (Paper presented at the Colloquium on Resources in Chinese Studies, Brighton, UK, 24-28 August 1987); Karen Wei, "OCLC CJK VS RLIN CJK: The Illinois Experience" (Speech delivered at the National Central Library, 18 August 1988).

8. Andrew Wang, Long distance telephone interview. Columbus, Ohio, 9 October 1988; Karen Wei, "OCLC CJK VS RLIN CJK: The Illinois Experience" (Speech delivered at the National Central Library, 18 August 1988).
9. Joseph Raben, "Databases for the Humanities," *Scholarly Publishing* (October 1986): 23-28.
10. Ching-chih Chen, "Potential of Videodisc Technology for International Information Transfer," *T'u Shu Kuan Hsueh Yu Tzu Hsun K'o Hsueh 圖書館學與資訊科學 [Journal of Library & Information Science]* 12, no. 2 (October 1986): 105-120.
11. Chin-chun Hsieh et al., "Full-Text Database for Chinese History Document" (Paper presented at 1988 International Conference on Computer Processing of Chinese and Oriental Languages, Toronto, Canada, 29 August – 1 September, 1988); Chin-chun Hsieh, "On the Development of Chinese Language Database for Sinology Studies" (Abstract draft of paper to be presented at International Conference on Resources for Chinese Studies at National Central Library, 30 November – 3 December, 1988); Hang-kuang Mao 毛漢光, "Ti Yi Ch'i Shih Chi Tzu Tung Hua Chien Chieh 第一期史籍自動化簡介," *Chi Suan Chung Hsin T'ung Hsun 計算中心通訊 [Newsletter of Computing Centre]* 2, no. 4 (16 February 1986): 13-14.
12. Shih-Thyen Tseng et al., "CED – A Machine Readable Chinese Dictionary" (Paper presented at the First Pacific Conference on New Information Technology for library and Information Professionals, Bangkok, Thailand, 16-18 June 1987).
13. Chung Yang Yen Chiu Yuan Li Shih Yu Yen Yen Chiu So, Chi Suan Chung Hsin 中央研究院歷史語言研究所，計算中心, "Han Tai Mu Yi Tzu Liao Ch'u Li Hsi T'ung 漢代墓彝資料處理系統," *Chi Suan Chung Hsin T'ung Hsun 計算中心通訊 [Newsletter of Computing Centre]* 2, no. 9 (1 May 1986): 39-40.
14. Yin-Chang Chuang 莊英章, Chu Sheng Pai Hang Hsu Yu Chia Ting Chieh Kou Tung T'ai – San Ko Hsiang Chen Te Pi Chiao Yen Chiu 出生排行序與家庭結構動態 — 三個鄉鎮的比較研究," *Chi Suan Chung Hsin T'ung Hsun 計算中心通訊 [Newsletter of Computing Centre]* 3, no. 1 (1 January 1987): 4-5; Leng-meng Lin et al., "Problem Solving for Analysis and Reasoning about Anthropology" (Paper presented at 1988 International Conference on Computer Processing of Chinese and Oriental Languages, Toronto, Canada, 29 August – 1 September, 1988).
15. Li-li Chang et al., "A Classification of Chinese Verbs for Language Pars-

ing" (Paper presented at 1988 International Conference on Computer Processing of Chinese and Oriental Languages, Toronto, Canada, 29 August – 1 September, 1988).

16. Yen-Hsien Chang 張炎憲, "Jih Chu Shih Tai T'u Ti Shen Kao Shu Tzu Liao Te Tzu Tung Hua 日據時代土地申告書資料的自動化," *Chi Suan Chung Hsin T'ung Hsun 計算中心通訊 [Newsletter of Computing Centre]* 4, no. 13 (1 July 1988): 99-100.
17. Jen-K'uei Li 李壬癸, "Taiwan T'u Chu Yu Yen Tzu Liao Tzu Tung Hua 台灣土著語言資料自動化," *Chi Suan Chung Hsin T'ung Hsun 計算中心通訊 [Newsletter of Computing Centre]* 3, no. 17 (1 September 1987): 116-120.
18. Chi-Wei Hang 杭極微, "Shuo Po Shih Lun Wen Ch'a Hsun Hsi T'ung Chien Chieh 碩博士論文查詢系統簡介," *Chi Suan Chung Hsin T'ung Hsun 計算中心通訊 [Newsletter of Computing Centre]* 4, no. 11 (1 June 1988): 84; P'ei-yen Huang [黃佩燕], "Shuo Po Shih Lun Wen T'i Yao Hsi T'ung Chien Chieh 碩博士論文提要系統簡介," *Chi Suan Chung Hsin T'ung Hsun 計算中心通訊 [Newsletter of Computing Centre]* 3, no. 7 (1 April 1987): 39-41.
19. Interview with Ching-chun Hsieh, Academia Sinica, Taipei, 22 September 1988.
20. Yu-hsiang Shih 石玉祥, "Pen Yuan Yen Chiu Jen Yuan Chu Tso Ch'a Hsun Hsi Tung 本院研究人員著作查詢系統," *Chi Suan Chung Hsin T'ung Hsun 計算中心通訊 [Newsletter of Computing Centre]* 4, no. 11 (1 June 1988): 85-86.
21. *National Central Library Automated Information Service Brochure* (Taipei: National Central Library, 1975); Nancy Ou-lan Chou (Nancy Ou-lan Hu) 胡歐蘭, "Kuo Chia Shu Mu Tzu Liao K'u Chi Ch'I Tzu Hsun Wan Chih Fa Chan 國家書目資料庫及其資訊網之發展 [The National Bibliographic Database and Its Network Development]" (Paper presented at Seminar on Library Automation and Information Networks, Taipei, Taiwan, ROC, 6-12 June 1988).
22. I-ming Shen, "The Development of Implementation of TALIS – An Integrated Chinese Library Automation System" (Paper presented at the Asia/Pacific Education Executive Conference, Taipei, Taiwan, ROC, 18-21 August 1987); Hung-Chu Huang 黃鴻珠, "Mai Ju Hsien Shang Kung Yung Mu Lu Te Li Cheng – Tan Chiang Ta Hsueh T'u Shu Kuan Te Ching Yen 邁入線上公用目錄的里程 — 淡江大學圖書館的經驗,"*Chung Kuo T'u Shu Kuan Hsueh Hui Pao 中國圖書館學會會報 [Bulletin of Library Association of China]* 42 (June 1988): 41-59 ; Li-Min Cheng 鄭麗敏, "Tan Chiang Ta Hsueh Fa Chan DOBIS / LIBIS / TALIS Chih Ching Yen 淡

江大學發展DOBIS / LIBIS / TALIS之經驗," *Chiao Yu Tzu Liao Yu T'u Shu Kuan Hsueh 教育資料與圖書館學 [Journal of Ecudation Media and Library Sciences]* 25, no. 4 (June 1988): 1-21.

23. *Kuo Li Chiao Tung Ta Hsueh T'u Shu Kuan Tzu Tung Hua Hsi Tung Chien Chieh 國立交通大學圖書館自動化系統簡介* (Hsin Chu: National Chiao Tung University Library, 1988).
24. *Science and Technology Information Center Brochure* (Taipei, 1988); Hsing Cheng Yuan Kuo Chia K'o Hsueh Wei Yuan Hui K'o Hsueh Chi Shu Tzu Liao Chung Hsin Pien 行政院國家科學委員會科學技術資料中心 編 [Science and Technology Information Center, National Science Council, Executive Yuan, ed.], *K'o Chi Hsing Ch'uan Kuo Tzu Hsun Wang Lu Tzu Kuei Hua Chi Fu Wu Kung Neng 科技性全國資訊網路之規劃及服務功能* (Taipei: STIC, NSC, 1987).
25. Karl M. Ku, Telephone interview. Taipei, 9 October 1988; Karl Min Ku 顧敏, "Li Fa Yuan So Yin Tz'u Hui Chien Chieh 立法索引詞彙簡介," *Chung Kuo T'u Shu Kuan Hsueh Hui Hui Wu Tung Hsun 中國圖書館學會會務通訊 [Library Association of China Newsletter]* 62 (31 May 1988): 14-15.
26. Wei-ling Dai, Long Distance Telephone interview. San Francisco: RLG, 22 September 1988; Nancy Ou-lan Chou (Nancy Ou-lan Hu), Hsiu-ying Chiang, "The Computerized Bibliography of Chinese Rare Books," *Chiao Yu Tzu Liao Yu T'u Shu Kuan Hsueh 教育資料與圖書館學 [Journal of Educational Media and Library Sciences]* 21, no. 2 (Winter 1984): 160-168; A Draft Plan on the International Union Catalog of Chinese Rare Books, 2 February 1982.

Paper presented in American Association for Chinese Studies 1988 Annual Conference, San Francisco, USA, 21-23 October 1988.

Reprinted with permission from *圖書館學與資訊科學 [Journal of Library & Information Science]* 14, no. 2 (October 1988): 158-177.

14

Biographical and Bibliographic Database of Chinese Studies

ABSTRACT

Chinese studies have gained academic interest all over the world, but there have not been enough reference tools available. From research in Taiwan and the author's efforts in the United States, a database has been developed in 1981, that is a Who's Who in Chinese Studies. The author urges scholars to get together and streamline the means of mutual interaction.

INTRODUCTION

The term "Chinese Studies," also known as "China Studies" or "Sinology," is used to refer to studies on China in the disciplines of humanities and social sciences. Such subjects as Chinese anthropology, archeology, arts, economics, education, geography, history, language, law, literature, philosophy, political science, religion, and sociology all fall into the broad category of Chinese Studies. It is a newly-developed term, originated in the Western hemisphere, comparable to the Chinese term of "Kuo Hsueh – national studies" and "Han Hsueh."[1] However, "Kuo Hsueh" is more limited in its coverage, as it concentrates on the period of ancient China only, whereas "China Studies" or "Chinese Studies or "Han

Hsueh" covers the above-mentioned topics ranging from ancient time to the modern era.[2]

During this presentation, "Chinese Studies" is used throughout the text for the purpose of consistency.

Chinese Studies has had a long history, and as a discipline it has gained increasing interest in the academic community all over the world.[3] By 1948-1949 in the United States, it had become an integral part of college and university area studies, with the help of foundation grants and government finding.[4] From the following figures, we can become aware of how much interest there is in Chinese Studies. As of 1989, in the United States alone, the Association for Asian Studies had a membership of 1,831 people who identified themselves as interested in Chinese Studies.[5] The Forty-Second Annual Meeting of the Association of Asian Studies, which took place on April 5-8, 1990, in Chicago, had forty-five panels, ten roundtables, and 121 paper presentations on China.[6]

There are almost one hundred American universities and colleges offering undergraduate and graduate courses in the field of Chinese Studies. In support of study and research in Chinese Studies, there are more than ninety libraries and almost fifty research centers affiliated with universities.[7]

Many foundations, such as the Ford, the Fulbright, the Guggenheim Memorial, the Henry Luce, and the NEH Foundation, the Council for Learned Societies, and the Center for Chinese Studies at Wang Institute of Graduate Studies, all have been enthusiastic in supporting research-related activities in the field. Such funded research projects have resulted in many significant findings and publications essential to the development of Chinese Studies.[8]

European academic endeavors in this area have also been impressive. The famous studies led by Joseph Needham resulted in the voluminous publications – *Science and Civilization in China and Science in Traditional China: A Comparative Perspective*,[9] which have a great impact upon Chinese Studies. The School of

Oriental and African Studies in London, the Centre de Recherche et de Documentation sur la Chine Comtemporaine in Paris, the Documentation Center for Contemporary China of the Sinological Institute at Leiden in the Netherlands, and the Institute of Asian Studies in Hamburg offer various courses in Chinese Studies. In addition, the British Library and the Bibliotheque Nationale provide a wealth of resources important to the study of China.[10]

In the Republic of China on Taiwan, we have also witnessed a surge of interest. During the period 1982-88, research on Chinese-related topics boomed. Prof. C. K. Wang's analyses of research projects, academic conferences, publications, degrees conferred, the establishment of the Center for Chinese Studies, and so forth, during this six-year period indicated their growing and glowing status in Taiwan, as shown by the following examples:[11]

1. **Research projects**

   A total of 264 research projects were conducted, with 25 percent of the projects in the field of history, 25 percent in Taiwan Studies, 19 percent in anthropology/sociology; and so on.

2. **Academic conferences**

   One hundred thirty-one Chinese Studies-related conferences were conducted, with a total presentation of 2,845 papers and an average of almost twenty-two conferences per year. Thirty-six conferences on Chinese history were held during the six-year period; literature came in second (twenty-two conferences) and Chinese philosophy ranked third.

3. **Publications**

   So far, very few up-to-date reference materials have been produced to facilitate research and communication in the field.[12] The apparent need for such types of reference tools led to the development of the database described below.

4. **Doctoral degrees conferred and professional recruitment**

   In addition to the 215 doctoral degrees conferred in the

> fields of Chinese literature, history, and philosophy in Taiwan in 1982-88, sixty-one students were sent abroad by the National Science Council to pursue further studies in Chinese Studies-related disciplines. The National Science Council also recruited seventy-three people who majored in related disciplines to come back to Taiwan either to work or to teach.

Increasingly, Chinese Studies has become an important discipline. However, not enough reference tools have been available. Bibliographic and biographical materials are instrumental to research projects; scholars need to communicate with one another on the same interest. Accordingly, scholars' names have been collected into a database by the end of 1986. It was updated by another survey in January 1987. the database now holds biographical and bibliographic information on 1,324 scholars in the field.[13]

DATABASE GENESIS

The database is based on both biographical and bibliographic information crucial to the study of China and the quality of scholarly research. Since 1981 the Center for Chinese Studies, located in the National Central Library in Taipei, has attempted to develop a database on Chinese–Studies scholars who reside in Taiwan. The Center started the project with a survey of Chinese scholars in Taiwan by sending questionnaires to pertinent faculty members at universities and researchers in research institutions. The questionnaire covered items such as name, birth date and place, education, experience, major, address, telephone numbers, and works (including books and articles). Data on 684 scholars in the field of Chinese Studies, including 1,413 monographs and 9,086 articles, were published in Taiwan in the same six-year period. 2,911 (28%) were on Chinese history; 1,620 (15%) on Chinese literature, and 1,285 titles (12%) on Chinese philosophy.

Realizing the urgent need for such reference material, from 1984 to 1987 the author collected information on some eight hundred China scholars who reside in the United States. In order to avoid duplication of efforts, an integrated but multi-purpose database is being designed as a Who' s Who type of reference tool which will be both in published and online formats. In the spring of 1990 a new questionnaire sent to these scholars for updating. It was estimated that the survey and modification of the software would both be completed by the fall of 1990. Subsequent to editing and processing, the preliminary product was expected to be available by 1991, with continuous bi-annual updating and publication in the future.

INFORMATION COVERAGE

The following information is covered in the database.

1. The field of biographical data cover system identification, Chinese name, English name, romanized name, alias, birthplace, sex, birth date, office and residence address, and telephone numbers, education including graduating department and institution, dissertation/thesis, highest degree obtained, expertise code, level of language proficiency, and awards granted.
2. The field of experience covers such information as current position, previous positions, and names of organizations in which they were held.
3. The field of bibliographic information provides room for 999 works for each entry. It records type of publication (monograph or article), title, date, place, publishers, and number of pages. For articles, periodical or collection title or title of proceedings, volume numbers, and page numbers are recorded.

DATABASE FUNCTIONS

The system is designed with the concept of user friendliness and flexibility in its functions of database maintenance, report generating and printing, and online retrieving. Biographical and bibliographic materials can be updated, edited, and deleted online with great ease. The following print-outs are available:[14]

1. List of Chinese Studies subjects.
2. List of Chinese Studies subtopics.
3. Classification numbers.
4. Individual verification sheet used for each biographee to make corrections..
5. Who's Who in Chinese Studies – arranged by Chinese names in the order of strokes and English or Romanized named in an alphabetical order, with both monographs and periodical articles arranged in a reverse chronological order.
6. List of scholars arranged by subjects in which they specialize.
7. Bibliography of individual scholar's works arranged in a reverse chronological order by publication date with indexes.
8. Bibliography of scholars' work arranged under subject in a reverse chronological order with indexes.

These printouts with various indexes can also be published separately as useful individual reference tools. Each of the following items can be searched online independently for immediate access; they can also be retrieved under multiple conditions or combinations of condition by using "And" (Boolean Logic) to link the following itemized information:

1. System identification number.
2. Names: Chinese, English, or Romanized.
3. Name of graduating university.
4. Name of graduating department.
5. Subject of specialty.
6. Specialization code.

7. Language.
8. Age.
9. Organization and department in which the scholar works.
10. Degree.

DATABASE STRUCTURE

The structure for the database of scholars residing in Taiwan, Republic of China, developed at the Center for Chinese Studies is basically a national database with identification of fields. Now, with the addition of scholars residing in the United States, the software will be modified to the structure of a full-text database. "And", "Or", "Not" (Boolean logic) will be applied.

While exploring the most efficient structure for this database, we have looked into various databases being developed for Chinese studies locally at the Academia Sinica.[15] These are helpful for the modification of the software for this particular database in Chinese Studies. I therefore feel that a brief description of these systems might be useful. It is hoped that all these full-text databases will eventually be linked with the Biographical and Bibliographic Database of Chinese Studies in order to facilitate accessibility to needed information with utmost efficiency.

BRIEF DESCRIPTION OF SELECTED EXISTING SYSTEMS/ DATABASES

In Taiwan, modern information technology is effectively applied to library automation, database building, and office automation. The author does not attempt to report on each and every one that is being developed and used. Only a few which are closely related to Chinese Studies will be described, as follows:

Legislative Information System (LEGISIS)

Developed by the Information Center of the Legislative Yuan on the VAX 8530 system, it offers three useful databases at the present time:[16]

1. LEGISIS THESAURUS : This database of some 2,000 terms serves as an online dictionary of legal terms.
2. The Full-Text Database of Acts, Laws, and Codes of the Republic of China consists of 560 types of legal documents (12,000 items), with description of each document's content and structure. The access points include dates, content summaries, categories, and subjects.
3. Interpellation System covers more than 14,000 interpellation made by the legislators since September 1984. All interpellations raised by legislators concerning administration, proposals, and budgets can be retrieved via the name of the legislator, pertinent subjects, government organization's name, keywords, and session numbers in which the interpellation were raised.

National Central Library Chinese Rare Books (Shan-pen)

Online Catalog plans to include some 15,000 titles of the printed and movable-type editions prior to the Ming Dynasty (A.D.1368-1644), rare editions after the Ch'ing Dynasty (A.D.1644-1911), manuscripts and editions revised by famous scholars, and hand-written edition, input into the database in accordance with the Chinese MARC Format. Its multiple access points include title, author, class/subject, preface or epilogue writer, engraving sponsor, engraving place, engraver, previous collectors, call number, dates of the author, type of edition, binding format code, accession number, and system identification number.[17] In addition, the National Central Library also provides an automated National Bibliography (including all Chinese books published in Taiwan since 1981), Periodical and Government Document indices (indexing 800 periodicals published in Taiwan area and nineteen official gazetters), and a *National Union List of Chinese Periodicals* covering 8,000 periodicals held by 170 local libraries. These are also basic tools for researchers in the Chinese Studies field.[18]

The Academia Sinica Also Has Built up the Following Databases:[19]

Ming/Ch'ing Dynasties Archival Materials Database

This IBM PC/AT based database contains approximately 200,000 official reports of Ming and Ch'ing Dynasties, supplying information on dates, reigns, emperor names, types and those responsible for drafting of reports.

Land Reports

This is a collection of archival materials on Land Reports gathered in the Hsinchu area by the Japanese Government during its occupation of Taiwan. This database, consisting of 472 volumes of 250,000 land reports, is essential to the study of Taiwan's economic history, the formation of land developments, and the relationship between landowners and tenants. Pertinent statistics can be generated to verify various hypotheses.

Database of Ancient Tombs

Using AT&T 3B/2, UNIX, and informatics/SDL database management systems, data pertaining to 3,040 tombs of the Han Dynasty have been processed. The database contains information on each individual tomb's date, structure, location, direction, path, decoration, inscription, accompanying burial items, method of burial, and the structure of the coffin. Related statistics on dates, location, and buried items pertaining to any of the above-mentioned items can be generated.

Chinese Electronic Dictionary

Based on *Kuo Yu Jih Pao Tze Tien (Gwoyeu Ryhbaw Tsyrdean)*, the most popular Chinese dictionary in Taiwan, the Computing Center of the Academia Sinica developed a database of Chinese dictions and names in "Chinese Electronic Dictionary" (CED). CED is to be used as a machine-readable tool for various Chinese information-processing applications, especially for the study of Chinese computation linguistics.

Full Text Database for Chinese History

This pioneering project of the Chinese electronic book was launched in July of 1984, aiming at processing Chinese historical texts of the twenty-five dynasties. These texts contain 60 million Chinese characters. As a prototype, *Shih Ho Chih (Treatise on Food and Money)* has been implemented.

The databases soon to be completed are *Shih Chi*, *Han Shu*, *Hou Han Shu*, *San Kuo Chih*, and *Shih Ho Chih*. It is expected that the entire database cluster will be completed by June 1990. Controlled vocabulary (keywords) and free-text searching are currently available. Controlled vocabulary (keywords) are classified into six categories : names, places, time, official titles, references, and major events. Six inverted list files were built to include these keywords and the pointers of the corresponding basic text elements.

Material sought and viewed on the terminal can be copied to the readers' own files and are to be used along with the readers' own notes. Concordances can be generated as well. Statistical analysis of Chinese character/word usage is the most appropriate application and welcome feature of this system.

CONCLUSION

From the above description, we realize that modern information technologies have been successfully applied to bibliographic control and database building of Chinese Studies resources. However, each application has been developed independently and in a tailor-made sense without an overall plan; they have been devised to meet the needs of one or two institutions. Some of them which are designed to be shared are not yet in a network mode, and are therefore still not shared.

In order to share resources and make the best use of existing information, it is imperative to come to a consensus that database structure should be designed to accommodate all needs, that new storage media such as CD–ROM and hypertext technology be adopted, and that the results of the forthcoming research on networking soon be made available for sharing. It is evident that the Center for Chinese Studies in Taipei plays a prime role in this important task. It is, therefore, recommended that : 1) a conference be called to discuss the various needs of Chinese Studies resources, and to identify necessary tools to be compiled and made available to readers through the use of modern technology; 2) short, medium, and long-range plans to be drawn accordingly for implementation, based on the conference resolutions; 3) standardization of terminologies, keywords, and subject heading in the field of Chinese studies be recognized as necessary; and that 4) redundancy of efforts be avoided and cooperative efforts promoted.

NOTES

1. Chen-ku Wang 王振鵠, "Chung Hua Min Kuo Han Hsueh Yen Chiu Ching K'uang (Shang) 中華民國漢學研究近況（上）," *Han Hsueh Yen Chiu T'ung Hsun 漢學研究通訊 [Newsletter for Research in Chinese Studies]* 8, no. 3 (September 1989): 165; Pang-Hsin Ting 丁邦新, "Kuo Nei Han Hsueh Yen Chiu Te Fang Hsiang Yu Wen T'i 國內漢學研究的方向與問題," *Chung Yuan Wen Hsien 中原文獻* 20, no. 7 (July 1988): 5-11.
2. Chen-ku Wang 王振鵠, "Chung Hua Min Kuo Han Hsueh Yen Chiu Ching K'uang (Shang) (Hsia) 中華民國漢學研究近況（上）（下）," *Han Hsueh Yen Chiu T'ung Hsun 漢學研究通訊 [Newsletter for Research in Chinese Studies]* 8, no. 3-4 (September, December 1989): 165-172, 239-246.
3. Tien-Ch'i Liao 廖天琪, "Tang Tai Chieh K'e Te Han Hsueh Yen Chiu 當代捷克的漢學研究," *Wen Hsin文星* 100 (October 1986): 139-141; Chun-Chieh Huang, Wei-Ying Ku 黃俊傑，古偉瀛, "Hsi Fang han Hsueh Yen Chiu Te Fa Chan 西方漢學研究的發展," *Shih Hsueh P'ing Lun 史學評論 [Chinese Historical Review]*, no. 12 (July 1986): 1-9; Yu Tai 戴玉, "Yuan Fang Te Teng Huo: Ma Han Mao T'an Te Kuo Han Hsueh 遠方的燈火: 馬漢茂談德國漢學," *Kuo Wen T'ien Ti 國文天地 [The World of Chinese*

Language and Literature] 7（December 1985）: 14-18; Wei-Lien Wang 汪威廉, "Yin Tu Te Chung Kuo Yen Chiu 印度的中國研究," *Kuo Li Chung Yang T'u Shu Kuan Kuan K'an 國立中央圖書館館刊 [National Central Library Bulletion]* New 18, no. 1 (June 1985): 55-58; Ching-Lan He 何金蘭, "Fa Kuo Han Hsueh Chih Tien Li Chi Ch'i Fa Chan 法國漢學之奠立及其發展," *Tamkang Hsueh Pao 淡江學報 [Tamkang Journal]* 26 (May 1988): 49-65; Ch'ing-Chang Lin 林慶彰, "Ching Hsueh Tsai Mei Kuo Chih Ken: Fang Han Hsueh Chia Ai Erh Man Chiao Shou 經學在美國植根: 訪漢學家艾爾曼教授," *Shu Mu Chi K'an 書目季刊 [Bibliography Quarterly]* 20, no. 3 (December 1986): 43-50; Yen-ch'iu Wang Pien 汪雁秋 編, *Hai Wai han Hsueh Tzu Yuan Tieh Ch'a Lu 海外漢學資源調查錄* (Taipei: Center for Chinese Studies, 1982).

4. Richard C. Howard, "The Development of American China Studies: A Chronological Outline," *International Association of Orientalist Librarians Bulletin* 32-33 (1988): 38 – 49.
5. Association for Asian Studies, Inc., ed., *Membership Directory* (Ann Arbor, Michigan: Association for Asian Studies, Inc., 1988).
6. Association for Asian Studies, Inc., ed., *Program of the 42nd Annual Meeting* (Ann Arbor, Michigan: Association for Asian Studies, Inc., 1990).
7. Association for Asian Studies, Inc., ed., *Committee on East Asian Libraries Membership Directory* (Ann Arbor, Michigan: Association for Asian Studies, Inc., 1989).
8. Richard C. Howard, "The Development of American China Studies: A Chronological Outline," 38 – 49.
9. Joseph Needham, *Science and Civilization in China* (Cambridge: Cambridge University Press, 1954-90); *The Shorter Science and Civilization in China: An Abridgement of Joseph Needham's Original Text* (Cambridge: Cambridge University Press, 1978-1986); Josseph Needjam, *Science in Traditional China: A Comparative Perspective* (Cambridge, MA: Harvard University Press, 1985), 4-7.
10. John T. Ma, *Chinese Collections in Western Europe: Survey of Their Technical and Readers' Service* (Switzerland: Inter Documentation Company, 1985), 4-7; Hung-Yuan Chu 朱浤源, "Yin Kuo Te Chung Kuo Tung: Liang Te Kuan Ch'a (1) 英國的中國通: 量的觀察（一）," *Ching Tai Chung Kuo Shih Yen Chiu Hsien K'ung 近代中國史研究現況* 2（September 1986）: 116-129.
11. Chen-ku Wang 王振鵠, "Chung Hua Min Kuo Han Hsueh Yen Chiu Ching K'uang (Shang) (Hsia) 中華民國漢學研究近況（上）（下），"

165-172, 239-246.

12. Ping-Chuan Yu 俞秉權, "Shih Chieh Ke Ti Chung Kuo Yen Chiu Tzu Liao Te Ti Li Fen Pu 世界各地中國研究資料的地理分佈," *Hong Kong T'u Shu Kuan Hsieh Hui Hsueh Pao 香港圖書館協會學報 [Journal of the Hang Kong Library Association]* 10（1986）: 65-69.
13. Ching-Ling Juan 阮靜玲, "Han Hsueh Yen Chiu Chung Hsin Kuo Nien Jen Ts'ai Tang Tzu Tung Hua Tso Yeh Chien Chieh 漢學研究中心國內人才檔自動化作業簡介," in *Han hsueh Yen Chiu Tzu Yuan Kuo Chi Yen T'ao Hui Ts'an K'ao Tzu Liao 漢學研究資源國際研討會參考資料*(1988).
14. Ibid.
15. Ching-Chun Hsieh 謝清俊, "Lun Han Hsueh Yen Chiu Yung Chung Wen Tzu Liao K'u Te K'ai Fa 論漢學研究用中文資料庫的開發," Han Hsueh Yen Chiu Tzu Yuan Kuo Chi Yen T'ao Hui Ts'an K'ao Tzu Liao 漢學研究資源國際研討會參考資料（1988）.
16. Karl M. Ku 顧敏, Telephone interview, Taipei, 22 March 1990; Min Ku 顧敏, "Li Fa So Yin Tz'u Hui Chien Chieh 立法索引詞彙簡介," *Chung Kuo T'u Shu Kuan Hsueh Hui Hui Wu Tung Hsun 中國圖書館學會會務通訊 [Library Association of China Newsletter]* 62（31 May 1988）: 14-15.
17. Ch'ing-Chih Li 李清志, "Kuo Li Chung Yang T'u Shu Kuan Shan Pen Shu Pien Mu Hsi Tung Chien Chieh國立中央圖書館善本書編目系統簡介," Han hsueh Yen Chiu Tzu Yuan Kuo Chi Yen T'ao Hui Ts'an K'ao Tzu Liao 漢學研究資源國際研討會參考資料（1988）.
18. *National Central Library Automated Information Service Brochure* (Taipei: National Central Library, 1988); Nancy Ou-lan Chou (Nancy Ou-lan Hu) 胡歐蘭, "Kuo Chia Shu Mu Tzu Liao K'u Chi Ch'I Tzu Hsun Wan Chih Fa Chan 國家書目資料庫及其資訊網之發展 [The National Bibliographic Database and Its Network Development]" (Paper presented at the Seminar on Library Automation and Information Networks, Taipei, Taiwan, 6-12 June 1988).
19. Ching-Chun Hsieh 謝清俊, "Lun Han Hsueh Yen Chiu Yung Chung Wen Tzu Liao K'u Te K'ai Fa 論漢學研究用中文資料庫的開發," Han Hsueh Yen Chiu Tzu Yuan Kuo Chi Yen T'ao Hui Ts'an K'ao Tzu Liao 漢學研究資源國際研討會參考資料(1988).

Paper presented at the Chinese-American Libraries Associtaion Conference on International Access to Specialized Information, Chicago, U.S.A., June 1990.

Reprinted with permission from *圖書館學與資訊科學 [Journal of Library & Information Science]* 17, no. 1 (April 1991): 26-38.

15

A Bibliography of Selected Works on Automated Library and Information Services in the Republic of China 1972-83

ABSTRACT

This bibliography contains selected Chinese and English works published during the period of 1970 to 1983 on automated information systems and services, computer-assisted information services, library automation, some essential works on computer technology, Chinese language and computer technology, standards related to the computer processing of library materials, resources sharing and networking in the Republic of China. It is not intended to be a comprehensive bibliography. Instead, the purpose to is point out some major literature helpful to the understanding of automated library and information services in the ROC in the past decade. The citations bearing romanized titles are of works either all or partially in the Chinese language.

INTRODUCTION

The development of library automation in the Republic of China began in 1973 when Science and Technology Information Center of the National Science Council processed and printed its *Union List of Scientific Serials in the Libraries of the Republic of China* in 1973 which marked the beginning of computer applications for libraries and information centers in the Republic of China. The idea to initiate researches on computer processing of vernacular language library materials was first conceived in 1974 and actually experimented with an integrated approach by building up a prototype bibliographic database meeting the needs of acquisition, cataloging and circulation (ACCI). In the library week of the same year, the Department of Library Science, National Taiwan University, demonstrated the storage and bibliographic retrieval capabilities of Chinese books. These early experiments indicated the feasibility of processing library materials in Chinese language.

The approaches employed by computer processing of Western language materials and Chinese language materials are completely different. In the application made for Western language materials, it followed the usual path which was to produce lists, statistics, etc. in a batch mode. The processing of vernacular materials, on the other hand, was started out with an on-line approach for the purpose of information storage and retrieval.

Since 1975, many different organizations have attempted to upgrade their Chinese information services with the aid of computers. Up to now, seven libraries and information centers have automated some of the operations. The current development covers all areas of library automation: acquisition, cataloging, circulation, reference, and serial control. The introduction of UDAS services, the use of DIALOG and ORBIT, and its initial installation at the university library and information center have greatly benefited the information user community.

The basics essential to library automation such as the various standards formation – revised cataloging rules, information interchange code, and machine readable cataloging formats – have won professional attention. The plans and creative concepts regarding future developments of library automation, information systems services, resources sharing and networking have also been drawn.

The state of art and these efforts reported in conferences, seminars, and journal articles, several important publications on the standards published in several editions in the Republic of China, some general reference works, and some essential works on computer technology, Chinese language and computer technology are not readily available in any one bibliography. For the purpose to facilitate an understanding of automated library and information services in this country, this bibliography is therefore compiled with future addition of annotations and continuous updating.

This bibliography contains selected Chinese and English works published during the period of 1970 to 1983 on automated information systems and services, computer-assisted information services, library automation, some essential works on computer technology, Chinese language and computer technology, standards related to the computer processing of library materials, resources sharing and networking in the Republic of China. It is not intended to be a comprehensive bibliography. Instead, the purpose to is point out some major literature helpful to the understanding of automated library and information services in the ROC in the past decade.

The citations are in Turabian's bibliographic reference style with addition of page numbers enclosed in parentheses following the citation and addition of conference or symposium places and dates. The citations bearing romanized titles are of works either all or partially in the Chinese language.

GENERAL

1. Tzu Hsun Kung Yeh Ts'e Chin Hui Pien 資訊工業策進會 編 [Institute for the Information Industry, ed.]. *Chung Hua Min Kuo Ch'i Shih I Nien Tzu Hsun Kung Yeh Nien Chien 中華民國七十一年資訊工業年鑑 [Information Industry Yearbook of the Republic of China, 1982]*. Taipei: Institute for the Information Industry, 1982. 228 pp.
2. Tzu Hsun Kung Yeh Ts'e Chin Hui Pien 資訊工業策進會 編 [Institute for the Information Industry, ed.]. *Chung Hua Min Kuo Tzu Hsun Kung Yeh Nien Chien: Ch'i Shih Nien Tu 中華民國資訊工業年鑑：七十年度*

[Information Industry Yearbook of the Republic of China, 1981]. Taipei: Institute for the Information Industry, 1981. 242 pp.

3. Kuo Li Chung Yang T'u Shu Kuan Pien 國立中央圖書館 編 [National Central Library, ed.]. *Chung Hua Min Kuo Tu Shu Kuan Nien Chien 中華民國圖書館年鑑 [Library Yearbook of the Republic of China]*. Taipei: National Central Library, 1981. 451 pp.
4. Chung Kuo T'u Shu Kuan Hsueh Hui Pien 中國圖書館學會 編 [Library Association of China, ed.]. *Chung Wen T'u Shu Tzu Liao Tzu Tung Hua Kuo Chi Yeh T'ao Hui Lun Wen Chi 中文圖書資料自動化國際研討會論文集 [Papers of the International Workshop on Chinese Library Automation]*, Taipei, 14-19 February 1981. Taipei: Library Association of China, 1981. 427 pp.
5. Kuo Li Chung Yang T'u Shu Kuan Pien 國立中央圖書館 編 [National Central Library, comp.]. *T'u Shu Kuan Shih Yeh He Tso Yu Fa Chan Yen T'ao Hui Hui I Chi Yao 圖書館事業合作與發展研討會會議紀要 [Proceedings of the 1980 Library Development Seminar]*, Taipei, 1-7 December 1980. Taipei: National Central Library, 1981. 547 pp.
6. ASIS Taipei Chapter. *Symposium on Computer Processing of Chinese Library Materials and Computer-Assisted Chinese Language Instruction at ASIS-82: Proceedings*, Columbus, Ohio, 19 October 1982. Taipei: ASIS Taipei Chapter, 1982. 123 pp.

AUTOMATED INFORMATION SYSTEMS AND SERVICES

1. Kuo Li Taiwan Shih Fan Ta Hsueh, Kuo Li Chiao Yu Tzu Liao Kuan Pien 國立台灣師範大學，國立教育資料館 編 [National Taiwan Normal University and National Institute of Educational Materials, eds.]. *Educational Resources Workshop Proceedings, Taipei*, 10-11 May 1980. Taipei: National Taiwan Normal University and National Institute of Educational Materials, 1980. 171 pp.
2. Fang, T'ung-sheng. "The Establishment and Use of Information System on Science and Technology in R.O.C." In *Symposium on Computer Processing of Chinese Library Materials and Computer-Assisted Chinese Language Instruction at ASIS-82: Proceedings*, Columbus, Ohio, 19 October 1982. Taipei: ASIS Taipei Chapter, 1982. (pp. 10-1-3.)
3. Fang, T'ung-sheng 方同生. "K'o Hsueh Ch'i K'an Lien Ho Mu Lu Tzu Liao T'ang Pao Kao 科學期刊聯合目錄資料檔報告 [Union List of Scientific and Technical Periodicals]." In *T'u Shu Kuan Shih Yeh He Tso Yu Fa Chan Yen T'ao Hui Hui I Chi Yao 圖書館事業合作與發展研討會會議紀*

要 *[Proceedings of the 1980 Library Development Seminar]*, Taipei, 1-7 December 1980. Taipei: National Central Library, 1981. (pp. 433-440.)

4. Fang, T'ung-shen 方同生. "T'ung I Ts'ai Kou Hsi Wen Tu Shu Tzu Liao Hsi T'ung Chi Hua 統一採購西文圖書資料處理系統計劃 [Centralized Acquisition System of Foreign Publications]." In *T'u Shu Kuan Shih Yeh He Tso Yu Fa Chan Yen T'ao Hui Hui I Chi Yao 圖書館事業合作與發展研討會會議紀要 [Proceedings of the 1980 Library Development Seminar]*, Taipei, 1-7 December 1980. Taipei: National Central Library, 1981. (pp. 441-445.)
5. Fung, Margaret C. "The Chinese Educational Resources Information Systems – A Case Report." In *Chung Wen T'u Shu Tzu Liao Tzu Tung Hua Kuo Chi Yeh T'ao Hui Lun Wen Chi 中文圖書資料自動化國際研討會論文集 [Papers of the International Workshop on Chinese Library Automation]*, Taipei, 14-19 February 1981. Taipei: Library Association of China, 1981. (pp. D1 - D10.)
6. Fung, Margaret C. 張鼎鍾. "Chung Wen T'u Shu Tzu Liao Tzu Tung Hua Tso Yeh 中文圖書資料自動化作業 [Chinese Library Automation]." In *T'u Shu Kuan Hsueh Yu Tzu Hsun K'o Hsueh Chih T'an T'ao 圖書館學與資訊科學之探討 [On library and Information Science]*. Taipei: Student Book Co., 1982. (pp. 61-70.)
7. Fung, Margaret C. 張鼎鍾. "Kuo Li Taiwan Shih Fan Ta Hsueh T'u Shu Kuan Kuo Chi Pai K'o Tzu Liao K'u Tso Yeh Kai K'uang 國立台灣師範大學圖書館國際百科資料庫作業概況 [Computer–Assisted Reference Service at the National Taiwan Normal University Library]." In *T'u Shu Kuan Shih Yeh He Tso Yu Fa Chan Yen T'ao Hui Hui I Chi Yao 圖書館事業合作與發展研討會會議紀要 [Proceedings of the 1980 Library Development Seminar]*, Taipei, 1-7 December 1980. Taipei: National Central Library, 1981. (pp. 450-451.)
8. Fung, Margaret C. "Library Automation in the Republic of China." *T'u Shu Kuan Hsueh Yu Tzu Hsun K'o Hsueh 圖書館學與資訊科學 [Journal of Library & Information Science]* 6 (April 1980): 1-16.
9. Fung, Margaret C. 張鼎鍾. *T'u Shu Kuan Hsueh Yu Tzu Hsun K'o Hsueh Chih T'an T'ao 圖書館學與資訊科學之探討 [On library and Information Science]*. Taipei: Student Book Co., 1982. 277 pp.
10. Fung, Margaret C. "State of Art: Library Automation in Taipei, R.O.C." *T'u Shu Kuan Hsueh Yu Tzu Hsun K'o Hsueh Chih T'an T'ao 圖書館學與資訊科學之探討 [On library and Information Science]*. Taipei: Student Book Co., 1982. (pp. 131-147.)

11. Fung, Margaret C. 張鼎鍾. "Wo Kuo Chiao Yu Tzu Liao K'u CERIS 我國教育資料庫CERIS [Chinese Educational Resources Information Systems CERIS]." In *Chiao Yu Tzu Liao Yen T'ao Hui Chi Lu 教育資料研討會記錄 [Educational Resources Workshop Proceedings]*, Taipei, 10-11 May 1980. Taipei: National Taiwan Normal University and National Institute of Educational Materials, 1980. (pp. 26–31.)
12. Fung, Margaret C. 張鼎鍾. "Wo Kuo Chiao Yu Tzu Liao K'u CERIS 我國教育資料庫CERIS [Chinese Educational Resources Information Systems]." In *T'u Shu Kuan Shih Yeh He Tso Yu Fa Chan Yen T'ao Hui Hui I Chi Yao 圖書館事業合作與發展研討會會議紀要 [Proceedings of the 1980 Library Development Seminar]*, Taipei, 1-7 December 1980. Taipei: National Central Library, 1981. (pp. 486 – 492.)
13. Hu, Nancy Ou-lan 胡歐蘭. *Ts'an K'ao Tzu Hsun Fu Wu 參考資訊服務 [Reference Information Services]*. Taipei: Student Book Co.,1982. 326 pp.
14. Huang, Hong-chu 黃鴻珠. "Wo Kuo Hsi Shu Ts'ai Kou Tien Nao Hua Tso Yeh Chih T'an Tao 我國西書採購電腦化作業之探討 [A Study on the Computerization of Foreign Publications Ordering Procedures in the R.O.C]." *T'u Shu Kuan Hsueh Yu Tzu Hsun K'o Hsueh 圖書館學與資訊科學 [Journal of Library & Information Science]* 5 (April 1979): 104 – 110.
15. Huang, Jack Kai–tung. "Freedom Council Information Abstracts." In *Chung Wen T'u Shu Tzu Liao Tzu Tung Hua Kuo Chi Yeh T'ao Hui Lun Wen Chi 中文圖書資料自動化國際研討會論文集 [Papers of the International Workshop on Chinese Library Automation]*, Taipei, 14-19 February 1981. Taipei: Library Association of China, 1981. (pp. D47-D56) .
16. Huang, Lin-chih 黃林芝. "Chung Shan K'o Hsueh Yen Chiu Yuan T'u Shu Kuan Tzu Tung Hua Chien Chieh 中山科學研究院圖書館自動化簡介 [Introducing Library Automation of Chung Shan Institute of Technology]." In *T'u Shu Kuan Shih Yeh He Tso Yu Fa Chan Yen T'ao Hui Hui I Chi Yao 圖書館事業合作與發展研討會會議紀要 [Proceedings of the 1980 Library Development Seminar]*, Taipei, 1-7 December 1980. Taipei: National Central Library, 1981. (pp. 446-449).
17. Huang, Shih-hsion 黃世雄. "Tan Chiang Ta Hsueh T'u Shu Kuan Tien Nao Hua Tso Yeh Hsi T'ung 淡江大學圖書館電腦化作業系統 [The Automated Library System in Tamkang University]." In *T'u Shu Kuan Shih Yeh He Tso Yu Fa Chan Yen T'ao Hui Hui I Chi Yao 圖書館事業合作與發展研討會會議紀要 [Proceedings of the 1980 Library Development Seminar]*, Taipei, 1-7 December 1980. Taipei: National Central Library, 1981. (pp. 523-525).

18. Huang, Yuan-ch'uan 黃淵泉. "Pen Kuan T'u Shu Tzu Liao Pien Mu Yeh Wu Yu Ch'i Tzu Tung Hua Tso Yeh Te Chan Wang 本館圖書資料編目業務與其自動化作業的展望 [Developments in the National Central Library's Book Cataloging and Other Library Automation Activities]." *Kuo Li Chung Yang T'u Shu Kuan Kuan K'an 國立中央圖書館館刊 [National Central Library Bulletin]* New 13 (December 1980): 30-37.
19. Lee, Lucy Te-chu 李德竹. "Chung Mei K'o Hsueh Tzu Liao Yun Yung Fa Chan Yen T'ao Hui 中美科學資料運用發展研討會 [Sino-U.S. Workshop on Scientific and Technical Information Needs and Resources]." *Kuo Li Chung Yang T'u Shu Kuan Kuan K'an 國立中央圖書館館刊 [National Central Library Bulletin]* New 6 (September 1973): 43- 46.
20. Lee, Lucy Te-chu, ed. 李德竹. *T'u Shu Kuan Hsueh Chi Tzu Hsun K'o Hsueh: Ch'ang Yung Tzu Hui 圖書館學及資訊科學: 常用字彙 [English Chinese Library and Information Terminology]*. Taipei: Feng-cheng Publishing Co., 1980. 291 pp.
21. Lin, Meng-chen 林孟真. *Wo Kuo Tzu Hsun Hsi T'ung Chih Chien Li Yu T'an T'ao 我國資訊系統之建立與探討 [The Establishment and Exploration of the Information Systems in the R.O.C.]*. Taipei: Wen Shih Che Publishing Co., 1982. 191 pp.
22. Loh, Yung–liang. "Computer Microfilm Retrieval System Used for Processing Chinese Criminal Data in the R.O.C." In *Chung Wen T'u Shu Tzu Liao Tzu Tung Hua Kuo Chi Yeh T'ao Hui Lun Wen Chi 中文圖書資料自動化國際研討會論文集 [Papers of the International Workshop on Chinese Library Automation]*, Taipei, 14-19 February 1981. Taipei: Library Association of China, 1981. (pp. D97 - D104).
23. Kuo Li Chung Yang T'u Shu Kuan 國立中央圖書館 [National Central Library]. "Chung Hua Min Kuo Chung Wen Ch'i K'an Lien Ho Mu Lu Tzu Liao Ch'u Li Chien Chieh 中華民國中文期刊聯合目錄資料處理簡介 [A Brief Introduction to the Union List of Chinese Periodicals of the R.O.C.]." In *T'u Shu Kuan Shih Yeh He Tso Yu Fa Chan Yen T'ao Hui Hui I Chi Yao 圖書館事業合作與發展研討會會議紀要 [Proceedings of the 1980 Library Development Seminar]*, Taipei, 1-7 December 1980. Taipei: National Central Library, 1981. (pp. 452-476).
24. National Science Council, ed. *Chung Mei K'o Chi Tzu Liao Ch'u Li Chi Yun Yung Yen T'ao Hui Pao Kao 中美科技資料處理及運用研討會報告* [Sino-U.S. Workshop on Scientific and Technical Information Needs and Resources in the Republic of China], Washingtion, D.C., 25-27 April 1973. Taipei: National Science Council, 1973. 139 pp.

25. Hsing Cheng Yuan Kuo Chia K'o Hsueh Wei Yuan Hui K'o Hsueh Chi Shu Tzu Liao Chung Hsin Pien 行政院國家科學委員會科學技術資料中心 編 [Science and Technology Information Center, National Science Council, Executive Yuan, ed.]. "*Chung Wen Tzu Hsun Tzu Tung Hua Tso Yeh Kai K'uang Chien Shu 中文資訊自動化作業概況簡述 [Brief Report on Chinese Automated Information Processing]*." In *Chung Wen T'u Shu Tzu Liao Tzu Tung Hua Kuo Chi Yeh T'ao Hui Lun Wen Chi 中文圖書資料自動化國際研討會論文集 [Papers of the International Workshop on Chinese Library Automation]*, Taipei, 14-19 February 1981. Taipei: Library Association of China, 1981. (I - XVIII).
26. "Services for Scientific Researches: Science and Technology Information Center." *NSC Review* (1980-1981): 92–97.
27. Chung Kuo T'u Shu Kuan Hsueh Hui Pien 中國圖書館學會 編 [Library Association of China, ed.]. "T'u Shu Kuan Tzu Tung Hua Tso Yeh Chi Hua 圖書館自動化作業計畫 [Library Automation Planning Program]." *Chung Kuo T'u Shu Kuan Hsueh Hui Hui Wu T'ung Hsun 中國圖書館學會會務通訊 [Library Association of China Newsletter]* 22 (1980): 9-10.
28. Wang, Chen-ku, and Seng, B. H. "Chinese Library Automation – An Overview." In *Symposium on Computer Processing of Chinese Library Materials and Computer-Assisted Chinese Language Instruction at ASIS-82: Proceedings*, Columbus, Ohio, 19 October 1982. Taipei: ASIS Taipei Chapter, 1982. (pp. 1-1-4).
29. Wei, Yung 魏鏞. *Fa Chan Tzu Hsun T'i Hsi, Ch'iang Hua Chueh Ts'e Kung Neng: Wo Kuo Hsing Cheng Tzu Hsun T'i Hsi Chih Chien Li Yu Chan Wang 發展資訊體系，強化決策功能：我國行政資訊體系之建立與展望 [Develop Information Systems, Strengthen Decision Making Capabilities: The Establishment and Development of Our National Management Information System]*. Taipei: Research, Development and Evaluation Commission, Executive Yuan, 1982.
30. Wu, Rui-lan Ku. "The Union List of Chinese Serials in the Republic of China – A Case Report." In *Chung Wen T'u Shu Tzu Liao Tzu Tung Hua Kuo Chi Yeh T'ao Hui Lun Wen Chi 中文圖書資料自動化國際研討會論文集 [Papers of the International Workshop on Chinese Library Automation]*, Taipei, 14-19 February 1981. Taipei: Library Association of China, 1981. (pp. D57-D82).
31. Wu, Wan-jiun. "The Agricultural Science and Technology Information Management System." In *Chung Wen T'u Shu Tzu Liao Tzu Tung Hua Kuo Chi Yeh T'ao Hui Lun Wen Chi 中文圖書資料自動化國際研討會論文*

集 *[Papers of the International Workshop on Chinese Library Automation]*, Taipei, 14-19 February 1981. Taipei: Library Association of China, 1981. (pp. D11-D46).

32. Wu, Wan-jiun 吳萬鈞. "Nung Yeh K'o Chi Tzu Hsun Kuan Li Hsi T'ung 農業科技資訊管理系統 [The Agricultural Science and Technology Information Management System]."In *T'u Shu Kuan Shih Yeh He Tso Yu Fa Chan Yen T'ao Hui Hui I Chi Yao 圖書館事業合作與發展研討會會議紀要 [Proceedings of the 1980 Library Development Seminar]*, Taipei, 1-7 December 1980. Taipei: National Central Library, 1981. (pp. 493-503).
33. Wu, Wan-jiun, Kao, Chiu-fang, Wang, Huan-hsin, and Hsu, Mei-chu. "Agri-Thesaurus of Agricultural Information System." In *Symposium on Computer Processing of Chinese Library Materials and Computer-Assisted Chinese Language Instruction at ASIS-82: Proceedings*, Columbus, Ohio, 19 October 1982. Taipei: ASIS Taipei Chapter, 1982. (pp. 6-1-6).
34. Wu, Wan-jiun, Shen, Hong-shyang, and Wee, Lily. "A Chinese Agricultural Information Management System." *The Information Community: An Alliance for Progress*. Edited by Lois F. Lunin, Madeline F. Henderson, and Harold Wooster. *Proceedings of the 44th ASIS Annual Meeting*, vol. 18, Columbus, Ohio, 25-30 October, 1981. White Plains, N.Y.: Knowledge Industry Publications, Inc. for American Society for Information Science, 1981. (pp. 62-64).

INFORMATION SERVICES – ONLINE RETRIEVAL

1. Chen, Shan-chieh 陳善捷. "Kuo Chi Pai K'o Kung Yung Yu Chien So 國際百科功用與檢索 [The Supply and Retrieval of UDAS]." *Tzu Hsun Yu Tien Nao 資訊與電腦 [Information and Computers]* 9 (March, 1981): 11-15.
2. Huang, Sophia Hong–chu 黃鴻珠. "Ts'ung Kuo Chi Pai K'o Te Ying Yung Chan Wang Wo Kuo Shu Mu Tzu Hsun Hsi T'ung Te Fa Chan 從國際百科的應用展望我國書目資訊系統的發展 [From the Utilization of UDAS to the Outlook Development of the Bibliographic Information Retrieval System in the R. O. C.]." *Chiao Yu Tzu Liao K'o Hsueh 教育資料科學 [Journal of Educational Media Science]* 18, no.2 (Winter 1980): 84-98.
3. Liu, Chin-lung 劉錦龍. "Ju Ho Yu Shiao Yun Yung Tzu Hsun Tzu Yuan – Kuo Chi Pai K'o Tien Nao Tzu Liao K'u Chih Li Yung 如何有效運用資訊資源 - 國際百科電腦資料庫之利用 [How to Effectively Use Information Resources – Use of UDAS]" *Chi Hsieh Yueh K'an機械月刊 [Machinery Monthly]* 7 (November 1981): 160-172.

4. Kuo Li Chung Yang T'u Shu Kuan, Hsing Cheng Yuan Ch'u Chi Chu Tien Tzu Tzu Liao Chu Li Chung Hsin Pien 國立中央圖書館，行政院主計處電子資料處理中心 編 [National Central Library, and Data Processing Center, Directorate General of Budget, Accounting and Statistics, eds.]. "Chung Hua Min Kuo Ch'i K'an Lun Wen So Yin Tzu Liao Ch'u Li Hsi T'ung Ch'u Pu Chi Hua Chien Chieh 中華民國期刊論文索引資料處理系統初步計畫簡介 [An Introduction to the Chinese Periodicals Indexing System]." In *T'u Shu Kuan Shih Yeh He Tso Yu Fa Chan Yen T'ao Hui Hui I Chi Yao 圖書館事業合作與發展研討會會議紀要 [Proceedings of the 1980 Library Development Seminar]*, Taipei, 1-7 December 1980. Taipei: National Central Library, 1981. (pp. 477-485).
5. Kuo Li Taiwan Shih Fan Ta Hsueh, Kuo Li Chiao Yu Tzu Liao Kuan Pien 國立台灣師範大學，國立教育資料館 編 [National Taiwan Normal University and National Institute of Educational Materials, eds.]. *Chiao Yu Tzu Liao Yen T'ao Hui Chi Lu 教育資料研討會記錄 [Educational Resources Workshop Proceedings]*, Taipei, 10-11 May 1980. Taipei: National Taiwan Normal University and National Institute of Educational Materials, 1980. 171 pp.
6. Kuo Li Taiwan Shih Fan ta Hsueh T'u Shu Kuan Pien 國立台灣師範大學圖書館 編 [National Taiwan Normal University Library, ed.]. *Kuo Chi Pai K'o Tzu Liao K'u ORBIT Chien So Shih Yung Shou Ts'e. 國際百科資料庫ORBIT檢索使用手冊 [User's Manual for ORBIT]*. Taipei: National Taiwan Normal University Library, 1982. 56 pp.
7. Hsing Cheng Yuan Kuo Chia K'o Hsueh Wei Yuan Hui K'o Hsueh Chi Shu Tzu Liao Chung Hsin Pien 行政院國家科學委員會科學技術資料中心 編 [Science and Technology Information Center, National Science Council, Executive Yuan, ed.]. *Kuo Chi Pai K'o Tzu Liao Chien So Fu Wu DIALOG Tzu Hsun Chien So Fu Wu Shou Ts'e. 國際百科資料檢索服務DIALOG資訊檢索服務手冊 [UDAS Information Retrieval Services: DIALOG Information Retrieval Services Manual]*. Taipei: Scientific and Technical Information Center, National Science Council, 1981. 29 pp.
8. Seng, Bao-hwan 沈寶環. "Wo Kuo K'o Chi T'u Shu Kuan Tzu Tung Hua Te Chan Wang 我國科技圖書館自動化的展望 [Development of Scientific and Technical Library Automation in the R.O.C]." *Chung Yang Jih Pao* 中央日報 [*Central Daily News* (Taiwan, ROC)], 27 December 1978.
9. Yates, Joann. "ORBIT System and Database Retrieving Skill." In *Chiao Yu Tzu Liao Yen T'ao Hui Chi Lu 教育資料研討會記錄 [Educational Resources Workshop Proceedings]*, Taipei, 10-11 May 1980. Taipei: Na-

tional Taiwan Normal University and National Institute of Educational Materials, 1980. (pp. 32-43).

STANDARDS – CATALOGING

1. T'u Shu Kuan Tzu Tung Hua Tso Yeh Kuei Hua Wei Yuan Hui Chung Kuo Pien Mu Kuei Tse Yen Chiu Hsiao Tsu Pien 圖書館自動化作業規劃委員會中國編目規則研究小組 編 [Chinese Cataloging Rules Working Group, Library Automation Planning Committee, ed.]. *Chung Kuo Pien Mu Kuei Tse 中國編目規則 [Chinese Cataloging Rules]*. Taipei: National Central Library, 1982. 60 pp.
2. Chinese Cataloging Rules Working Group, Library Automation Planning Committee, ed. "The Shaping of the Chinese Cataloging Rules." In *Chung Wen T'u Shu Tzu Liao Tzu Tung Hua Kuo Chi Yeh T'ao Hui Lun Wen Chi 中文圖書資料自動化國際研討會論文集 [Papers of the International Workshop on Chinese Library Automation]*, Taipei, 14-19 February 1981. Taipei: Library Association of China, 1981. (pp. C33-C66).
3. Lan, C. C., and Wu, M. D. "The New Chinese Cataloging Rules as the Foundation of Chinese MARC." In *Symposium on Computer Processing of Chinese Library Materials and Computer-Assisted Chinese Language Instruction at ASIS-82: Proceedings*, Columbus, Ohio, 19 October 1982. Taipei: ASIS Taipei Chapter, 1982. (pp. 4-1-5).

STANDARDS - CCCII

1. Agenbroad, James E. "Personal Names and the Chinese Character Code for Information Interchange, Vol. 1: (CCCII / 1) – Adequacy and Implications." In *Chung Wen T'u Shu Tzu Liao Tzu Tung Hua Kuo Chi Yeh T'ao Hui Lun Wen Chi 中文圖書資料自動化國際研討會論文集 [Papers of the International Workshop on Chinese Library Automation]*, Taipei, 14-19 February 1981. Taipei: Library Association of China, 1981. (pp. A1-A8).
2. Agenbroad, James E. "Personal Names and the Chinese Character Code for Information Interchange, Vol. 1: (CCCII / 1) – Adequacy and Implications." *T'u Shu Kuan Hsueh Yu Tzu Hsun K'o Hsueh, 圖書館學與資訊科學 [Journal of Library & Information Science]* 7 (October 1981): 152-160.
3. Chung Wen Tzu Hsun Ch'u Li Yung Tzu Yen Chi Hsiao Tsu Pien 中文資訊處理用字小組 編 [The Chinese Character Analysis Group, ed.]. *Chung Wen Tzu Hsun Chiao Huan Ma 中文資訊交化換碼 [Chinese Character Code for Information Interchange]*, 1 vol. Taipei: Library Associa-

tion of China, 1980.

4. Hsing Cheng Yuan Kuo Tzu Cheng Li Hsiao Tsu Pien 行政院國字整理小組 編 [The Chinese Character Analysis Group, Executive Yuan, ed.]. *Chung Wen Tzu Hsun Chiao Huan Ma Tzu Hsing Piao 中文資訊交換碼字形表 [Symbols and Character Tables of Chinese Character Code for Information Interchange]*, 1 vol. Taipei: The Chinese Character Analysis Group, Executive Yuan, 1981.
5. Kuo Tzu Cheng Li Hsiao Tsu Pien 國字整理小組 編 [The Chinese Character Analysis Group, ed.]. *Chung Wen Tzu Hsun Chiao Huan Ma I T'i Tzu Piao 中文資訊交換碼異體字表 [Variant Forms of Chinese Character Code for Information Interchange]*, 2nd ed., vol. 2. Taipei: The Chinese Character Analysis Group, 1982.
6. Hsieh, Ching-chun, Huang, Jack Kai-tung, Yang, Chen-chau, and Chang, Chung–tao. "The Design and Application of the Chinese Character Code for Information Interchange – (CCCII)." In *Chung Wen T'u Shu Tzu Liao Tzu Tung Hua Kuo Chi Yeh T'ao Hui Lun Wen Chi 中文圖書資料自動化國際研討會論文集 [Papers of the International Workshop on Chinese Library Automation]*, Taipei, 14-19 February 1981. Taipei: Library Association of China, 1981. (pp. 1-17).
7. Hsieh, Ching-chun, Huang, Jack Kai-tung, Yang, Chen-chau, and Chang, Chung-tao. "The Design and Application of the Chinese Character Code for Information Interchange – (CCCII)." *T'u Shu Kuan Hsueh Yu Tzu Hsun K'o Hsueh 圖書館學與資訊科學 [Journal of Library & Information Science]* 7 (October 1981): 129-143.

STANDARDS-MARC FORMAT

1. T'u Shu Kuan Tzu Tung Hua Tso Yeh Kuei Hua Wei Yuan Hui Chung Wen Chi Tu Pien Mu Ke Shih Kung Tso Hsiao Tsu Pien 圖書館自動化作業規劃委員會中文機讀編目格式工作小組 編 [Chinese MARC Working Group, Library Automation Planning Committee, ed.]. *Chung Kuo Chi Tu Pien Mu Ke Shih 中國機讀編目格式 [Chinese MARC Format]*. Taipei: Library Association of China and National Central Library, September 1982. 342 pp.
2. Chinese MARC Working Group, Library Automation Planning Committee, ed. "Chinese MARC Format and Bibliographic Databases." In *Symposium on Computer Processing of Chinese Library Materials and Computer-Assisted Chinese Language Instruction at ASIS-82: Proceedings*, Columbus, Ohio, 19 October 1982. Taipei: ASIS Taipei Chapter,

1982. (pp. 5-1-27).

3. Chinese MARC Working Group, Library Automation Planning Committee, ed. *Chinese MARC Format for Books*, 1st ed. Taipei: Library Association of China and National Central Library, February 1981. 162 pp.
4. T'u Shu Kuan Tzu Tung Hua Tso Yeh Kuei Hua Wei Yuan Hui Chung Wen Chi Tu Pien Mu Ke Shih Kung Tso Hsiao Tsu Pien 圖書館自動化作業規劃委員會中文機讀編目格式工作小組 編 [Chinese MARC Working Group, Library Automation Planning Committee, ed.]. *Chung Wen Chi Tu Pien Mu Ke Shih 中文機讀編目格式 [Chinese MARC Format for Books]*, 2nd ed. Taipei: Library Association of China and National Central Library, July 1984. 205 pp.
5. T'u Shu Kuan Tzu Tung Hua Tso Yeh Kuei Hua Wei Yuan Hui Chung Wen Chi Tu Pien Mu Ke Shih Kung Tso Hsiao Tsu Pien 圖書館自動化作業規劃委員會中文機讀編目格式工作小組 編 [Chinese MARC Working Group, Library Automation Planning Committee, ed.]. *Chung Wen Chi Tu Pien Mu Ke Shih 中文機讀編目格式 [Chinese MARC Format for Books]*. Taipei: Library Association of China and National Central Library, September 1982. 307 pp.
6. T'u Shu Kuan Tzu Tung Hua Tso Yeh Kuei Hua Wei Yuan Hui Chung Wen Chi Tu Pien Mu Ke Shih Kung Tso Hsiao Tsu Pien 圖書館自動化作業規劃委員會中文機讀編目格式工作小組 編 [Chinese MARC Working Group, Library Automation Planning Committee, ed.]. *Chung Wen T'u Shu Chi Tu Pien Mu Ke Shih 中文圖書機讀編目格式 [Chinese MARC Format for Books]*. 1st ed. Taipei: Library Association of China and National Central Library, February 1981. 140 pp.
7. T'u Shu Kuan Tzu Tung Hua Tso Yeh Kuei Hua Wei Yuan Hui Chung Wen Chi Tu Pien Mu Ke Shih Kung Tso Hsiao Tsu Pien 圖書館自動化作業規劃委員會中文機讀編目格式工作小組 編 [Chinese MARC Working Group, Library Automation Planning Committee, ed.]. *Chung Wen T'u Shu Chi Tu Pien Mu Ke Shih 中文圖書機讀編目格式 [Chinese MARC Format for Books]*. 2nd ed. Taipei: Library Association of China and National Central Library, July 1981. 176 pp.
8. T'u Shu Kuan Tzu Tung Hua Tso Yeh Kuei Hua Wei Yuan Hui Chung Wen Chi Tu Pien Mu Ke Shih Kung Tso Hsiao Tsu Pien 圖書館自動化作業規劃委員會中文機讀編目格式工作小組 編 [Chinese MARC Working Group, Library Automation Planning Committee, ed.]. *Chung Wen Chi Tu Pien Mu Ke Shih: Shih Yung Shou Ts'e中文圖書機讀編目格式：使用手冊 [Chinese MARC Format for Books: User's Manual]*. Taipei:

Library Association of China and National Central Library, 1981. 53 pp.

9. Fung, Margaret C. "The Development of Chinese MARC in Taipei." *Chiao Yu Tzu Liao K'o Hsueh 教育資料科學 [Journal of Educational Media Science]* 19 (Summer 1982): 357-368.
10. Lee, Lucy Te-chu 李德竹. "Chung Wen T'u Shu Chi Tu Pien Mu Ke Shih Yen Ting Kung Tso Pao Kao 中文圖書機讀編目格式研訂工作報告 [Report on Chinese MARC Format for Books]." In *T'u Shu Kuan Shih Yeh He Tso Yu Fa Chan Yen T'ao Hui Hui I Chi Yao 圖書館事業合作與發展研討會會議紀要 [Proceedings of the 1980 Library Development Seminar]*, Taipei, 1-7 December 1980. Taipei: National Central Library, July 1981. (pp. 518-519).
11. Lee, Lucy Te-chu, Hu, Nancy Ou-lan, Huang, Sophia Hong-chu, Huang, Jack Kai-tung, and Wu, Ming-der. "Chinese MARC: Its Present Status and Future Development." In *Chung Wen T'u Shu Tzu Liao Tzu Tung Hua Kuo Chi Yeh T'ao Hui Lun Wen Chi 中文圖書資料自動化國際研討會論文集 [Papers of the International Workshop on Chinese Library Automation]*, Taipei, 14-19 February 1981. Taipei: Library Association of China, 1981. (pp. C9 – C26).
12. Lee, Lucy Te-chu, Hu, Nancy Ou-lan, Huang, Hong-chu, Huang, Jack Kai-tung, and Wu, Ming-der. "Chinese MARC: Its Present Status and Future Development." *T'u Shu Kuan Hsueh Yu Tzu Hsun K'o Hsueh 圖書館學與資訊科學 [Journal of Library & Information Science]* 7, no.1 (April 1981): 1-18.

CHINESE LANGUAGE AND COMPUTER TECHNOLOGY

1. Chang, Chung-tao, Huang, Jack Kai-Tung, Hsieh, Ching-chun, and Yang, Chen-chau. "The Design of a Cross Reference Database for Chinese Character Indexing." In *Chung Wen T'u Shu Tzu Liao Tzu Tung Hua Kuo Chi Yeh T'ao Hui Lun Wen Chi 中文圖書資料自動化國際研討會論文集 [Papers of the International Workshop on Chinese Library Automation]*, Taipei, 14-19 February 1981. Taipei: Library Association of China, 1981. (pp. 1-9).
2. Chang, Chung-tao, Huang, Jack Kai-tung, Hsieh, Ching-chun, and Yang, Chen-chau. "The Design of a Cross Reference Database for Chinese Character Indexing." *T'u Shu Kuan Hsueh Yu Tzu Hsun K'o Hsueh 圖書館學與資訊科學 [Journal of Library & Information Science]* 7 (October 1981): 144-151.
3. Chin, Hsiang-heng 金恆祥. "Ts'ung Wo Kuo Wen Tzu Chih Yen Chin Lai

T'an Hsing Mu 從我國文字之演進來談形母 [On the Development of the Ideographic Element in Chinese Characters: Discussion on Hsing Mu in Chinese Computers]." In *Chung Wen T'u Shu Tzu Liao Tzu Tung Hua Kuo Chi Yeh T'ao Hui Lun Wen Chi 中文圖書資料自動化國際研討會論文集 [Papers of the International Workshop on Chinese Library Automation]*, Taipei, 14-19 February 1981. Taipei: Library Association of China, 1981). (pp. B39a-B52).

4. Chou, Ho. "A Study of the Phonetic and Ideographic Elements of the Chinese Characters." In *Symposium on Computer Processing of Chinese Library Materials and Computer-Assisted Chinese Language Instruction at ASIS-82: Proceedings,* Columbus, Ohio, 19 October 1982. Taipei: ASIS Taipei Chapter, 1982. (pp. 8-1-9).
5. Chou, Ho, and Lin, Jen-chain 周何，林礽乾. "Chung Wen Tien Nao Yung Tzu Sheng Hsi Yen Chiu Pao Kao中文電腦用字聲系研究報告 [Study on the Phonetic Components of Characters Used in Computers]." In *Chung Wen T'u Shu Tzu Liao Tzu Tung Hua Kuo Chi Yeh T'ao Hui Lun Wen Chi 中文圖書資料自動化國際研討會論文集 [Papers of the International Workshop on Chinese Library Automation]*, Taipei, 14-19 February 1981. Taipei: Library Association of China, 1981. (pp. B33a-B38).
6. Chou, Nelson. "Chinese Word – Division: A Proposal to the East Asian Program of Research Libraries Group." In *Chung Wen T'u Shu Tzu Liao Tzu Tung Hua Kuo Chi Yeh T'ao Hui Lun Wen Chi 中文圖書資料自動化國際研討會論文集 [Papers of the International Workshop on Chinese Library Automation]*, Taipei, 14-19 February 1981. Taipei: Library Association of China, 1981. (pp. B99-B102).
7. Chou, Nelson. "Information, Computers and Chinese Language." In *Chung Wen T'u Shu Tzu Liao Tzu Tung Hua Kuo Chi Yeh T'ao Hui Lun Wen Chi 中文圖書資料自動化國際研討會論文集 [Papers of the International Workshop on Chinese Library Automation]*, Taipei, 14-19 February 1981. Taipei: Library Association of China, 1981). Taipei: Library Association of China, 1981. (pp. B53-B62).
8. Chou, Tsin-fu 周駿富. "T'u Shu Kuan Te Chung Wen Tien Nao She Chi 圖書館的中文電腦設計 [The Chinese Computer Design for Libraries]." In *T'u Shu Kuan Shih Yeh He Tso Yu Fa Chan Yen T'ao Hui Hui I Chi Yao 圖書館事業合作與發展研討會會議紀要 [Proceedings of the 1980 Library Development Seminar]*, Taipei, 1-7 December 1980. Taipei: National Central Library, 1981. (pp. 504 -517).
9. Hsieh, C. C., Chang, C. T., and Tseng, S. S . "Chinese Character Database:

Its Design, Implementation and Application." In *Symposium on Computer Processing of Chinese Library Materials and Computer-Assisted Chinese Language Instruction at ASIS-82: Proceedings*, Columbus, Ohio, 19 October 1982. Taipei: ASIS Taipei Chapter, 1982. (pp. 7-1-18).

10. Hu, Li-ren, Chang, Yuan-wei, and Huang, Jack Kai-tung 胡立人，張源渭，黃克東. *Chung Wen So Yin Hu Huan Piao 中文索引互換表 [Chinese Indexes Interchange Table]*. Taipei: System Publication Co., 1981. 105 pp.
11. Hu, Li-ren, Chang, Yuan-wei, and Huang, Jack Kai-tung 胡立人，張源渭，黃克東. *Chung Wen San Chiao Pien Hao Fa Hsun Lien Shou Ts'e 中文「三角編號法」訓練手冊 [Training Manual for the Three Corner Coding Method].* Taipei: System Publication Co., 1979. 131 pp.
12. Kiang, Te-yao and Ch'eng, Tao-ho 江德耀，程道和. *Chung Kuo Wen Tzu Te Hsin Fen Hsi Fa Chi Lien Tai Chien P'an Shu Ju HsiT'ung 中國文字的新分析法及連帶鍵盤輸入系統 [A New Analysis Scheme of Chinese Characters and the Associated Keyboard Input System].* Taipei: K'o Chi T'u Shu Ku Fen Yu Hsien Kung Szu, 1979. 167 pp.
13. Kiang, Te-yao and Ch'eng, Tao-ho 江德耀，程道和. "Chung Wen Shu Ju Fang Shih Te Chien T'ao Ho P'in Hsing Fu Hao Te Chien Li 中文輸入方式的檢討和拼形符號的建立 [Study of the Chinese Input Systems and the Establishment of Chinese Character Composing Signs (CCCS)]." In *Chung Wen T'u Shu Tzu Liao Tzu Tung Hua Kuo Chi Yeh T'ao Hui Lun Wen Chi 中文圖書資料自動化國際研討會論文集 [Papers of the International Workshop on Chinese Library Automation]*, Taipei, 14-19 February 1981. Taipei: Library Association of China, 1981. (pp. B1-B32).
14. Lee, Hsiao-ting and Chou, Tsin-fu 李孝定，周駿富. "Ts'ung Chung Kuo Wen Tzu Te Chieh Kou Ho Yen Pien Kuo Ch'eng T'an Chung Wen Tien Nao Yung Tzu Te Cheng Li 從中國文字的結構和演變過程談中文電腦用字的整理 [Discussion on the Arrangement of Characters Used in Computer from the Viewpoint of Chinese Character Structure and Evolutionary Changes]." In *Chung Wen T'u Shu Tzu Liao Tzu Tung Hua Kuo Chi Yeh T'ao Hui Lun Wen Chi 中文圖書資料自動化國際研討會論文集 [Papers of the International Workshop on Chinese Library Automation]*, Taipei, 14-19 February 1981. Taipei: Library Association of China, 1981. (pp. B83-B94).
15. Lin, Shu 林樹. "Chung Wen Tzu Ken Yu Tzu Hsun Ch'u Li 中文字根與資訊處理 [On the Application of the Basic Component Set of Chinese Charcters]." In *Chung Wen T'u Shu Tzu Liao Tzu Tung Hua Kuo Chi Yeh*

T'ao Hui Lun Wen Chi 中文圖書資料自動化國際研討會論文集 [Papers of the International Workshop on Chinese Library Automation], Taipei, 14-19 February 1981. Taipei: Library Association of China, 1981. (pp. B73-B82).

COMPUTER TECHNOLOGY

1. Hsing Cheng Yuan yen Chiu fa Chan K'ao He Wei Yuan Hui 行政院研究發展考核委員會 [Research, Development and Evaluation Commission, Executive Yuan]. *Wo Kuo Chung Wen Tien Nao Hsi T'ung Chih Fa Chan: Hsien K'ung Tiao Ch'a Chi Wei Lai Chan Wang. 我國中文電腦系統及發展: 現況調查及未來展望 [Development of Chinese Language Computer Systems in the ROC: Current Status and Future Developments]*. Taipei: RDEC, 1979. 152 pp.
2. *Chinese Data Processing and Text Handling: The Next Frontier. Proceedings of the International Computer Conference, Hong Kong, 1980*. Hong Kong: International Computer Conference, Hong Kong, 1980. 2 vols. Vol. I, 287 pp.; Vol. II, 246 pp.
3. Tzu Hsun Kung Yeh Ts'e Chin Hui Pien 資訊工業策進會 編 [Institute for the Information Industry, ed.]. *Chung Wen Tien Nao Fa Chan Tiao Ch'a Fen Hsi Pao Kao. 中文電腦發展調查分析報告 [Analytic Report on Chinese Computer Development]*, 2 vols. Taipei: Institute for the Information Industry, 1982. Vol. II, 95 pp.
4. Lin, Meng-chen 林孟真. "Wo Kuo Tzu Hsun Ch'u Li Hsien K'uang 我國資訊處理現況 [The Current Status of Data Processing Systems in the R. O. C.]." In *T'u Shu Kuan Shih Yeh He Tso Yu Fa Chan Yen T'ao Hui Hui I Chi Yao 圖書館事業合作與發展研討會會議紀要 [Proceedings of the 1980 Library Development Seminar],* Taipei, 1-7 December 1980. Taipei: National Central Library, 1981. (pp.357-432).
5. Yang, C. C.; Hsieh, C. C., and Lin, D. T. "Chinese Computer Technology in Taiwan – An Overview." In *Symposium on Computer Processing of Chinese Library Materials and Computer-Assisted Chinese Language Instruction at ASIS-82: Proceedings*, Columbus, Ohio, 19 October 1982. Taipei: ASIS Taipei Chapter, 1982. (pp. 3-1-13).

RESOURCES SHARING AND NETWORKING

1. Wang, Yen-ch'iu 汪雁秋 [Chang, Teresa Wang]. "Ju Ho Chia Ch'iang Wo Kuo Ch'u Pan P'in Kuo Chi Chiao Huan Kung Tso 如何加強我國出

版品國際交換工作 [How to Strengthen International Exchange of Publications].” In *T'u Shu Kuan Shih Yeh He Tso Yu Fa Chan Yen T'ao Hui Hui I Chi Yao 圖書館事業合作與發展研討會會議紀要 [Proceedings of the 1980 Library Development Seminar]*, Taipei, 1-7 December 1980. Taipei: National Central Library, 1981. (pp. 176-209).

2. Ch'en, Ping-chao 陳炳昭. “Wo Kuo Chin Shih Nien Lai K'o Chi T'u Shu Kuan Kuan Chi Chien Ho Tso Kuan Hsi Chih Hui Ku Yu Chan Wang 我國近十年來科技圖書館館際間合作關係之回顧與展望 [A Recollection and Future Prospect of the Cooperative Efforts of Scientific and Technical Libraries in the Past Decade].” In *T'u Shu Kuan Shih Yeh He Tso Yu Fa Chan Yen T'ao Hui Hui I Chi Yao 圖書館事業合作與發展研討會會議紀要 [Proceedings of the 1980 Library Development Seminar]*, Taipei, 1-7 December 1980. Taipei: National Central Library, 1981. (pp. 210-218).
3. Fung, Margaret C. 張鼎鍾. “Tzu Tung Hua Tzu Hsun Wang Yu Kuo Chia Chien She 自動化資訊網與國家建設 [Automated Information Network and National Development].” In *T'u Shu Kuan Shih Yeh He Tso Yu Fa Chan Yen T'ao Hui Hui I Chi Yao 圖書館事業合作與發展研討會會議紀要 [Proceedings of the 1980 Library Development Seminar]*, Taipei, 1-7 December 1980. Taipei: National Central Library, 1981. Taipei: National Central Library, 1981. (pp. 351-356).
4. Fung, Margaret C. 張鼎鍾. “Wen Hua Chien She Sheng Chung Te Tzu Hsun Kung Neng 文化建設聲中的資訊功能 [Information Activities of the Cultural Development Program].” In *T'u Shu Kuan Hsueh Yu Tzu Hsun K'o Hsueh Chih T'an T'ao 圖書館學與資訊科學之探討 [On library and Information Science]*. Taipei: Student Book Co., 1982. (pp. 33-55).
5. Huang, Shih-hsion 黃世雄. “Fa Chan Tzu Hsun Kung Yeh Ying Chung Shih Te Chi Ko Wen T'i 發展資訊工業應重視的幾個問題 [Some Issues to be Emphasized in Developing the Information Industry].” *Chung Yang Jih Pao 中央日報* [*Central Daily News* (Taiwan, ROC)], 21-22 December 1980, 2.
6. Lee, Hwa-wei 李華偉. “Chien Li Ch'uan Kuo T'u Shu Tzu Hsun Wang Ch'u I 建立全國圖書資訊網芻議 [Preliminary Suggestions on the Establishment of a National Information Network].” *Chung Yang Jih Pao 中央日報* [*Central Daily News* (Taiwan, ROC)], 26, 27 February 1974, 9-10.
7. Lee, Hwa-wei. “A Sketch for a Computerized National Library and Information Network.” In *Chung Wen T'u Shu Tzu Liao Tzu Tung Hua Kuo Chi Yeh T'ao Hui Lun Wen Chi 中文圖書資料自動化國際研討會論文集 [Papers of the International Workshop on Chinese Library Automation]*,

Taipei, 14-19 February 1981. Taipei: Library Association of China, 1981. (pp. E1-E12).

8. Lei, Shu-yun 雷叔雲. "Ch'i Pu Chung Te Chung Hua Min Kuo Jen Wen Chi She Hui K'o Hsueh T'u Shu Kuan Chi Tzu Liao Tan Wei Kuan Chi Ho Tso Tsu Chih 起步中的「中華民國人文暨社會科學圖書館及資料單位館際合作組織」[The Interlibrary Cooperative Organization among Libraries of Humanities and Social Sciences]." In *T'u Shu Kuan Shih Yeh He Tso Yu Fa Chan Yen T'ao Hui Hui I Chi Yao 圖書館事業合作與發展研討會會議紀要 [Proceedings of the 1980 Library Development Seminar]*, Taipei, 1-7 December 1980. Taipei: National Central Library, 1981). (pp. 219-220).
9. Lin, Meng-chen 林孟真. "T'u Shu Kuan Tzu Tung Hua Te Kuan Chi Ho Tso 圖書館自動化的館際合作 [Interlibrary Cooperation for Library Automation]." *Chung Teng Chiao Yu 中等教育* 31 (October, 1980): 36- 41.
10. Wang, Chen-ku 王振鵠. "Chiao Yu Tzu Liao Chih Ho Tso Chiao Liu." 教育資料之合作交流 [The Cooperative Sharing and Interchange of Educational Materials]." In *Chiao Yu Tzu Liao Yen T'ao Hui Chi Lu 教育資料研討會記錄 [Educational Resources Workshop Proceedings]*, Taipei, 10-11 May 1980. Taipei: National Taiwan Normal University and National Institute of Educational Materials, 1980. (pp. 103-106).

Reprinted from the paper presented at The First Asian-Pacific Conference on Library Science, Session I Library Service and Resource-Country Report. Taipei, National Central Library, 13-19 March 1983. (pp. 81-105).

16

Information Systems and Services in China

ABTRACT

Extracted and abridged from the l0th chapter of the l8th volume of the *Annual Review of Information Science and Technology* entitled *Information Systems and Services in China and Japan* co-authored with Donald V. Black published by ASIS in 1983, this portion of the paper on China covers description and discussion of information systems and services in the Republic of China (Taiwan) and the People's Republic of China (China mainland). General background, recent and current status, current information system/services, computer technology for information services and the future trends are presented. The literature reviewed begins at the 1920s up to 1983.

INTRODUCTION

Information systems are defined as a coordinated set of activities (people, machines, etc.) organized for the delivery information from a source to a recipient. Information services are those activities of an information system that result in the transfer of information from source to recipient. Because this is the first *ARIST* chapter to cover China in depth, the literature reviewed begins with the 1920s. The most recent citation is 1983. No attempt has been made to cover the available literature exhaustively. Most of the excluded literature is in Chinese and is not available in Western language. Further, the original sources are not, for the most part, available in the United States or in Europe.

REPUBLIC OF CHINA

ROC is unique for its long and continuous cultural tradition. Philosophies beginning in the 6th century B. C. still serve as models.[1] Standardization of the written language, weights and measures, roads, and the like, as well as large construction projects like the Great Wall, occurred in the Ch'in dynasty (221-206 B. C.). A legal code drafted in the T'ang dynasty (618-907) served as a model for later Chinese codes until the 20th century. An impressive corpus of scientific and technical knowledge has been documented,[2] and great cultural achievements in the fine arts as well as literature are not only revered but have been emulated throughout history.[3]

Modern China began on October 10, 1911, with the overthrow of the Ch'ing dynasty (1644-1911). On January 1, 1912, the Republic of China was founded, and it is now established in Taiwan because of the Communist takeover of the mainland area after World War II.[4] Since then, ROC has experienced considerable economic and educational progress. Compulsory nine-year education and an emphasis on continued higher education, 12 major development projects (including that of the strategic information industry) and a series of social and political reforms have contributed to stability. Now ROC is transforming itself from a labor-intensive to a technology-intensive economy. The severing of U. N. and other diplomatic ties has created special difficulties, yet there have been continued advances in information systems and services.

Cultural Background

As early as the Chou dynasty in the 6th century B. C., Chinese libraries existed in the form of book archives, private collections, and royal libraries.[5] In subsequent dynasties, China maintained imperial collections that were the depository of national literature for use by the imperial families, high officials, and renowned scholars,[6] and they gained special stature during the Ch'ing dynasty (1644-1911).[7] Since the beginning of the 20th century, Chinese libraries have progressed through the following stages[8]: 1) (1901-1911): Chinese leaders realized the importance of libraries to national modernization. On their recommendations, the government began the modern Chinese library movement, which has been a major force in mass education, by establishing the first national and public libraries in 1905.[9] The first regulations for federal and provincial libraries were announced in 1909, and public libraries thus gained legal status. 2) (1912-1937): The Ministry of Education assumed supervisory authority over libraries. From the beginning of the Republic to the onset of the Sino–Japanese War, libraries enjoyed an era of growth. Library-related regulations and laws were announced in 1915, 1927, and 1930. The first professional U. S. trained librarian, promotion of library education, and the establishment of training facilities and courses at several universities indicated a recognition of professional status for librarians. The library association, organized in 1925, became an organ for professional communication and publicity. 3) (1937-1949): The major accomplishment of the this period (disrupted by war and revolution) was the large-scale international book donation drive.

After Taiwan was recovered from Japanese occupation in 1945 and after the seat of the Nationalist government moved to Taipei in 1949, library matters fell into three periods[10]: 1) (1945-1951): recovery from the war; 2) (1952-1970): a time of growth during which the National Central Library was reinstated, library buildings were erected, the library association was reconstituted, and library schools were added to universities and colleges; and 3) (1972 to present): a period of maturity, with practices of interlibrary cooperation, execution of a cultural development program, and stipulation of standards for library automation.

Recent and Current Trends

A survey by the National Central Library reported 167 public libraries, 135 academic libraries, 369 high school and vocational school libraries, and 219 special libraries.[11] Compared with data from an earlier survey, the 1981 figures show 119% growth in special libraries.[12] However, the earlier survey did not take branch libraries into account, while the later survey included all branches but did not include 2,380 grade school and 1,235 junior high school libraries.

Surveys on different types of libraries also portrayed the various stages, problems, and improvements in librarianship and library services in Taiwan area. 1980 survey of school libraries[13] compared domestic and foreign school library standards in evaluative and descriptive ways,[14] and public library survey of 1978 indicated an improvement in library services[15] since the 1974 survey.[16] S. C. Ma discusses and summarizes those surveys and their recommendations for future progress.[17]

The progress of college and university libraries in Taiwan from 1952 to 1977 was succinctly summarized[18] by using data collected in three surveys.[19] Lan comments on special libraries surveys.[20]

Major events of Chinese librarianship from January 1912 to December 1971 are itemized by Chang & Huang.[21] The same records are repeated in the 1981 yearbook with additions dating from 1972 to 1980.[22] An overview of ROC library activities (including historical background, current library status, library services, library science and education, and professional activities – with appendices on library laws and standards) is documented for the first time in a yearbook format.[23]

In 1978 information on 255 public, private, academic, government, and special libraries in Taiwan was published.[24] It included user services and future plans as well as the usual library statistics.

The latest library directory for the Taiwan area lists libraries by type, providing handy information on librarians' names, postal codes, addresses, telephone numbers and special features in tabular form.[25] Although there is a table of contents, lack of an index is a common major drawback of these directories.

Current information Systems and Services (IS & S)

Information services in Taiwan began to receive well-deserved attention in the early 1970s with the formation of the Science and Technology Information Center (STIC) and the 1973 Sino-U. S. Workshop on Scientific and Technical Information Needs and Resources in ROC taken place in Washington, D. C.[26] The workshop was instrumental in ROC's scientific and technical information (STI) activities concerning planning, policy-making, cooperation among international non-governmental organizations, centralized acquisitions, use of databases, development of STI systems, personnel training, and so forth. Increased awareness of the need for information services and activities for developing computerized information systems have progressed significantly since 1979.

Development of automated information services in libraries was furthered by a preliminary plan created in 1980[27] and by the formation of library automation planning committee. Progress in computer applications for libraries and requirements for processing Chinese library materials were reported by Fung,[28] who did the initial planning and continuing promotion for the automation project.[29] This overview has been updated by Wang & Seng.[30] Summarizing data collected from July 1, 1978 to June 31, 1979, M. C. Lin categorizes Chinese data processing activities into that of scholarly and research information, STI, business information, administrative information, reservation information, and automated library systems.[31]

One of the stronger information systems is the Agriculture Science Information Center's (ASIC) Agricultural Science and Technology Information Management System (ASTIMS). W. J. Wu describes this system in detail.[32] It includes databases of personnel in agricultural science and technology (FASTEP), research projects (FASTEJ), research reports (FASTER), and agricultural science and technology literature in Chinese and English.[33] The system has been enhanced by the completion of an Agri-Thesaurus.[34]

The in-house information systems of the Chung Shan Institute of Technology library (CLSI) is described by L. C. Huang.[35] It includes serials control, acquisitions, cataloging, information retrieval, circulation, and selective dissemination of information (SDI) services.

Freedom Council Information Abstracts (FCIA) is a database of abstracts of publications covering major events and information on ROC. Supported by private endowments, FCIA was designed on the same concept as the New York Times Information Bank and was implemented in 1978 on a Wang MVP 2200 but was discontinued in 1981.[36]

The National Bureau of Criminal Investigation's computer microfilm retrieval system used for criminal data illustrates and attempt to combine data processing equipment with microfilm to enhance output in Chinese characters. Loh gives illustrations of this sophisticated, efficient, and effective system.[37]

The National Central Library led the national automated library information system for bibliographic control. Its MARC (Machine Readable Cataloging) bibliographic database of Chinese library materials, begun in 1981, had more than 6,000 records in 1982 and is available on tape. The *Union List of Chinese Periodicals*, compiled at the end of 1979, covers 7,453 periodical titles in 171 libraries. A detailed description of the system was presented in Chinese at a 1980 conference[38] and in English at a 1981 international workshop.[39]

Based on its *Educational Literature Abstracts*, in 1978 National Taiwan Normal University Library (NTNU) pioneered in building subject literature databases with its Chinese Educational Resources Information System (CERIS), which uses the TOTAL Database Management System on Perkin Elmer 3220 computers. Fung briefly describes CERIS's structure with flowcharts and illustrations in both Chinese and English.[40]

STIC's Management Information System of Science and Technology Resources includes databases of: 1) science and technology experts, 2) research projects, 3) research reports, and 4) research facilities as well as a *Union List of Scientific Serials* (12,328 titles from 187 institutions) and a *Union Catalog of Western Books in Science and Technology*.[41] In addition, T. S. Fang delineates the National Science Council's conceptual system for centralized acquisition of library materials in western languages, which will process all government-funded acquisitions of non-Chinese materials.[42]

S. H. Huang describes briefly Tamkang University's efforts in automating its acquisitions and serials control functions and its outlook for future development.[43] The brief discussion by H. C. Huang on the problems in computerizing acquisitions of foreign publications by Chinese private colleges and universities is a practical analysis.[44]

Information retrieval services offered by the major U. S. vendors have been made available in the Taiwan area under the acronym of UDAS (Universal Database Access Service). Service began on December 28, 1979. National Taiwan Normal University Library pioneered in providing this service to the public on May 10, 1980.[45] STIC also began Computer Assisted Information Service (CAIS) in December 1981.[46] S. H. Huang gives an introduction to the bibliographic information retrieval system, including the features and procedures for establishing databases in general.[47] Useful information on searching procedures, needed searching skills, available databases, charges, and so forth, are described in detail by Liu[48] and by S. C. Chen.[49]

The Research, Development and Evaluation Commission the Republic of China in 1979 delineated plans for the development of a Chinese-language computerized decision-support system and a national management information system (MIS). They consist of six information subsystems: national status, general administration, science and technology, economic development, communications development, and national defense and security.[50] Wei presents an update in 1982 that is the only official report on the topic.[51]

Computer Technology for Information Services

The study of computer processing of Chinese characters started in 1971, but it was not until recently that a practical application level was reached.[52] An excellent survey, which supersedes an equally good older survey,[53] provides evidence of progress in the capabilities of Chinese computer I/O (input/output) devices and user satisfaction and improvements in Chinese data processing.[54] The 1979 survey reported the status only, without statement on the aspect of evaluation.

An overall picture of and various statistics on computer technology and issues in the Chinese information industry are presented by the comprehensive information industry yearbook. The 1982 yearbook indicates that in 1982, 49% of the total of all hardware was installed in Taipei; of that 49%, 42% was installed in private industry, 18.9% in schools and research institutions, 16.9% in public enterprises, 11.7% in computer companies, and 10.5% in government agencies.[55]

Issues related to Chinese-language data processing, including hardware design, I/O devices, linguistic problems and cross reference databases for Chinese characters are discussed comprehensively in presentations at two international conferences held in Taipei and Hong Kong.[56] Additional informative and technical conference papers are also listed with sources of availability in the 1982 yearbook.[57]

The Three Corner Coding System and Chinese Index Interchange Tables exemplify the most important schemes for indexing and their use in Chinese computer I/O methods.[58]

Standards

Standards are essential to the success of Chinese library automation and automated services.[59] The Chinese Character Code for Information Interchange (CCCII)[60] was designed according to ISO 626 and 2022 to cover approximately 83,000 Chinese characters, other related ethnic language characters (e. g., Manchurian, Mongolian, Tibetan), and all variant characters.[61] The new set of Chinese cataloging rules incorporates AACR2 (Anglo-American Cataloging Rules, 2nd edition) and ISBD (International Standard Bibliographic Description) to meet automation requirements.[62] The 1982 report updates the one for 1981. The Chinese MARC Format, based on UNIMARC, is modified to accommodate the unique features of Chinese library materials and to meet the special requirements of East Asian libraries abroad.[63] The Chinese MARC Format for books and an integrated MARC format for books and non-books are available in Chinese and in English. This edition supersedes the former two editions of February and July 1981.

Interlibrary cooperation

Interlibrary cooperation in the past decade that began among seven scientific and technical libraries in 1972 has grown in eight years to encompass 72 institutions. The history, function, interlending activities, present problems, and future outlook are presented in detail with charts and graphs by Ch'en.[64] Lei reports briefly an attempt in 1978 to organize a consortium in humanities and social sciences that now includes 35 libraries.[65]

Of the many international cooperative efforts in librarianship in

ROC, international exchange of publications seems to have the most direct and influential effect on library services. At present, exchange is conducted with 957 libraries in 79 countries. The historical background, present status, procedures, problems, and future solutions of international exchange are discussed in detail by T. W. Chang, who is in charge of this operation at the National Central Library.[66]

Networking

With the advent of automated library systems and libraries' needs for interdependence, networking has gained increasing attention in ROC. S. H. Huang,[67] Fung,[68] and M. C. Lin[69] promote the idea, and H. W. Lee,[70] Fung,[71] and M. C. Lin[72] all outline realistic proposals for national networking from different viewpoints.

Improving library services

Many leaders in Chinese librarianship have pointed out basic ways to improve library services.[73] Other references that discuss improvements are T. C. Chang,[74] Fung,[75] Li,[76] C. K. Wang,[77] and The Commission on National Development Research the Republic of China.[78]

The Cultural Development Program begun in 1978 calls for the establishment of cultural centers, including libraries and museums. C. K. Wang[79] and Research, Development and Evaluation Commission[80] propose plans basic to the development of libraries in the cultural centers. Fung suggests strategic plans for information services and systems in the program.[81] C. K. Wang reports in outline the actual implementation of the Cultural Development Program at the national, provincial, municipal, and local levels up to December 1980 and their future anticipated progress.[82]

Future Trends

A number of useful works provide both good overviews and in-depth analyses by ROC experts on various topics in information. The Library Development Seminar of 1980[83] contains a collection of 35 papers, most in Chinese, that deal with library activities, cooperation and exchange, library education and automation, and information systems. The International Workshop on Chinese Library Automation[84] includes 31 papers (both Chinese and English) that cover CCCII, Chinese-language processing and computers, Chinese cataloging rules, Chinese MARC format, Chinese library automation and information systems, and efforts in international cooperation. Ten papers from another symposium[85] address library automation, Chinese language and computer technology, new Chinese cataloging rules, Chinese MARC format, specific information systems, thesaurus building, computer-aided Chinese cataloging rules, and computer-aided Chinese language instruction. Abstracts and full text of some of the papers are also available in the ASIS Meeting Proceedings.[86] A detailed and current report (in Chinese) provides comprehensive data and statistics on Chinese libraries and library-related matters.[87] The yearbooks published by the National Central Library,[88] also supply a wealth of material on librarianship, Chinese library history, current library status, activities, education, regulations, and standards for all types of libraries. The most important published standards are *CCCII* (Volumes 1-2),[89] *Chinese MARC Format* 1982,[90] and *Chinese Cataloging Rules* 1982.[91] For thorough coverage, detailed technical reports, and statistics about computers and information processing in ROC, the best source is the annual yearbook of the Institute for Information Industry.[92]

Considerable progress has been made and is continuing in ROC to develop modern information systems and services. Libraries are the present foundation of available services.

PEOPLE'S REPUBLIC OF CHINA (PRC)

Before World War II, the history of information services or libraries in PRC is identical to that of ROC. Despite the common tradition, the development of IS&S after PRC was established has been markedly different.

Recent and Current Trends

Since 1949, extreme change has affected every institution and organization in PRC. Developments in IS&S that would have typical of an underdeveloped country were abruptly halted by the Great Proletarian Cultural Revolution of 1966-1968. Tell[93] and Broadbent[94] give a good picture of the activities during 1949-4968. J. T. Ma gives the best view of the development in the 1950s and cites a number of papers in his bibliography.[95] Hawkins gives an interesting overview of various IS&S activities at the ad hoc level that illustrates the necessity to begin anew in developing IS&S in PRC.[96] Hawkins's bibliography is especially useful in gaining a proper perception of educational activities in that country. Lacking good information facilities, radio broadcasting and regional publications become a primary means of disseminating information. Hawkins examines four networks for transforming techniques: 1) research and development (R&D); 2) formal education, 3) extension and dissemination; and 4) nonschool information dissemination. This paper provides an excellent background for a number of more traditional information science papers by Tell[97] and Chandler.[98] The view given by Tell of the struggle to rebuild an information infrastructure is very wide ranging, covering public libraries, libraries in schools, universities, factories, trade unions, military establishments, and research organizations, and the rebirth of a national library association. The most important special feature of Tell's paper is the bibliometric study she performed to obtain a rough idea of how far behind their western colleagues they were in access to good information sources. Tell also provides a very good bibliography, although some of the references are in one or another Scandinavian language.

Many papers describe recent tours of PRC that give a personalized view of PRC's libraries and information centers — e.g., the paper by C. C. Chen.[99] Such papers are interesting reading but more in-depth studies are needed.

Several individuals have had more extensive missions in PRC and provide detailed accounts of particular aspects of PRC social structure, sometimes directly on aspects of information science. Meier, in a lengthy paper mainly devoted to communications and computer technology (both hardware and software) quotes portions of an address by Fang Yi, Vice-Premier of the State Council, at the Chinese National Conference on Science and Technology, held in Beijing in March 1978.[100] Entitled the *Outline National Plan for the Development of Science and Technology, Relevant Policies and Measures*, it launched a momentous program to "approach or reach the advanced world levels of the 1970s in a number of important branches of science and technology." The most important part of this address was the statement: "It is essential to equip information institutions with modern facilities in the shortest possible time. In eight years we will set up a number of documentation retrieval centers and databases and build a preliminary nationwide computer network of scientific and technical information and documentation retrieval centers." How well has PRC progressed since then? Evidence is contained in the papers below.

Chandler describes the founding of the Society of Chinese Libraries in July 1979 and discusses the content of the first issue of the new *Bulletin of Library Science*, without citing titles of the articles.[101] Chandler's paper gives extensive details on the National Library of Peking, special libraries, the Institute of Scientific and Technical Information of China (ISTIC), the Chinese Academy of Sciences, various other city, provincial, public libraries, and many university libraries. In most instances the descriptions contain statistics on size, budget, holdings, and the like. Unfortunately, neither Chandler nor Meier provides a bibliography.[102]

In 1980, UNESCO sent a two-man team to PRC to advise on the establishment of the functional units of ISTIC, which will be responsible for such activities as acquisitions and abstracting and indexing (A&I) services. In the followup report, Brawne & Schwarz provide a surprising amount of information about the information services of the institute and the planned new systems and services as well as the role and structure of the institute.[103] Their bibliography provides a list of recent ISTIC publications and a brief discussion of the computer facilities of PRC and Beijing.

Broadbent gives a concise overview of the status of library and information services in PRC for the period from just before the Great Proletarian Cultural Revolution to early 1981.[104] The only real area of interest is the description of activities of an attempt to translate western languages into Chinese. Broadbent accurately assesses the status of most areas of information services. The bibliography is short.

In 1982, representatives from PRC appeared on the program at two international meetings. Z. Lin, Director of ISTIC, presented a paper full of statistics demonstrating the progress in rebuilding an information infrastructure.[105] He reported 43 national specialized information institutes, 28 provincial information institutes, and 219 information units dispersed in different cities and countries. Also, in 1981 there were over 2,000 information clearinghouses and 134 periodical titles published in information retrieval. Xu discusses the problems of resource sharing and a national library network.[106] A Chinese classification system has been developed and will be used by 90% of the libraries and information centers. Xu also describes a Chinese thesaurus published in 1981. It comprises a total of 90,000 descriptors and 17,000 "see" references. Xu gives no bibliography.

Huang & Zhao give a very good description of the interlibrary loan (ILL) service of the National Library.[107] Because of PRC's vast territory, large population, and sparse collections, ILL is a necessity. Huang and Zhao list some union catalogs that have been developed to further ILL activity.

The paper by Shi & Yan describes the recent development

of the library and information systems of the Chinese Academy of Science.[108] The academy includes more than 140 library and information units, 117 library and information divisions belonging to the different institutes affiliated with the academy. There is a total staff of more than 2,400 and over 16 million volumes in the collection. None of the papers given by representatives of PRC contains a bibliography.

Xingyun has provided the first "official" comprehensive overview of the present situation in PRC.[109] He gives an extensive history of libraries and information work with some interesting examples. Many statistics are given, some of which are a bit astounding – e.g., that there are 50,000 "information professionals" at present. Xingyun enumerates many official statements of tasks, principles, etc., one of which is "to develop international exchange and cooperation in information work." In view of the steadfast refusal of several "information professionals" to communicate with the senior author, that statement is open to interpretation.

CONCLUSION

The Republic of China, while attempting to retain ancient cultural traditions, has adopted many of the advances in information technology and has made significant progress in developing new techniques of information handling and in enhancing her information industry.

The People's Republic of China has attempted to sever its ties to the past and build a new national system of information services. While progress is being made, there is no evidence that they have recognized the importance of a well-organized system of bibliographic control and a long-range planning effort to accelerate the pace with which some sort of information technology becomes widely known and used.

The next few years will be interesting indeed to see what developments occur in IS&S in these countries. Does the information structure mirror the level of economic and technological development, or is it vice versa? Which is cause and which effect?

NOTES:

1. William T. De Bary, *Sources of Chinese Tradition*, 2 vols. (New York, NY: Columbia University Press, 1960).
2. Joseph Needham, *The Shorter Science and Civilization in China* (Cambridge, England: Cambridge University Press, 1978), (Abridgement by C. A. Ronan; Includes illustrations and maps).
3. Lawrence Sickman and Alexander Soper, *Art and Architecture of China*, 3rd ed. (Baltimore, MD: Penguin, 1968), 349. (Includes illustrations).
4. Edmund Clubb, *Twentieth Century China*, 3rd ed. (New York: Columbia University Press, 1978), 559. .
5. K'aiming Ch'iu, "National Libraries in China," Library Quarterly 3 (April 1933): 146; Tsin-fu Chou 周駿富, *Chung Kuo T'u Shu Kuan Chien Shih 中國圖書館簡史 [A Brief History of Chinese Libraries]* (Taipei, Taiwan, ROC: Student Book Company, 1974), 87-140.
6. K'aiming Ch'iu, "National Libraries in China," *Library Quarterly* 3 (April 1933): 146.
7. Chien-cheng Sung 宋建成, "Ching Tai T'u Shu Kuan Shih Yeh Fa Ch'an Shih 清代圖書館事業發展史 [The History of Library Development in the Ching Dynasty]" (master degree's thesis of Graduate Institute of History, College of Chinese Culture, 1972), 177; Cheuk-woon Taam (Cho-Yuan Tan), *The Development of Chinese Libraries under the Ch'ing Dynasty, 1644-1911* (Shanghai, China: CMC, 1955), 194. (Reprinted, San Francisco, CA: Chinese Materials Center, 1977.)
8. Wen-yu Yen and Ching Su 嚴文郁，蘇精, "*Chung Kuo T'u Shu Kuan Shih Yeh Te Fa Chan 中國圖書館事業的發展* [The Development of Chinese Librarianship]," in Chung Hua Min Kuo T'u Shu Kuan Nien Chien 中華民國圖書館年鑑, ed. Kuo Li Chung Yang T'u Shu Kuan 國立中央圖書館 [National Central Library] (Taipei: National Central Library, 1981), 1-10; Tsin-fu Chou 周駿富, *Chung Kuo T'u Shu Kuan Chien Shih 中國圖書館簡史 [A Brief History of Chinese Libraries]* (Taipei, Taiwan, ROC: Student Book Company, 1974), 87-140.
9. Tsin-fu Chou 周駿富, *Chung Kuo T'u Shu Kuan Chien Shih 中國圖書館簡史 [A Brief History of Chinese Libraries]* (Taipei, Taiwan, ROC: Student Book Company, 1974), 87-140; T. C. Tai, Development of Modern Li-

braries in China (Peiping, China, 1929), 9-16. (Libraries in China Series).

10. Chen-ku Wang 王振鵠, "San Shih Nien Lai Te Taiwan T'u Shu Kuan Shih Yeh 三十年來的台灣圖書館事業 [Librarianship in Taiwan in the Last 30 Years]," *T'u Shu Kuan Hsueh Yu Tzu Hsun K'o Hsueh 圖書館學與資訊科學 [Journal of Library & Information Science]* 1, no. 2 (October 1975): 41-69; Chen-ku Wang 王振鵠, Wo Kuo T'u Shu Kuan Shih Yeh Chih Hsien K'uang Yu Chan Wang: Taiwan Ti Ch'u T'u Shu Kuan Shih Yeh Hsien K'uang 我國圖書館事業之現況與展望：台灣地區圖書館事業現況與展望 [The Current Status and Future Prospects of Libraries in the Taiwan Area]," in *Chung Hua Min Kuo T'u Shu Kuan Nien Chien 中華民國圖書館年鑑* , ed. Kuo Li Chung Yang T'u Shu Kuan 國立中央圖書館 [National Central Library] (Taipei: National Central Library, 1981), 11-17. (Includes various tables); Chen-ku Wang 王振鵠, "Wo Kuo T'u Shu Kuan Shih Yeh Chih Hsien K'uang Yu Chan Wang 我國圖書館事業之現況與展望 [The Current Status and Future Prospects of Chinese Librarianship]," in *T'u Shu Kuan Shih Yeh He Tso Yu Fa Chan Yen T'ao Hui Hui I Chi Yao 圖書館事業合作與發展研討會會議紀要* (Taipei: National Central Library, 1981), 53-60.
11. Shu-yun Lei 雷叔雲 et al., *Tai Min Ti Ch'u T'u Shu Kuan Hsien K'uang Tiao Ch'a Yen Chiu 台閩地區圖書館現況調查研究 [Survey of Libraries in Taiwan and Fukien]* (Taipei: National Central Library, 1982), 384. (Includes various tables).
12. Kuo Li Chung Yang T'u Shu Kuan Pien 國立中央圖書館 編 [National Central Library, ed.], "Taiwan Ti Ch'u T'u Shu Kuan Shih Yeh Hsien K'uang 台灣地區圖書館事業現況 [The Current Status of Librarianship in the Taiwan Area]," in *Chung Hua Min Kuo T'u Chu Kuan Nien Chien Tiao Ch'a Lu 中華民國圖書館年鑑調查錄* (Taipei: National Central Library, 1980), 238.
13. Kuo Li Taiwan Shih Fan Ta Hsueh T'u Shu Kuan Chi She Hui Chiao Yu Hsueh Hsi Pien 國立台灣師範大學圖書館暨社會教育學系 編 [National Taiwan Normal University. Library and Department of Social Education, eds.], *Taiwan Ti Ch'u Chung Hsiao Hsueh T'u Shu Kuan (Shih) Hsien K'uang Tiao Ch'a Pao Kao 台灣地區中小學圖書（室）館現況調查報告 [Report on the Survey of School Libraries in the Taiwan Area]* (Taipei: National Taiwan Normal University Library, 1981), 81.
14. Nancy Ou-lan Hu 胡歐蘭, "Taiwan Ti Ch'u Chung Hsiao Hsueh T'u Shu Kuan (Shih) Hsien K'uang Tiao Ch'a Yen Chiu 台灣地區中小學圖書（室）館現況調查研究 [A Survey of School Libraries in the Taiwan

Area]," *T'u Shu Kuan Hsueh Yu Tzu Hsun K'o Hsueh 圖書館學與資訊科學 [Journal of Library & Information Science]* 7, no. 1 (April 1981): 72-98.

15. Chung Kuo T'u Shu Kuan Hsueh Hui. Kung Kung T'u Shu Kuan Wei Yuan Hui Pien 中國圖書館學會公共圖書館委員會 編 [Library Association of China. Public Libraries Committee, ed., "Taiwan Ti Ch'u Ke Chi Kung Kung T'u Shu Kuan Hsien K'uang Tzu Liao I Lan Piao 台灣地區各級公共圖書館現況資料一覽表 [Survey Tables of Public Libraries in the Taiwan Area]," *Chung Kuo T'u Shu Kuan Hsueh Hui Hui Pao 中國圖書館學會會報 [Bullentin of the Library Association of China]* 30 (December 1978): 199. (Includes various tables)
16. Chung Kuo T'u Shu Kuan Hsueh Hui. Kung Kung T'u Shu Kuan Piao Chun Ni Ting Hsiao Tsu Pien 中國圖書館學會公共圖書館標準擬定小組 編 [Library Association of China. Public Library Standards Working Group, ed.], *Chung Hua Min Kuo T'ai Min Ti Ch'u Sheng (Shih) Hsien Shih Hsiang Cheng Ch'u T'u Shu Kuan Hsien K'uang Tiao Ch'a Pao Kao 中華民國台閩地區省（市）縣市鄉鎮區圖書館現況調查報告 [Survey of Public Libraries in the Taiwan and Fukien Areas]* (Taipei: Library Association of China, 1976), 10.
17. Shao-chuan Ma 馬少娟, "Tsung Wo Kuo Kung Kung T'u Shu Kuan Hsien Kuang Tiao Cha Yu Pi Chiao Tan Chiu Chin Hou Fa Chan Chih Tao 從我國公共圖書館現況調查與比較探究今後發展之道 [An Exploration into the Future Development of Public Libraries in the ROC through Survey and Comparisons]." *Chiao Yu Tzu Liao K'o Hsueh Yueh K'an 教育資料科學月刊 [The Bulletin of Educational Media Science]* 8, no. 5/6 (December 1975): 24-28; 9, no. 1 (January 1976): 26-33; 9, no. 2 (February 1976): 21-26.
18. Nancy Ou-lan Hu 胡歐蘭, "Liu Shih Chi Nien Taiwan Ta Chuan Yuan Hsiao T'u Shu Kuan Hsien Kuan T'iao Ch'a Fen Hsi 六十幾年台灣大專院校圖書館現況調查分析 [Current Analytical Survey of College and University Libraries in Taiwan of 1978]," *Chung Kuo T'u Shu Kuan Hsueh Hui Hui Pao 中國圖書館學會會報 [Bulletin of the Library Association of China]* 30 (December 1978): 97-114.
19. Chen-ku Wang 王振鵠, *Taiwan Ch'u T'a Chuan Y'uan Hsiao T'u Shu Kuan Hsien K'uang Tiao Ch'a Pao Kao 台灣區大專院校圖書館現況調查報告 [Report of a Current Survey of College and University Libraries in Taiwan]* (Taipei: Chiao Yu Pu T'a Chuan T'u Shu Kuan Piao Chun Ni Ting Kung Tso Hsiao Tsu, October 1975), 60. (Includes various tables); Tzu-chung Li 李志鍾, "Ch'uan Kuo T'u Shu Kuan Yeh Wu Pao Kao 全

國圖書館業務報告 [Report of Librarianship in the ROC]," in *Ti I Tz'u Ch'uan Kuo T'u Shu Yeh Wu Hui Chi Yao 第一次全國圖書業務會紀要* (Taipei: National Central Library, April 1972), 25-27; (Taipei: National Central Library, 1972), 39-93; Chen-ku Wang 王振鵠, "Taiwan Ta Chuan T'u Shu Kuan Hsien K'uang Chih Tiao Ch'a Yen Chiu 台灣大專圖書館之調查研究 [A Survey of College and University Libraries in Taiwan]," *T'u Shu Kuan Hsueh Yu Tzu Hsun K'o Hsueh 圖書館學與資訊科學 [Journal of Library & Information Science]* 2, no. 1 (April 1976): 74-101. (Includes tables)

20. Chien-chang Lan 藍乾章, "Erh Shih Wu Nien Lai Te Chuan Men T'u Shu Kuan 二十五年來的專門圖書館 [Special Libraries in the Last 25 Years]," *Chung Kuo T'u Shu Kuan Hsueh Hui Hui Pao 中國圖書館學會會報 [Bullentin of the Library Association of China]* 29 (November 1977): 77-81. (Includes tables)
21. Ching-lang Chang and Yuan-ch'uan Huang 張錦郎，黃淵泉, *Chung Kuo Chin Liu Shih Nien Lai T'u Shu Kuan Shih Yeh Ta Shih Chi 中國近六十年來圖書館事業大事記 [The Chronology of Chinese Librarianship in the Past Sixty Years]* (Taipei: Taiwan Shang Wu Ying Shu Kuan, 1974), 225.
22. Ching-lang Chang and Yuan-ch'uan Huang 張錦郎，黃淵泉, *T'u Shu Kuan Shih Yeh Ta Shih Chi 圖書館事業大事記 [Chronology of Chinese Librarianship]* (Taipei: National Central Library, 1981), 355-401.
23. Kuo Li Chung Yang T'u Shu Kuan Pien 國立中央圖書館 編 [National Central Library, ed.], *Chung Hua Min Kuo T'u Shu Kuan Nien Chien 中華民國圖書館年鑑 [Library Yearbook of the Republic of China]* (Taipei: National Central Library, 1981), 451. (Includes [facsimiles of] legal documents related to Chinese libraries)
24. Kuo Li Chung Yang T'u Shu Kuan Pien 國立中央圖書館 編 [National Central Library, ed.], *Ch'uan Kuo T'u Shu Kuan Chien Chieh 全國圖書館簡介 [Brief Introduction to Libraries in the Republic of China]* (Taipei: National Central Library, 1978), 315. (Includes photos of 4 major libraries)
25. Kuo Li Chung Yang T'u Shu Kuan Pien 國立中央圖書館 編[National Central Library, ed.], *Chuan Kuo T'u Shu Kuan Chi Tzu Liao Tan Wei Min Lu 全國圖書館及資料單位名錄 [Directory of Libraries and Information Agencies in the ROC]* (Taipei: National Central Library, 1982), 54.
26. Lucy Te-chu Lee 李德竹, "Chung Mei K'o Hsueh Tzu Liao Yun Yung Fa Chan Yen T'ao Hui 中美科學資料運用發展研討會 [Sino-US Workshop on Scientific and Technical Information Needs and Resources in the ROC]," *Kuo Li Chung Yang T'u Shu Kuan Kuan K'an 國立中央圖書館館*

刊 [National Central Library Bulletin] New 6, no. 2 (September 1973): 43-46; National Science Council (NSC), *Chung Mei K'o Chi Tzu Liao Ch'u Li Chi Yun Yung Yen T'ao Hui Pao Kao [Sino-US Workshop on Scientific and Technical Information Needs and Resources in the Republic of China: Report of the Workshop]* (Washington, DC., 25-27 April 1973); (Taipei: National Science Council, 1973), 139. (Text in Chinese, notes, agenda and participants in English)

27. Chung Kuo T'u Shu Kuan Hsueh Hui Pien 中國圖書館學會 編 [Library Association of China, ed.], "T'u Shu Kuan Tzu Tung Hua Tso Yeh Chi Hua 圖書館自動化作業計畫 [Library Automation Planning Program]," *Chung Kuo T'u Shu Kuan Hsueh Hui Hui Wu T'ung Hsun 中國圖書館學會會務通訊 [Library Association of China Newsletter]* 22 (1980): 9-10.
28. Margaret C. Fung, "Library Automation in the Republic of China," *T'u Shu Kuan Hsueh Yu Tzu Hsun K'o Hsueh 圖書館學與資訊科學 [Journal of Library & Information Science]* 6, no.1 (April 1980): 1-16.
29. Margaret C. Fung 張鼎鍾, *T'u Shu Kuan Hsueh Yu Tzu Hsun K'o Hsueh Chih T'an T'ao 圖書館學與資訊科學之探討 [On library and Information Science]* (Taipei: Student Book Co., 1982), 227. (Articles in Chinese and in English); Nancy Ou-lan Hu 胡歐蘭, *Ts'an K'ao Tzu Hsun Fu Wu 參考資訊服務 [Reference Information Services]* (Taipei: Student Book Co., 1982), 326; Meng-chen Lin 林孟真, *Wo Kuo Tzu Hsun Hsi T'ung Chih Chien Li Yu T'an T'ao 我國資訊系統之建立與探討 [The Establishment and Exploration of the Information Systems in the ROC]* (Taipei: Wen Shih Che Publishing Co., 1982), 191.
30. Chen-ku Wang and B. H. Seng, "Chinese Information Networks — An Overview," in *Information Interaction: Proceedings of the American Society for Information Science (ASIS) 45th Annual Meeting: Volume 19,* 17-21 October 1982, Columbus, OH, ed. Anthony E. Petrarca, Celianna I. Taylor, and Robert S. Kohn (White Plains, NY: Knowledge Industry Publications, Inc. for ASIS, 1982). (Abstract only). Paper also entitled: *Chinese Library Automation — An Overview*.
31. Meng-chen Lin 林孟真, "Wo Kuo Tzu Hsun Ch'u Li Hsien K'uang 我國資訊處理現況 [The Current Status of the Data Processing Systems in the ROC]," in *T'u Shu Kuan Shih Yeh He Tso Yu Fa Chan Yen T'ao Hui Hui I Chi Yao 圖書館事業合作與發展研討會會議紀要 [Proceedings of the 1980 Library Development Seminar]*, Taipei, 1-7 December 1980 (Taipei: National Central Library, 1981), 357-432.
32. Wan-jiun Wu, "The Agricultural Science and Technology Information

Management System," in *Chung Wen T'u Shu Tzu Liao Tzu Tung Hua Kuo Chi Yeh T'ao Hui Lun Wen Chi 中文圖書資料自動化國際研討會論文集 [Papers of the International Workshop on Chinese Library Automation]*, Taipei, 14-19 February 1981 (Taipei: Library Association of China, 1981), D11 - D46; "Nung Yeh K'o Chi Tzu Hsun Kuan Li Hsi T'ung 農業科技資訊管理系統 [The Agricultural Science and Technology Information Management System]," in *T'u Shu Kuan Shih Yeh He Tso Yu Fa Chan Yen T'ao Hui Hui I Chi Yao 圖書館事業合作與發展研討會會議紀要 [Proceedings of the 1980 Library Development Seminar]*, Taipei, 1-7 December 1980 (Taipei: National Central Library, 1981), 493-503. (Includes flowcharts, tables)

33. Rui-lan Ku Wu, "The Union List of Chinese Serials in the Republic of China: A Case Report," in *Chung Wen T'u Shu Tzu Liao Tzu Tung Hua Kuo Chi Yeh T'ao Hui Lun Wen Chi 中文圖書資料自動化國際研討會論文集 [Papers of the International Workshop on Chinese Library Automation]*, Taipei, 14-19 February 1981 (Taipei: Library Association of China, 1981), D57-D82.
34. Wan-jiun Wu et al., "Agri-Thesaurus: A Chinese Thesaurus for the Agricultural Science and Technology Information Management System," in *Information Interaction: Proceedings of the American Society for Information Science (ASIS) 45th Annual Meeting: Volume 19*, 17-21 October 1982, Columbus, OH, ed. Anthony E. Petrarca, Celianna I. Taylor, and Robert S. Kohn (White Plains, NY: Knowledge Industry Publications, Inc. for ASIS, 1982), 342-344. Also available as: "Agri-Thesaurus: A Chinese Thesaurus for the Agricultural Science and Technology Information Management System," in *Symposium on Computer Processing of Chinese Library Materials and Computer-Assisted Chinese Language Instruction at ASIS-82: Proceedings*, Columbus, Ohio, 19 October 1982. (Taipei: ASIS Taipei Chapter, 1982), 6-1-6.
35. Lin-chih Huang 黃林芝, "Chung Shan K'o Hsueh Yen Chiu Yuan T'u Shu Kuan Tzu Tung Hua Chien Chieh中山科學研究院圖書館自動化簡介 [Introducing Library Automation of Chung Shan Institute of Technology]," in *T'u Shu Kuan Shih Yeh He Tso Yu Fa Chan Yen T'ao Hui Hui I Chi Yao 圖書館事業合作與發展研討會會議紀要 [Proceedings of the 1980 Library Development Seminar]*, Taipei, 1-7 December 1980 (Taipei: National Central Library, 1981), 446-449.
36. Margaret C. Fung, "Library Automation in the Republic of China," *T'u Shu Kuan Hsueh Yu Tzu Hsun K'o Hsueh 圖書館學與資訊科學 [Journal of Library & Information Science]* 6, no.1 (April 1980): 1-16. (In Eng-

lish); Jack Kai-tung Huang, "Freedom Council Information Abstracts," in *Chung Wen T'u Shu Tzu Liao Tzu Tung Hua Kuo Chi Yeh T'ao Hui Lun Wen Chi 中文圖書資料自動化國際研討會論文集 [Papers of the International Workshop on Chinese Library Automation]*, Taipei, 14-19 February 1981 (Taipei: Library Association of China, 1981), D47-D56; Meng-chen Lin 林孟真, "Wo Kuo Tzu Hsun Ch'u Li Hsien K'uang 我國資訊處理現況 [The Current Status of the Data Processing Systems in the ROC]," in *T'u Shu Kuan Shih Yeh He Tso Yu Fa Chan Yen T'ao Hui Hui I Chi Yao 圖書館事業合作與發展研討會會議紀要* (Taipei: National Central Library, 1981), 357-432.

37. Yung-lang Loh, "Computer Microfilm Retrieval System Used for Processing Criminal Data in the ROC" in *Chung Wen T'u Shu Tzu Liao Tzu Tung Hua Kuo Chi Yeh T'ao Hui Lun Wen Chi 中文圖書資料自動化國際研討會論文集 [Papers of the International Workshop on Chinese Library Automation]*, Taipei, 14-19 February 1981 (Taipei: Library Association of China, 1981), D97-D104 (Includes flowcharts and illustrations).
38. Kuo Li Chung Yang T'u Shu Kuan Pien 國立中央圖書館 編 [National Central Library, comp.], *T'u Shu Kuan Shih Yeh He Tso Yu Fa Chan Yen T'ao Hui Hui I Chi Yao 圖書館事業合作與發展研討會會議紀要 [Proceedings of the 1980 Library Development Seminar]*, Taipei, 1-7 December 1980 (Taipei: National Central Library, 1981) (Taipei: National Central Library, 1981). (Text in Chinese and English).
39. Rui-lan Ku Wu, "The Union List of Chinese Serials in the Republic of China: A Case Report," in *Chung Wen T'u Shu Tzu Liao Tzu Tung Hua Kuo Chi Yeh T'ao Hui Lun Wen Chi 中文圖書資料自動化國際研討會論文集 [Papers of the International Workshop on Chinese Library Automation]*, Taipei, 14-19 February 1981 (Taipei: Library Association of China, 1981), D57-D82.
40. Margaret C. Fung, "Library Automation in the Republic of China," *T'u Shu Kuan Hsueh Yu Tzu Hsun K'o Hsueh 圖書館學與資訊科學 [Journal of Library & Information Science]* 6, no.1 (April 1980): 1-16. (In English); Margaret C. Fung, "The Chinese Educational Resources Information Systems — A Case Report," in *Chung Wen T'u Shu Tzu Liao Tzu Tung Hua Kuo Chi Yeh T'ao Hui Lun Wen Chi 中文圖書資料自動化國際研討會論文集 [Papers of the International Workshop on Chinese Library Automation]*, Taipei, 14-19 February 1981 (Taipei: Library Association of China, 1981), D1-D10. (In English); Margaret C. Fung 張鼎鍾, *T'u Shu Kuan Hsueh Yu Tzu Hsun K'o Hsueh Chih T'an T'ao 圖書館學與資訊科學之*

探討 [On library and Information Science] (Taipei: Student Book Co., 1982), 227. (Articles in Chinese and in English)

41. Tung-sheng Fang 方同生, "K'o Hsueh Ch'i K'an Lien Ho Mu Lu Tzu Liao T'ang Pao Kao 科學期刊聯合目錄資料檔報告 [Union List of Scientific and Technical Periodicals]," in *T'u Shu Kuan Shih Yeh He Tso Yu Fa Chan Yen T'ao Hui Hui I Chi Yao 圖書館事業合作與發展研討會會議紀要 [Proceedings of the 1980 Library Development Seminar]*, Taipei, 1-7 December 1980 (Taipei: National Central Library, 1981), 433-440. (Text in Chinese; Includes sample input sheet and flowchart); Meng-chen Lin 林孟真, *Wo Kuo Tzu Hsun Hsi T'ung Chih Chien Li Yu T'an T'ao 我國資訊系統之建立與探討 [The Establishment and Exploration of the Information Systems in the ROC]* (Taipei: Wen Shih Che Publishing Co., 1982), 191; National Science Council (NSC). Services for Scientific Research: Science and Technology Information Center. *NSC Review* (1980-1981): 92-97.
42. Tung-sheng Fang 方同生, "T'ung I Ts'ai Kou Hsi Wen Tu Shu Tzu Liao Hsi T'ung Chi Hua 統一採購西文圖書資料處理系統計劃 [Centralized Acquisition System of Foreign Publications]," in *T'u Shu Kuan Shih Yeh He Tso Yu Fa Chan Yen T'ao Hui Hui I Chi Yao 圖書館事業合作與發展研討會會議紀要 [Proceedings of the 1980 Library Development Seminar]*, Taipei, 1-7 December 1980 (Taipei: National Central Library, 1981), 441-445.
43. Shih-hsion Huang 黃世雄, "Tan Chiang Ta Hsueh T'u Shu Kuan Tien Nao Hua Tso Yeh Hsi T'ung 淡江大學圖書館電腦化作業系統 [The Automated Library System in Tamkang University]," in *T'u Shu Kuan Shih Yeh He Tso Yu Fa Chan Yen T'ao Hui Hui I Chi Yao 圖書館事業合作與發展研討會會議紀要 [Proceedings of the 1980 Library Development Seminar]*, Taipei, 1-7 December 1980 (Taipei: National Central Library, 1981), 523-525.
44. Hong-chu Huang 黃鴻珠, "Wo Kuo Hsi Shu Ts'ai Kou Tien Nao Hua Tso Yeh Chih T'an Tao 我國西書採購電腦化作業之探討 [A Study on the Computerization of Foreign Publications Ordering Procedures in the R.O.C]," *T'u Shu Kuan Hsueh Yu Tzu Hsun K'o Hsueh 圖書館學與資訊科學 [Journal of Library &Information Science]* 5 (April 1979): 104 – 110. (Text in Chinese, abstract in English).
45. Kuo Li Taiwan Shih Fan Ta Hsueh, Kuo Li Chiao Yu Tzu Liao Kuan Pien 國立台灣師範大學，國立教育資料館 編 [National Taiwan Normal University and National Institute of Educational Materials, eds.], *Chiao*

Yu Tzu Liao Yen T'ao Hui Chi Lu 教育資料研討會記錄 [Educational Resources Workshop Proceedings], Taipei, 10-11 May 1980 (Taipei: National Taiwan Normal University and National Institute of Educational Materials, 1980), 171. (Text in Chinese and English)

46. Science and Technology Information Center, "Chung Wen Tzu Hsun Tzu Tung Hua Tso Yeh Kai K'uang Chien Shu 中文資訊自動化作業概況簡述 [Brief Report on Chinese Automated Information Processing]," in *Chung Wen T'u Shu Tzu Liao Tzu Tung Hua Kuo Chi Yeh T'ao Hui Lun Wen Chi 中文圖書資料自動化國際研討會論文集 [Papers of the International Workshop on Chinese Library Automation]*, Taipei, 14-19 February 1981 (Taipei: Library Association of China, 1981), I - XVIII.
47. Shih-hsion Huang 黃世雄, "Fa Chan Tzu Hsun Kung Yeh Ying Chung Shih Te Chi Ko Wen T'i 發展資訊工業應重視的幾個問題 [Some Issues to be Emphasized in Developing the Information Industry]," *Chung Yang Jih Pao 中央日報* [*Central Daily News* (Taiwan, ROC)], 21-22 December 1980, 2.
48. Ching-lung Liu 劉錦龍, "Ju Ho Yu Shiao Yun Yung Tzu Hsun Tzu Yuan – Kuo Chi Pai K'o Tien Nao Tzu Liao K'u Chih Li Yung 如何有效運用資訊資源 – 國際百科電腦資料庫之利用 [How to Effectively Use Information Resources – Use of UDAS]," *Chi Hsieh Yueh K'an 機械月刊 [Machinery Monthly]* 7 (November 1981): 160-172.
49. Shan-chieh Chen 陳善捷, "Kuo Chi Pai K'o Kung Yung Yu Chien So 國際百科功用與檢索 [The Supply and Retrieval of UDAS]," *Tzu Hsun Yu Tien Nao 資訊與電腦 [Information and Computers]* 9 (March, 1981): 11 – 15.
50. Hsing Cheng Yuan Yen Chiu Fa Chan K'ao He Wei Yuan Hui Pien 行政院研究發展考核委員會 編 [Research, Development and Evaluation Commission, Executive Yuan, ed.], *Wo Kuo Chung Wen Tien Nao Hsi T'ung Chih Fa Chan: Hsien K'uang Tiao Ch'a Chi Wei Lai Chan Wang 我國中文電腦系統之發展：現況調查及未來展望 [Development of Chinese Language Computer Systems: Current Status and Future Outlook]* (Taipei: Research, Development and Evaluation Commission, 1979), 152. (In Chinese, one paper in English; includes charts, illustrations, tables).
51. Yung Wei 魏鏞, Fa Chan Tzu Hsun T'i Hsi, Ch'iang Hua Chueh Ts'e Kung Neng: *Wo Kuo Hsing Cheng Tzu Hsun T'i Hsi Chih Chien Li Yu Chan Wang 發展資訊體系，強化決策功能：我國行政資訊體系之建立與展望 [Develop Information Systems, Strengthen Decision Making Capabilities: The Establishment and Development of our National Management Information System]* (Taipei: Research, Development and Evaluation

Commission, Executive Yuan, 1982), 28. (Includes charts, diagrams).

52. C. C.Yang, C. C. Hsieh, and D. T. Lin, "Chinese Computer Technology in Taiwan, ROC — An Overview," in *Information Interaction: Proceedings of the American Society for Information Science (ASIS) 45th Annual Meeting: Volume 19,* 17-21 October 1982, Columbus, OH, ed. Anthony E. Petrarca, Celianna I. Taylor, and Robert S. Kohn (White Plains, NY: Knowledge Industry Publications, Inc. for ASIS, 1982), 383. (Abstract only). Full text available in reference: American Society for Information Science (ASIS), Taipei Chapter, ed., *Symposium on Computer Processing of Chinese Library Materials and Computer-Assisted Chinese Language Instruction at ASIS-82: Proceedings*, Columbus, Ohio, 19 October 1982. (Taipei: ASIS Taipei Chapter, 1982), 3- 1-13.

53. Hsing Cheng Yuan Yen Chiu Fa Chan K'ao He Wei Yuan Hui Pien 行政院研究發展考核委員會 編 [Research, Development and Evaluation Commission, Executive Yuan, ed.], *Wo Kuo Chung Wen Tien Nao Hsi T'ung Chih Fa Chan: Hsien K'uang Tiao Ch'a Chi Wei Lai Chan Wang 我國中文電腦系統之發展：現況調查及未來展望 [Development of Chinese Language Computer Systems: Current Status and Future Outlook]*, 152. (In Chinese, one paper in English; includes charts, illustrations, tables).

54. Tzu Hsun Kung Yeh Ts'e Chin Hui Pien 資訊工業策進會 編 [Institute for the Information Industry, ed.], C*hung Wen Tien Nao Fa Chan Tiao Ch' a Fen Hsi Pao Kao 中文電腦發展調查分析報告 [Analytic Report on Chinese Computer Development]*, 2 vols (Taipei: Institute for the Information Industry, 1982).

55. Tzu Hsun Kung Yeh Ts'e Chin Hui Pien 資訊工業策進會 編 [Institute for The Information Industry, ed.], *Chung Hua Min Kuo Tzu Hsun Kung Yeh Nien Chien: Ch'i Shih Nien Tu 中華民國資訊工業年鑑: 七十年度 [Information Industry Yearbook of the Republic of China, 1981]* (Taipei: Institute for the Information Industry, 1981), 242. (Text in Chinese; Includes various tables, charts, graphs); Tzu Hsun Kung Yeh Ts'e Chin Hui Pien 資訊工業策進會 編 [Institute for the Information Industry, ed.], *Chung Hua Min Kuo Ch'i Shih I Nien Tzu Hsun Kung Yeh Nien Chien 中華民國七十一年資訊工業年鑑 [Information Industry Yearbook of the Republic of China, 1982]* (Taipei: Institute for the Information Industry, 1982), 228. (Includes various charts, tables, graphs).

56. Internationl Computer Conference: Hong Kong, ed., *Chinese Data Processing and Text Handling - The Next Frontier: Proceedings of the Hong Kong Computer Society and the Chinese Language Computer Society*

International Computer Conference: Hong Kong, 12-15 October 1980, Hong Kong (Hong Kong: International Computer Conference, 1980). 2 vols (Volume I: 287; Volume II: 246). (Includes charts, graphs, tables; Text partially in Chinese); Chung Kuo T'u Shu Kuan Hsueh Pien 中國圖書館學會 編 [Library Association of China, ed.], *Chung Wen T'u Shu Tzu Liao Tzu Tung Hua Kuo Chi Yeh T'ao Hui Lun Wen Chi 中文圖書資料自動化國際研討會論文集 [Papers of the International Workshop on Chinese Library Automation],* Taipei, 14-19 February 1981 (Taipei: Library Association of China, 1981), 408. (Text in Chinese and in English).

57. Tzu Hsun Kung Yeh Ts'e Chin Hui Pien 資訊工業策進會 編 [Institute for the Information Industry, ed.], *Chung Hua Min Kuo Ch'i Shih I Nien Tzu Hsun Kung Yeh Nien Chien 中華民國七十一年資訊工業年鑑 [Information Industry Yearbook of the Republic of China, 1982]*, 228. (Includes various charts, tables, graphs)
58. Li-ren Hu, Yuan-wei Chang, and Jack Kai-tung Huang 胡立人，張源渭，黃克東, *Training Manual for the Three Corner Coding Method* (Taipei: System Publication Co., Ltd., 1979), 131. (In Chinese and English; includes tables); Li-ren Hu, Yuan-wei Chang, and Jack Kai-tung Huang 胡立人，張源渭，黃克東, *Chinese Indexes Interchange Table* (Taipei: System Publication Company, Ltd., 1981), 105. (In Chinese and English); Te-yao Kiang and Tao-ho Ch'eng 江德耀、程道和, *Chung Kuo Wen Tzu Te Hsin Fen Hsi Fa Chi Lien Tai Chien P'an Shu Ju Hsi T'ung 中國文字的新分析法及連帶鍵盤輸入系統 [A New Analysis Scheme of Chinese Characters and the Associated Keyboard Input System]* (Taipei: K'o Chi T'u Shu Ku Fen Yu Hsien Kung Szu, 1979), 167.
59. Margaret C. Fung, "Library Automation in the Republic of China," *T'u Shu Kuan Hsueh Yu Tzu Hsun K'o Hsueh 圖書館學與資訊科學 [Journal of Library & Information Science]* 6, no. 1 (April 1980): 1-16.
60. Ching-chun Hsieh et al., "The Design and Application of the Chinese Character Code for Information Interchange (CCCII)," *T'u Shu Kuan Hsueh Yu Tzu Hsun K'o Hsueh圖書館學與資訊科學 [Journal of Library & Information Science]* 7, no. 2 (October 1981): 129-143. (Includes graphs, illustrations).
61. Chung Wen Tzu Hsun Ch'u Li Yung Tzu Yen Chi Hsiao Tsu Pien 中文資訊處理用字小組 編 [The Chinese Character Analysis Group, ed.], *Chung Wen Tzu Hsun Chiao Huan Ma 中文資訊交化換碼 [Chinese Character Code for Information Interchange]*, 1 vol. (Taipei: Library Association of China, 1980). (Includes various tables and separate Character Code

sheet); Hsing Cheng Yuan Kuo Tzu Cheng Li Hsiao Tsu Pien 行政院國字整理小組 編 [The Chinese Character Analysis Group, Executive Yuan, ed.], *Chung Wen Tzu Hsun Chiao Huan Ma Tzu Hsing Piao 中文資訊交換碼字形表 [Symbols and Character Tables of Chinese Character Code for Information Interchange]*, 1 vol. (Taipei: The Chinese Character Analysis Group, Executive Yuan, 1981); uo Tzu Cheng Li Hsiao Tsu Pien 國字整理小組 編 [The Chinese Character Analysis Group, ed.], *Chung Wen Tzu Hsun Chiao Huan Ma I T'i Tzu Piao 中文資訊交換碼異體字表 [Variant Forms of Chinese Character Code for Information Interchange]*, 2nd ed., vol. 2 (Taipei: The Chinese Character Analysis Group, 1982).

62. T'u Shu Kuan Tzu Tung Hua Tso Yeh Kuei Hua Wei Yuan Hui Chung Kuo Pien Mu Kuei Tse Yen Ting Hsiao Tsu Pien 圖書館自動化作業規劃委員會中國編目規則研訂小組 編 [Cataloging Rules Working Group, Library Automation Planning Committee, ed.], "The Shaping of the Chinese Cataloging Rules," in *Chung Wen T'u Shu Tzu Liao Tzu Tung Hua Kuo Chi Yeh T'ao Hui Lun Wen Chi 中文圖書資料自動化國際研討會論文集 [Papers of the International Workshop on Chinese Library Automation]*, Taipei, 14-19 February 1981 (Taipei: Library Association of China, 1981), C33-C66. (Text in English with cataloging rules in Chinese); C. C. Lan and M. D. Wu, "New Chinese Cataloging Rules as the Foundation of the Chinese MARC," in *Information Interaction: Proceedings of the American Society for Information Science (ASIS) 45th Annual Meeting: Volume 19*, 17-21 October 1982, Columbus, OH, ed. Anthony E. Petrarca, Celianna I. Taylor, and Robert S. Kohn (White Plains, NY: Knowledge Industry Publications, Inc. for ASIS, 1982), 155-157. Also available in *Symposium on Computer Processing of Chinese Library Materials and Computer-Assisted Chinese Language Instruction at ASIS-82: Proceedings*, Columbus, Ohio, 19 October 1982. (Taipei: ASIS Taipei Chapter, 1982), 4-1-5.

63. Chinese MARC Working Group, Library Automation Planning Committee, ed., "Chinese MARC Format and Bibliographic Databases," in *Information Interaction: Proceedings of the American Society for Information Science (ASIS) 45th Annual Meeting: Volume 19*, 17-21 October 1982, Columbus, OH, ed. Anthony E. Petrarca, Celianna I. Taylor, and Robert S. Kohn (White Plains, NY: Knowledge Industry Publications, Inc. for ASIS, 1982), 58-59. Also available in *Symposium on Computer Processing of Chinese Library Materials and Computer-Assisted Chinese Language Instruction at ASIS-82: Proceedings*, Columbus, Ohio, 19 October 1982.

(Taipei: ASIS Taipei Chapter, 1982), 5-1-27. (Includes illustrations); Margaret C. Fung 張鼎鍾, *T'u Shu Kuan Hsueh Yu Tzu Hsun K'o Hsueh Chih T'an T'ao 圖書館學與資訊科學之探討 [On library and Information Science]* (Taipei: Student Book Co., 1982), 227. (Articles in Chinese and in English).; Lucy Te-chu Lee 李德竹, "Chung Wen T'u Shu Chi Tu Pien Mu Ke Shih Yen Ting Kung Tso Pao Kao 中文圖書機讀編目格式研訂工作報告 [Report on Chinese MARC Format for Books]," in *T'u Shu Kuan Shih Yeh He Tso Yu Fa Chan Yen T'ao Hui Hui I Chi Yao 圖書館事業合作與發展研討會會議紀要 [Proceedings of the 1980 Library Development Seminar]*, Taipei, 1-7 December 1980 (Taipei: National Central Library, 1981), 518-519; Lucy Te-chu Lee, et al., "Chinese MARC: Its Present Status and Future Development," in *Chung Wen T'u Shu Tzu Liao Tzu Tung Hua Kuo Chi Yeh T'ao Hui Lun Wen Chi 中文圖書資料自動化國際研討會論文集 [Papers of the International Workshop on Chinese Library Automation]*, Taipei, 14-19 February 1981 (Taipei: Library Association of China, 1981), C9-C26. (Includes tables). Also available: *T'u Shu Kuan Hsueh Yu Tzu Hsun K'o Hsueh 圖書館學與資訊科學 [Journal of Library & Information Science]* 7, no. 1 (April 1981): 1-18. (Includes charts and illustrations).

64. Ping-chao Ch'en 陳炳昭, "Wo Kuo Chin Shih Nien Lai K'o Chi T'u Shu Kuan Kuan Chi Chien Ho Tso Kuan Hsi Chih Hui Ku Yu Chan Wang 我國近十年來科技圖書館館際間合作關係之回顧與展望 [A Recollection and Future Prospect of the Cooperative Efforts of Scientific and Technical Libraries in the Past Decade]," in *T'u Shu Kuan Shih Yeh He Tso Yu Fa Chan Yen T'ao Hui Hui I Chi Yao 圖書館事業合作與發展研討會會議紀要 [Proceedings of the 1980 Library Development Seminar]*, Taipei, 1-7 December 1980 (Taipei: National Central Library, 1981), 210-218. (Includes graphs and tables).
65. Shu-yun Lei 雷叔雲, "Ch'i Pu Chung Te Chung Hua Min Kuo Jen Wen Chi She Hui K'o Hsueh T'u Shu Kuan Chi Tzu Liao Tan Wei Kuan Chi Ho Tso Tsu Chih 起步中的「中華民國人文暨社會科學圖書館及資料單位館際合作組織」 [The Interlibrary Cooperative Organization among Libraries of Humanities and Social Sciences]," in *T'u Shu Kuan Shih Yeh He Tso Yu Fa Chan Yen T'ao Hui Hui I Chi Yao 圖書館事業合作與發展研討會會議紀要 [Proceedings of the 1980 Library Development Seminar]*, Taipei, 1-7 December 1980 (Taipei: National Central Library, 1981), 219-220.
66. Yen-ch'iu Wang 汪雁秋 [Teresa Wang Chang], "Ju Ho Chia Ch'iang Wo

Kuo Ch'u Pan P'in Kuo Chi Chiao Huan Kung Tso 如何加強我國出版品國際交換工作 [How to Strengthen International Exchange of Publications]," in *T'u Shu Kuan Shih Yeh He Tso Yu Fa Chan Yen T'ao Hui Hui I Chi Yao 圖書館事業合作與發展研討會會議紀要 [Proceedings of the 1980 Library Development Seminar]*, Taipei, 1-7 December 1980 (Taipei: National Central Library, 1981), 176-209. (Includes illustrations)

67. Shih-hsion Huang 黃世雄, "Fa Chan Tzu Hsun Kung Yeh Ying Chung Shih Te Chi Ko Wen T'i 發展資訊工業應重視的幾個問題 [Some Issues to be Emphasized in Developing the Information Industry]," in *Chung Yang Jih Pao 中央日報 [Central Daily News* (Taiwan, ROC)], 21-22 December 1980, 2; Shih-hsion Huang 黃世雄, "Wo Kuo T'u Shu Kuan Shih Yeh Wei Lai San Shih Nien Chih Chan Wang 我國圖書館事業未來三十年之展望 [The Future Outlook of Chinese Librarianship in the Next Thirty Years]," *Chung Yang Jih Pao 中央日報 [Central Daily News* (Taiwan, ROC)], 19 December 1982, 2.
68. Margaret C. Fung 張鼎鍾, "Tzu Tung Hua Tzu Hsun Wang Yu Kuo Chia Chien She 自動化資訊網與國家建設 [Automated Information Network and National Development]," in *T'u Shu Kuan Shih Yeh He Tso Yu Fa Chan Yen T'ao Hui Hui I Chi Yao 圖書館事業合作與發展研討會會議紀要 [Proceedings of the 1980 Library Development Seminar]*, Taipei, 1-7 December 1980 (Taipei: National Central Library, 1981), 351-356.
69. Meng-chen Lin 林孟真, "Wo Kuo Tzu Hsun Ch'u Li Hsien K'uang 我國資訊處理現況 [The Current Status of Data Processing Systems in the R. O. C.]," in *T'u Shu Kuan Shih Yeh He Tso Yu Fa Chan Yen T'ao Hui Hui I Chi Yao 圖書館事業合作與發展研討會會議紀要 [Proceedings of the 1980 Library Development Seminar]*, Taipei, 1-7 December 1980 (Taipei: National Central Library, 1981), 357-432.
70. Hwa-wei Lee 李華偉, "Chien Li Ch'uan Kuo T'u Shu Tzu Hsun Wang Ch'u I 建立全國圖書資訊網芻議 [Preliminary Suggestions on the Establishment of a National Information Network]," in *Chung Yang Jih Pao 中央日報 [Central Daily News* (Taiwan, ROC)], 26 February 1974, 9-10; Hwa-wei Lee, "A Sketch for a Computerized National Library and Information Network," in *Chung Wen T'u Shu Tzu Liao Tzu Tung Hua Kuo Chi Yeh T'ao Hui Lun Wen Chi 中文圖書資料自動化國際研討會論文集 [Papers of the International Workshop on Chinese Library Automation]*, Taipei, 14-19 February 1981 (Taipei: Library Association of China, 1981), El-El2.
71. Margaret C. Fung 張鼎鍾, *T'u Shu Kuan Hsueh Yu Tzu Hsun K'o Hsueh Chih T'an T'ao 圖書館學與資訊科學之探討 [On library and Information*

Science] (Taipei: Student Book Co., 1982), 227. (Articles in Chinese and in English).

72. Meng-chen Lin 林孟真, *Wo Kuo Tzu Hsun Hsi T'ung Chih Chien Li Yu T'an T'ao 我國資訊系統之建立與探討 [The Establishment and Exploration of the Information Systems in the ROC]* (Taipei: Wen Shih Che Publishing Co., 1982), 191.
73. Fu-ts'ung Chiang 蔣復璁, "Chung Kuo T'u Shu Kuan Shih Yeh Te Hui K'u Yu Ch'an Wang 中國圖書館事業的回顧與展望 [The Recollection and Future Outlook of Chinese Librarianship]," *Kuo Li Chung Yang T'u Shu Kuan Kuan K'an 國立中央圖書館館刊 [National Central Library Bulletin]* New 7 , no. 2 (September 1974): 4-6; Bao-hwan Seng 沈寶環, "Wo Kuo T'u Shu Kuan Shih Yeh Fa Chan Te T'u Ching 我國圖書館事業發展的途徑 [The Ways to Develop Chinese Librarianship]," *Chiao Yu Yu Wen Hua 教育與文化* 414 (April 1974): 9-11.
74. Tung-che Chang 張東哲, "Chia ch'iang Fa Chan Wo Kuo T'u Shu Kuan Shih Yeh Chi T'iao Chang Ai Chiao Shao Te T'u Ching 加強發展我國圖書館事業幾條障礙較少的途徑 [Ways of Expediting the Development of Our Library and Information Programs],"in *T'u Shu Kuan Shih Yeh He Tso Yu Fa Chan Yen T'ao Hui Hui I Chi Yao 圖書館事業合作與發展研討會會議紀要 [Proceedings of the 1980 Library Development Seminar],* Taipei, 1-7 December 1980 (Taipei: National Central Library, 1981), 61-74.
75. Margaret C. Fung 張鼎鍾, *T'u Shu Kuan Yu Tzu Hsun 圖書館與資訊 [Libraries and Information]* (Taipei: Feng Cheng Publishing Co., 1979), 244. (Text in Chinese and English); Margaret C. Fung 張鼎鍾, *T'u Shu Kuan Hsueh Yu Tzu Hsun K'o Hsueh Chih T'an T'ao 圖書館學與資訊科學之探討 [On library and Information Science]* (Taipei: Student Book Co., 1982), 227. (Articles in Chinese and in English).
76. Tzu-chung Li 李志鍾, "Fa Chan Ch'uan Kuo T'u Shu Kuan Yeh Wu Te Chi Tien I Chien 發展全國圖書館業務的幾點意見 [Opinions on Developing Nationwide Library Operations]," *Chung Yang Jih Pao 中央日報* [*Central Daily News* (Taiwan, ROC)], 25 February 1973, 2.
77. Chen-ku Wang 王振鵠, "Lun Chuan Mien Fa Chan T'u Shu Kuan Shih Yeh Chih T'u Ching 論全面發展圖書館事業之途徑 [Ways to Develop Librarianship as a Whole]," *Chiao Yu Tzu Liao K'o Hsueh Yueh K'an 教育資料科學月刊 [The Bulletin of Educational Media Science]* 4, no 4 (October 1972): 2-3.
78. Kuo Chia Chien She Yen Chiu Wei Yuan Hui Pien 國家建設研究委員會編 [Commission on National Development Research, ed.], *Tang Ch'ien Wen*

Hua Chien She Chung T'u Shu Kuan Te Kuei Hua Yu She Chih Chih Yen Chiu 當前文化建設中圖書館的規劃與設置之研究 *[A Study on the Planning and Establishment of Libraries in the Cultural Development Program]* (Taipei: ROC Commission on National Development Research, 1981), 98.

79. Chen-ku Wang 王振鵠, "Wen Hua Chung Hsin T'u Shu Kuan Chih Kuei Hua 文化中心圖書館之規劃 [The Planning of the Library of the Cultural Center]," *Chung Kuo T'u Shu Kuan Hsueh Hui Hui Pao* 中國圖書館學會會報 *[Bullentin of the Library Association of China]* 30 (3 December 1978): 1-3.
80. Kuo Chia Chien She Yen Chiu Wei Yuan Hui Pien 國家建設研究委員會 編 [Commission on National Development Research, ed.], *Tang Ch'ien Wen Hua Chien She Chung T'u Shu Kuan Te Kuei Hua Yu She Chih Chih Yen Chiu* 當前文化建設中圖書館的規劃與設置之研究 *[A Study on the Planning and Establishment of Libraries in the Cultural Development Program]*, 98.
81. Margaret C. Fung 張鼎鍾, *T'u Shu Kuan Hsueh Yu Tzu Hsun K'o Hsueh Chih T'an T'ao* 圖書館學與資訊科學之探討 *[On library and Information Science]* (Taipei: Student Book Co., 1982), 227. (Articles in Chinese and in English)
82. Chien Wang 王健, "Wen Hua Chien She Chi Hua Shih Shih Hsien K'uang 文化建設計劃實施現況 [The Performance of the Cultural Development Project]," in *T'u Shu Kuan Shih Yeh He Tso Yu Fa Chan Yen T'ao Hui Hui I Chi Yao* 圖書館事業合作與發展研討會會議紀要 *[Proceedings of the 1980 Library Development Seminar]*, Taipei, 1-7 December 1980 (Taipei: National Central Library, 1981), 101-106.
83. Kuo Li Chung Yang T'u Shu Kuan Pein 國立中央圖書館 編 [National Central Library, comp.], *T'u Shu Kuan Shih Yeh He Tso Yu Fa Chan Yen T'ao Hui Hui I Chi Yao* 圖書館事業合作與發展研討會會議紀要 *[Proceedings of the 1980 Library Development Seminar]*. (Text in Chinese and English)
84. Chung Kuo T'u Shu Kuan Hsueh Hui Pien 中國圖書館學會 編 [Library Association of China, ed.], *Chung Wen T'u Shu Tzu Liao Tzu Tung Hua Kuo Chi Yeh T'ao Hui Lun Wen Chi* 中文圖書資料自動化國際研討會論文集 *[Papers of the International Workshop on Chinese Library Automation]*, Taipei, 14-19 February 1981 (Taipei: Library Association of China, 1981), 408. (Text in Chinese and in English)
85. American Society for Information Science (ASIS). Taipei Chapter, ed., *Symposium on Computer Processing of Chinese Library Materials and Computer-Assisted Chinese Language Instruction at ASIS-82: Proceed-*

ings, Columbus, Ohio, 19 October 1982. (Taipei: ASIS Taipei Chapter, 1982), 1 vol.

86. Anthony E. Petrarca, Celianna I.Taylor, and Robert S. Kohn, eds., *Information Interaction: Proceedings of the American Society for Information Science (ASIS) 45th Annual Meeting: Volume 19*, 17-21 October 1982, Columbus, OH (White Plains, NY: Knowledge Industry Publications, Inc. for ASIS, 1982), 431pp.
87. Kuo Li Chung Yang T'u Shu Kuan Pein 國立中央圖書館 編 [National Central Library, ed.], *Ch'uan Kuo T'u Shu Kuan Hsien K'uang Tiao Ch'a Yen Chiu 全國圖書館現況調查研究 [Survey of Libraries in Taiwan ROC]* (Taipei: National Central Library, 1982), 384. (Includes various tables).
88. Kuo Li Chung Yang T'u Shu Kuan Pien 國立中央圖書館 編 [National Central Library, ed.], *Chung Hua Min Kuo T'u Shu Kuan Nien Chien 中華民國圖書館年鑑 [Library Yearbook of the Republic of China]*, 451. (Includes [facsimiles of] legal documents related to Chinese libraries)
89. Chung Wen Tzu Hsun Ch'u Li Yung Tzu Yen Chi Hsiao Tsu Pien 中文資訊處理用字小組 編 [The Chinese Character Analysis Group, ed.], *Chung Wen Tzu Hsun Chiao Huan Ma 中文資訊交化換碼 [Chinese Character Code for Information Interchange]*, 1 vol.; Hsing Cheng Yuan Kuo Tzu Cheng Li Hsiao Tsu Pien 行政院國字整理小組 編 [The Chinese Character Analysis Group, Executive Yuan, ed.], *Chung Wen Tzu Hsun Chiao Huan Ma Tzu Hsing Piao 中文資訊交換碼字形表 [Symbols and Character Tables of Chinese Character Code for Information Interchange]*, 1 vol.
90. T'u Shu Kuan Tzu Tung Hua Tso Yeh Kuei Hua Wei Yuan Hui Chung Kuo Chi Tu Pien Mu Ke Shih Kung Tso Hsiao Tsu Pien 圖書館自動化作業規劃委員會中國機讀編目格式工作小組 編 [Chinese MARC Working Group, Library Automation Planning Committee, ed.], *Chung Kuo Chi Tu Pien Mu Ko Shih 中國機讀編目格式 [Chinese MARC Format]* (Taipei: National Central Library, 1982), 342. (Includes tables, appendices index)
91. T'u Shu Kuan Tzu Tung Hua Tso Yeh Kuei Hua Wei Yuan Hui Chung Kuo Pien Mu Kuei Tse Yen Chiu Hsiao Tsu Pien 圖書館自動化作業規劃委員會中國編目規則研究小組 編 [Chinese Cataloging Rules Working Group, Library Automation Planning Committee, ed.], *Chung Kuo Pien Mu Kuei Tse 中國編目規則 [Chinese Cataloging Rules]* (Taipei: National Central Library, 1982), 60.
92. Tzu Hsun Kung Yeh Ts'e Chin Hui Pien 資訊工業策進會 編 [Institute

for the Information Industry, ed.], *Chung Hua Min Kuo Ch'i Shih I Nien Tzu Hsun Kung Yeh Nien Chien* 中華民國七十一年資訊工業年鑑 *[Information Industry Yearbook of the Republic of China, 1982]*, 228. (Text in Chinese; Includes various charts, tables, graphs)

93. Marianne Tell, *A Note about China's Scientific and Technological Information System* (Stockholm, Sweden: Royal Institute of Technology Library, July 1980), 49. (Report no. TRITA-LIB-1102). ERIC: ED 197703.
94. Kieran P. Broadbent, "The Modernization of Information Services in the People's Republic of China," *Journal of Information Science* (The Netherlands) 3, no. 5 (November 1981): 227-233.
95. John T. Ma, "Libraries in the People's Republic of China," *Wilson Library Bulletin* 45 (June 1971): 970-975.
96. John N. Hawkins, "Rural Education and Technique Transformation in the People's Republic of China," *Technological Forecasting and Social Change* 11 (1978): 315-333.
97. Marianne Tell, *A Note about China's Scientific and Technological Information System*. (Stockholm, Sweden: Royal Institute of Technology Library, July 1980), 49. (Report no. TRITA-LIB-1102). ERIC: ED 197703.
98. George Chandler, "The Chinese Library System," *International Library Review* 12, no. 4 (1980): 393-427.
99. Ching-Chih Chen, "Recent Developments in Library and Information Science in China," *Bulletin of the American Society for Information Science* 6, no. 4 (April 1980): 10-11.
100. John H. Meier, "Information Technology in China," *Asian Survey* 20, no. 8 (August 1980): 860-875.
101. George Chandler, "The Chinese Library System," *International Library Review* 12, no. 4 (1980): 393-427.
102. John H. Meier, "Information Technology in China," *Asian Survey* 20, no. 8 (August 1980): 860-875.
103. Michael Brawne and Stephan Schwarz, *Development of the Institute of Scientific and Technical Information of China* (ISTIC) (Paris, France: UNESCO, 1981), 84. (UNESCO Technical Report no. FMR/PGI/81/104(Rev).
104. Kieran P. Broadbent, "The Modernization of Information Services in the People's Republic of China," *Journal of Information Science* (The Netherlands) 3, no. 5 (November 1981): 227-233.
105. Zixin Lin, "China's Scientific and Technical Information Work and Application of New Information Technology" (Paper presented at the Inter-

national Federation for Documentation (FID) 41st Congress, Hong Kong, 12-16 September 1982), 13. (Session F, Paper no. 22).

106. Wenxu Xu, "Chinese Library Networks: Retrospect and Prospect" (Paper presented at the International Federation for Library Associations and Institutions (IFLA) 48th General Conference, Montreal, Canada, 22-28 August 1982), 7.

107. Junqui Huang and Qikang Zhao, "Inter-Library Loan Service of the National Library of China" (Paper presented at the International Federation of Library Associations and Institutions (IFLA) 48th General Conference, Montreal, Canada, 22- 28 August 1982), 9.

108. Jian Shi and Yan Lizhong "The Development of [the] Library and Information System of the Chinese Academy of Sciences" (Paper presented at the International Federation of Library Associations and Institutions (IFLA) 48th General Conference, Montreal, Canada, 22-28 August 1982), 11.

109. Luo Xingyun, "Libraries and Information Services in China," *Journal of Information Science* (The Netherlands) 6, no. 1 (March 1983): 21-31.

Co-authored with Donald V. Black.

Reprinted with permission from *The Annual Review of Information Science and Technology* V. 18. White Plains, NY: Knowledge Industry Publications, Inc. for American Society for Information Science, c1983. (pp. 307-314 & 330-354).

17

The Dynamics of Growing Public Libraries in Taiwan Area

ABSTRACT

This paper attempts to report the status of public libraries in Taiwan area with brief geographical and demographic descriptions. A brief history of public library development and its current status are presented with statistics to illustrate the impacts of national development policy, education, and economic development upon the growth of public libraries in Taiwan area.

INTRODUCTION

Before presenting the status of public libraries in Taiwan area, we would like to provide you with some basic information about this area which covers the island of Taiwan and two off-shore islands, Kinmen and Matsu, with a total land area of 13,968.8 square miles. Taiwan island is located at the southeastern coast of the China mainland, separated by the Taiwan Straits about 200 km from Fukien province. The southern tip of the island is 350 km north of the Philippines, and the northern tip is 1,000 km southwest of Japan.

The Chinese settled in Taiwan ages ago but mass migration was led by Cheng Chen-kung in 1661. Taiwan became part of

China since 1886. The island was occupied by Japanese since 1895 for fifty years until it was returned to Chinese government in 1945. After the seat of the ROC moved to Taiwan in 1949, there are now two special municipalities (Kaohsiung and Taipei), sixteen counties, five cities, 399 towns and villages. The current population of this area has reached 19 million with an average of 520 persons per square meter. A high density of population is indeed evident.

The population, however, is comparatively young because quarter of the population is still in school. It also indicated an educated population because less than nine percent of the population is illiterate since the advent of the nine-year compulsory education initiated in 1968. This paper will explore the types, functions, and development of public libraries in such a conducive environment.

Types of Public Libraries in Taiwan Area

Discussed here are libraries for public use which include national libraries, provincial and municipal libraries, county and city libraries, town and village libraries, libraries of the cultural centers and libraries of social educational institutions. These libraries, subordinate to governmental organizations, are publicly funded. There are also privately-funded libraries for public use, some of them have collections of subject specializations and some of general interest.

The Development of Public Libraries in Taiwan Area

Era of 1901-1977

Public libraries began in 1901 with the establishment of Taiwan Collection (台灣文庫 – Taiwan Wen Ku) funded by private sources. In 1914, it was merged by Taiwan Provincial Government and became the first government-supported public library. Since the announcement of Rules and Regulations of Private and Public Libraries by Taiwan Provincial Government in 1923, public libraries mushroomed in a speedy manner. The development of public libraries in Taiwan was also greatly enhanced by the establishment of the Library Association in 1927.

In accordance with 1943 statistics, there were ninety-four public libraries, of which ninety were supported by government and four by private sectors. They were quite a few public libraries, but the collections were mostly in Japanese and comparatively very small. Circulation was poor.

Toward the end of World War II, Taiwan was greatly damaged by bombing. Most of the libraries suffered great loss. After the war when Taiwan was recovered by China, libraries did not function at all because of financial constraints and the impractical nature of the Japanese collection. Libraries were reinstated toward the end of the 1940s when the government structure was redefined. It was at this time that public libraries' organization and regulations were gradually formulated. County and City Library Organizational Regulations announced by Taiwan Provincial Government in 1951 required the establishment of libraries in counties and cities. According to the statistics of 1952, there were three provincial libraries, fourteen county and city libraries, with a total collection of 437,241 volumes. Almost all the counties and cities had public library services by that time.

The revision of the above mentioned regulations in 1968 enabled the libraries to have more librarians. Since the announcement of Village and Town Libraries Organizational Regulations in 1969, the legal status of village and town libraries was clearly founded and thus promoted the establishment of village and town libraries.

The 1976 statistics indicated that there were fifty-four public libraries in Taiwan. The collection raised from 1,066,207 volumes in 1968 to 1,864,181 volumes in 1976; an increase of 75% was an encouragement.

In 1977, Cultural Construction Project, stipulated by national development policy, was announced as one of the Twelve National

Development Projects; public libraries, being an integral part of the project, have thus stepped into a new era of growth.

Cultural Construction and Public Libraries

With the purpose of enriching people's knowledge and upgrading their livelihood, the Cultural Construction Project has plans to establish a cultural center in each of the cities and counties within five years of 1977. *Outlines of Establishing County and City Cultural Center Plans* announced by the Executive Yuan specified the following:

1. Relocation of the National Central Library,
2. Establishment of a cultural center with emphasis on library in each of the counties and cities in the province of Taiwan,
3. Establishment of a library in each of the administrative district in Taipei,
4. Establishment of Chiang Kai-shek Cultural Center in Kaohsiung with establishment of a branch library at each administrative district.

From 1978 up to now, the most prominent development of libraries rested at the building of new quarters of libraries. Up to 1986, there are eighteen cultural centers all over counties and cities with a total footage of 15,583 square miles at a cost of US$102 million.

Kaohsiung Municipal Chiang Kai-shek Cultural Center, opened to the public in April 1981, the earliest library of a cultural center, has a collection of 106,868 volumes. In Kaohsiung and Taipei, these two special municipalities, among twenty-seven administrative districts, there are only three districts which do not yet have branch libraries. New libraries are actually either under construction or being planned for construction.

National Central Library started construction in 1982 and was completed in 1985 with plans to serve the public commencing September 28, 1986.

In addition to the hardware construction, a1l libraries have made significant improvements in collection and funding.

In the past three summers, professional assistance has been given to cultural center libraries in that four library schools have been sending their students to aid technical services under the direction of their faculty members. *Cultural Center Handbook* is also being prepared by the National Central Library in order to provide administrative guidelines. In addition, Ministry of Education and Provincial Library in Taichung also held seminars for the purpose of giving short term cultural center professional training.

CONCLUSION

Public libraries, being instrumental to the upgrading of citizens' intellectual level, to the popularization of education, to the wholesome development of the society, and to meeting needs of all public and private sectors, have won nationwide attention and government support.

From the above description, we can see the impressive development in public libraries:

1. The number of public libraries has grown from 17 in 1952 to 307 in 1986, a 1706% increase.
2. The collection raised from 1,066,207 volumes in 1976 to 1,864,181 in 1986, an increase of 75%.

As a result of the above two figures, we can draw a conclusion that funding has also been increased many folds even though the staff quota allowance for professional librarians has not been significantly upgradeded to coop with the growing collections and mushrooming libraries.

We are pleased to conclude with the following observations that the development of public libraries has been enhanced by the rules and regulations, government policy support, economic and social prosperity, professional organization, extension of compulsory education, and coordinated efforts in library automation.

Rules and Regulations

These rules and regulations set up by the government have played important roles to the development of public libraries. The formulations and revisions of County and City Libraries Organizational Regulations and Village and Town Libraries Organizational Regulations have directly increased the number of village and town libraries. In turn, these regulations have great impacts upon the quality of public services.

Government Policy Support

Various support given by government policy have greatly enhanced the growth of both the hardware and software of libraries. Such type of policy support has been evidenced by the Cultural Construction Project. Its impacts upon libraries have been proven by the fact that the number of libraries has been increased and provincial and national libraries have been improved.

The Economic and Social Prosperity of the Country

Taiwan area's economic take-off began in the mid 1960s. Since then, the per capita income has reached US$3,142 in 1985 in comparison with US$221 in 1966. With economic bloom, private sectors, being the wealthier ones in the country, have established more libraries for public use. Since 1970, there have been an increase of public libraries funded by private resources, the increase of religious bodies and electronic manufacturing companies have made significant contributions, they have funded thirty-five public libraries and AV libraries for public use. As we realize, private funding has less limitations; as a result, libraries with private resources, are enabled to collect more expensive materials, e.g. AV materials in addition to the regular collections of printed materials.

Professional Organization

The Library Association of China was re-established in 1953. Its revival has helped the drafting of public library standards, rules, and regulations putting to public libraries which indeed assist professional training and upgrading of library qualities.

Extension of Compulsory Education and Increasing Consciousness of the importance of Education

Compulsory education was expanded to nine years since 1968. A highly educated population put more demands upon libraries.

Coordinated Efforts of Library Automation

Library Automation Project led by the Library Association of China and National Central Library has enjoyed its fruits. Under the coordinated efforts and the leadership of NCL, public libraries system seems to be benefited from the standards adopted by NCL and its experiences.

REFERENCES

1. Hu, An-i 胡安彝. "Erh Shih Wu Nien Lai Te Kung Kung T'u Shu Kuan 二十五年來的公共圖書館 [Public Libraries in the Past Twenty-five Years]." *Chung Kuo T'u Shu Kuan Hsueh Hui Hui Pao 中國圖書館學會會報 [Bullentin of the Library Association of China]* 29 (1977): 51-64.
2. Lei, Shu-yun 雷叔雲. *Tai Min Ti Chu T'u Shu Kuan Hsien Kuang Tiao Cha Yen Chiu 台閩地區圖書館現況調查研究 [Survey of the Current Status of Libraries in Taiwan and Fukien Areas]* (Taipei: National Central Library, 1982).
3. Ma, Shao-chuan 馬少娟. "Tsung Wo Kuo Kung Kung T'u Shu Kuan Hsien Kuang Tiao Cha Yu Pi Chiao Tan Chiu Chin Hou Fa Chan Chih Tao 從我國公共圖書館現況調查與比較探究今後發展之道 [An Exploration into the Future Development of Public Libraries in the ROC through Survey and Comparisons]." *Chiao Yu Tzu Liao K'o Hsueh Yueh K'an 教育資料科學月刊 [The Bulletin of Educational Media Science]* 8, nos. 5/6 (1975): 24-28; 9, no. 1 (1976): 26-33; 9, no. 2 (1976): 21-26.
4. Ma, Shao-chuan 馬少娟. "Taiwan Ch'u Kung Kung T'u Shu Kuan Shih

Lueh, 1895-1976 台灣區公共圖書館史略, 1895-1976 [A Brief History on Public Libraries in Taiwan, 1895-1796]." *Chiao Yu Tzu Liao K'o Hsueh Yueh K'an 教育資料科學月刊 [The Bulletin of Educational Media Science]* 11, no. 3 (1977): 29-32; 12, no. 2 (1977): 31-35; 12, no. 3 (1977): 36-40; 12, no. 4 (1977): 28-39.

5. Sung, Chien-cheng 宋建成. "San Shih Nien Lai Te Kung Kung T'u Shu Kuan 三十年來的公共圖書館 [Public Libraries in the Past Thirty Years]." *Chung Kuo T'u Shu Kuan Hsueh Hui Hui Pao 中國圖書館學會會報 [Bulletin of the Libray Association of China]* 35 (1983): 20-32.
6. Ibid.
7. Taiwan Sheng Li Tai Chung T'u Shu Kuan Pien 台灣省立台中圖書館編 [National Taichung Library, ed.]. *Taiwan Sheng Ko Hsien Shih Wen Hua Chung Hsin T'u Shu Kuan Hsing Cheng Yu Shih Wu Yen Tao Hui Chih Shih 台灣省各縣市文化中心圖書館行政與實務研討會記實 [Seminar on Administration and Practice of Cultural Center Libraries in Taiwan]* (Taichuhg: Taiwan Provincial Taichung Library, 1985).
8. Taiwan Sheng Li Tai Chung T'u Shu Kuan Pien 台灣省立台中圖書館 編 [National *Taichung Library, ed.]. Taiwan Sheng Ko Hsian Cheng Hsien Hsia Shih Li T'u Shu Kuan Kai Kuang 台灣省各鄉鎮縣轄市立圖書館概況 [General Status of Village, Town, County Libraries]* (Taichung: Taiwan Provincial Taichung Library, 1975).
9. "Ti Fang Tu Shu Kuang Tiao Cha Piao 地方圖書館調查表 [A Survey of Local Libraries]." *Chung Kuo T'u Shu Kuan Hsueh Hui Hui Pao 中國圖書館學會會報 [Bulletin of the Library Association of China]* 5 (1955): 13-14.
10. Chung Kuo T'u Shu Kuan Hsueh Hui. Kung Kung T'u Shu Kuan Wei Yuan Hui Pien 中國圖書館學會公共圖書館委員會 編 [Library Association of China. Public Libraries Committee, ed.]. "Taiwan Ti Chu Ko Chi Kung Kung T'u Shu Kuan Hsien Kuan Tzu Liao I Lan Piao 台灣地區各級公共圖書館現況資料一覽表 [Directory of Public Libraries in Taiwan Area]." *Chung Kuo T'u Shu Kuan Hsueh Hui Hui Pao 中國圖書館學會會報 [Bulletin of the Library Association of China]* 30 (1978): 199.
11. Wang, Chen-ku. "Library and Information Services in Taiwan, ROC." *National Central Library Newsletter*, vol. 17, no. 1 (May 1985): 1-5.

Co-authored with Christina K. C. Chen 陳國琼 (Lecturer, National Institute of the Arts).

Reprinted from the paper presented in the 1986 IFLA Annual Conference, Tokyo, Japan, 24-29 August 1986.

Part IV

MISCELLANEOUS

- Current Problems of International Book Numbers for Bibliographic Control
- Cultivation of Humanistic Spirit, Moral Standards, and Social Morales
- Library and Information Science Curriculum
- Global Librarianship in the Information Age
- Access and Human Rights of People with Disability in Taiwan
- Status of Women in the Republic of China

18

Discussion on the Current Problems of International Book Numbers for Bibliographic Control at International Symposium on Information Technology

Being a firm believer in the importance of bibliographic control and a devoted advocate of standards, the discussant makes a favorable discussion on Dr. Kies' paper entitled "The Current Problems in the International Book Numbers for Bibliographic Control." Dr. Kies' detailed comments on problems/confusions and suggestions for solution are worthy of attention.

DISCUSSION

As a person who is a firm believer in the importance of bibliographic control and a devoted advocate of standards, I feel very much honored to serve as a discussant on Dr. Kies' paper entitled "The Current Problems in the International Book Numbers for Bibliographic Control." As you will agree with me, this paper is both informative and enlightening.

Dr. Kies gave a thorough analysis and insignt into International Standard Book Number (ISBN) which is one of the fundamental means used for bibliographic control. She provided us with its historical background, its evolution, its structure, its purposes, its significance and various associated existing problems. Dr. Kies traced its evolution to the Third International Conference on Book

Market Research and Rationalization in the Book Trade in 1996, the announcement of ISO's 2108, the U.S. adoption of ISBN and subsequent change to ISBN in the U.S.

Using the U.S experience, Dr. Kies explicitely pointed out the problems that are encountered with ISBN. The problems and confusion caused by the redundant assignments of ISBN are as follows:

1. The lack of ISBN historical legends on the copyright page,
2. The misuse of ISBN – Different ISBNs are assigned to editions of the same text, of the same texts published by publishers in various countries, and of softwares,
3. The publishers' misunderstanding toward the function of ISBN. The ISBN is only used for inventory control by many publishers,
4. The assignment of ISBN to a set as a whole and to different volumes/titles in a set or in a series,
5. The confusion of ISBN and ISSN.

We, library professionals in Taiwan, Republic of China, have also experienced the same difficulties as Dr. Kies testified. We tried to apply for a designation number for the past ten years. After repeated efforts, we were finally assigned a country number in July, 1989. Within such a short period of time, we also experienced the same delimma as described by Dr. Kies, especially in the case of juvenile books, with serials, or series types of works, with translations, and with editions that have only cosmetic changes.

As we all are aware, ISBN is used as an identification, a great tool for disseminating information on publications, for communicating and for accessing to information. It is a means employed for bibliographic control. With such confusions as identified by Dr. Kies, it is really very sad to see such defeats of purpose. It seems that certain control over this tool of bibliographic control itself is needed.

Dr. Kies offered some suggestions for solutions. All four

suggestions are feasible means to exercise better control over the confusion caused by misuse, or by violation of the guidelines or by mis-assignments of ISBN:

1. The recording of ISBN history on the title page or colophon page,
2. The recording of ISBN on all bibliographic or information list on publications,
3. The use of optional digits for specific purposes that publishers have with this publication,
4. Continued discussions between publishers and librarians regarding problems encountered inadopting ISBN.

I cannot agree more with Dr. Kies regarding the solutions that she proposed. However, I would like to add some more suggestions or ways for implementation for your deliberation:

1. The ISBN Headquarters in Germany should take initiatives in coordinating actions to be taken among librarians, publishers, and other related national agencies,
2. The Headquarters should provide clearer and more definite guidelines regarding the assignments of ISBNs,
3. The ISBN Headquarters need to supply all national agencies with the software that they use, so that each national agency will have a consistent and authoritative ways of handling this matter,
4. At the present time, ISBN is employed to identify a wide range of non-book materials as well. Additional numbers other than ISBN or ISSN should probably be explored.

If we want to use ISBNs as successful means of bibliographic control, better control mechanism of these numbering systems has to be devised, provided and observed.

We are grateful to Dr. Kies for voicing the issues, for providing insights into the problems and possible solutions. Her enlightening suggestions at this Symposium, hopefully, can lead to a timely review and certain effective actions to be taken by the Headquarters in Germany after discussions and coordination among various parties involved and countries concerned. I wish to congratulate Dr. Kies for her excellent presentation.

Ladies and Gentlemen, may I also take this opportunity to express our heartfelt appreciation to the organizers for this Symposium, to Thammasat University Libraries for their meticulate arrangements and perfect organization of successful Symposium.

Reprinted from the discussion presented at the International Symposium on Information Technology, Bangkok, Thailand, 5 Sepember 1989.

19

The Cultivation of Humanistic Spirit, Moral Standards, and Social Morales from the Perspective of Librarianship

ABSTRACT

This paper attempts to identify some of the basic causes of the recent abnormal social phenomena in Taiwan — the lack of a humanistic spirit, moral standards and acceptable social mores. A brief description of government's cultural policies planned as remedies is presented. The cultivation of humanistic spirit, the promotion of ethical conduct and the improvement of social mores through library and information related activities are briefly presented as remedial measures.

INTRODUCTION

China has traditionally been known to be a nation of courtesy and righteousness. Chinese people pride themselves on being loyal, pious, benevolent, trustworthy, righteous, and peace-loving. Emphasis has always been placed on "man." A person's duties, a person's being; the relations between sovereign and subjects, between father and son, between husband and wife, among brothers, and among friends have been essentials of the Chinese society. These treasured human relations and "human-centered" beliefs have recently been shattered by many factors.

May Fourth Movement introduced “Science” and “Democracy” which brought new values and new dimensions to Chinese culture. Foreign aggression, world wars, and internal conflicts have brought about a different mentality.

During the past forty years, the political, economic, and social developments (land reform, technological advances, and democratic endeavors) have built Taiwan into a state of prosperity and won the fame of the ”Taiwan Experience” as a model for other nations.

The prosperity in Taiwan has induced many people to reach out for a luxurious material life. The termination of Martial Law, the lifting of many restrictions as a result of the promotion of democracy, free and international economy, the lifting of the restrictions on foreign exchange, on importation of liquor and cigarettes, on the press, on the formation of political parties, on visits to the mainland and on tourist visa issuance, etc., have facilitated the development of an open society which has led us into a transformational age of many changes.

Well illustrated by Alvin Toffler in his book entitled *The Third Wave*, the collapse of the Second Wave society undermines the needs for community, structure and meaning. A new civilization is emerging in our lives...brings with it new family styles; changed ways of working, loving, and living; a new economy; new political conflicts; and beyond all this an altered consciousness as well.[1] As a result, conflict, disorder, misunderstanding, irregularity in human relationship and organization and aimlessness prevail in the society.

PHENOMENA AND CAUSES

The transformational age presents us with progress as well as some negative changes of values which have initiated many abnormal phenomena.

Such social disorders evidenced in the cultural maladjustment and dismantling of social conventions have exerted a serious impact upon the stable and healthy development of the ROC.

Soon after we began to enjoy a free life style, the economic miracle, and technological advancement, our society became economically rich but culturally a desert. It has experienced appalling disorders: Kidnapping, armed robberies, murders, traffic problems, pollution, rapes, gambling, cheating, bribery, smuggling; and saddest of all, physical fights, violence, and insults to human dignity in the Legislative Yuan and National Assembly are some of the disgusting phenonema among the many unpleasant issues that we have to face. In the Legislative Yuan and National Assembly, people's representatives have set appalling examples which have greatly damaged the government's image and exerted an undesirable impact upon the general public. If not corrected in time, it is not overly pessimistic to predict that the country will soon be led to self-destruction.

Many scholars have studied the issues and concluded that these problems are caused by the absence of humanistic spirit, the lack of moral standards, and the want of refined social mores.

THE TRINITY

The humanistic spirit leads to ethical conduct, reinforces a fine quality of life and thus leads to a fine social mores. They are parts of a trinity, three aspects of one entity. All of them are interrelated and and interdependent.

The word "culture" 文化 is derived from: 觀乎天文以察時變，觀乎人文以化成天下(Change of weather can be observed from astronomical phenomena; how the world is formed and transformed can be detected by looking at humanism).[2] The culture created by human beings is a humanistic one and its spirit is defined as the humanistic spirit.[3] The broad definition of "humanistic spirit" is thus originated from culture.

In a narrower definition, "humanism" denotes human nature, human relations, man's position, the value of human life which, having been studied, developed, and ascertained, gradually generates humanistic spirit. Well defined by Dr. Wei-fan Kuo, humanism means the cultural objects and products created and generated by human beings to enrich their lives.[4]

The humanistic spirit, therefore, places emphasis on "man," his "being," his responsibilities, the quality of human personality and the five relations of human beings (五倫): the relations between father and son, between sovereign and subjects, between husband and wife, among brothers, and among friends.(父子有親，君臣有義，夫婦有別，長幼有序，朋友有信)

A man in forming his character, forms the character of others; in enlightening himself, he enlightens others. (立己立人，成己成物)

As the result of materialistic civilization enhanced by science and technology, people are tempted to search for materialistic enjoyment. Materialistic satisfaction seems to be people's only goal in life. Under such circumstances, Taiwan appears to an economic giant but a moral pygmy.

Affirmative recognition of human dignity and value, emphasis on cultivation of the personality, emphasis on human reations, emphasis on human virtues, developing of a person's inner virtue, and refining of external behavior, nurturing of man's habits to work hard for what they want are instrumental to the humanistic spirit which leads to ethical conduct and ultimately forms the proper social mores.

EFFORTS MADE

Dr. K. T. Li identified the need to pay attention to the development of an additional human relation, i.e. the relation between oneself and the public (群已). He urges us to be thrifty with public resources, to be protective of the public environment, and to be supportive of public orderliness. Dr. I-fu Ju further identified the importance of the relation between one group and other groups, (群倫) i.e. relation between one country and the other countries.[5] These new relations are factors enhancing the establishment of a harmonious society.

The government has repeatedly declared the importance of cultural development which, in essence, aims at the cultivation of humanistic spirit, ethical living, and fine social mores.

Dismayed by the current social disorder, the government has tried to devise various correcting measures. In September of 1989, the Primier, Dr. Lee Huan, reported his proposal of four policies and eleven implementation guidelines to the Legislative Yuan.[6] The four policies pertain to: 1) cultural development, 2) political development, 3) economic development and, 4) social development. Cultural development aims at the following: [7]

1. Enabling people to establish correct concept towards life and life style,
2. Enabling people to upgrade the qualities of their lives and their living standards,
3. Enabling people to observe both the traditional moral principles and to be aware of the importance of the relations between oneself and the public,
4. Enabling people to learn how to handle living resources: how to properly use money after they acquire it, how to best use their leisure time and how to enjoy a rewarding spiritual life;
5. Enabling people to enjoy numerous artistic and literary events,
6. Enabling people to honor laws, to be thrifty and enterprising, to be rid of speculating and lazy attitudes.
7. Enabling people to love and protect our cultural assets and to respect the major accomplishments of world civilization,
8. Enabling people to fully develop their artistic talents, helping the artists and art groups to participate in international art activities for the purpose of promoting Chinese culture and its contribution to world culture.

With these purposes in mind, Council for Culture Affairs proposes three projects and formulates eighteen implementing guidelines with details:

1. Upgrading social quality:
   (1) To guide and correct social mores,
   (2) To promote modern moral principles,
   (3) To initiate "leisure culture,"
   (4) To beautify the living environment,
   (5) To improve the quality of media.
2. Enhancing humanistic disposition and discipline:
   (1) To promote humanistic thinking,
   (2) To upgrade the quality of education,
   (3) To emphasize "Personality" education,
   (4) To provide education on how to use leisure time,
   (5) To reinforce family education,
   (6) To improve teachers' education.
3. Promoting artistic and literary activities:
   (1) To maintain and protect cultural assets,
   (2) To encourage and assist cultural enterprises,
   (3) To upgrade folk culture,
   (4) To popularize the refined culture,
   (5) To strengthen international exchange activities,
   (6) To influence world culture with the practice of Chinese culture.

Under these guidelines, some 165 programs have also been suggested for implementation. The wide range of programs are definitely effective measures.

LIBRARY'S ROLE IN THE TASK

The above mentioned cultural development programs laid down a blueprint for what we can do to get to a more ideal society. Under each category, the library, a cultural, an educational and social institution, can play an important role in implementing these programs. However, very few concrete tasks for libraries are mentioned in these programs. We should be very thankful that the previous the Twelfth Cultural Development Program initiated in 1977 has built many libraries including town libraries and those in cultural centers.

A library, in the traditional sense, is an institution which acquires, organizes, and preserves all types of materials for the use of their respective patrons: [8]

1. For public use if it is a public library — an institution of social education,
2. For faculty, staff and students' use if it is an educational institution (school, college or university),
3. For researchers' and staff use if it is a research or special library.

The library has since been given other functions than the above ones. It now serves as a community center which provides materials/information in all formats (printed, non-print, non-book materials, and even materials in electronic formats), recreational programs such as video and movie shows, puppet shows, story hours, concerts, etc., and continuing educational activities such as lectures, speeches, workshops, exhibition of rare and new materials, etc.

All library activities can be used for the cultivation of humanistic spirit, moral standards, and fine soicial mores as follows:

1. Quality materials/information collecting and disseminating: The library collects good and inspiring books or materials, organizes them, promotes them and disseminates them through circulation, book reviews, reading guidance services and other library-related activities.

   Bibliotherapy, in the past, was used as treatment of mentally-sick persons with the use of books. Now, it can very well be used for the general public under the circumstances.

2. Librarians and their services:
   Librarians serve as interfaces between books/materials and users. Librarians are entrusted with the duties to provide the right book/information to the right reader at the right time. Patrons can be led to read interesting books or factual materials, so that they can nurture the much-needed humanistic spirits, observe ethics of living and learn how to behave properly. When one reader affected, he will influence others around him, establish ethics suitable to modern life, and thus form acceptable mores in the community — such as a literary society (書香社會).
   A library's extension services, such as lectures, workshops, and reading clubs are not only ways to provide continuing education to patrons but also a good means to provide best use of the patrons' leisure time.
3. The library environment:
   The library is a community in itself, providing an environment to be shared by patrons. To follow established regulations, to be considerate of other people's rights and welfare can be learned in the library through the friendly guidance of librarians. Such habits can be formed in a small community like the library and be expanded to the society at large.

NECESSARY PRE-REQUISITES

The important factors which make the above three aspects possible are: quality books/materials, qualified librarians, and adequate buildings. The government has measures to promote good publications by granting awards. Eventually, there will be more good books for selection. Each city and town has already built its public library; all cultural centers and educational institutions have library facilities. However, libraries are not yet well-equipped to render the services as expected because of the following reasons:

1. Lack of a legal foundation and criteria for evaluation — there is no library law upon which library can relay and there is no authorized library standards to be used as criteria either as the basis to start a library or to evaluate a library's performance.
2. Lack of staff — most libraries are suffering from a shortage of qualified personnel. Libraries are required to hire only those who have passed civil examination. The importance of professional training and professional status are not properly recognized. The turnover rate of professional librarians is therefore very frequent and high. Furthermore, libraries do not have an adequate quota for professional librarians. With limited and unqualified staff, how can we expect the library to provide quality services?
3. Lack of leadership and a centralized coordinating body — Each library is subordinate to its respective official organ which reports to different levels of administrative and educational departments. Fox example, the Bureau of Education has authority over school libraries in the city, Ministry of Education has authority over college and university libraries and cultural center libraries report to different authorities. The vertical supervisory function is there; but there is no horizontal coordination which is highly needed among various different types of libraries for better coordinated services.

RECOMMENDATIONS

Cultivation of humanistic spirit, ethical conduct, and fine social mores calls for total implementable programs as proposed by the Council for Cultural Affairs and active participation by all sectors concerned. Library and information centers, being one of the best means for the purpose, should definitely and actively participate in these programs.

It is suggested that the Council for Cultural Affairs gets all libraries actively involved in its existing programs. The following activities are suggested to be immediately implemented first:

1. Teaching citizens how to use library by requiring students of all levels to take a course in library instruction and by scheduling demonstrations and presentations on TV or through the Open University.
2. Publicizing library activities, persuading people to use libraries by offering incentives, such as best readers' awards, frequent borrowers' awards, and friends of the library awards, etc.
3. Organizing reading clubs within the community led by celebrated leaders; making reading a popular and prestigious hobby.

In order to get the best result, it is necessary to solve the problems confronting librarianship by:

1. Upgrading professional librarians' status to that of educators.
2. Upgrading library professional education to graduate levels; revising library/information science curricula; increasing the number of library schools; designating normal educational institutions of various levels to train teacher/librarians, and providing continuing education to practicing librarians in evening schools.
3. Formulating library laws and standards with provisions for periodical revisions and updating.
4. Setting up a standing organization to coordinate library/ information activities, and to formulate related policies.
5. Organizing a high level conference on library and information science for the formulaion of national library/ information policy, by taking the White House Conference on Library and Information Science as an example.

When we try to source remedies, it is best to identify all possibilities which should include library as one of the effective means and tools. Put libraries into good use and ask them to perform in this important cultural rehabilitation task. Charge libraries their due responsibilities in cultivating humanistic spirit, promoting living ethics, and to form acceptable social mores. In the meantime, to solve the problems which prevent libraries from rendering satisfactory deserve serious deliberations and immediate action.

NOTES

1. Alvin Toffeler, *The Third Wave* (New York: William Morrow and Company, 1980), 25, 383.
2. Chou Yi Tse Kua Hsiang Chuan 周易責卦象傳.
3. Wei-te Chen 陳維德, "Lun Jen Wen Ching Shen 論人文精神 [On Humanism]," *K'ung Meng Yueh K'an 孔孟月刊 [Cong Meng Monthly]* 2, no.6 (February 1963): 12.
4. Wei-Fan Kuo 郭為藩, *K'o Chi Shih Tai Te Jen Wen Chiao Yu 科技時代的人文教育 [Humanistic Education in the Scientific and Technological Age]* (Taipei: Yu Shih, 1989), 31.
5. Yi-yuan Li 李亦園, "Hsien Tai Lun Li Te Ch'uan T'ung Chi Ch'u 現代倫理的傳統基礎 [The Tranditional Basis of Contemporary Ethics]," *Chung Hua Wen Hua Fu Hsing Yueh K'an 中華文化復興月刊 [Chinese Cultural Renaissance Monthly]* 214 (January 1986): 11-17.
6. Executive Yuan, ed., *Wen Hua Chien She Fang An: Kuo Chia Chien She Ssu Ta Fang An Tzu Yi 文化建設方案: 國家建設四大方案之一 [Cultural Construction Plan: One of the Fourth National Construction Plan]* (Taipei, Executive Yuan, 1990).
7. Ibid.
8. James S.C. Hu and Tsu-shan Wu 胡述兆，吳祖善, *T'u Shu Kuan Hsueh Tao Lun 圖書館學導論 [Introduction to Library Science]* (Taipei: Han Mei Book, lnc., 1989), 1.

Reprinted with permission from *The Proceedings of Chinese-American Academic and Professional Convention*. New York: CAPPCON, 1990. pp. 274-277.

20

Library and Information Science Curricula Planning in the Republic of China

ABSTRACT

This paper presents a brief historical background of library and information science education and its relationship with curricula planning in the Republic of China. The author identifies curricula problems confronting library and information science education from the perspectives of faculty members and students.

Principles, trends and recommendations on library and information science curricula planning are presented as a basis for discussion with the purpose of reaching some kind of consensus for the planning/revision of library and information science curricula in the Republic of China.

INTRODUCTION

Chinese culture has always been known for its emphasis on education, knowledge, and intellectual excellence. Books, as a result, are pivotal to the heritage of the Chinese people. Chinese libraries were, in the past, considered privileged institutions available to privileged people only.

Librarianship at that time was synonymous with custodianship; librarians were people who served as "keepers of books" only.

It was not considered as a profession; librarians were trained on the jobs. It was purely apprenticeship at the time.

Since the concepts of democracy and science were introduced to China, libraries' educational functions have received their due recognition, and their functions of providing popular education have been duly identified, the services and management of libraries have stepped into a new era. Library science education has thus been developed in order to train quality librarians capable of administering libraries and providing needed services.

The education of librarians has aimed at theory, application of theory, and practice ever since library science has been developed into a discipline for the study of theory and applications needed in the development and operations of library with scientific methods. Since the advent of modern technology and information science, the curricula designed to meet the new demands have thus become more complex due to the increasingly multi-disciplinary nature.

In China there was no formal education of librarians implemented before 1920. Greatly influenced by American practice, Mary Elizabeth Wood first initiated education for Chinese librarians at Boone University in 1920.[1] The curriculum was mostly patterned after the U.S. system.

From 1925 on, many institutions of higher education in China, before, during and after the Sino-Japanese War started library science departments/programs, such as Shanghai Kuo-ming University, Nanking University, National College of Social Education, Provincial Chiangsu College of Education, and National Peking University, etc.[2]

In Taiwan, Republic of China, library science course was first offered at the Foreign Language and Literature Department of the National Taiwan University in 1954;[3] formal university-level library science education was first offered in the Division of Library Science at the Social Education Department of the Taiwan Provincial Normal College (now National Taiwan Normal University) in

1955, followed by National Taiwan University, where an independent department was established in 1961.[4]

The World College of Journalism inaugurated its library technicians programs at the junior college level in 1964. Fu-jen Catholic University started its Library Science Department in 1970 and Tamkang University established its Department of Educational Media and Library Science in 1971. A master's program at National Taiwan University was established in 1980, and a doctoral program was inaugurated in 1989. The University of Chinese Culture offers some library science-related graduate courses in its Graduate Institute of History leading to both master's and doctoral degrees. National Taiwan Normal University offers several library/information science-related courses in its Graduate Institute of Social Education since 1985.[5]

Tamkang University's Graduate Institute in Educational and Media Science has been approved for inauguration by the Ministry of Education and the status of the World College of Journalism will be upgraded to four-year college level. In addition to such above-mentioned formal education, continuing education has been regularly offered by the Library Association of China, institutes and seminars sponsored by other professional associations, organizations, universities or colleges are also conducted as needs arise.[6]

EDUCATIONAL OBJECTIVES AND CURRICULUM PLANNING

During the apprenticeship period, practical experience was particularly emphasized. When formal education for librarians was instituted, attention was directed to curriculum planning. Education and curriculum planning are closely related and are interactive as cause and effect. Education intends to instruct, inform, train, develop, and indoctrinate; whereas curriculum planning is an institutionalized plan for education.[7]

Curriculum is the general overall plan of the content or specific materials of instruction that the school offers to the student by way of qualifying him for entrance into the profession.[8] It is an organized system of learning opportunities. It should be built around the organizing principles, the concepts and methods of inquiry which give the structure to a subject and attempt to make a coherent system of its aspects in the universe.[9]

In formulating a curriculum, it is necessary to base its rationale and implementation upon the educational philosophy of that particular discipline and the objectives of the educational program from which curriculum planning is generated. In general, the curriculum is organized to move from the most inclusive to the more particular and factual.[10] The curriculum should identify the methods of acquiring knowledge which are relevant to the field—sociological, bibliographic, mathematical, linguistical.[11] It should help students to integrate the whole program into body of knowledge which is effective in solving professional problems.

The three-way division of educational labor – college, professional school and practice provide a useful guideline for curriculum planning.[12] It encourages cooperation between professional schools and colleges in the formation of stable knowledge structures of basic disciplines and in promoting experience for practitioners as a way of learning.

LIBRARY SCHOOL OBJECTIVES AND CURRICULUM PLANNING

The mission of library education is to educate quality and competent librarians for the purpose of carrying out quality professional duties and professional services which include management of libraries, preservation and transmission of cultural heritage, organization of materials, providing reference and information services, teaching patrons the use of libraries, etc. The objective of library school is focusing around chosen professional problem of communicating human knowledge.

The ultimate goal of education for librarianship should be directed to educating students to be able to think and act upon the issues presented to them as administrators, planners, or practitioners. The emphasis of education should be intellectual and theoretical, so that librarians can think creatively about whatever area of librarianship they may be concerned with.[13] All service professions are in need of knowledge, skill and experience.[14]

Knowledge and skills cover the fundamentals and specific subject knowledge, whereas experience is the professional action which cover: 1) professional action (including human action system – biological, personality, social interactions, and cultural interactions); 2) clientele; 3) institutional and social environment.[15] There are the so-called core courses – those aspects of theory and practice which all libraries have in common; more specialized work might follow involving an expanded use of analysis, evaluation, and problem solving a variety of areas....[16] It has long been recognized by the library profession that the broad and general undergraduate background is an integral part of librarian's education. Dr. Harris B.H. Seng believes that prospective librarian should be equipped with:

1. A solid subject background,
2. A thorough knowledge of library science,
3. A workable knowledge of information science,
4. A fundamental knowledge of psychology, and
5. An understanding of environment and ergonomics (the needs of the country or region as a whole and the library and information infrastructure of the country or of the region).[17]

Professor Lancaster made an analysis and came up with valuable suggestions on the curriculum of information science. During the Conference on Library Automation and Information Networks in 1988, he also identified some important requirements of library/information science educational program and the competencies as follows:[18]

1. A program of study in information science should produce

graduates, capable of managing secondary distribution functions (libraries, information centers) more effectively, including the implementation and management of technological change.

2. Another requirement is to produce graduates able to apply automation to a wide range of library/information center applications.
3. A third is for people who can design and implement various types of database.
4. Finally, there is the need to build up a cadre of people able to perform research on information problems.

Professor Bernard S. Schlessinger identified the desired content of the core curriculum for information science/library science education in the 1990s by looking at: 1) competencies deemed necessary for professionals by practitioners through an analysis of job advertisements, 2) competencies deemed necessary for professionals by library educators as reflected in present core curricula, and 3) competencies deemed necessary by literature surveys of employers.[19] In his opinion, the needed courses can be categorized as follows:

1. Resources-Orientation including collection development, reference, bibliographic instruction, preservation, archives, media, audio-visuals, government documents, and maps, etc.,
2. Organization-Orientation including cataloging, classification and technical services,
3. Management-Orientation including budget, planning, and supervision, etc.,
4. Information Science-Orientation including automation systems and database searching, and
5. Youth/Children's Service-Orientation.[20]

Eight years ago, Dr. Tefko Saracevic's description of Case Western

Reserve University's curricula revision actually was quite similar to those suggested by Dr. Schlessinger:[21]

1. Information technology and tools including technology, processing, and programming, etc.,
2. System and network including system analysis, networks, database structure, etc.,
3. Management including basic management, issues in management of information services, economics of information, bibliometrics, marketing and user studies of information services, etc.,
4. Information sources covering the content and use of reference materials, representative organization methods (indexes and classification systems) and information structure (types of materials.)

The existing library education in the Republic of China falls into the following categories: 1) Undergraduate program, 2) Graduate Program (both master's program and doctoral program) and 3) Continuing education. It is different from the U.S. practice in the following aspects: 1) In the U.S., professional school offered in fifth year is primarily responsible for providing professional education; the skills of application of principles usually trained in the sixth year. What qualifications are needed for librarians and how can they be acquired have always been our professional concerns here.

CURRICULA PLANNING AND COURSES OFFERED IN CHINA

In China, as early as 1935, Mr. Ching-hsing Lee outlined the system of library science. In his opinion, the courses can be divided into: 1) Historical library science and 2) Systematic library science as follows:[22]

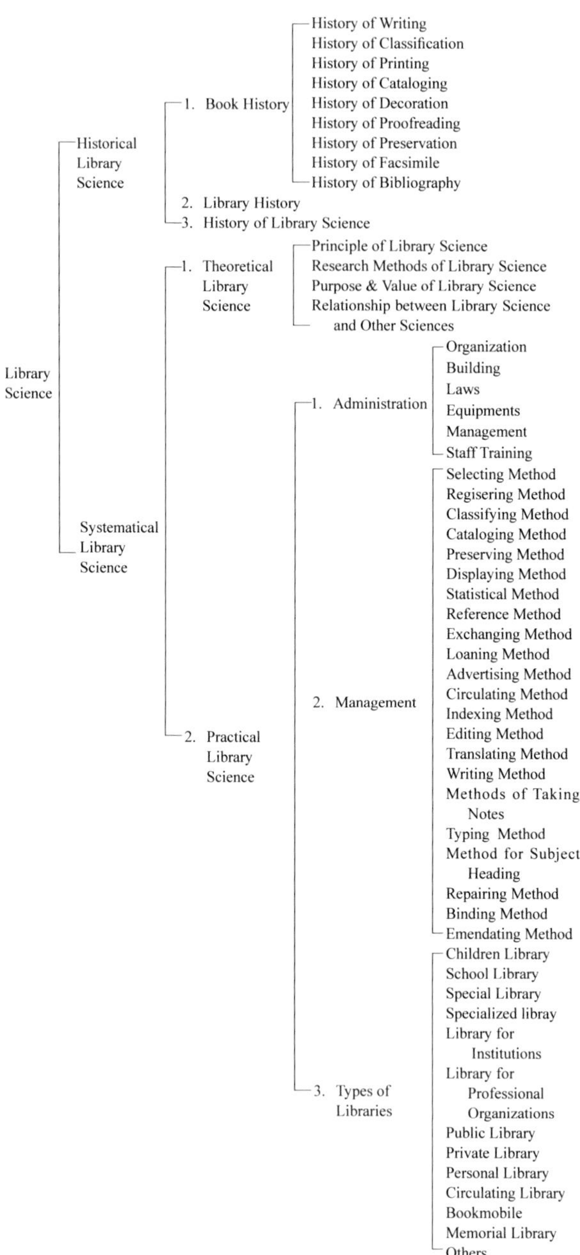
Library Science
Historical Library Science
1. Book History
History of Writing
History of Classification
History of Printing
History of Cataloging
History of Decoration
History of Proofreading
History of Preservation
History of Facsimile
History of Bibliography
2. Library History
3. History of Library Science
Systematical Library Science
1. Theoretical Library Science
Principle of Library Science
Research Methods of Library Science
Purpose & Value of Library Science
Relationship between Library Science and Other Sciences
2. Practical Library Science
1. Administration
Organization
Building
Laws
Equipments
Management
Staff Training
2. Management
Selecting Method
Regisering Method
Classifying Method
Cataloging Method
Preserving Method
Displaying Method
Statistical Method
Reference Method
Exchanging Method
Loaning Method
Advertising Method
Circulating Method
Indexing Method
Editing Method
Translating Method
Writing Method
Methods of Taking Notes
Typing Method
Method for Subject Heading
Repairing Method
Binding Method
Emendating Method
3. Types of Libraries
Children Library
School Library
Special Library
Specialized libray
Library for Institutions
Library for Professional Organizations
Public Library
Private Library
Personal Library
Circulating Library
Bookmobile
Memorial Library
Others

This system is actually archaic because it was devised more than half a century ago when information science and advanced technology were not available then.

REQUIRED LIBRARY SCIENCE COURSES STIPULATED BY THE MINISTRY OF EDUCATION

With the purpose of assuring the quality of education and the educational standards for various disciplines throughout the country, the Ministry of Education constantly evaluates, revises curriculum of all departments in order to meet new demands, needs and developments.

Ever since that advent of formal library schools in the college level, the Ministry of Education has revised the library school curriculum eight times; the latest one took place in 1988. Forty-eight credits of required courses have been stipulated as follows:[23]

Required Courses Stipulated by Ministry of Education in 1988

Course Title	Credits	Year to be Offered Freshman		Sophomore		Junior		Senior	
		*A	*B	*A	*B	*A	*B	*A	*B
Introduction to Library Science	2	2							
Introduction to Information Science	2		2						
*Chinese Reference Sources	4	2	2						
Western Reference Sources	4			2	2				
*Cataloging and Classification I	6			3	3				
*Cataloging and Classification II	6					3	3		
Introduction to Computer Science	4	2	2						
Bibliography	4			2	2				
*Non-Book Materials (including Management of AV Materials)	4			2	2				
Selection & Acquisition of Library Materials	4					2	2		
Library Management	4							2	2
Library Field Work	0							0	0
Library Automation	4							2	2
Total	48	12	18	10	8				

Remarks: *Two-hour practicum is added to each of these courses without additional credits;
*A = semester 1; *B = semester 2

Some of the changes made in 1988 have demonstrated great improvements:

1. To combine Chinese and Western Classification and Cataloging into one course and rename it as "Cataloging and Classification I and II."
2. To teach "Introduction to Computer Science" and "Chinese Reference Sources" in the freshman year.
3. To move the course of "Western Reference Sources" from the junior year to sophomore year.
4. The total required courses are reduced from 50 to 48 credits.

Librarians do need broad knowledge and a subject major. For undergraduate library school students in the ROC, students are allowed to select a minor in order to enhance their knowledge in various specialized subject fields.

During their freshman year, they are required to take Chinese, English, Chinese history and thoughts of Dr. Sun Yat-sen which will provide them with a broad knowledge background and language skill.

LIBRARY/INFORMATION RELATED COURSES OFFERED BY THE FIVE LIBRARY SCIENCE DEPARTMENTS IN THE REPUBLIC OF CHINA

The library/information science courses taught in departments of library science can be grouped into five categories similar to that offered by some of the Western library schools:[24] 1) The fundamental (foundation) courses for library science; 2) Library management courses; 3) Technical services-related courses; 4) Readers' services-related courses; and 5) Information Science-related courses.

Looking at the courses offered at the National Taiwan University, we can obtain a bird's eye view on the current status of library/information science curricula in the Republic of China because they cover both undergraduate and graduate programs.[25]

Examining the catalogs of these five library science departments in the ROC as listed on Table I-V, we are pleased to note that library schools offer a variety of electives in addition to the required courses.[26]

Table I to V clearly indicate that National Taiwan University (NTU) offers more fundamental courses, management courses, readers' service-related courses. National Taiwan Normal University (NTNU) being a teachers' university, offers the most needed professional courses for school librarians which are essential in preparing students to be teacher-librarians, Fu-jen Catholic University (FJCU) pays equal attention to all five categories, Tamkang University (Tamkang) pays more attention to information science-related and educational media courses, World College of Journalism aims at training entry level librarians or library technicians before its current plan of upgrading to four-year college level. In proportion, it reduced the credits of Western Cataloging, Chinese Cataloging, Library Collection Building, Chinese Reference Sources, and Western Reference Sources. It seems to be a local arrangement for a department which trains library technicians. The Department of Library Science at the National Taiwan University is the only institution which now offers both independent master's and doctoral programs for library and information science. Tables VI-X show the course titles and their pertinent credits for the master's program;[27] these courses are either to be taken as required or electives during the course of their study. Table XI lists all doctoral courses planned by NTU. Actual elective courses offered each year vary a great deal depending on the availability of faculty members.[28]

PROBLEMS CONFRONTING STUDENTS AND FACULTY MEMBERS

Education of librarians in the Republic of China has been quite successful in comparison with the status reported by Dr. Saracevic on some of the developing countries.[29] It has been an accepted fact that most of those who have completed undergraduate programs here go to the States to pursue further studies in the U.S. graduate schools are doing outstanding academic work just the same as the other native students.[30] We always believe in making improvements. Only from problem locating, can we find solutions and move ahead. It is, therefore, always helpful to call attention to the problems and try to find a solution for them. From my personal experience as a faculty member teaching library science for almost twenty years, the following problems came to my attention. These observations will be shared with colleagues first and then some recommendations/suggestions will be made as basis for discussion.

Arrangement of Courses

Through highly competitive University/College Joint Examination, the undergraduate library/information program admits high school students whose general knowledge background and specialized subject knowledge are quite limited for the profession of librarians. As a result, in the freshman year, students are required to take the above-mentioned general courses and to pick a minor which is considered as a remedial measure. Students are allowed to take two to three library/information sciences courses in the freshman year. The sophomore and junior years are usually packed with professional courses. For the library science majors at the National Taiwan Normal University, they are required to pick a minor in a subject that they will teach in high schools (e.g. history, language, geography, mathematics, chemistry, etc.). In addition to library science courses, they are required to take general background courses (e.g. Chinese, English, Thoughts of Dr. Sun Yat-sen, etc.), education courses (e.g. instructional materials, teaching methods, etc.,) and other courses related to the subject that they will teach in high schools as mentioned above. The sophomore and junior years become the most hectic time for library science students.

There are assignments for each of these courses. With such a heavy work load, most of the students find it hard to cope. As a result, the work load somewhat decreases their interest in the profession. Homework is very important to the study of library science, the need to do exercises cannot be overlooked. However, continuous uncoordinated assignments and reports somewhat reduce their initiative in actively acquiring knowledge and studying on their own. To hand in their homework on time seems to be their only goal. Little motivation is generated from their homework. The subject knowledge they obtain from the limited hours offered by the minor do not help them much in strengthening their subject background because most of their courses they select from the minors are not monitored.

Parallel Teaching and Redundancy of Chinese and Western Readers' Services Courses

It is a great improvement that Chinese Classification and Cataloging and Western Classification and Cataloging are combined into one course offered in two semesters since the last revision of curriculum standard in 1989. However, the same combination has not been made on the modern Chinese and Western Basic Reference Sources. They are offered separately and thus much effort and time are wasted. Mr. Shann-jye Chen and Professor Chien-chang Lan also identified the same problem.[31]

Insufficient Courses Offered for the Processing of Classical Chinese Works and for the In-depth Understanding of Information Resources of Chinese Classics

Enhancing Chinese librarians' ability in these areas is indeed in need of close attention.

Unsatisfactory Field Work or Practicum

Students are required to have some practical or hands-on experience at libraries in a real life situation. Most such type of practice work is done haphazardly. Sometimes, inadequate opportunities are given to library science department students by some of the libraries affiliated with the universities. Some department offices or the faculty members find places for the students to do some field work during the semester or during summer vacations. The libraries which accept the students for the field work might not have adequate professionals or able staff members to supervise the students' work. Most of the students get assigned to non-professional work or routine work where they cannot apply the theory they learn in the class to actual work at the libraries where they practice. Some library science departments offer their departmental libraries for students to practice in. However, these libraries' collections and services are usually limited and cannot replace the field work offered by a library which renders all types of services and library materials.

Duration of Study

In Taiwan now, for those graduate students whose undergraduate major is library science, it usually takes them two years to complete the master's program because of the strict requirements of a thorough understanding of the discipline and writing of a thesis. For those graduate students whose undergraduate majors are in other disciplines than library science, it will take them even longer period of time to take up the required undergraduate courses. The lengthened period of study seems to be the graduate students' common concerns.

The Non-MOE Required Second Foreign Language Course

Language is an asset to librarians who need to process materials language in foreign languages and to locate information from materials published in other languages than Chinese and English.

A second foreign language is no longer a MOE requirement in the Chinese library science curriculum. Some universities make it a requirement on their own.

Segregation of Theory and Application of Technology

Take Library Automation or Cataloging and Classification Class as an example, students are taught various MARC formats. They learn how to fill out a MARC format worksheet; they do not necessarily have online cataloging experience.

Inadequate Textbooks Written in Chinese

Even though great improvements have already been made in the last five years by many far-sighted colleagues and prolific writers, the amount is not enough to meet the great demand.

The Improper Use of Short Term Continuing Education Courses

The purpose of short courses and summer institutes should be targeted to continuing education only. They are now often treated as an alternate or replacement for formal library school education.

RECOMMENDATIONS AND SUGGESTIONS

As Dr. C. C. Chen pointed out that "... it is easy to witness a realization of all these new technologies as time progresses, it is important to keep in mind that the whirlwind pace of new technological developments have generally greatly outpaced our ability and effort to conceptualize and develop new appropriate educational programs and curricula for preparing our information professional for the efficient, full and productive use of these new technologies, ... the challenge to us as educators in restructuring our educational conceptual model, in continuously updating our curriculum, in offering continuing education opportunities, and in conducting research, is indeed, great."[32]

Based on the above conviction, I am making some suggestions/recommendations in the spirit of brainstorming. Your comments and ideas in making them more feasible and reasonable for possible consideration or implementation are greatly appreciated.

Impact of Technology Library Schools' Names or Subordination

Revision of library school's names to be corresponding with the curricula changes in technology and the use of automated systems in libraries have so far promoted two phenomena in American library schools:

1. Integration of library science and information science by adding "Information Science" to the name, i.e. "School of Library and Information Science." Eighty percent of the United States and Canadian Schools have added some phrase including the word "Information" to their names.[33]
2. Separation of these two disciplines into two different departments, one aims at the education of traditional library science and the other focuses its attention to information science.

Integration of library and information science might be a better choice for our country as short term practice, because there have already been department of information science in the College of Engineering or department of information management in the College of Management or Business at universities here. An additional separate department in the College of Arts might cause some confusion and poor coordination. In fact, information science-related courses have already become important ingredients of the library schools in the Republic of China. The adding of "Information Science" to their names seems more appropriate.

For the long term educational planning, it would be ideal to establish a separate Library/Information Science College or departments to accommodate three devisions: library science, information science and museum science. Dr. James Hu thinks that disciplines of library science and information science are somewhat interrelated. They should take some common courses as pre-requisites before making an independent yet concentrated studies on these two areas.[34]

Special Concentrations of Various Library Schools and Inter-institutional Cooperation

There are now five independent departments for library science in the country, aside from the required or general courses, each of them should offer some specially-emphasized or unique courses, so that faculty members and resources can be greatly enhanced through this type of concentrated efforts.

Arrangements should be made between national universities and also among private institutions with the approval of the Ministry of Education allowing students to be able to take courses for credits at other universities of the same categories. So that students from universities which do not offer such courses can also be benefited through inter-institutional cooperative arrangements. This is commonly done among universities in the United States. The same arrangement is not completely impossible either. Deliberation on this idea for the upgrading of library/information science education seems to be necessary.

Revision of Curricula to Cope with Changes

The last revision of curriculum standard was done two years ago. Improvements were quite evident. However, more graduate programs are to be inaugurated and more new courses or concentrations are offered in other countries. In order to meet new demands and newly-developed trends, it is advisable to take another overall look at the current curriculum and come up with new required or core courses for different levels of studies.

Just as Professor Lancaster once advised me that various aspects of automation could be incorporated into various courses;[35] on-line retrieval from databases could be incorporated with "Reference Services", automated acquisition system could be a part of "Building Library Collection" or "Acquisition" course. Through integration, manual and automated systems can be learned at the same time. Library automation per se should be offered either as a general background overview course giving students basic concepts of automation or a highly technically-oriented course or a course on the administration of automated services. Students are thus enabled to write specifications/proposals and to evaluate both software and hardware equipments.

Balanced course arrangement, added courses on Chinese classics, user-related, and leadership courses are highly recommended.

Re-Categorization of Courses in Place of the Former Ways of Grouping

The following suggested categorizations made by Dr. Schlessinger can be used as references of our master's curriculum planning:[36]

1. Foundation of Information/Library Science — Such as intellectual freedom, philosophy, communications, ethics, technology, etc.
2. Information Resource Development — Community analysis, media selection and evaluation, collection evaluation, censorship, weeding, standards, media acquisition, publishing, technology in collection management.
3. Information Organization I — Theory of organization, theory of cataloging, theory of classification, theory of indexing, an in-depth treatment of descriptive cataloging, a numerical and a subject classification system, cataloging support databases.
4. Information Organization II — In-depth treatments of major numerical and subject classification systems, subject versus indexing, major cataloging-support database, records management, organization of specialized materials.
5. Information Resources I — Types of materials, theory of reference and information retrieval, communication and effective interaction, introduction to online searching.
6. Information Resources II — In-depth treatment of re-

sources in major disciplines, including the use of subject-specific database treatments.

7. Information Tools and Application I — Theory and uses of system analysis, introduction to computers and networking.
8. Information Tools and Applications II — Applications of mainframe, mini, and micro computers for libraries, telecommunications, information processing.
9. Writings in Information/Library Science — Writing abstracts, annotations, reviews, research reports, annual reports, grant applications, use of graphics and tables.
10. Research — Research methods, research design, critical analysis of research reports, types of research, and statistical analysis, etc.
11. Management I — Theories of management, planning, leadership, facilities and building planning, public relations and marketing technology in management, introduction to budgeting.
12. Management II — In depth treatments of personnel management and fiscal management in information centers and libraries.

The Offering of Different Levels of Library/Information Science Education

Knowledge is power, information is an asset; accurate and timely information becomes an important part for human life and existence. All work of people depend on different types of information providers. Librarian/information scientists, being one of the information providers, have to cater to different needs.

Within libraries or information centers, there are many different types of workers shouldering different responsibilities. There are various ways of identifying library personnel: professionals, para-professionals, technicians, and clericals; academic librarians, public librarians, school librarians, children's librarians, catalogers, reference librarians, bibliographers and system librarians, etc.

Different levels of education should be made available for different types of librarians and different types of work. For a public library in a remote town, the qualifications of that public librarians are different from those working in metropolitan public libraries. Education of school librarians should be different from that of academic librarians.

With the upgrading of World College of Journalism, we need other junior college or vocational schools to train library technicians, para-professionals; we need to have departments in teachers' colleges to train school librarians; we need to keep the undergraduate programs at universities to prepare librarians for entry level positions, junior catalogers, junior reference librarians, and junior library administrators; we also need to establish more graduate programs educating people for academic librarians, library planners, leaders, library school faculty members, subject bibliographers, information specialists and researchers. For these various calibres of professionals, we need to devise different curricula to meet the different educational objectives.

Short term training class should be open to practising librarians with the purpose of conducting continuing education only. It should never take the place of formal education for librarians. As a result, curriculum planning for such short courses should be carried out with care and attention.

Special Funds Needs to be Set Up for the Encouragement of Chinese Textbook Writing and Publishing

The perfection of our services depends upon a sound educational system and well-designed curriculum only with which can competent professionals be educated to enhance the advancement of library/information services in order to meet various needs prevailing in the society. Ideal education and fine curriculum planning for Chinese librarians/information scientist are indeed our major concern as well as a great challenge to us.

Table I Fundamental Courses Offered by the Five Departments of Library Science in the ROC

COURSE TITLE	NTU	NTNU	FJCU	Tamkang	World College
Introduction to LS (2)	*	*	*	*	*
Bibliography (4)	*	*	*	*	*
History of Libraries (2)	+			+	
Special Topics in Library Science (2)	*	+			
Mass Communication (2)	*(old)				
(Introduction to Communication (2))	*(new)				
Research Methods and Thesis Writing (2)	*	+		*	
Library and Mass Communications (2)					*
Journalism (4)					*
System Analysis (2)	+		+	+	
Selected Readings on Library Science in English (2)	+		*		
Collectanea (3)	+				
International Librarianship (2)				+	
Comparative Librarianship (2)				+	
Emendation and Edition Studies (2)				+	
History of Books & Printing (2)					*
Library Education (2)		+			
AV Education (2)				*	
English for Librarians (2)	+				
Printing & Publishing (2)	+				
Museum Science (3)		+			
Library Statistics (3)	*(new)				

Remarks: * = required course; + = elective course
Number of credits are indicated in parentheses

Table II Management Courses Offered by the Five Departments of Library Science in the ROC

COURSE TITLE	NTU	NTNU	FJCU	Tamkang	World College
Library Management (4)	*		*	*	
Library Administration (2)		*			*
Measurement and Evaluation of Library Operations (2)	+			+	
Library Field Work	*(0)	*(3)	*(1)	*(2)	
University Libraries	+(3)	+(2)			
College Libraries (2)				+	
Public Libraries	+(3)	+(2)	+(3)	+(2)	
Children's Libraries	+(3)		+(2)		
Special Libraries	+(3)		+(2)	+(2)	
School Libraries	+(3)	*(2)		+(2)	
Medical Libraries			+(3)	+(2)	
Business Libraries (3)			+		
Archival Management (2)	+	+	+	*	*(4)
Law Materials Management (3)	+				
Data Management		*(2)			*(4)

Remarks: * = required course; + = elective course
Number of credits are indicated in parentheses

Table III Techinical Services-Related Courses Offered by the Five Departments of Library Science in the ROC

COURSE TITLE	NTU	NTNU	FJCU	Tamkang	World College
Selection & Acquisition of Library Materials (4)	*	*	*	*	*(2)
Cataloging & Classification I (6)	*(new)	*(new)	*(new)	*(new)	
Cataloging & Classification II (6)	*(new)	*(new)	*(new)	*(new)	
Dewey Decimal Classification (2)	+				
U. S. Library of Congress Classification (2)	+		+	*	
Materials in Japanese Language (4)	+				
Indexing & Abstracting (2)	+		+	*	
Subject Heading (2)			+		
AV Material Classification & Cataloging (2)				+	
Photography (2)				+	
Educational Television (2)				+	
Production of Multi-Media (2)				+	
Microform Application (2)				+	*(1)
Planning & Producing AV Materials (3)	+				
Study of Classification Systems (2)	+				

Remarks: * = required course; + = elective course
Number of credits are indicated in parentheses

Table IV Readers Services-Related Courses Offered by the Five Departments of Library of Science in the ROC

COURSE TITLE	NTU	NTNU	FJCU	Tamkang	World College
Chinese Reference Sources (4)	*	*	*	*	*(2)
Western Reference Sources (4)	*	*	*	*	*(2)
Non-book Materials (4)	*(new)	*(new)	*(new)	*(new)	
Introduction to Reference Services (2)	+				
Literature of the Humanities (4)	+		+	+	
Literature of Social Sciences (4)	+		+	+	
Literature of Science and Technology (4)	+		+	+	
Reading Materials for Children and Young Adults (20)		+			
Children's Books (3)	+				
Young Adult Literature (2)	+				
Selected Readings for Children (2)	+				
Japanese Reference Sources (6)	+				
Classics Reading Guidance (2)				+	
Extension Services (2)			+		
Government Publications	+(3)			*(2)	
Public Services (2)		+			
Interpersonal Communication & Readers' Services (2)	+				
Introduction to AV Materials (3)	+				
Library Service for Special Readers (2)	+				
Picture books (2)	+				
Storytelling (2)	+				

Remarks: * = required course; + = elective course
Number of credits are indicated in parentheses

Table V Information Science Related Courses Offered by the Five Departments of Library of Science in the ROC

COURSE TITLE	NTU	NTNU	FJCU	Tamkang	World College
Introduction to Information Science (2)	*	*	*	*	*(4)
Introduction to Computer Science (4)	*	*	*	*	
Library Automation (4)	*	*	*	*	*
Information Retrieval (2)		+			
Information Technology (2)			+		
Personal Computer & Library (2)			+	+	
Word Processing (2)			+	*	+
Computer Programming Application (2)				*	+
Information Center & Services (4)				*	
Information Network (2)				+	
Principles & Planning of CAI Courses (2)				+	
Special Topics on Automation (2)				+	
Practical Computer Science (2)					*
Theory & Practice of Computer (4)					+
Online Database Retrieval (2)			+		
Computer Application for Libraries (3)	+				
Computer Programming (3)	+				
Chinese Character Indexing (2)	+				
Introduction to Data Processing for Libraries (3)	+				

Remarks: * = required course; + = elective course
Number of credits are indicated in parentheses

Table VI Fundamental Courses for NTU's Master Program

Course Title	Required	Elective	Credits
Thesis	*		6
Research Method	*		2
Thesis Writing		+	2
History of Books		+	2
Issues of Modern Librarianship		+	2
Operations Research		+	3
History of Chinese Printing		+	2
Study of Chinese Block Editions		+	2
Statistics for Librarians		+	3
Library Education		+	2
Information science Education		+	2
Comparative Librarianship		+	2
Special Topics in Chinese Bibliography		+	2
Library Building		+	2
Special Topics on Intellectual Property		+	2
AV Education		+	2

Remarks: * = required course; + = elective course

Table VII Management Courses for NTU's Master Program

Course Titles	Required	Elective	Credits
Seminar on Library Administration	*		2
Seminar on Public Libraries		+	2
Management of Cultural Center		+	2
Seminar on Academic Libraries		+	2
Management of Computer Centers		+	2
Seminar on University Libraries		+	2
Information Marketing & Publicity		+	2
Legal Issue for Information Handling		+	2
Information Management		+	3

Table VIII Technical Services-Related Courses for NTU's Master Program

Course Title	Required	Elective	Credits
Study on the Management and Emendation of Chinese Classics		+	2
Collection Development		+	2
Cataloging of Chinese Classics		+	2
Seminar on Technical Services	*		2
Thesaurus Construction		+	2

Table IX Readers' Services-Related Courses for NTU's Master Program

Course Title	Required	Elective	Credits
Seminar on Reader's Services	*		2
Chinese Biographical Materials		+	2
Chinese Classical Reference		+	2
Study of Chinese Rare Books		+	2
Behavior & Communication		+	2
Library Resource Sharing		+	2

Table X Information Services-Related Courses for NTU's Master Program

Course Title	Required	Elective	Credits
Seminar on Information Science	*		2
Online Information Searching		+	3
Information Management System		+	3
Database Management		+	3
Database and File Structure		+	2
Seminar on Chinese Computer & Data Processing		+	3
Indexing of Chinese Characters with the Computer		+	2
Indexing Chinese Characters		+	2
Study of Chinese Computer		+	2
Computer Data Structure		+	2
Information Storage and Retrieval		+	2
Introduction to Database Management		+	2
Seminar on Computer Science		+	2
Seminar on Special Topics in Library/Information System		+	2

Table XI Courses and Credits for NTU's Doctoral Program

Course Title	Required	Elective	Credits
Bibliographic Literature of China		+	2
Dissertation	*		2
Independent Studies		+	2
Information Policy		+	2
Library and Information Industry		+	2
Library and Information Science Research Trends		+	2
Library and Information Society		+	2
Orientation to Doctoral Program		+	2
Philosophy for Librarianship		+	2
Research Methodology		+	2
Seminar on Behavioral Foundations		+	2
Seminar on Communication and Library Services		+	2
Seminar on Comparative Librarianship		+	2
Seminar on Information Management		+	2
Seminar on Library Education		+	2
Seminar on Library/Information Laws and Regulations		+	2
Seminar on National Libraries		+	2
Seminar on the Organization and Emendation of Chinese Classics		+	2
Seminar on Printing and Publishing		+	2
Seminar on Theories of Classification		+	2
Special Topics on AV Materials		+	2
Special Topics on Chinese Bibliography		+	2
Special Topics on Chinese Block Editions		+	2
Special Topics on History of Chinese Printing		+	2
Special Topics on Information Science		+	2
Special Topics on Library Management		+	2
Theories of AV Education		+	2

NOTES

1. George Huang, "Miss Mary Elizabeth Wood: Pioneer of the Library Movement in China," *Tu Shu Kuan Hsueh Yu Tzu Hsun K'o Hsueh 圖書館學與資訊科學 [Journal of Library & Information Science]* (April 1975): 67-78.
2. Li-ling Kuo 郭麗玲, *Chung Mei T'u Shu Kuan Chiao Yu Pi Chiao 中美圖書館教育比較 [Comparative Study on Chinese and American Library Education]* (Taipei: Feng Cheng Publishing Co., 1978), 56.
3. James S.C. Hu, "Library Education in the Republic of China," in *Library & Information Science Education: An International Symposium* (Taipei: National Taiwan University, 1986), 38.
4. Cheng-ku Wang 王振鵠, "San Shih Nien Lai Te Taiwan T'u Shu Kuan Chiao Yu 三十年來的台灣圖書館教育 [Thirty Years of Library Education in Taiwan]," *Chung Kuo T'u Shu Kuan Hsueh Hui Pao 中國圖書館學會會報 [Bulletin of Library Association of China]* 35 (18 December 1983): 9-19.
5. Li-ling Kuo 郭麗玲, *Chung Mei T'u Shu Kuan Chiao Yu Pi Chiao 中美圖書館教育比較 [Comparative Study on Chinese and American Library Education]*, 48.
6. Shih-hsion Huang, "Continuing Education & Staff Development for Librarians in the Republic of China," in *Library & information Science Education: An International Symposium* (Taipei: National Taiwan University, 1986), 206-207.
7. Neal Harlow, "Designs on the Curriculum," in *Education for Librarianship: The Design of the Curriculum of Library Schools* (Illinois: University of Illinois, 1971), 4.
8. Lester Asheim, "New Trends in the Curriculum of Library Schools," in *Education for Librarianship: The Design of the Curriculum of Library Schools* (Illinois: University of Illinois, 1971), 64-65.
9. Neal Harlow, "Designs on the Curriculum," in *Education for Librarianship: The Design of the Curriculum of Library Schools*, 6.
10. Ibid., 8.
11. Ibid.
12. Ibid., 9.
13. Sarah R. Reed, "The Curriculum of Library Schools Today: A Historical Review," in *Education for Librarianship: The Design of the Curriculum of Library Schools* (Illinois: University of Illinois, 1971), 32.
14. Jesse H. Shera, *Introduction to Library Science: Basic Element of Library*

Science (Littleton, Colorado: Libraries Unlimited, 1976), 151.

15. Ibid., 152.
16. Neal Harlow, "Designs on the Curriculum," 11
17. Harris B.H. Seng, "Problems Confronting Library Science Education in the Republic of China," in *Library & Information Science Education: An International Symposium* (Taipei: National Taiwan University, 1986), 70.
18. F. W. Lancaster, "The Curriculum of Information Science," in *Library Automation and Information Networks 1988: Proceedings of a Seminar*, Taipei, Taiwan, ROC, 6-12 June 1988 (Taipei: The ROC Committee for Scientific and Scholarly Cooperation with the U. S., Academia Sinica, National Central Library, 1989), 207.
19. Bernard S. Schlessinger, June H. Schlessinger, and Rashelle Schlessinger Karp, "Information Science/Library Science Educations Programs in the 1990s: A Not-So-Modest Proposal," *Library Administration & Management* 5, no. 1 (Winter 1991): 16.
20. Ibid.
21. Tefko Saracevic, "Tzu Hsun Shih Tai Chung Te T'u Shu Kuan Chiao Yu 資訊時代中的圖書館教育 [Library Education in the Information Age]," trans. Mei-hua Yang 楊美華 譯, *T'u Shu Kuan Hsueh Yu Tzu Hsun K'o Hsueh 圖書館學與資訊科學 [Journal of Library & Information Science]* 8, no. 2 (October 1982): 226-7.
22. James S.C. Hu and Tsu-shan Wu 胡述兆，吳祖善, *T'u Shu Kuan Hsueh Tao Lun 圖書館學導論 [Introduction to Library Science]* (Taipei: Han Mei Book, lnc., 1989), 33; quoted in Chien-chang Lan 藍乾章, "Wo Kuo Tsao Ch'i Te T'u Shu Kuan Hsueh 我國早期的圖書館學 [The Early Stages of Library Science in China]," *T'u Shu Kuan Hsueh K'an (Fu Tai) 圖書館學刊(輔大) [Journal of Library Science (Fu-jen Catholic University)]* 12 (September 1983): 7.
23. Lucy Te-chu Lee 李德竹, " Chiao Yu Pu Han Pen Hsi Hsin Hsiu Ting Chih T'u Shu Kuan Hsueh Hsi Pi Hsiu K'o Ch'eng 教育部和本系新修訂之圖書館學系必修課程 [Ministry of Education and Department of Library Science of National Taiwan University Newly Revised Required Curriculua]," *Shu Fu 書府* 11 (June 1990): 7-8.
24. James S.C. Hu and Tsu-shan Wu 胡述兆，吳祖善, *T'u Shu Kuan Hsueh Tao Lun 圖書館學導論 [Introduction to Library Science]* (Taipei: Han Mei Book, lnc., 1989), 34-36.
25. Kuo Li T'ai Wan Ta Hsueh Pien 國立台灣大學 編 [National Taiwan University, ed.], *Introduction to Department and Graduate Institute of Li-*

brary Science (1990).

26. Kuo Li Taiwan Ta Hsueh Pien 國立台灣大學 編 [National Taiwan University, ed.], *The 1990 Curriculum Schedule of Department and Graduate Institute of Library Science/College of Liberal Arts* (1990); Kuo Li Taiwan Shih Fan Ta Hsueh Pien 國立台灣師範大學 編 [National Taiwan Normal University, ed.], The *1990 Curriculum Schedule of Department of Social Education* (1990); Kuo Li Taiwan Shih Fan Ta Hsueh Pien 國立台灣師範大學 編 [National Taiwan Normal University, ed.], *Introduction to Department and Graduate Institute of Social Education* (June 1988); T'ien Chu Chiao Fu Jen Ta Hsueh Pien 天主教輔仁大學 編 [Fu-jen Catholic University, ed.], *The 1990 Curriculum Schedule of Department of Library Science* (1990); Tamkang Ta Hsueh Pien 淡江大學 編 [Tamkang University, ed.], *The 1990 Curriculum Schedule of Department of Educational Media & Library Science* (1990); Shih Chieh Hsin Wen Chuan K'o Hsueh Hsiao Pien 世界新聞專科學校 編 [The World College of Journalism, ed.], *The 1990 Student Manual* (1990).
27. Kuo Li Taiwan Ta Hsueh Pien 國立台灣大學 編 [National Taiwan University, ed.], *Introduction to Department and Graduate Institute of Library Science* (1990).
28. Ibid.
29. Tefko Saracevic, Gilda M. Braga, and Matthew A. Afolayan, "Issues in Information Science Education in Developing Countries," *Journal of the American Society for Information Science* (May 1985): 195.
30. James S. C. Hu, Remarks made on 16 March 1990.
31. Shann-jye Chen 陳善捷, "T'u Shu Kuan Hsueh K'o Ch'eng An P'ai Chih T'an Tao「圖書館學課程」安排之探討 [On the Arrangement of Curriculum of Library Science in Several Colleges of the Republic of China]," *Chiao Yu Tzu Liao Yu T'u Shu Kuan Hsueh 教育資料與圖書館學 [Journal of Education Media and Library Science]* 18, no. 1 (September 1980): 125-6; Chien-chang Lan 藍乾章, "T'u Shu Kuan Hsueh Hsi Hsin Ting Pi Hsiu K'o Mu P'ing I 圖書館學系新訂必修科目評議 [Comments on the Newly Revised Library & Information Science Courses Developed by Library Schools]," *Chung Kuo T'u Shu Kuan Hsueh Hui Hui Pao 中國圖書館學會會報 [Bulletin of the Library Association of China]*, no. 35 (December 1983): 70.
32. Ching-chih Chen, "The New Technology and Its Potential for Information Professionals & Effects," in *Library and Information Science Education: An International Symposium* (Taipei: National Taiwan University, 1986), 37.

33. Richard K. Gardner, "Library and Information Science Education: The Present State and Future Prospects," in *Education of Library and Information Professionals: Present and Future Prospects* (Littleton, Colorado: Libraries Unlimited, 1987), 34-35.
34. James S.C. Hu, Telephone remarks made on 25 March 1991.
35. F.W. Lancaster, Remarks made on 7 June 1988.
36. Bernard S. Schlessinger, June H. Schlessinger, and Rashelle Schlessinger Karp, "Information Science/Library Science Educations Programs in the 1990s: A Not-So-Modest Proposal," 17-18.

Reprinted with permission from *The Proceedings of the International Conference on New Frontiers in Library and Information Services* V. 2, 9-11 May 1992. (pp. 823-856).

21

Global Librarianship in the Information Age

ABSTRACT

The author, being the Louise Maxwell Award recipient in 1994, delivers this speech to congratulate and encourage the SLIS graduates at Indiana University. Gratitude is expressed to the faculty members and the Alumni Association. The need for global information system is pointed out. With speaker's experience and the speedy advancement of technology, attention is called to the multidisciplinary nature of librarianship and the necessity of life-long learning for the preparation of global librarianship in the information age of the 21st century.

INTRODUCTION

Dean Cronin, President Betty Martin of the SLIS Alumni Association, Faculty Members, 1994 SLIS Graduates, Friends, Ladies and Gentlemen:

First of all, I wish to congratulate all of you, the 1994 graduates for this important and memorable day. The commencement signifies the completion of an important phase of your education, your professional/academic achievements with the grant of advanced academic degree, and the start of another stage of your life. It is a wonderful feeling that you have successfully overcome various challenges during the course of study and receive the credential of a master's degree from this fine institution of higher education. I would also like to congratulate the outstanding faculty members at SLIS for educating such promising and quality librarians and information scientists.

I feel very much honored today that the SLIS Alumni Association bestows upon me the 1994 Louise Maxwell Award in recognition of my achievements/contributions in the field of library science.

I am sure that many SLIS graduates share my personal feeling today, i.e. we really should attribute our accomplishments to the faculty members and fellow classmates. In addition to our own efforts, it is their inspiration, guidance, good role models and exchange of opinions that made our achievements possible. I, especially, wish to express my heartfelt thanks to Dr. Kaser and Dr. Abrera for their personal concerns, encouragement and guidance.

Eleven years after graduation, I am pleased to have this opportunity to return to Indiana University to witness the rapid growth and remarkable achievements of SLIS.

At the time when several leading library schools have been closed due to economic depression, it is extremely exciting to see that SLIS is expanding and growing. As the President of SLIS Alumni Association, Betty Martin, wrote in the last *Alumni Newsletter*: "New programs and new partnerships are moving the school forward to meet opportunities that are on the horizon for information sciences."[1] All of these facts make us feel so proud to be an IU SLIS alumnae. While we are expecting the first generation cybrarians to be produced by SLIS as recently indicated by Dean Cronin,[2] we are also happy to learn from Betty Martin that "there remains at SLIS an appreciation for libraries and librarians — a more traditional role and there continues to have a commitment to produce library professionals who may find their goals closely linked to the arts and humanities and who must satisfy local expectations."[3]

It is probably due to such an equal emphasis on the mastery of both information technology and traditional librarianship that makes SLIS a program so attractive to people who are interested in pursuing advanced studies for this profession. As we are going to step into the information age of the 21st century in less than six years, I would like to share with you my views on "Global Librarianship in the Information Age of the 21st century."

All parts of the world are aware of the need for the Global Information System in the future;[4] it is advocated that information technology will be applied to activities at home, offices, factories, hospitals, and restaurants, etc. Almost every facility will be equipped with modern technological devices to assure efficiency and effectiveness. Libraries, of course, will be no exception; they will be one-stop information shopping center which provide twenty-four hours services.[5]

Libraries are now global in nature for the simple reason that they no longer suffer under the constraints of time and space which handicapped the libraries in the past. In the past, libraries emphasized collections; at the present time, they consider information retrieval pivotal to library operations. The fast advances of modern technology have indeed greatly benefited library and information services. It makes librarians' life easier in one way or the other; less and less original cataloging or manual search for answers to reference questions are done at libraries after they are hocked up with bibliographic utilities and/or online databases.

Now, we no longer are confined in one library building to use library resources or to search for information with the blessings of information technology. Universal availability and accessibility of information are feasible through the magic of modern information technological devices, such as databases generated by computers, networking resulted from upgraded telecommunication devices, and all types of electronic media. Libraries become to interdependent systems locally, nationally and internationally. There is no boundary among libraries anymore and no libraries exist in isolation. International standardized rules and regulations (such as MARC Formats and ISBN) telecommunication protocols resulted by the increasing demand of resources sharing and the advent of information technology have made our profession a global one. H. G. Well's idea of "world brain" suggests all human information and knowledge will be consolidated and into integrated resources to be utilized by people all over the world.[6]

Nevertheless, rapid changes of information technology generates various other challenges to information professionals. We need to keep pace with the fast-changing technological developments. To be a qualified information worker, one needs to be prepared to meet the challenges caused by these modern technological devices — various systems, various programming languages, various searching techniques, etc. In short, we need to be knowledgeable of information related technology.

However, it is important to note that technology is just a means for better management, better services, it is not an end itself.

We want to get our libraries automated, we want to build up databases, we want to develop various packages for automation. Remember, we do all these for the purpose of making resources readily available or accessible to users. It is equally important to note that our profession requires both basic multi-disciplinary knowledge and in depth subject specialization in order to provide quality services to information users. To know human behavior, we need to study psychology; to better administer libraries, we need to learn from business administration; to make libraries visible, we need to master the theory and practice of marketing. To render better services to subject specialists, we need to have strong subject background of that particular field.

Even though people can obtain information more easily with the use of technological devices, we cannot refrain from our duties to serve as a mediator between resources and users, as a consultant to information seekers or library users and as information engineers to information systems.

The five basic principles of library services that Raganathan suggested remains to be true. I, therefore, do believe and the integration of modern information technology and traditional librarianship are instrumental to the upgrading of information services to a higher echelon. Since libraries are one of the important constituents of the social infrastructure for human learning, information professionals must also constantly educate ourselves in order to play an important role as information gateway in support of universal communication made across culture, discipline and language. Thus, I cannot but emphasize the importance of life-long education in order to face the various challenges of the information age. Take myself as an example, I first came to the United States to pursue advanced study in the field of education at the University of Oregon. I then for the first time discovered the importance of wealth of knowledge that library science provides. I immediately transferred my major to library science even though I was about to receive the master degree then. I completed library studies and received my master's degree from Marywood College and started working as cataloger at St. John's University Library and Brookline Public Library. I took a salary cut when I took up the position at Harvard-Yenching Library because I wanted to acquire the management knowledge and skills unique to East Asian collections. During my subsequent posts as assistant librarian, university deputy library, director of university libraries, faculty member at schools of library and information science, I have always tried to receive continuing education by attending summer schools at the American and British universities and academic institutions, seminars workshops and international conferences which have kept me up to date and enabled me to be more proficient in our profession. At the age of 47, I quit from a tenured position of full professorship and came to IU to enter the doctoral program.

After three years' hard work, I received my doctoral degree from IU; during the course of my subsequent positions, I again did my post doctoral studies at University of Illinois and as a result, I completed a book on library automation in Chinese which has been widely used in Taiwan. For the past four years, being one of the ministers in charge of civil service and a professor of library and information science at two universities in Taipei, it remains to be my interest and drive to grasp every learning opportunity. I have found that life-long education fulfills my dreams and aspirations, assists me in overcoming difficulties and strengthens my capabilities. It is indeed gratifying and rewarding. I would now like to conclude my talk with a Chinese old saying: "There is no limitation for learning." We do need to refuel ourselves constantly by pursuing continuing education throughout our lives in preparation for global librarianship in the information age of the 21st century. Thank you.

Notes

1. Betty Martin, "Alumni Can Be Justifiably Proud of Alma Mater," *Indiana University School of Library and Information Science Alumni Newsletter* 32, no. 1 (Fall/Winter 1993): 2.
2. Blaise Cronin, "First-Generation Cybrarians to Come out of SLIS," *Indiana University School of Library and Information Science Alumni* Newsletter 32, no. 1 (Fall/Winter 1993): 2.
3. Ibid.
4. Clifford A. Lnych, "Library Automation and National Research Network," *EDUCOM Review* (Fall 1989): 21-26.
5. Patricia Battin, "The Electronic Library: A Vision for the Future," *EDICOM Bulletin* (Summer 1984): 12-17, 34.
6. Nancy Herron, "The Paperless Society," in *Encyclopedia of Library and Information Science*, vol. 41 (New York: Marcel Dekker, 1986), 277-278.

Reprinted from the address delivered at the Luncheon in Honor of the 1994 SLIS Graduates.

22

Efforts of Promoting Information Access and Human Rights of Disability in Taiwan

ABSTRACT

The efforts of promoting information access and human rights of the disabled people in the R.O.C. on Taiwan are described and discussed thoroughly under the following captions: The population of the disabled, their legal protection, employment security, special civil service examination, library services, medical/educational assistance, and foundation for the hearing impaired. The paper is concluded with a remark: "Care for the disabled should be based on legal protection, government and community supports as well as the public and private efforts."

INTRODUCTION

The Republic of China, founded in 1911 by Dr. Sun Yat-sen, has had a history of 88 years. Since the occupation of China mainland by the Communists in 1949, the ROC government moved to Taiwan where "Taiwan Experience" and "Taiwan Miracle" have clearly demonstrated the economic, social and political progresses.

On an island occupying a total area of 36,000 sq. km., with little natural resources, the successful nationwide economical, political, and social developments brought people wealth, democracy and freedom.

POPULATION OF THE DISABLED PEOPLE

In 1998, out of the 22 million population in Taiwan, the amount of people with disability amount to 553,454, which is 2.52% of the entire population. In comparison with the previous year 53,316, there has been an evident increase of 0.25%. 78.47% of the disabled male are educated, and 59.44% of the entire disabled female are educated.[1]

LEGAL PROTECTION

Protection Law for the Disabled

Human rights of the people with disability have acquired nationwide attention as early as 1980 with the proclamation of the Protection Law for the Disabled. The law has since been amended four times with the last amendment on April 26, 1997. There are eight chapters and seventy-five articles giving clear definition of the disabled, stipulation the offices in charge, communicating channels, medical assistance, educational rights, employment, welfare, and fines, etc. Almost all facets of life confronted by the disabled are clearly stipulated by the Law.[2]

Special Education Law

This set of laws proclaimed on May 14, 1997, consisting 33 articles, protects the rights of both the handicapped and talented people to receive appropriate education.[3]

Copyright Law

In January 21, 1999, the copyright law has been revised. Article 53 of our newly revised copyright law stipulates that publications can be reproduced with braille, recording or computer by government approved organizations. This new revision grants organizations to reproduce publications for the blind.[4]

In addition, there are many welfare programs provided to the disabled by the Ministry of Interior and by Taipei Municipal Government with administrative orders. Information is available on: http://www.basa.teg.gov.tw/diswelfar.htm.[5]

EMPLOYMENT PROTECTION

It is stipulated that all the private business entities comprising of more than 100 employees must hire one disabled person. Two percent of the government positions must be given to the disabled with exception of police department, fire department and customs office. If a government or private organization dose not observe such stipulation, the office has to pay US$466 for each position that the disabled is not hired. The government total employees amount to 669,948, according to the statistics gathered in March 1999, 13,502 disabled persons are civil servants, approximately 2.02% of the entire government employee population.[6]

SPECIAL CIVIL SERVICE EXAMINATION FOR THE DISABLED

Starting from 1996, special civil service examination has been given to the disabled by the Ministry of Examination. In 1996, 47 disabled have been qualified for government work and have been hired by various offices. For example, a blind person was hired by our office — the Supervisory Board of Civil Servants Pension Fund — to work as a typist, he then successfully passed the Examination for Social Workers. He is now a qualified social worker working for the Taipei Municipal Government. In 1999, 2,750 people with disability participated in this special examination. 129 of them have passed the examination for position available. An additional 129 disabled people will enter the government arena.[7]

LIBRARY SERVICES

Taiwan Branch of the National Central Library

Many private and government efforts have by made to provide library services to the visually disabled. Starting from July 1, 1975, Taiwan Branch of the National Central Library (NCL) established the Material Center for the Blind, producing books with braille and recording, teaching the blind to learn the braille, to use computers and to retrieve information. Searching and providing reading materials to the blind, and providing nationwide information network are made accessible by using special computers designed for the blind. With its rich collection: recording: 50,713 reels, 12,177 volumes of Chinese braille books and 912 titles of digital books reproduced by Tamkang University are available to the blind through BBS of the NCL Taiwan Branch Library. The successful library services rendered to the blind by this library in 1998 can be identified by the following statistics:[8]

Library materials circulated	Number of borrowers	Amount circulated
Braille	9,868 readers	48,677 volumes
Recording	9,850 readers	128,412 items

Tamkang University

With excellent facilities and faculty assistance, the University pays great attention to the education of disabled students, especially to the blind students by establishing a resources center for the blind, planning a digital library for the blind, developing computer for the blind, information network for the blind, and reproducing books into braille or recording.[9]

Book Center for the Hearing Impaired People, ROC Association for the Hearing Impaired

This Center, located in the center of Taipei City and sponsored by the Chinese National Association of the Deaf, R.O.C. (CAD), provides information on job opportunities, information on examinations for the disabled, and information on career planning for the hearing impaired on a membership basis. The hearing impaired people can get access to the collection and job information by joining the Association as members with nominal membership dues.[10]

MEDICAL AND EDUCATIONAL ASSISTANCE

Training Center

The Chinese Women's Anti-Aggression League, the largest women's organization founded by Madame Chiang Kai-shek, initiated its new program to train pre-school hearing impaired children (three to six year old kids) in the insulated classroom of its affiliated nursery. Staffed with professionals from the Veterans General Hospital and the National Taiwan Normal University, the program has been proven successful in its teaching the hearing impaired children to speak by watching the lips of the teacher and actual actions, cultivating their habit to speak up and increasing their interest in learning. The training enabled many children to be enrolled in regular class of normal children and they even have learned to answer to phone or to give instructions to fellow classmates. The classes are participated by parents and the children for continuous training outside of classrooms. For the children of hearing impaired in elementary schools in the age bracket between six and twelve years, the program also offers courses for them to learn English, Chinese and the use of computers.[11]

Foundation for the Hearing Impaired

Under the supervision and planning of the League, a foundation was set up three years ago to lend the following assistance to the hearing impaired persons:

1. Providing advice on pre-school hearing problems.
2. Providing professional hearing guidance.
3. Holding teaching hearing impaired seminars for parents.
4. Providing books and videos on the topics of the hearing impaired.
5. Circulating children's book and toys.
6. Providing individualized training programs for the hearing impaired.
7. Providing group hearing impaired training programs.
8. Providing hearing examination and evaluation of hearing aids.
9. Lending hearing aids.
10. Providing scholarship to aid the hearing impaired.
11. Providing financial assistance to students in their purchase of hearing aids or their medical expenses.

Zonta International's efforts

Zonta International Taipei II Club donated equipment to the School for the Disabled continuously for many years. With such contribution from various clubs and social welfare organizations, the School for the Disabled has been able to provide quality education to these unfortunate people.

CONCLUSION

Care for the disabled people based upon legal protection, supports from the government and communities are very important. In Taiwan, we have had very good results with public and private efforts.

NOTES

1. Department of Statistics, Ministry of the Interior ed., *The 1994 Investment Report on the Disabled Life Status in Taiwan Area* (Taipei, November 1994), 12-13.
2. The Protection Law for the Mentally & Physically People with Disablility proclaimed by the President's Office, Hua-tsang I Tzu (1) 8600101190 (華總義（一）字第8600101190號), 23 April 1997.
3. The Special Education Law proclaimed by the President's Office, Hua-tsang I Tzu (1) 8600112820 (華總義（一）字第8600112820號), 14 May 1997.
4. The Copyright Law proclaimed by the President's Office, 21 January 1998.
5. The Ministry of Personnel Administration, *The Analysis Report on the Disabled Working Right*, 15 June 1999.
6. Ibid.
7. Ministry of Examination, *The Minutes of the Second Meeting of the Examination for the Disabled*, 9 June 1999.
8. Kuo Li Chung Yang T'u Shu Kuan Taiwan Fen Kuan Mang Jem Tzu Liao Chung Hsin Pien 國立中央圖書館台灣分館盲人資料中心 編 [National Central Library Taiwan Branch, the Material Center for the Blind, ed.], *The Brief Introduction – Service Statistic for the Visually Disabled Readers*, 1998.
9. Http://www.tkbling.tku.edu.tw/tkbwork.htm.
10. Http://www.cnad.org.tw/about.htm.
11. The Chinese Women's Anti-Aggression League ed., *The Brochure of the CWAAL Programs for Children of Hearing Impaired*, October 1994, Taipei.

Reprinted from the paper presented in 1999 American Library Association Annual Conference, New Orleans, USA, 24 June – 1 July 1999.

23

Status of Women in the Republic of China

ABSTRACT

This address presents the status of women in the Republic of China. It reports female education, vocational training, job opportunity, legal protection, social supports implemented in the ROC with concrete figures.

INTRODUCTION

On an island of 36,000 sq. km., with a women population of 10 million five hundred seventy nine thousand persons in the Republic of China, Taiwan has been well known by the so-called "Taiwan Miracle" which demonstrated economic, social and political progresses. The success of "Taiwan Miracle" is credited to the popularization of education and quality human resources. Women in Taiwan, being highly educated, have contributed greatly to the successful "Taiwan Experience."

EDUCATION

At end of 1997, according to the statistics prepared by the Ministry of Education, 47 percent of junior college graduates, 43 percent and college and university graduates, and 28 percent of graduate school graduates were women.

VOCATIONAL TRAINING AND JOB OPPORTUNITIES

Form July 1997 to May 1998, 1,739 women graduated form 13 vocational training centers as full time students and 3,466 as evening class students. An additional 6,115 women completed vocational programs organized by local county or city governments.

During that period of time Employment and Vocational Training Administration of the Council of Labor Affairs, provided job hunting assistance to 31,269 women.

There are now 241,923 female civil servants. Out of government employees, a little more that 30% are women. Female working for other types of profession than government employees and agricultural sector amount to 2,367,635 persons.

Up to now, in the Legislative Yuan, only 13.9% of the legislators are held by women. Only 18.4% of the representatives of National Assembly are women, the highest number of women participating in the City Council is only 23.5 % of the entire city councilors. In comparison with male government employees, less women are hired for the positions of high ranks. The government tries to upgrade the legal status of women by stipulating an article in our Constitution, demanding 1/3 of the people's representation (National Assembly women and female legislators) quota be given to women. Such civil representation in the National Assembly and Legislative Yuan indeed will upgrade the status of women and enable them to serve the country and the people more effectively.

LEGAL PROTECTION

Civil Code was revised, giving both parents equal priority with regard to parental rights and obligations to younger children, and giving the wife full rights over property registered under her name.

Since June 24, 1998, Domestic Violence Prevention Law went into effect, central government, Ministry of the Interior, and all levels of local governments must organize domestic violence prevention committee including judicial, police, medical, educational; and volunteer services organizations will be integrated into a complete prevention system.

Article 7 of our Constitution states that all people in the Republic of China are legally equal. In addition to that, Equal Working Act for Both Sexes was studied, debated by the Legislative Yuan and one of the articles in that Act regarding "allowing nursing time" is quite uniquely protecting female workers' right.

Related law such as the Child and Youth Sexual Transaction Prevention Act, targets teenage prostitution supplementing the Penal Code was proclaimed on May 11, 1999 to protect female teenagers. A ten year imprison can be given to a person who commits such crime.

SOCIAL SUPPORTS

Many women organizations, societies and associations have great concern over the status of women in the Republic of China. Just to name a recent event as an example: starting from July, 1998, Zonta International, a worldwide service organization of executives in business and the professions, working together to advance the status of women, recognizing the rising incidents of violence against women and children and the need to take action to eradicate all forms of violence, started a program named Zonta International Strategies to Eradicate Violence against Women and Children (ZISVAW). With the Mediation Training for Children, children are trained to deal with conflict and to resist violent and abusive behaviors, especially toward girls and women. In response to this, Zonta International Clubs in the Republic of China held a forum on violence against women and children on April 27, 1999-May 3, 1999, discussing and sharing experiences regarding such an important issue.

CONCLUSION

In spite of the ancient tradition that women in China were quite invisible and their position was indeed very inferior for thousands of years. But ever since the founding of the Republic, both the government and private sectors have realized the importance of equality between male and female. Females are popularly educated and their responsibilities are quite heavy. A high percentage of female population receive college and university education and post bachelor education. Their performances and contributions in all walks of life have demonstrated excellence and superb quality. Both public and private sectors in our society have demonstrated great support to female in all endeavors. We feel proud of what women can do in the Republic of China.

Reprinted from an address presented in 1999 General Federation of Women's Clubs International Convention: San Francisco, California.

INDEX

1. Personal and corporate names, conferences, publication titles, authors' names, special terms and terminologies mentioned in the text are indexed.
2. Selected indexed terms are arranged alphabetically with the exception of articles (the, a, an).
3. Titles of publications are in italics.
4. "See" and "See also" cross references are provided for two related terms.

A

B

C

D

E

F

G

H

I

J

K

L

M

N

O

P

T

U

V

W

X

Y

Z

 Library & Information Science AG0069

The Collected Works of Margaret C. Fung, Ph.D.

by Margaret C. Fung

Published by Showwe Information Co., Ltd.
Address: 1F., No.25, Lane 583, Rueiguang Rd., Neihu District,
Taipei City 114, Taiwan (R.O.C.)
TEL: +886-2-2657-9211
FAX: +886-2-2657-9106
E-mail: service@showwe.com.tw
Domestic retail price: NT$500

Printed in Taiwan
June, 2004

讀　者　回　函　卡

感謝您購買本書，為提升服務品質，煩請填寫以下問卷，收到您的寶貴意見後，我們會仔細收藏記錄並回贈紀念品，謝謝！

1.您購買的書名：______________________

2.您從何得知本書的消息？

☐網路書店　☐部落格　☐資料庫搜尋　☐書訊　☐電子報　☐書店

☐平面媒體　☐ 朋友推薦　☐網站推薦　☐其他________

3.您對本書的評價：(請填代號　1.非常滿意 2.滿意 3.尚可 4.再改進)

封面設計____　版面編排____　內容____　文/譯筆____　價格____

4.讀完書後您覺得：

☐很有收獲　☐有收獲　☐收獲不多　☐沒收獲

5.您會推薦本書給朋友嗎？

☐會　☐不會，為什麼？____________________________

6.其他寶貴的意見：________________________________

____

____

____

讀者基本資料

姓名：________________　年齡：_____　性別：☐女　☐男

聯絡電話：_____________　E-mail：________________

地址：____

學歷：☐高中(含)以下　☐高中　☐專科學校　☐大學

☐研究所(含)以上　☐其他____________

職業：☐製造業　☐金融業　☐資訊業　☐軍警　☐傳播業　☐自由業

☐服務業　☐公務員　☐教職　☐學生　☐其他________

請貼
郵票

To：114

台北市內湖區瑞光路 583 巷 25 號 1 樓

秀威資訊科技股份有限公司　　　收

寄件人姓名：

寄件人地址：□□□

(請沿線對摺寄回,謝謝!)

秀威與 BOD

BOD（Books On Demand）是數位出版的大趨勢，秀威資訊率先運用 POD 數位印刷設備來生產書籍，並提供作者全程數位出版服務，致使書籍產銷零庫存，知識傳承不絕版，目前已開闢以下書系：

一、BOD 學術著作—專業論述的閱讀延伸
二、BOD 個人著作—分享生命的心路歷程
三、BOD 旅遊著作—個人深度旅遊文學創作
四、BOD 大陸學者—大陸專業學者學術出版
五、POD 獨家經銷—數位產製的代發行書籍

BOD 秀威網路書店：www.showwe.com.tw
政府出版品網路書店：www.*gov*books.com.tw

永不絕版的故事・自己寫・永不休止的音符・自己唱